Workers, Capital, and the State in British Columbia: Selected Papers

THIS COLLECTION OF ESSAYS offers a comprehensive examination of the working-class experience in British Columbia and contains essential background knowledge for an understanding of contemporary relations between government, labour, and employees. It treats workers' relationship to the province's resource base, the economic role of the state, the structure of capitalism, the labour market, and the influence of ethnicity and race on class relations.

Using different analytical categories and based on primary research, the individual studies provide new assessments of the development of capitalist relations of production; the way new economic developments changed old and traditional cultures; the connection between the demand for labour and the immigration policy; the impact of technology on work relations; and the various responses of labour to the policies of the state and capital groupings.

Articles focusing on episodes from the 1870s to the present deal with major staple industries such as the early fur trade, fishing, mining, and forestry and with the struggle of labourers against their employers in communities such as New Westminster and Fraser Mills and in specific sectors such as telecommunications and education. Many of the analyses show that ethnicity acts both as a focus of integration and resistance against external forces in the larger society and as a point of division and antagonism internal to the working class.

The activities of the working class and its relationships to other parts of society are of primary importance in explaining social and economic change in the province and in the country. *Workers, Capital, and the State in British Columbia* will be of interest to students of class, labour, and community relations.

RENNIE WARBURTON is a member of the department of sociology, University of Victoria. DAVID COBURN is in the department of behavioural sciences, University of Toronto.

Workers,
Capital,
and the State
in British Columbia

SELECTED PAPERS

edited by
RENNIE WARBURTON
and
DAVID COBURN

UNIVERSITY OF BRITISH COLUMBIA PRESS
VANCOUVER 1988

WORKERS, CAPITAL, AND THE STATE IN BRITISH COLUMBIA:
SELECTED PAPERS

© The University of British Columbia Press 1988

This book has been published with the help of a grant from the Social
Science Federation of Canada, using funds provided by the Social Sciences
and Humanities Research Council of Canada.

Canadian Cataloguing in Publication Data

Main entry under title:

Workers, capital, and the state in British Columbia

Includes bibliographical references and index.
ISBN 0-7748-0283-9

1. Labor and laboring classes - British Columbia.
Social conflict - British Columbia.   3. British
Columbia - Economic conditions.   I. Warburton,
Rennie, 1937-   II. Coburn, David, 1938-
HD8109.B72W67 1988   305.5′62′09711   c88-091109-3

International Standard Book Number 0-7748-0283-9
Printed in Canada

Contents

Preface

In the Spring 1980 issue of *B.C. Studies*, Allan Smith argued that studies of British Columbia history could be divided into three separate but overlapping phases. The first phase was characterized by a bourgeois Victorian emphasis on material progress and moral improvement, the province's place in the British Empire, and the achievements of celebrated pioneers. An intermediate phase saw the application of staples theory with a focus on explaining British Columbia's "development" through the exploitation of trapping, fishing, and forest industries, together with its "regional character and continental connections." The third phase, from the 1960's on, showed historians and social analysts preoccupied with ethnic and class relations. We see a more recent, incipient fourth phase where the focus is on gender relations as fundamental to understanding British Columbia. In approaching the province's development from a political economy perspective, this book is a continuation of the two latest phases, although the treatment of gender is less central than we would like.

The feature of the class structure examined in this volume is the formation and transformation of the British Columbia working class, which includes all those who work for wages and who do not control or profit from their control over the means of production.

This is an edited book based on the work of a number of different authors. The contributors were not given a particular theoretical perspective from which to present their specific studies. Thus, these papers were originally written from a varied set of approaches and for diverse purposes and many of the authors would perhaps not agree in whole or in part with the perspective from which we view their writings. Reliance on writers with varied perspectives means that it is a challenge to encompass all their analyses within a specific framework. Nevertheless it is our contention that these studies, and those of others, can be understood within a single, broad, theoretical perspective and that this perspective, with modifications, is the one best able to explain the various data presented here and the course of British Columbia development in general.

The essence of our own approach, one increasingly adopted in recent years, is that the nature of British Columbia and its society has been constrained and moulded by the needs of capital and the demands of labour. A result of the onset and changing character of capitalism both without and within the province, the class nature of British Columbia is the chief characteristic of its social structure. Class interests, class relationships, and the class struggle are the major factors helping us to understand why the province developed in the way that it has.

Although our initial orienting framework focused on the role of the two major classes of the bourgeoisie and the working class, such a model is, of course, an overly simplistic one. In British Columbia, and in any specific society, the reality is more complex. The papers in this volume, even as applied to the working class alone, point to a more differentiated class structure due mainly to divisions within the working class such as those of ethnicity, gender, or status and to the rise of what some would contend is a "new middle class" of white-collar workers (but which we feel are status groups within the working class. In the interaction of theory and actual historical processes neither theory nor the ideas people hold about British Columbia are likely to remain intact.

This volume, which was stimulated by recent work in Canadian political economy, is only a beginning to the application of class theory to the understanding and explanation of provincial development. Both description and explanation are undeveloped. However, we hope it is a stimulant to extension, criticism and correction. For us, editing these papers has indicated areas worthy of further investigation and topics which so far seem to have been relatively neglected. For example, within the working class the role of white collar workers, both early in provincial history and more recently, is problematic. There is very little work on the history of petty commodity producers. Just as the working class is divided and fragmented, the provincial bourgeoisie is also composed of various fractions and these need more study. The role of ethnicity and gender vis-à-vis class is a continuing concern. The relationships between factors internal and external to British Columbia have yet to be fully explicated. Finally, the interactions between social structure and such areas as ideology and the polity are sources of questions and possible investigation.

However, despite these complexities, we believe that a fairly simple theory of class conflict and the exigencies of capital accumulation is the initial approach best able to make sense of a variety of concrete historical happenings in British Columbia from strikes in the salmon fisheries and coal mines early in the century, to race riots, to the post-war rise of militant white-collar unions and to processes and events not treated in this volume such as the role of Social Credit and N.D.P. governments, Operation Solidarity, and the 1987 General Strike.

Acknowledgements

We first wish to acknowledge the other authors of the articles in this volume, without whom it would not exist. They have been both co-operative and patient. If this publication has merit it is largely because of their work. We would also like to acknowledge the influence of earlier writings on British Columbia, particularly those by Paul Phillips, Phillip Resnick, Martin Robin, and Pat Marchak. Readers such as those by Ward and McDonald and Ralston and Friesen that adopt perspectives different to our own also have proven useful.

In the wider Canadian context a stimulus has been provided by the burgeoning interest in political economy and labour history over the past two decades, exemplified respectively in the journals *Studies in Political Economy* and *Labour/Le Travail*. Among their central concerns have been the experiences of working people such as native Indians, Chinese storekeepers, fishermen, loggers, teachers, and telephone operators, particularly in their dealings with employers, competitors, and government agencies.

We would like specifically to acknowledge the financial support of the Social Sciences and Humanities Research Council of Canada, both for our own researches and for sponsoring this publication through the Social Science Federation of Canada. Thanks are also due to *Canadian Dimension*, *B.C. Studies*, and the *Canadian Review of Sociology and Anthropology* for permission to reprint Chapters 3, 12, and 13 respectively.

We are grateful to Bill Carroll for comments on earlier drafts of the concluding chapter and to anonymous reviewers for the S.S.F.C. and the University of British Columbia Press for critical comments on the manuscript. Last but not least, our thanks to Mollie Arnold and Barbara Millward, who typed various versions of the manuscript, and to Jane Fredeman and Laura Coles of U.B.C. Press for editorial improvements.

R. W.

D. C.

Contributors

ELAINE BERNARD, Labour Studies Programme, Simon Fraser University.

DAVID COBURN, Department of Behavioural Sciences, University of Toronto.

JAMES CONLEY, Department of Sociology, University of Western Ontario.

CYNTHIA CORNISH, Graduate Student, Department of Sociology, University of Victoria.

GILLIAN CREESE, Department of Anthropology and Sociology, University of British Columbia.

ALAN DUTTON, Doctoral Student, Department of Sociology and Anthropology, Simon Fraser University.

MICHAEL KEW, Department of Anthropology and Sociology, University of British Columbia.

JOHN MALCOLMSON, Research Analyst, B.C. Teachers' Federation.

PATRICIA MARCHAK, Department of Anthropology and Sociology, University of British Columbia.

JEANNE MEYERS, M.A. (History), LL.B., Articling with Leo McGrady, Barrister and Solicitor, Vancouver.

PAUL PHILLIPS, Department of Economics, University of Manitoba.

ALLEN SEAGER, Department of History, Simon Fraser University.

RENNIE WARBURTON, Department of Sociology, University of Victoria.

1

Introduction

RENNIE WARBURTON
and
DAVID COBURN

In the two decades preceding the onset of the current economic depression, workers and their families in British Columbia enjoyed the considerable benefits of living in one of Canada's most prosperous regions. Lucrative international markets for the sale of forest, mineral, and energy resources gave corporations ample opportunity to accumulate capital despite the high wage rates secured by the labour movement in the province. Allen (1986:20-25) has argued that B.C.'s prosperity has been more a result of its location within a single, national, well-integrated labour market than simply a product of the increasing export of natural resources. It is worth noting, however, that much of the surplus from the production and sale of these resources was appropriated elsewhere, in the form of profits, investment capital, and debt payments (Resnick, 1974:10).

Throughout the post-war period per capita income in B.C. had been one of the highest in Canada. Paradoxically, however, this prosperity was accompanied by a high unemployment level, regional inequalities within the province, and bitter, polarized, class-based antagonisms. Thus, while a large section of the population prospered and a very small minority remained, or became, very rich, many people marginal to the labour force have had to endure hardship. Working-class women and members of ethnic minorities continue to be particularly likely to experience marginal employment. As well, many native people are not fully absorbed into the wage-earning labour force or are dependent on welfare. Native communities in general suffer high unemployment, social problems, and high suicide rates.

These class, gender, and ethnic issues have been exacerbated in the economic crisis of the 1980's. As Marchak points out in her contribution to this book, many workers have been laid off because of plant closures as companies have reorganized to protect themselves during the recession. The Social Credit government has directly allied itself with business interests in attacking hard-won workers' rights, benefits, and social services, using the recession as an excuse for a broad assault on the social, political, and economic position of working men and women. Cuts in health, education, social programmes, and cultural activities indicate how vulnerable social services are when the economy falters. Just at a time when they are most needed, benefits are reduced or withdrawn, some of the funds being deployed to help finance incentives or subsidies to corporations. At the same time, lowered social expenditures and layoffs of workers in the health, education, and welfare systems create even more problems, both social and personal. Economic difficulties are increased because attacks on salary levels reduce the overall capacity to consume. All of this is justified in the name of restraint and economic recovery.

The consequences of this contradictory development of prosperity followed by economic downturn include: widespread unemployment, underdevelopment of secondary industry, a beleaguered trade union movement, continuing labour-management confrontation, and soured relations between the governing Social Credit party and its opponents, including the parliamentary opposition, workers' and women's organizations, and community groups.

The contributions to this volume show that many elements in the present situation are not new: examples can be found at various points in British Columbia's history. Conflict has long been entrenched in the province's economy and society. Recent examples of struggle between labour and capital are but the contemporary manifestations of the antagonisms endemic to the competitive structure of capitalist development. This is one reason why studies of the experiences and struggles of wage-earning people should have a central place in the history of British Columbia.

The following papers were chosen on the basis of our awareness of ongoing work on British Columbia in the tradition established by the new Canadian political economy and labour history (Palmer, 1983, 1986; Drache and Clement, 1985; Marchak, 1985).

There are significant gaps in the collection. We particularly regret that there are not more papers dealing with the working experiences of women. (Several papers in Latham and Pazdro's [1984] collection make up for this deficiency.) There is also insufficient analysis of the economic activity of native people, the non-manual workforce, the petit bourgeoisie, and the capitalist class itself. We are hopeful that current and future social science and historical research will enable these gaps to be filled.

The volume is intended to demonstrate the value of detailed investigations of class structure and class conflict in the history and sociology of the province. We strongly disagree with those who maintain that class struggle is not as important as, for example, race, or that it no longer occupies the central position it once held in earlier phases of the province's history (Ward, 1980). Because the majority of people in the province are wage-earners or their dependents, that is, members of the working class, their future is directly tied to employees' fortunes regarding job opportunities, working conditions, remuneration, and other benefits. And since these are largely determined by struggles between employees and the companies for which they work, class relations are centrally important.

The papers are presented in more or less chronological order from the pre-Confederation, gold-mining, colonial period to present-day advanced capitalism. The articles deal in varying degrees with relations between workers and their employers, between workers and the state, and between workers and each other. Overall the picture shows occasions when British Columbia's workers were divided by ethnicity, gender, political orientation, union rivalries, or degree of ownership of their means of production. At other times these divisive tendencies have been overridden by strong elements of working-class solidarity.

Turning to the specific contents of the articles, Malcolmson's chapter on the state in the nineteenth century provides further evidence against the contention that the liberal-democratic state is a neutral arbiter standing above particular interests and intervening on behalf of the population as a whole (Panitch, 1977). Whether the Hudson's Bay Company, which represented Britain in the fur-trade period, the ensuing colonial administration, or the eventual federal-provincial-municipal complex, the state has assisted entrepreneurs to accumulate capital. Lucrative land grants accompanied the granting of rail line charters and were a prime means of enabling outside capital from the United Kingdom, eastern Canada, and the United States to penetrate the resource hinterland of British Columbia.

Kew's paper demonstrates how relations between the Canadian state and native peoples were a key factor in the process of European settlement and the introduction of capitalist social relations which came with it (Warburton and Scott, 1985). A central feature of the early period were land purchases made by British property-owners; even political office depended on property qualifications and British citizenship (Mackie, 1984:237-38). These criteria made it virtually impossible for most native people to assume a dignified and responsible place in the socio-economic order. The land which they had used for thousands of years had become a commodity to be sectioned, owned, bought, and sold—by those Europeans who were allowed to own it! At the same time as they were being dispossessed of the land from which they gained a living, native groups were being confined to relatively small "Indian reserves." The many land claims which presently lie before the courts are a legacy of that era. The marginal position in the economy held by many, but by no means all, native groups in the province is to a large degree a consequence of the lack of opportunities offered to them and the denial to them of political power. For, as Kew demonstrates, the Indian Act not only helped to destroy native cultures by turning distinct groups like the Kwakiutl, Haida, and Coast Salish into the general category of "Indians," but it also regulated their existence and severely limited the scope they had for independent decision-making.

As outlined in Phillips's paper, early mining in the province saw individual miners digging or panning for gold or other minerals, which constituted a form of independent commodity production. But the shift to lode-mining (underground mining) on a large scale led to wage-earning work becoming the dominant economic activity. Harsh working conditions, low pay, and the unionizing experience of miners from the United Kingdom and the United States all made miners aware of their class circumstances as they became involved in industrial disputes, strikes, and workers' political movements. The absence in the earlier formative period of a large number of farmer/settlers or groups capable of mediating, buffering, or reducing the significance of, capital-labour confrontations, as well as the rapid onset of wage-based capitalism, helped to make acute class conflict an established feature of the province's history. Phillips observes that worker militancy was also provoked by intransigent capitalists who refused to improve working conditions and hired Asians, who were prepared to accept lower wages than European workers.

Immigrant workers from China, Japan, and India have been the victims of some of the most acute exploitation and racist hostility in the province's history. Creese's account of Asian workers in various types of employment emphasizes the competitive threat they presented to Euro-Canadian workers and the political ramifications of the measures taken against them by the state, notably special taxes, immigration quotas, and exclusionary laws. Exclusion of Asians from political, trade union, and cultural organizations threw them back on to their own cultural and organizational resources. These included the Chinese benevolent associations for self-help purposes and retention or revival of customs and family traditions. Creese emphasizes that exclusionary ethnic communities and practices are not so much expressions of cultural differences as they are ways that immigrants cope with difficult and sometimes oppressive experiences.

The significance of competition between workers of different ethnic backgrounds is also brought out by Conley in his article on conflict and the problems of labour supply in the seasonal salmon-fishing industry at the beginning of this century. Japanese and native Indian fishermen became caught up in struggles over fish prices not only with employers but also with Euro-Canadian fishermen. But the episodes he examines, like some of the situations studied by Knight (1978), show evidence of co-operation between members of different ethnic groups, suggesting that their mere co-presence does not always lead to conflict. Conley's analysis shows the diversity of employment found among the working class and the breaking down of independent commodity production owing to the power of the canning companies. He also shows how the federal government aided the canning companies by persuading Indian fishermen to break ranks with other fishermen during the 1893 strike. It also regulated a boat-rating system in the northern fishery that limited the number of boats a cannery could fish, thus helping to overcome problems of over-capacity and labour supply.

Seager's discussion of worker unrest in New Westminster during the first three decades of this century attributes the causes of this unrest to primitive workplace relations and forms of production. He points out that workers in New Westminster worked in diverse industries. This industrial diversity produced a range of worker organizations, providing evidence that the kinds of action seen by Drache (1984) to be typical of resource peripheries were actually also present in other industrial capitalist contexts.

Meyers's article is a case study of certain social consequences of assaults on workers which accompany capitalist recession. Capital-labour relations in Maillardville/Fraser Mills had been stable during the prosperous period that followed the First World War, and the resulting community solidarity evidenced in the 1931 strike proved a valuable source of resistance. It enabled the strikers to resist pressures to capitulate from employers, the state, and even the local Roman Catholic priest! The support given to the strike by the wives and other women is noteworthy since the "neglected majority" have so frequently been omitted from accounts of labour disputes and working-class experience. Meyers also draws attention to the role of the communist union leadership in avoiding outbreaks of racist animosity among the workers.

Dutton and Cornish examine the interplay of class and ethnicity among farmworkers in their struggles against employers. Agriculturalists have been particularly successful in lobbying successive provincial governments to maintain legislation favourable to employer interests. As a consequence farm employees suffer some of the worst types of exploitation found in British Columbia today. The process of forming the Canadian Farmworkers' Union in response to this situation has been a tough, uphill battle.

In her previous work Marchak has made significant contributions to our knowledge of the province's forest industry. Her essay in this collection brings that work up to date. It shows how the provincial state has encouraged corporate growth and the disappearance of numerous small firms by issuing cutting licences selectively and granting direct capital subsidies to the large forest companies. The failure to implement the principles of sustained yield management, to which lip service has been paid since the Sloan Commissions of the 1940's and 1950's, has also been part of the favourable treatment given to the largest enterprises. The recent discovery that the province's timber resource is depleted and that marketable timber is in short supply is thus partly the result of the state having subsidized forest companies by not insisting that they grow as much as they cut. Marchak shows the international context of the problems facing the industry and advocates increased community control and specialized manufacturing as solutions to some of the difficulties.

Automation is a threat to many workers' jobs. The 1981 strike of telephone workers described by Bernard involved the use of non-striking supervisory, professional, and other non-bargaining workers in order to maintain services during the strike. The fear of job loss during the preceding decade had been expressed in several disputes as the company attempted to make production more efficient and profits higher by modifying working conditions and the organization of work and by hiring outside contractors. The workers' resistance to these changes goes to the very heart of class conflict, since it involves the rights of the company, based on its proprietorial status, to determine its own future and those of its employees.

Telephone workers are typical of the growing numbers of "white-collar" or "non-manual" employees found in the state and corporate bureaucracies. Warburton and Coburn outline the increasing prevalence of these workers in the province's labour force during the twentieth century and offer an explanation of that process.

Warburton's overview of the experience of teachers as workers since the founding of the province is a case study of a prominent "white-collar" group. He shows the contradiction between elements in the professional image of teachers and their actual treatment by their state employers. The present dispute between the Van der Zalm government and the school teachers should be more understandable given this historical background.

The concluding chapter outlines the capitalist mode of production and uses parts of that framework to draw together some of the major themes contained within the various papers. It emphasizes the introduction and establishment of capitalist social relations, class conflict, the links between class struggle and ethnic relations, and the complex role of the state.

This is a work in historical sociology. It is a study of particular class-based social groups and organizations and their inter-relations in times past. Because social structures are the products of past as well as present human actions, a sociology without history is suspect. Sociological research on capitalist societies, however, must include historically grounded analysis of social institutions within the logic of capitalist economic development (Dickinson and Russell, 1986:1). But the collection can also be described as sociological history. Because human beings have always existed in social relationships with each other—not merely class relations but also those involving gender, community, generation, and many other bases for social interaction—we believe that history which is not sociological is basically deficient.

Studies of the relations between labour, capital, and the state are particularly suited to the modern history and sociology of British Columbia; the province's development is directly connected to particular class relations, the origins of which are examined in the opening chapter by Malcolmson.

REFERENCES

Allen, Robert C. 1986.
"The B.C. Economy: Past, Present and Future." Chap. 1 in Robert C. Allen and Gideon Rosenbluth (eds.), *Restraining the Economy: Social Credit Economic Policy for B.C. in the Eighties*. Vancouver: New Star.
Dickinson, James and Bob Russell (eds.). 1986.
Family, Economy and State: The Social Reproduction Process under Capitalism. Toronto: Garamond.
Drache, D. 1984.
"The Formation and Fragmentation of the Canadian Working Class: 1820-1920." *Studies in Political Economy* 15:43-90.
Drache, D. and W. Clement. 1985.
The New Practical Guide to Canadian Political Economy. Toronto: Lorimer.

Knight, Rolf. 1978.
Indians at Work. Vancouver: New Star.
Latham, B. and Pazdro R. (eds.). 1984.
Not Just Pin Money: Selected Essays on the History of Women's Work in British Columbia. Victoria: Camosun College.
Mackie, Richard S. 1984.
"Colonial Land, Indian Labour and Company Capital: The Economy of Vancouver Island, 1849-1858." M.A. thesis, University of Victoria.
Marchak, Patricia. 1985.
"Canadian Political Economy." *Canadian Review of Sociology and Anthropology*, December 22, 5:673-709.
Palmer, Bryan. 1983.
Working Class Experience: The Rise and Reconstitution of Canadian Labour, 1800-1980. Toronto: Butterworths.
Palmer, Bryan. 1986.
"Listening to History Rather than Historians: Reflections on Working-Class History." *Studies in Political Economy*, Summer, No. 20:47-84.
Panitch, L. 1977.
The Canadian State: Political Economy and Political Power. Toronto: University of Toronto Press.
Resnick, P. 1974.
"The Political Economy of British Columbia: A Marxist Perspective." In P. Knox and P. Resnick (eds.), *Essays in B.C. Political Economy*. Vancouver: New Star.
Warburton, R. and S. Scott. 1985.
"The Fur Trade and the Beginnings of Capitalism in British Columbia. *Canadian Journal of Native Studies*, 5:27-46.
Ward, W. Peter. 1980.
"Class and Race in the Social Structure of British Columbia, 1870-1939." *B.C. Studies* 45:17-35.

2

Politics and the State in the Nineteenth Century

JOHN MALCOLMSON

INTRODUCTION

From the earliest periods of European contact, the development of British Columbia—first as a company preserve, later as a colonial outpost and finally, from the late nineteenth-century forward, as a province within the Canadian Confederation—has been predicated upon the fortunes of its dominant resource industries. The development of these sectors has, in turn, provided a kind of socioeconomic context for the emergence of early state structures in Canada's Pacific region. In addition, the resource industries made necessary the earliest forms of regional state intervention in the economy: provision of a legal framework to regulate access to land and staple resources, and state sponsorship of road and rail line construction.

Yet, despite the overall importance of the state and its role within this context, little attempt has been made to analyze the general nature of the regional state in early British Columbia. Moreover, little attention has been paid to the origin and development of the state in Canada's Pacific and to the forces which, in the past, have made for periodic changes in the institutional form of the state itself. At times, various writers have focused on different aspects of state activity, such as early transportation development, taxation and state finance, and settlement promotion.[1] Others have approached various facets of the early political process, such as the struggle for responsible government, relations with federal powers, and the origins of provincial party politics.[2] Yet seldom has any real attempt been made to relate these different areas to questions regarding the institutional character or form of the state and the corresponding exercise of state power. It is precisely for this reason that the present essay will, following a brief theoretical section, attempt to develop the beginnings of such an analysis as it pertains to the historical experience of British Columbia from the period of the fur trade up to the close of the nineteenth century.

THEORETICAL PERSPECTIVES ON THE STATE

Over the course of the past fifteen years, Marxist theory has "rediscovered" the state in capitalist society as an object of disciplined scientific inquiry. Much of the work undertaken over this period has had an explicitly theoretical orientation. And in the attempt to develop an adequate Marxist theory of the state and of political power, there have emerged differing and, in some senses, competing perspectives on why the state in capitalist society can be viewed as a capitalist state.

In the work of Ralph Miliband, the analysis focuses on elite linkages and recruitment networks which make for a constant flow of personnel and ideology back and forth between the higher corporate echelons and the state apparatus. In summing up the results of his study, Miliband states that

> it has remained a basic fact of life in advanced capitalist countries that the vast majority of men and women in these countries have been governed, represented, administered, judged and commanded in war by people drawn from other economically and socially superior and relatively distant classes.[3]

In the course of his analysis, Miliband does go some distance toward demolishing the analytical pretentions of contemporary liberal-pluralist theory with its concept of the state as a neutral arbiter of competing social interests. However, he does not go far toward formulating a distinctively Marxist theory of the state. As Holloway and Picciotto note, there is little in Miliband other than an attempt to demonstrate "that the bourgeois theorists have got the facts wrong."[4]

The work of Nicos Poulantzas contains a more serious attempt to provide a theoretical basis for the analysis of the capitalist state. Poulantzas rejects a preoccupation with patterns of elite recruitment as a means of deciphering the class character of state structures. Instead, he concentrates on the structural articulation of political, economic, and ideological levels in society, an articulation which grants the capitalist state a position of "relative autonomy" within society.

> This autonomy has theoretical consequences for the object of our study. It makes possible a regional theory (in the very strict sense) of an instance of this mode, e.g. a theory of the capitalist state; it permits us to constitute the political into an autonomous and specific object of science.[5]

Much of Poulantzas's work from this point consists of an elaboration of concepts specific to this analysis of the political level, concepts such as "hegemony," "power bloc," and "class fraction." Building on many of the ideas first developed by Antonio Gramsci, he does contribute valuable insights to a theory of the capitalist state.

However, apart from a number of vague references to an articulation of levels determined "in the last instance" by the economic realm, there exists in Poulantzas little precise theoretical analysis of the place occupied by the state within the capitalist mode of production. Consequently, throughout his work, Poulantzas remains curiously silent on a number of important theoretical issues, including the historic genesis of the state, its changing role in the accumulation process, and the manner in which this accumulation process effectively circumscribes the field of effective state intervention.

Despite the differences which obviously separate Miliband and Poulantzas in their respective theoretical positions, both share a failure to situate the state adequately within the socioeconomic context provided by capitalist society. Out of this failure emerges an incomplete consideration of class formation and class struggle as it pertains to the development of the state.

It is precisely this latter problem—the need to analyze all aspects of the state in relation to underlying class forces and relations—which has recently been taken up by theorists like Wright, Hirsch, and Holloway and Picciotto. Some of these analyses emphasize the role of the state itself as a participant in the process of class struggle.[6] Others examine the impact that class struggle has on the very nature of the state.[7] Still others examine, in the contemporary context, the class dynamics involved in state intervention geared to reconstituting the requisite conditions for continued capital accumulation amidst conditions of crisis and declining profitability.[8]

Given the direction and intent of this paper, there is no need to pursue the intricacies of these latter approaches in fine detail. Suffice it to say that a central insight to be drawn from these debates concerns the need to view the state as both a product of and a participant in the process of social class struggle. From this vantage point, the institutional character of the state bears a direct relation to prevailing configurations of social class forces in society. In addition, fundamental alterations in these configurations brought on by changes in the process of capital accumulation transform the state itself. For these reasons, political analyses must go beyond considerations relating to the content of state policies or actions; they must, in fact, examine the total state as well as its actions and interventions.

THE EARLY STATE IN B.C.

From the earliest European settlements, class relations in British Columbia have been a product of prevailing forms of the labour process involved in the extraction of regional staples. With the fur staple, most of the actual labour process involved in trapping animals and transporting pelts lay outside the direct control of the Hudson's Bay Company, the dominant economic and political power in the region. It was, therefore, not the direct exploitation of human labour within the process of production which constituted the decisive hinge in this system of mercantile accumulation; it was rather the exploitation of a monopoly position of trade with the native population. Within this social context, there existed little scope for a process of internal class differentiation. Furthermore, given the absence of any significant extension of commodity production beyond the company's control, there existed no reason for an institutional separation of "state" and "economy" within the region. The establishment of Vancouver Island as a crown colony in 1849 served to formalize the fusion of political and economic realms; the administrative power and control afforded by such a system conduced well to the maintenance of the dominant relations of mercantile accumulation. It was, however, all dependent upon the maintenance of the underlying locus of staple production in the fur trade.

On the political level, this system reflected a British imperial interest in consolidating control over the lands to the north of the Oregon territories. The company was not the ideal agency for such an undertaking, but its involvement in the area and the scope of resources at its disposal rendered its participation essential. Prior to the 1849 arrangement, the British government had ceded control over the territories later to become British Columbia to the company, which in addition to its exploits in the fur trade oversaw sideline activities in the mining of Vancouver Island coal and the cutting of coastal timber for spars. However, the company's main interest lay in the fur trade, an interest that was generally opposed to settlement, economic diversification, and development.

For this reason, the discovery of placer gold, first in the Queen Charlotte Islands and later in the Fraser River area, threw the entire edifice of mercantile accumulation and power into jeopardy. In the early 1850's, following a flurry of gold mining activity in the Queen Charlotte Islands, the colonial governor instituted a licensing system for miners, establishing the state's jurisdiction over the disposition of mineral deposits and providing a basis for future state policy in this area.[9] In a matter of months in 1858 and 1859, the influx of a large and transitory mining population to the B.C. interior led to an extension of independent commodity production on the mainland, a mode predicated upon individual and co-operative forms of the labour process. Groups of miners undertook the joint development of mining claims along the gold bearing rivers of the colony.[10] A new class of independent producers emerged at the hub of the placer gold economy, and the colonial authority extended its regulatory jurisdiction to encompass the new staple orientation. In Victoria, a new merchant bourgeoisie quickly emerged in response to the increasing requirements for provisions among the mainland mining communities.[11] All these new productive processes and class relations lay beyond the reach of effective administration by the Hudson's Bay Company. Consequently, the old mercantile structures soon gave way to a new system of colonial state power; in the process, the institutional and structural linkages binding "state" and "economy" into a single entity were severed. For the first time in British Columbia history, the regional state structure emerged as a distinct political form.

The new colonial state was, however, still subordinate to an external state entity, only this time the subordination was direct, no longer mediated through a mercantile trade monopoly. In effect, the transition to this new state form represented a British response to the socioeconomic and political repercussions of a shift in the region's dominant staple orientation; the altered configuration of social classes within the regional economic formation rendered this transition essential. In this sense, the prevailing institutional form of the state can be seen as directly related to the internal balance of class forces.

During the subsequent colonial period, state intervention was geared largely to the development of a legal framework to regulate land settlement and staple extraction.[12] In addition, the state was active in helping to fund the construction of an interior road network to link up the newly established centres of mining activity.[13] These interventions served a dual purpose. First of all, they helped sustain a system of generalized commodity production on the mainland, at least for the duration of the gold rush, which was the only viable form of economic development given the absence of any significant large-scale investment. Secondly, it helped further British imperial interests by enforcing the crown's claims to the region with an actual presence, settlement, and control, of the area.

This system of commodity production went into crisis with the declining availability of placer gold. As a result, the state experienced declining revenues and mounting deficits.[14] The colonial state on the mainland found itself unable to press ahead with its programme of road construction.[15] The island and mainland colonies were united in 1866 in an attempt to remedy the problem, but in the absence of any significant economic revival, the fiscal crisis persisted through the remaining years leading up to British Columbia's entry into Confederation. As an option for the future of the colonies, Confederation held out the prospect of renewed prosperity on the western end of a new transcontinental rail link. A general reactivation of economic activity could therefore be expected to follow upon the colony's transition to provincial status.

An examination of the political process leading up to the year 1871, however, shows that entry into Confederation was not the only option facing the Pacific colony in the late 1860's. Fearing an anticipated loss of power and prestige, certain sections of the colonial elite favoured retention of the colonial status quo.[16] Farmers, although small in number and weak in political influence, were also anxious lest a departure from colonial status and protection might lead to increased foreign competition and economic decline. On the other hand, sections of the merchant bourgeoisie in Victoria favoured the option of annexation to the United States, hoping that this might lead to increased economic development and a reactivation of Pacific trading links.[17]

However, despite this sort of opposition and public debate, the pro-Confederation position prevailed. Two important factors lay behind this. The first was the continued influence of British imperial policy, with its emphasis upon the maintenance of a modified form of British control over the west coast area.[18] The second factor concerned efforts made by reformers like John Robson and Amor de Cosmos to dovetail the push for British Columbia's entry into Confederation with the struggle for a form of responsible government within the colony.[19] Miners in the interior, many of whom were of American background, favoured responsible self-government. In addition, for nascent resource capital—such as the Dunsmuir coal and rail interests on Vancouver Island or the Hendry and McNair timber interests of New Westminster—responsible government within Canadian Confederation promised increased access to the regional political process and an opportunity to press for provincial government encouragement of private development projects. In this way, the change in political structures represented by Confederation heralded the advent of relationships and policies conducive to accelerated capital accumulation and economic development.

The interplay of these two factors was reflected in the Confederation agreement. On the one hand, the colony of British Columbia was to enter the Dominion of Canada as a province. In this manner the British were able to secure their overall objective and thus safeguard present and future interests in the area. On the other hand, a system of responsible government was to be established, a reflection of the growing power and influence of the reform forces. Thus the alteration in the form of the state that Confederation and responsible government represented can be seen as directly related to an internal process of class struggle: the representatives of interests favouring opposing solutions to the region's depressed economic circumstances were pitted against each other. The fact that the reform-Confederation forces were victorious, however, was in large measure a product of external factors, most notably the British imperial interest in seeing British Columbia's entry into Canada. For this reason, it is essential when interpreting the sequence of events leading to B.C.'s 1871 union with the Dominion of Canada to place the class struggles discussed above within a broader, international context.

With Confederation came the prospect of a transcontinental rail link, increased settlement, and prosperity based upon the expanding frontiers of large-scale capital investment in provincial resource development. Prior to the completion of the rail line in 1886, however, the province's economy continued to rest upon a generalized system of independent commodity production first established in the colonial gold rush period. Capitalist relations of production were evident during this time but were largely confined to the province's coal industry on Vancouver Island. For the most part, production on this scale and class relations characteristic of a developed capitalist mode were not to be found throughout the rest of the province's resource industries.

Through this early period, the provincial state continued to develop and extend a legal framework for the regulation of land and resource alienation. Given the preponderance of the independent commodity mode, these laws increased the access of individual small-scale producers to settlement land and natural resources. In the process, the provincial state was forced to abandon any immediate hope of establishing public finance upon a durable foundation of resource revenue. The result was an increased provincial reliance upon federal government subsidization.[20]

This situation changed dramatically in the post-1886 period. Large-scale capital investment followed closely on the heels of the completed Canadian Pacific Railway (C.P.R.) link. In the forestry sector, for example, the North Pacific Lumber company entered production in 1889 near the C.P.R. line east of Vancouver with a capitalization of $100,000, a timber stand of 90,000 acres, and a work force of 1,980 men. Similarly, the Fraser River Mill owned by the Ross and McLaren interests from eastern Canada opened in the early 1890's to service growing export markets.[21] In the mining sector, investment activity was concentrated in the East Kootenay region and was closely connected to the extension of regional branch rail lines which helped render the development of lode mining economically feasible. Between 1890 and 1900, B.C. mineral production grew sevenfold in value as American, British and eastern Canadian capital poured in to avail itself of the expanding and lucrative opportunities.[22] Typical of the late nineteenth-century lode operations were the Le Roi, Centre Star, and War Eagle mines, staked by American prospectors and subsequently capitalized through the promotion of share subscriptions in the United States, and the Kootenay Bonanza and American Flag mines developed with British capital just before the turn of the century.[23] During the same period, the C.P.R.-owned Consolidated Mining and Smelting Company gained a foothold in the province's southeast corner with the acquisition of smelting operations at Trail and later at Rossland. Subsequent years saw C.P.R. interests extend control over a variety of regional mineral developments, including the War Eagle and Centre Star mines in Rossland in 1906, the St. Eugine mine at Moyie in 1906, and the Sullivan mine at Kimberley in 1908.[24]

In a relatively short time, therefore, B.C.'s resource industries were entirely transformed as the large capitalist interests displaced independent and small-scale production. In effect, this signified the opening stages of a transition to the dominance of capitalist productive relations across the entire resource field. In fact, given the relative size, power, and position of the Canadian Pacific rail and mining interests, the argument can be advanced that B.C. found itself launched on a hastened transition to monopolistic capitalist structures during this period.[25]

Within this development process, the city of Vancouver began to emerge as a regional administrative metropole with its own local bourgeoisie well ensconced in the financial field, in real estate and mining promotion, and in various other intermediary sectors. As has been noted, most of the capital invested in the resource sectors came from outside the province—from eastern Canada, Britain, and the United States.[26] The system that emerged reflected a *de facto* "accommodation" between the different sections of local, national, and foreign capital. Within this context, regional capitalists and entrepreneurs entered the fields of real estate promotion and urban infrastructure development (gas and water works) with some limited involvement in resource processing. In addition, provincial interests, centred mainly in Vancouver, took up the provision of various intermediary, service, and "go between" functions (mining brokerage, wholesale trade and financial services) linked to interior and coastal resource development. Eastern Canadian capital, on the other hand, had consolidated a strong presence in the transportation, financial, and resource sectors, while foreign (mostly American and British) interests had largely gravitated to the areas of mine and forestry development.[27] In subsequent years, this system would consolidate itself, thus providing an underlying basis for the development of the distinctive character of contemporary British Columbia political economy.

Throughout the post-1886 period the provincial state authority continued to modify and refine various statutes regulating land tenure and resource alienation. In the area of settlement policy, provincial laws continued to facilitate access to agricultural land for those willing to work it; it was during this period that much of the best land was actually taken up. Some of this represented land previously included in different conveyances for the assistance of rail line construction throughout the province. As it turned out, the largest settlement acreages in these conveyances eventually ended up under the control of the C.P.R.[28] For this reason, the province was unable to regulate directly the terms and conditions governing agricultural settlement on much of the province's limited acreage.

In the area of resource development, provisions for increased royalty payments and stringent mandatory improvement expenditures on crown-granted land used for mining show the provincial state playing an active role in reinforcing existing tendencies towards large-scale capitalist production.[29] With forestry, licensing changes introduced shortly after the turn of the century enabled large and mostly foreign-based capital to consolidate control over the development rights on vast acreages.[30] In the final analysis, in both of these sectors the trend towards greater capitalization held out the prospect of increased resource revenue for the state. Given this situation, the system of independent commodity production generalized in the pre-C.P.R. period declined rapidly in economic importance under the twin pressures of legislative discouragement and increased competition from larger capitalist interests.

It was, however, in the area of intraprovincial rail line promotion that the state went farthest in helping to hasten the advent of the monopoly capitalist mode. Rail lines were essential for the profitable expansion of logging operations and lode mineral production.[31] Consequently, late nineteenth-century politics in British Columbia was largely the story of a crowded succession of rail line charters whisked through the legislative assembly in private members' bills with promises of lucrative land grants and cash subsidies. Although few of the intended lines were ever built, the impact of those completed was substantial in helping to facilitate the penetration of foreign and eastern Canadian capital investment into the province's resource hinterland.[32]

Under the impact of this type of investment and amidst a flurry of main and branch line rail construction, British Columbia became a province dominated by capitalist relations of production. In the process, the stage was set for a period of rapid and sustained growth as the province entered the twentieth century. It is important, however, to note the effect this transition had upon the regional class structure. As has been stated, in the period leading up to 1886, the provincial economy rested upon a mode of independent commodity production. The succeeding capitalist mode was radically different insofar as it entailed a generalization of the wage relation and a separation of the direct producers from control over the process and results of their social labour. In other words, capitalism created an industrial working class in the resource sectors. Data from the federal census of 1901 revealed, for example, the existence of thirty-two gold lode mines in the province in that year, each employing an average of 60 workers, fourteen copper mines each averaging 63 workers, and thirty-four silver-lead mines each employing on average 37 workers. In coal mining, the level of productive concentration was much greater with the province's eight producing mines averaging some 540 workers each.[33]

The impact of this process of capital concentration and proletarianization upon the political climate and culture of the province was nothing short of profound. Through the last decades of the nineteenth century, British Columbia emerged as a vast and sprawling battlefield of class conflict with workers and their fledgling organizations pitted against the power of the employers and their associations.[34] Faced with an increasing incidence of bitter and often violent strike activity, the state took steps to guarantee the stability and social cohesion required by established interests and potential investors, using legal sanctions to break working class resistance in certain situations. In others, such as the miners' 1877 strike against the Dunsmuir interests and the Wellington coal strike of 1890, militia violence and state-sponsored repression were employed for the same purpose.[35] Developments such as these suggest that the state's role in organizing a legal framework for society was relevant not only for determining the conditions of resource alienation and development but also in defending and maintaining the established structures of class rule and power.

The process of class struggle and conflict was not confined to the province's mines and mills through this period. Beginning in the late nineteenth century, labour representatives managed to win election to the provincial legislative assembly. There, a system of shifting pre-party alignments provided a propitious environment for the attainment of prolabour reforms and concessions. A prime example of this type of reform was the successful struggle for an eight-hour working day in the metal mines, a measure passed through the legislature in 1899.[36]

As long as labour participation in the political process centred around this type of pressure-group reformism, it could be accommodated within existing political arrangements. However, the last years of the nineteenth century saw the beginnings of a basic shift in working-class organization and ideology throughout B.C. Such was a process closely bound up with the emergence of industrial unionism in the form of the Western Federation of Miners in the interior mining communities. This shift found a political expression in the emergence of new groups and parties which rejected a preoccupation with issues of piecemeal reform as they embraced openly socialist perspectives on the nature of modern capitalist exploitation.[37]

Faced with this growth of a radical labour challenge, establishment groups and interests in the provincial assembly moved to adopt a system of formal party alignments and divisions.[38] In this manner, the threat of an independent, class-conscious labour movement was contained, at least at the state level. Describing some of the factors that led to this development, one author wrote,

> So long as governments changed in kaleidoscopic fashion and House members crossed the floor at whim, industrial promoters, whether in the mining, railway, fishing or lumber industries were reluctant to invest for fear of changed conditions. Railway contracts were made and unmade, mining laws passed and altered. Investments could not be planned and undertaken where the legal environment was not predictable.[39]

This transition to fixed party distinctions and the subsequent adoption of the disciplinary and organizational modes of parliamentary party operation signified yet another transformation of the institutional form of the provincial state. It also offers another indication of the manner in which developments pertaining to society's dominant productive mode—in this case, advancing capitalist concentration and capital/labour class polarization—necessitated such a transition. In the final analysis, the province witnessed a fundamental political and institutional shift from a parliamentary system based upon loose and shifting alliances to one resting upon fixed party distinctions and rivalries. This latter arrangement was more ideally suited to the task of maintaining a stable investment climate as the province entered the twentieth century.

The transition to a party system in B.C. provincial politics represents a change in the organizational form of the state that falls in line with the two transitions cited earlier: from mercantile to colonial and from colonial to provincial. All three transitions bear a direct relation to the interconnected processes of economic crisis and economic restructuring, class development and class struggle as they impact upon political structures. In this way, the analysis of political change in B.C., particularly as it pertains to changes in the form and operation of state power, finds itself closely linked to an analysis of the underlying socioeconomic reality of the province. Within each period, state intervention, through the provision of legal regulation and the promotion of infrastructure development, helped facilitate an expansion of the productive forces. In late nineteenth-century British Columbia, this expansion signalled the emergence and growing dominance of distinctively capitalist relations of production in the resource fields. Much of the investment capital underpinning resource development came from outside the province, and the entire process consolidated British Columbia's traditional role as a resource hinterland supplying an ever-increasing external demand for staple resource products.

So, as the province entered the twentieth century, its dominant resource sectors found themselves firmly established on a trajectory of capitalist expansion and development. Within this context, the provincial state continued to encourage the process of capital accumulation just as it had earlier helped lay the groundwork for the emergence of the resource-based economy. The end product was a provincial economic base firmly established on the foundation of forestry and mining. A legacy of the nineteenth century, this orientation was destined to leave its lasting imprint on the twentieth as well.

CONCLUSION

This paper has attempted to develop a theoretically informed overview of the early state in British Columbia. Clearly, more work needs to be undertaken to examine in greater detail the precise contours of nineteenth-century political relations. In addition, such an analysis could be extended forward in time to develop an understanding of how dominant patterns and trends evolved into the twentieth century.

Essential to the success of projects of this type, however, is the incorporation of insights drawn from a theoretical framework that stresses the centrality of class relations and class struggle and particularly the intersection of these critical factors with the development of political forms and processes. Only in this way can the analysis of state structures and political relations hope to find an adequate grounding in socioeconomic reality.

NOTES

1. In the area of transportation development, see Helen Ferguson, "The Development of Communications in Colonial British Columbia as Affected by British Interest" (M.A. thesis, Department of History, University of British Columbia, 1939) and Robert Cail, *Land, Man and the Law* (Vancouver: University of British Columbia Press, 1974). In the area of state finance, see Paul Phillips, "Confederation and the Economy of British Columbia," in George Shelton (ed.), *British Columbia and Confederation* (Victoria: Morriss, 1967). In the area of settlement promotion, see Leonard Wrinch, "Land Policy of the Colony of Vancouver Island, 1849-1886" (M.A. thesis, University of British Columbia, 1932), and Phyllis Mikkelsen, "Land Settlement Policy on the Mainland of British Columbia, 1858-1874" (M.A. thesis, University of British Columbia, 1950).
2. In the area of responsible government, see Stella Higgins, "British Columbia and the Confederation Era," in Shelton, *British Columbia and Confederation*, Jack Scott, *Sweat and Struggle: Working Class Struggles in Canada* (Vancouver: New Star, 1974), and Isabel Bescoby, "A Colonial Administration: An Analysis of Administration in British Columbia, 1869-71," in K. Ralston and J. Friesen (eds.), *Historical Essays on British Columbia* (Toronto: McClelland and Stewart, 1976). For federal-provincial relations, see Margaret Ormsby, *Relations Between British Columbia and the Dominion of Canada, 1871-1885* (Ann Arbor: University Microfilms, 1972) and Harold Johns, "British Columbia's Campaign for Better Terms, 1871-1907" (M.A. thesis, University of British Columbia, 1935). And, in the field of party politics, see Walter Sage, "Federal Parties and Provincial Political Groups in British Columbia, 1871-1903," *Pacific Historical Review* 1, no. 2, (1932):424-443, Edith Dobie, "Party History in B.C., 1903-1933," in Ralston and Friesen, *Historical Essays on British Columbia*, pp.70–81, and Eleanor Mercer, "Political Groups in British Columbia, 1803-1898" (M.A. thesis, University of British Columbia, 1937).
3. Ralph Miliband, *The State in Capitalist Society* (London: Quartet, 1973), p. 62.
4. John Holloway and Sol Picciotto, "Introduction," in J. Holloway and S. Picciotto (eds.), *State and Capital: A Marxist Debate* (London: Edward Arnold, 1978), pp. 4-5.
5. Nicos Poulantzas, *Political Power and Social Classes* (London: Verso, 1978), p. 29.
6. E. Wright, G. Esping-Andersen, and R. Friedland, "Modes of Class Struggle and the Capitalist State," *Kapitalistate*, nos. 4-5 (Summer 1976).
7. See Joachim Hirsch, "The State Apparatus and Social Reproduction," in Holloway and Picciotto, *State and Capital: A Marxist Debate*, pp. 57-107.

8. See the range of literature surveyed by Bob Jessop, "Recent Theories of the Capitalist State," *Cambridge Journal of Economics,* 1 (December 1977):353–73.
9. See Ferguson, "The Development of Communications in Colonial British Columbia," pp. 21-23.
10. W. J. Trimble, *The Mining Advance into the Inland Empire* (Madison: University of Wisconsin Press, 1914), pp. 223 ff. See also W. Clement, "The Subordination of Labour in Canadian Mining," in W. Clement (ed.), *Class, Power and Property* (Toronto: Methuen, 1983) for a description of the reality of independent commodity production in early Canadian mining development.
11. J. M. S. Careless, "The Business Community in the Early Development of Victoria, British Columbia," in Ralston and Friesen, *Historical Essays on British Columbia,* pp. 179-80.
12. Wrinch, "Land Policy of the Colony of Vancouver Island," and Mikkelsen, "Land Settlement Policy on the Mainland of British Columbia."
13. Ferguson, "The Development of Communications in Colonial British Columbia," pp. 39-40, 94-95.
14. See Phillips, "Confederation and the Colony of British Columbia." Phillips's article draws upon information provided by the colonial "Blue Books" to outline the economic predicament faced by the colonial administration in the immediate pre-Confederation period.
15. Ferguson, "The Development of Communications in Colonial British Columbia," p. 106.
16. This area is discussed in Bescoby, "A Colonial Administration" and in Susan D. Scott, "The Attitude of the Colonial Governors and Officials Towards Confederation," in Shelton, *British Columbia and Confederation,* pp. 143-64.
17. Stella Higgins, "British Columbia and the Confederation Era," in Shelton, *British Columbia and Confederation,* p. 19.
18. See David M. Farr, *The Colonial Office and Canada, 1867-1887* (Toronto: University of Toronto Press, 1955).
19. The confluence of these two struggles is examined in greater detail in John Malcolmson, "Resource Development and the State in Early British Columbia" (M.A. thesis, Simon Fraser University, 1980), pp. 42ff.
20. For a detailed breakdown of provincial state revenue during this period which reveals the full extent of the federal subsidy in its varied forms, see *British Columbia in the Canadian Confederation,* a submission presented to the Royal Commission on Dominion-Provincial Relations by the Government of the Province of British Columbia (Victoria: King's Printer, 1938) p. 243.
21. G.W. Taylor, *Timber* (North Vancouver: J. J. Douglas, 1975), p. 39.
22. *Statistics of Industry in British Colmbia* (Victoria: Economic Council of British Columbia, 1938), tables M2 and M8.
23. Harold Innis, "Settlement and the Mining Frontier," in W. A. Mackintosh and W. L. G. Joerg (eds.), *Canadian Frontiers of Settlement* (Toronto: Macmillan, 1936), p. 227, and Tom Naylor, *The History of Canadian Business* (Toronto: Lorimer, 1975), p. 92.
24. Harold Innis, "Settlement and the Mining Frontier," pp. 282-83, and H. Angus, F. Howay, and W. Sage, *British Columbia and the United States* (Toronto: Ryerson, 1942), p. 282.
25. When the extent of the C.P.R.'s land conveyances is taken into account, the company ranks as one of the largest corporations in the entire world in terms of assets for the late nineteenth-century period. See R. Galois, "The Social Structure in Space: The Making of Vancouver Island, 1886-1901" (Ph.D. diss., Simon Fraser University, 1979).
26. The sources of capital investment in B.C. resource industries in the late nineteenth century are discussed in D. G. Paterson, "European Finance Capital and British Columbia: An Essay on the Role of the Regional Entrepreneur," *B.C. Studies* 21

(Spring 1974):33-47; D. G. Paterson, *British Direct Investment in Canada* (Toronto: University of Toronto Press, 1976); and Angus, Howay, and Sage, *British Columbia and the United States*.

27. For a detailed examination of this system, see Galois, "The Making of Vancouver Island," pp. 203-42.
28. Angus, Howay, and Sage, *British Columbia and the United States,* pp. 253-63 provides a discussion of the process of branch line absorption by the C.P.R. during this time. See also R. Cail, *Land, Man and the Law*, Chapter 10, for an analysis of the nature and extent of land subsidization for rail construction in B.C.
29. R. Cail, *Land, Man and the Law*, pp. 73ff.
30. British Columbia, "Report of the Forestry Commission," *B.C. Sessional Papers*, 12th Parliament, 2d Session, 1911, p. D30ff. The evolution of forest tenure in B.C. is also discussed in G. Ainscough, "The British Columbia Forest Land Tenure System," in W. McKillop and W. Mead (eds.), *Timber Policy Issues in British Columbia* (Vancouver: University of British Columbia Press, 1976).
31. See Angus, Howay and Sage, *British Columbia and the United States*, for a discussion of this area.
32. Martin Robin, *The Rush for Spoils: The Company Province, 1871-1933* (Toronto: McClelland and Stewart, 1972), p. 63. Also, see Tom Naylor, *The History of Canadian Business, 1867-1914*, Vol. 2 (Toronto: Lorimer, 1975), p. 25.
33. *Census of Canada*, 1901 (Ottawa: King's Printer, 1903), Vol. 2, Table 58.
34. Three studies which deal with the growth of late nineteenth-century labour radicalism in B.C. are J. Scott, *Sweat and Struggle: Working Class Struggles in Canada* (Vancouver: New Star Books, 1974), R. McCormack, *Reformers, Rebels and Revolutionaries* (Toronto: University of Toronto Press, 1977), and Martin Robin, *Radical Politics and Canadian Labour* (Kingston: Industrial Relations Centre, Queen's University, 1968).
35. Jack Scott, *Sweat and Struggle,* 1, pp. 195-98; Paul Phillips, *No Power Greater* (Vancouver: B.C. Federation of Labour and the Boag Foundation, 1967), pp. 5-7; Harold Griffin, *British Columbia: The People's Early Story* (Vancouver: Tribune, 1958), pp. 48-49.
36. T. Loosemore, "The British Columbia Labour Movement and Political Action, 1879-1906" (M.A. thesis, University of British Columbia, 1954).
37. A prime example of this tendency was the emergence of the Marxist-oriented Socialist Party in B.C. On this, see McCormack, *Reformers, Rebels and Revolutionaries*, pp. 31 ff. and Loosemore, "The British Columbia Labour Movement," pp. 198-200.
38. A discussion of the nature of pre-party politics in B.C. up to the period of transition to party distinctions is offered in Sage, "Federal Parties and Provincial Political Groups," Mercer, "Political Groups in British Columbia," and E. Dobie, "Some Aspects of Party History in British Columbia," *Pacific Historical Review* 1, no. 2 (1932):235-251. See also the discussion offered in Malcolmson, "Resource Development and the State," pp. 122-45.
39. Robin, *The Rush for Spoils*, p. 85.

3

Making Indians

MICHAEL KEW

In the early 1800's, when Canadian and British fur traders extended their routes to what is now British Columbia, there were approximately 70,000 Indians in the area. These few people were distributed among some twenty-five territorial groupings each speaking a mutually unintelligible language.[1] Additionally they conformed in culture to three major divisions: Northwest Coast, Plateau, and Sub-Arctic.

Looking closer still we find that Indians were divided into an uncounted number of political groupings of varying size. These ranged from small, loosely integrated local bands of families occupying immense territories, as among Beaver Indians, to occasional confederations of several village groups of a thousand or more people, as found on the coast and lower reaches of large rivers. Over much of the province the major political unit was a group of people centred in a winter village. Each group used resources from, and in that sense occupied, large and imprecisely delimited areas of land. Centralized authority was the exception rather than the rule.

In British Columbia today there are 189 politically separate units called bands and 1,620 parcels of land called reserves. In total these comprise 843,479 acres and range in size from less than one to several thousand. Reserves are widely scattered throughout the province, although they are generally more numerous and smaller near the coast.

The proliferation of reserves in British Columbia (more than half of the total for Canada) is understandable in light of the original linguistic and political divisions, the patterns of land use, and the history of colonization. To some extent in the plateau and markedly on the coast, Indians were closely attached to places: permanent village sites, food gathering locations, fishing stations, and so on.

The first whites on the scene were fur traders with whom Indians found it profitable to interact—interests were complementary. The upsurge of white immigration, which came with the gold rush of 1858 and the rush to find other easy spoils on the frontier, be they minerals, fish, or timber, brought about much more discord and some bloodshed.

As settlement proceeded, governments had to face the issue of conflict over rights to Indian land. Colonial officers had begun to survey and reserve tracts of land occupied by Indians in areas prone to white settlement; for a time Governor James Douglas favoured a policy of purchasing Indian rights in land by treaty agreements. But sufficient funds were not available locally, nor were they forthcoming from the imperial government. The colony entered Confederation in 1871, and as part of the terms of union the new province agreed to grant land for Indian reserves, while the federal government was to assume responsibility for administering these lands and Indian Affairs generally.

In this process the earlier recognition of Indian title to land was conveniently forgotten and Indian protests were allowed to go unanswered. No treaties such as those being negotiated throughout the other western provinces by federal agents were made in British Columbia, with the exception of participation by Indians east of the Rocky Mountains in Treaty No. 8 (1899).[2] British Columbia Indians generally agree that they still hold unextinguished aboriginal rights to most of the land—a position with which the Canadian government concurs and for which reason it has instructed the office of Indian Claims to negotiate settlement of the issue in British Columbia.

What eventually happened was that the two governments, acting in concert, designated most occupied villages and some small seasonal campsites as reserves set apart for the special use of Indians. Although some consultation with Indians occurred in this process, from the Indians' point of view it was unilateral action by governments and their agents.

This allotment policy allowed the Indians to remain dispersed in small scattered groups more or less in areas of traditional residence, as the settlers took up large areas in between. From the white point of view this was a sensible procedure. It also looks in retrospect rather more humane than the enforced removal and confinement of Indians that occurred in parts of the United States and in the Canadian plains. Of course it also meant that the Indians, dispersed in small groups, remained militarily insignificant and never effectively threatened the security of settlers.

The maintenance of many small local residence places for Indians was a most suitable solution to the state's problem of what to do with the Indian, and it fitted neatly with his attachment to his traditional home and desire to extract in old ways a portion of sustenance from the land. The dispersed population, able to fish and hunt, provided pockets of local labour ready to work for minimal wages when required by the fishing, farming, and timber industries.

But here as elsewhere in North America, Indians presented other vexing problems to white immigrants and their leaders. The Indians were heathens, uneducated and uncivilized. They drank to excess when they could, abandoning their usual restrained demeanor. They disregarded fences and camped where it was convenient—"squatters" on their own land. Federal legislation, eventually known as the Indian Act, became the prime means for dealing with problems like these. The legislation applied to British Columbia's Indians from the time of entry into Confederation.

The Indian Act is a collection of laws or rules proclaimed by the government. Sanctions are provided for those who break the law, for like all legislation, it is backed by the power of the state: the police, the courts, penal services, and ultimately the military. But no Acts of Parliament are simply bundles of "thou shall" or "thou shalt not" statements. The Indian Act carefully defines terms and specifies courses of action for administrative bodies which it created—most pointedly the Department of Indian Affairs. (At various times in its history, this agency has been a department to itself and a branch of other departments such as Secretary of State, Interior, Citizenship and Immigration, and, perhaps most revealing of all, a branch of the Department of Mines and Resources.) The specified courses of action include the right to make "regulations" and to act in accordance with these. Thus the means are provided for the administrative agency to create a second order of "laws" to get on with the business at hand. In short, the act is a charter which provides the Department of Indian Affairs and Northern Development with power to establish procedures and rules and to administer them. With definitions, regulations, and charter, it creates a social system and defines people's views of people.

Let us consider some of the actual definitions within the act, looking first at the meaning of "Indian." In common sense terms an Indian is someone with more or less brown skin and black straight hair, who is descended from original inhabitants of North America. Some white Canadians may recognize that Indians still speak special languages, and some may know there are old-fashioned Indians around who practise strange customs. For the Indian himself, he is Indian first of all because that is how he was born and reared. If his family call themselves Indians and others around agree, that's how the individual knows his Indianness. As he grows, he attains a working understanding of how he is unique and distinct from those who are not Indian.

What does the Indian Act say? Picture yourself a young Indian reading the act for the first time in order to find out. On the second page you find that: "'Indian' means a person who pursuant to this act is registered as an Indian or is entitled to be registered as an Indian."[3]

Not much help, so you press on. You learn that a register of names is kept by the Department of Indian Affairs and that certain persons are entitled to have their names entered in that register. In short, if you are the child of a man registered as an Indian, or his wife, or the illegitimate child of a woman so registered, then you too may be registered. You also find that the original register of names lists people considered Indian in an unspecific sense when the act came into force. But quite clearly you are definitely an Indian only when your name is on the register. Nothing is said of race, culture, or language—the common-sense indicators. And it's clearly not sufficient to think of yourself as Indian to be one.

Some rather intriguing possibilities follow. You find that the act requires females to take the status of their husbands; if you are an Indian female and marry a non-Indian, your name may be erased from the registered list. By the act of marriage you can become a non-Indian. Similarly if you are a white woman, or any female non-Indian, and you marry a registered Indian, you become, willy nilly, an Indian. And it is possible, indeed it has happened, that a woman, born a white English-speaking citizen of Great Britain, has become not only a Canadian Indian but also, in due course, an Indian Chief.

At the same time in most provinces there are many people, even whole communities of thousands, who speak an Indian language as their first tongue and are otherwise identifiable as Indians, who are not legally Indians. These include the Metis of the prairie provinces—the descendents of people whose names were not entered on lists or whose leaders were not party to treaties signed in those areas. Paradoxically, some communities of such people are much more Indian in their own views than many bands of registered Indians. Thus, the corporate view of Indian is far removed from any common-sense view.

Having specified precisely who it affects, the Indian Act goes on to shape community social structure and political organization. It defines a unit called a band, a nominal list of persons who hold in common the rights to the use of reserve land and money that may have accumulated from sale of land and resources. Membership in the band, like the status of registered Indian, is a matter of patrilineal descent and marriage—wives again taking the band membership of husbands. Upon marriage a woman usually moves away to live with her husband, attaining rights in his band's wealth and giving up rights in her own. She may receive a per capita share of her band's money but no portion or settlement for the value of her reserve lands.

All this is neat and sensible to patriarchal Anglo-Saxon businessmen, but initially it made varying degrees of nonsense to Indians—particularly matrilineal people like the Haida of the Queen Charlotte Islands, who ascribed membership to kin groups exclusively through the female line.

The major wealth of the bands resides in their reserves although these contain only minute fractions of their original territory. As we read further in the act we find they do not even own the reserves in a legal sense, although they certainly understand the reserves to be theirs by right of traditional occupancy. In fact, all the Indian reserves in Canada are owned by the Crown, that is to say, the federal government, which in turn guarantees rights of use and occupancy as specified by the Indian Act. But Indian rights do not extend to sale, lease, subdivision, and so on, except to the extent, generally speaking, that such actions are approved by the chain of command of the Indian Affairs Department.

The numbers and locations of reserves are permanently fixed. The band is therefore a limited group of people with attachments to fixed places, although we should note that Indians may reside off reserves without relinquishing band membership. Should new industry develop in a certain place and a town come into existence with sources of employment, reserves are not created to accommodate Indians. If they are to participate in such development, Indians must leave land and homes, unsold, as well as their kin and friends and the one place which they have been allowed to see as their safe homeland. And, of course, when resources of fur, big game, and fish become inadequate to meet the needs of the people—as has happened in remote reserves in the hinterlands and the coast—the reserves with their populations remain, inadequately subsidized by welfare allowances.

Another new idea which the act introduced across Canada is that of local government by persons in elected or appointed offices. The administrators of the act had to do business with Indians; that is, they had to have Indian signatures on documents from time to time, according to procedures laid out in the act, often quite irrelevant to the ways the Indians themselves did their own business. From the white man's viewpoint what was needed was a representative of the band—a chief. Not all Indian societies had such offices, and the simplest procedure was to create them. So where chiefs were non-existent or intractible, administrators appointed them. What they got were not actual leaders of the Indians but handy "yes" men or the spokesmen of factional divisions.

While the act includes definitions which remade Indians and helped to shape their local social structures, the ones we have mentioned so far were essentially products of rational-legal and administrative patterns of doing things effectively. The aim was not to make Indians into people with names on a list but to identify in a controllable way a client group which could be dealt with effectively. However, the act also includes clauses quite purposefully aimed at changing Indian cultures, at making Indians over, as Harold Cardinal puts it, in the *Unjust Society,* into "brown white men." The most blatant of these have been repealed, but they have had enduring consequences and illustrate succinctly the motives of cultural manipulation underlying the act.

Probably the most notorious prohibitions the act ever contained were the clauses forbidding Indians the purchase, possession, and consumption of alcohol. These applied in British Columbia until 1951 when Indians were permitted to drink in public beverage rooms and lounges but nowhere else. Finally in 1956, the province decided not to prosecute offences still extant in the act, and the Indian since then has had in effect more or less the same rights as other citizens in this regard.

Why the attention to liquor? First, there was and is a great myth that Indians are physically less capable of withstanding the effects of alcohol. This of course is nonsense. Drinking behaviour and the ability to consume liquor may vary with health and weight but not with race. Cultural, learned ways of reacting to liquor are, however, widely variable. In addition to the myth, liquor has long been known as a waster of money, a temptor of workmen, and a debaucher of women. And sure enough the Indians often behaved exuberantly and even rather nastily when they drank. They created unpleasant spectacles in the streets. One should note parenthetically that Indians were introduced to booze in the first place by some pretty exuberant drinkers: fur traders, sailors, and loggers. Furthermore, the condition of prohibition, long in force, is a notably ineffective way to encourage genteel consumption of pleasurable things.

The intent of the law was to protect Indians from debauchery and to guide them singly and collectively into a self-sufficient and morally correct way of life. An unintended consequence was to make Indians liable before the courts for acts which non-Indians freely performed. Far from raising the Indian's moral standing, the corporate rules paradoxically defined Indians as criminals and left us with a tragic legacy of effects we have yet to assess fully.

Another prohibition, directly affecting the coastal tribes, was the law against the potlatch, the rituals of gift exchange and feasting which were at the root of the Northwest Coast socioeconomic systems. The anti-potlatch law was aimed in part at stopping traditional religious rituals which were often performed at large inter-village feasts and stood squarely in the way of the goal of fitting the Indians to the Christian mould. Indians who held potlatches were poor church attendants. The Indian Act is still openly partial to Christianity and missionaries; in federal schools on Indian reserves, teachers may be required, according to the act, to be of the same denomination as the majority of band members, and so, as a normal course, the churches reach rather effectively into the classrooms.

By far the most impressive and disturbing aspects of potlatches, however, were that they appeared to be spendthrift giveaways of food and wealth. Not understanding the patterns of reciprocity involved in these exchanges, whites were outraged to see an Indian fisherman work hard for several seasons, amass a large stock of foodstuffs and goods, and then give it all away at one fell swoop during a great happy festival to be left apparently destitute and a candidate for "relief." To the white man it seemed a contradiction of the whole Protestant business ethic.

Before it was removed from the act in 1951, the anti-potlatch law had varying effects on the Indians. It stopped potlatching in some areas, discouraged members of many communities from participation, and incidentally opened or deepened factional rifts. On the other hand, it drove some potlatching activities underground, where they achieved added significance to the people as protests against the authority of the white world. Potlatches were not done away with by law; rather the law became an additional factor, common to all coast tribes, in shaping the course of their change.

The portions of the act most destructive of Indian culture and society, however, were those dealing with education. Schooling was made compulsory long before adequate schools were available to accommodate Indian children, and teachers, truant officers and other officials were given extraordinary power of enforcement, including removal of children from custody of parents.[4] Under the act, Indian children who are expelled from school or fail to attend regularly are juvenile delinquents, and may be dealt with accordingly.[5] Until the mid 1950's, Indian schools were segregated, generally had less well qualified teachers, and most were residential schools: large boarding schools in central locations to which children were removed for ten months of the year. It was conventional policy for teachers and staff, usually either Roman Catholic or Protestant missionaries, to prohibit and punish the speaking of Indian languages within the premises; thus, lessons were invariably in English. These schools did two things: they weakened or destroyed Indian languages and the cultural beliefs embodied and conveyed in those languages; and they altered the structure of home communities by removing children and interrupting vital socialization processes that occurred in a community setting. This further weakened Indian culture.

My favourite example of the arrogant legislative approach to changing peoples' ways of life is a clause which also disappeared with the 1951 revision of the act. It gave a court the power to restrain and subsequently to impose a fine of $25.00 or thirty days in jail to any Indian who, "by inordinate frequenting of a poolroom . . . misspends or wastes his time or means to the detriment of himself, his family or household."[6] This is a prime example of a rational, consistent approach carried to such an extreme as to outdo itself and become completely self-defeating. The intention is to invoke the force of courts against deviation from an ideal model of behaviour. To a white bureaucrat or businessman, perhaps himself with a continual shadow of guilt about "wasting" time, a fine of $25.00 or thirty days looks like a good enough reason to get out of the pool room and get busy at the woodpile. But to others not imbued with the same value for a dollar and guilt about idleness, nothing could be more absurd than the idea that wasting time is a crime, nothing, that is, but the second idea that an appropriate punishment for it should be thirty days in jail!

This law illustrates nicely the colonizers' attitude towards the colonized which permeates the Indian Act. But sharper teeth resided in other acts of parliament and legislature, such as those which denied federal and provincial voting rights to Indians. In British Columbia, Indians were not granted provincial franchise until 1949, and it was not until 1960 that the federal franchise was extended to all Indians. In the federal election of 1962 the Indians were, for the first time, freely able to vote for the governments which made the legislation directing their lives.

The politically weak and subordinate position of Indians vis-à-vis the department of Indian Affairs and the white world is ensured by the still existing sections which restrict Indians' ability to use reserve land, to spend money held in a band's name, to enact bylaws, and to plan community businesses—in short, to undertake anything of importance or significance for themselves. In all such actions, hovering more or less imminently in the background, is the personage of the Indian agent and his staff, who may veto and must approve and process almost anything that a band council wishes to do on behalf of its membership.

In most relationships with whites, this structural subordination of the Indians is repeated: Indians are the receivers of services, the subordinate clients of white agencies of health, education, welfare. They are employees of white businesses, workers supervised by white foremen, debtors of white storekeepers and loan companies.

Not only do the rational rules of the corporate state define the Indian as a person with his name on a list in an office filing cabinet—to speak of the reality of the definition—but they are also the core of a system which created and perpetuates the dependent and subordinate condition of *being* Indian.

In case there is a mistaken notion that Indians are living a prosperous life, well cared for by a benevolent state, we should take note of a few hard facts. Statistics Canada noted in 1980 that native Indians had incomes far below those of other Canadians, referring to studies showing that natives who were employed earned only 84 per cent of the mean income of Canadian wage earners, and that proportionately fewer Indians enjoyed earned incomes—unemployment among Indians being more than four times the rate for non-Indians.[7] There is nothing in the trends of recent years to suggest that the findings of the 1966 study directed by Professor H. B. Hawthorn are not fully applicable today. At that time, the average per capita earned incomes of Indians were only one-fifth those of non-Indians. Social assistance programmes have come to play an ever-increasing role and Statistics Canada reports that in 1973-74 "an estimated 55 per cent of all registered Indians received some form of social assistance."[8] These statistics do not describe real communities very well. There is certainly great variation in ranges of Indian income and employment; what is starkly apparent to researchers and administrators in contact with reserve communities, however, is the pervasive poverty, entrenched unemployment, and consequent simmering sense of deprivation. This is most forcefully attested by rates of suicide and accidental death among Indians. In 1977, the rate of suicide per 100,000 was 17 for British Columbia as a whole and 48 for registered Indians.[9] Accidental death has been the leading cause of death among native Indians for several years; according to the Medical Services Branch of the Department of National Health and Welfare (the branch of federal government presently charged with supervisory responsibility for registered Indian health services), alcohol abuse is estimated to be a contributing factor in 80 per cent of such cases.[10] Although the Indian population as a whole is increasing, there are still serious problems. Infant mortality of registered Indians in British Columbia in 1981 was still at 36.1 per thousand live births, while the rate for the province as a whole has been around 17 in recent years.

However, there are good things to be said about being Indian and living in an Indian community. Kinship bonds, social networks, and cultural systems are supportive in a psychological as well as economic sense. To a considerable extent, Indians create communities in which people look after one another; Indian communities in this sense of the term also extend into urban areas and their skid-road sectors, often many miles distant from home reserves. Nevertheless, no Canadian should believe the platitude that Indians are content to live the way they do or that the paternalistic government takes good care of them. Indian life expectancy is significantly lower than that of non-Indians. Chronic illness, frustration, self-destructive violence, and sudden death are routine parts of Indian experience. These are not the stuff of an abundant life.

It should be obvious that Canada's Indian policy has failed to bring the Indians into the mainstream of Canadian life. Indeed if we look again at the act we note an immediate paradox. The act was intended, in part, to make the Indians more like whites so they could assimilate or integrate fully with the larger society. This is not written into the act, but it has been an understood and often stated policy. But such an aim is contradicted from the outset in the very terms of reference and definitions which create Indians as a special new category of people. Indians are made into legal things and attached to specific legal places in inflexible ways. Indian land is made into reserves, and reserves are, by definition, segregated places of residence. As long as they exist, equality of integration and assimilation are ultimately impossible. The Indian Act guarantees the persistence of Indians.

In a sort of extension of this contradiction, Indian Affairs employees have been fond of saying their job has been to help the Indian develop to the point where he can look after his own affairs—the agent is "trying to work himself out of his job." That, of course, is quite improbable. People in bureaucracies are much more likely to make work than to complete finite tasks. In fact, the aims and goals of corporate organizations aren't couched in finite terms; they are continual: they provide a *service*; they *maintain* law and order.

To complicate this whole issue, it is not only the Indian Affairs department that is interested in maintaining some aspects of the present relationship; now the Indians are too. This became patently clear in 1969, when the federal government released a proposal for a new policy on Indian Affairs which included sweeping revisions of the act including disbanding the Department of Indian Affairs within five years. Apparently awakening to the paradox of defining Indians as a special kind of people and admitting that it was discriminatory legislation, the government proposed to alter this feature.

Indian leaders across Canada responded to the proposal immediately and negatively. One of them, Harold Cardinal, reasoned that the existing bureaucracy would simply be replaced by a series of provincially constituted ones, and that instead of one enemy the Indians would have ten—a fairly astute prognosis. Indians also expressed fears about loss of certain small privileges which the federal act guarantees: for example, Indians do not pay inheritance taxes or taxes on income they earn from employment on reserves; there is no land tax levied on those parts of the reserves occupied by Indians. Of course, all other forms of taxation—for example, the hidden taxes in the retail prices for goods and services—are paid by Indians. Finally and most emphatically, the Indian leaders clearly stated that they feared the loss of the status of Indian. They did not talk about being Iroquois or Kwakiutl or Cree. They were saying that they wanted to continue to be *Indians* and did not wish to assimilate and otherwise lose those characteristics which set them apart from white men.

With poetic justice we have come full circle. The state created *Indians* as Canadians know them in a conceptual sense, and the state had a large hand in shaping material circumstances of dispossession and political subjugation which create the common condition of Indian life in Canada. Indians originally were themselves—the Dene, Haida, or Gitksan, as they termed themselves. Now the state would rid itself of its own creation, the status of Indian and all that means, but the Indians are fighting to retain this as a slender guarantee of their own separate identity.

NOTES

*This paper is reprinted with permission from *Canadian Dimension*.

1. Wilson Duff, *The Indian History of British Columbia*, Vol. 1, *The Impact of the White Man*, Anthropology in B.C. Memoir No. 5 (Victoria: Provincial Museum of B.C., 1964).
2. P. A. Cumming and N. H. Mickenberg (eds.), *Native Rights in Canada* (Toronto: Indian-Eskimo Association of Canada and General Publishing, 1972).
3. *Indian Act*, Revised Statutes of Canada, 1970, c.1-6, s.2(1).
4. Ibid., s.119 (1-6).
5. Ibid., s.120.
6. *Indian Act*, Revised Statutes of Canada, 1947, s.140A.
7. Statistics Canada, *Perspectives Canada III* (Ottawa: Supply and Services, 1980), p.175.
8. H. B. Hawthorn (ed.), *A Survey of Contemporary Indians of Canada* (Ottawa: Department of Indian Affairs, 1966), p.175.
9. Canada. Department of National Health and Welfare, *Medical Services, Annual Report—Pacific Region, 1977* (Vancouver, n.d.), p.7.
10. Ibid.

4

The Underground Economy:
The Mining Frontier to 1920

PAUL PHILLIPS

INTRODUCTION

In British Columbia's formative years, it was the mining industry that propelled economic development, encouraged the integration of the colony into Confederation, and placed its particular political-economic stamp on social and class relations. In 1907, in fact, W. A. Bailie-Grohman claimed: "The history of British Columbia is brief. Gold made and gold unmade it."[1] But gold was just one of the products of the ground, and while its meteoric rise during the gold rush of the 1850's and 1860's commands much attention from economic and social historians, it was the much less glamorous coal and base metal mines that had more lasting and significant effects on the social and economic fabric of the province in the seven decades culminating in the First World War.

The mining industry encompasses a diverse range of products, among the most important being precious metals (gold and silver), base metals (copper, lead, zinc, and nickel), iron ore, and coal. Of these, only iron ore and nickel were not significant in the early history of B.C. In addition, there are two very different forms of gold mining, placer mining and lode mining, forms which had dissimilar implications for the socio-economic structure of the province. Placer mining involved the recovery of free gold, washed out of ore-bearing rock by erosion, from alluvial deposits along the river and creek beds. It is usually associated with "panning" for gold, though panning was more commonly a prospecting technique and placer mining was usually done with rocker cradles and riffle boxes. Lode mining (sometimes referred to as quartz mining) involved underground mining in bedrock, the original host rock of the placer gold, to get at the source or "mother lode."

Coal and base metal mining had much in common with lode mining, in terms of technology and social relations, and relatively little in common with placer mining. Placer mining attracted a highly mobile breed of independent miners who worked the gravel deposits, usually starting at the mouth of a river and working their way towards the source. Capital requirements were limited and entry to the gold fields was relatively easy as claims were generally small, essentially on a "first come, first served" basis. The independence and footloose nature of gold rush miners has become the subject of many myths, particularly of violence and lawlessness (such as in the entertaining poetry of the Canadian poet, Robert Service). While there is some basis in history for this myth, the B.C. gold rushes were remarkably devoid of lawlessness.

Still, the small scale of production, the relatively infrequent use of wage labour, and the independence and mobility of the miners created a unique social milieu, an impermanent, "classless" society of young single men, heavily infused with the gambler's spirit. Though the gold rush was to have, in Harold Innis's terms, a "cyclonic" effect on the B.C. political economy, its social effects proved more transitory as underground mining regained its predominance.

Underground mining differed markedly in its characteristics. Sinking deep shafts in bedrock and providing machinery for ventilating, hoisting, and pumping, facilities for concentrating and smelting, transportation services, and marketing organizations all required large-scale organization and considerable reserves of capital. The miners were predominantly wage labour; the mine owners were independent or corporate capitalists. Whereas placer mining was dominated by a class of independent producers, underground mining was dominated by a class society of workers and (often absentee) owners. Whereas placer mining bred an impermanent, mobile society, underground mining had a degree of permanence which created the conditions for the development of continuing communities. The role of the independent miner was largely reduced to that of prospector.

The cultures of the two types of miners, therefore, were markedly different. However, it was the culture of the underground miner that was to make its indelible mark on British Columbia society.

EARLY DEVELOPMENT

Prior to the gold rush in the late 1850's, the area which is now British Columbia was primarily a fur trade preserve under the monopoly of the

Hudson's Bay Company (H.B.C.). Though fur was the company's main economic interest, the H.B.C. did make some attempts to diversify, primarily to reduce the cost of importing supplies by replacing them with local products or by providing a return cargo in addition to the high value, low bulk furs. This included attempts to develop coal mining, first to supply local needs for heating and for the company's coasting steamers, and later for the growing export market in San Francisco, during the California gold boom.

The Hudson's Bay Company's first attempt to develop coal deposits dates back to 1835, at Fort Rupert on the isolated, northeastern coast of Vancouver island. One cannot say that the coal was discovered then because the company learned of the existence of the outcrops of coal from local Indians. Nevertheless, the company did begin attempts at commercial exploitation, though with little success because of the poor quality of the small coal seams. However, intermittent efforts continued because of the heavy cost of importing steam coal from Britain, culminating in the importation of a small number of Scottish miners in 1849 to develop the seams. The experiment was not a success; disputes broke out almost immediately between the feudally organized H.B.C. and the craft-conscious Scots miners, who objected not only to the working and living conditions and low wages but also to being assigned unskilled labourers' work.[2] Open conflict broke out in 1850, and some of the miners, including the lead hand, John Muir, abandoned Fort Rupert, leaving the coal seam undeveloped.[3] Attempts continued for a short while, apparently with the assistance of a new Scots immigrant mine official, Robert Dunsmuir, who was to become notorious in future years.[4] But labour troubles and the poor quality of coal led James Douglas, H.B.C. agent and governor of the Vancouver Island colony, to explore the possibilities of coal development near Nanaimo, some sixty miles north of the company headquarters in Victoria.

Again, it was a native who provided the intelligence. In 1849, an Indian having his gun repaired in Victoria informed the blacksmith that it was unnecessary to import coal from afar when plenty was available at Nanaimo. For his information, he had his gun repaired and was given a bottle of rum. The H.B.C. immediately appropriated the native resource, and the company, the Dunsmuirs, and later coal barons who exploited the Nanaimo fields all received fortunes.

Nevertheless, the development of the Nanaimo coal field proceeded fairly slowly. Production began in 1852 when some 1,840 (long) tons were shipped out, apparently mined by both native and British workers.[5] But the Indians proved unamenable to industrial discipline and, in 1854, a contingent of Staffordshire miners was brought over to augment the remaining Scottish group from Fort Rupert. Poor working conditions, low wages, and long hours proved no more acceptable to the new group. Dissatisfaction, fanned by the rumours of fortunes to be made in the gold fields, led to unorganized strike activity in 1855. Robert Dunsmuir aided the company's resistance for which he received his reward:

> So ended the first strike at Nanaimo, and following this, two of the men who had been against it, Dunsmuir and Ed Walker, applied to Governor Douglas to work on their own. Permission was granted and on October 12, 1855, Dunsmuir commenced his first independent operation.[6]

The operation was a reward of coal rights on one thousand acres in the Nanaimo area. It was not until 1869, however, that Dunsmuir found the seam that was to fulfil his wildest dream of wealth and power.

These early mining developments did little to change the economic or social face of the region. The colony remained a fur-trade area, supplemented by a few agricultural, coal mining, timber, and fishing enterprises, all within the paternal pocket of the H.B.C. On the eve of the Fraser River gold rush, British Columbia comprised only around five hundred people of European descent clustered around Victoria, and approximately forty to fifty thousand natives combining traditional pursuits with participation in the fur trade.

THE CYCLONE: PLACER GOLD

In 1848 at Sutter's Creek in California, gold had been found, touching off the great California gold rush and transforming San Francisco into a booming commercial city. As the fields became crowded and the deposits were played out, hopeful miners worked up the westward flowing rivers to their sources or moved north to test their luck on new waterways. A short-lived rush occurred on the Queen Charlotte Islands in 1852, but its impact was minor and transitory as the gold quickly gave out. One institution that did come out of the 1852 rush, however, was to be significant later: the licensing of miners, which provided some order to an inherently disordered industry.

The economic cyclone began in 1856 when gold was found in the lower reaches of the Fraser River. The news soon travelled to California where hydraulic techniques, lode mining and exhaustion of the placer fields had left a large reserve of independent miners still in search of the elusive find. It was 1858, however, before the great influx of fortune seekers arrived in B.C., led by a contingent of 450 who departed San

Francisco on the steamer *Commodore* in April. Before the end of the summer, they were followed by some 25,000 to 30,000 others.[7] The commercial centre, indeed the only real settlement in the region, was the Hudson's Bay Company enclave at Victoria, which felt the full impact of the storm. Population increased well over 1,000 per cent, with an even greater inflationary effect on the prices of land and provisions, which rose 3–4,000 per cent per month. But it was not only miners who made their way north. They were immediately followed by commercial and financial businesses, largely from San Francisco, and by American provisions and supplies, including lumber from the Puget sound area for the consequent building boom.

The great population influx into Victoria in 1858 was short-lived, however, as the miners quickly moved on to the gold fields of the mainland. The population in Victoria declined to around 1,500 by 1859; with the decline came falling land prices and business activity. Victoria knew its first depression, as it watched the departure of a number of businesses that had invaded the centre just one year earlier.

Such a pattern was, of course, inevitable given the volatility of the gold rush phenomenon. In the following years a more stable base was established, though it was still dependent on placer gold. In addition to being the administrative centre for the region, Victoria became the transhipment point for supplies to the gold fields, and it was declared a free port in 1860 to foster the warehouse trade and thus combat the 1859 slump. By 1862, it was also the financial centre, with three banks whose major role was in the export of gold. Indeed, two of the three banks evolved out of the express business in handling the precious metal.

Victoria's population again swelled and prices rose rapidly with the discovery of gold in the Cariboo district in 1860. This time, the discovery of gold so far inland added a new dimension. The Fraser River is navigable only as far as the Fraser Canyon; beyond Emory's Bar, just above Hope, goods had to be packed or taken by canoe, and the resulting prices for supplies in the region could only be described as astronomical. Improvements to the transportation system into the colony's interior were required, improvements that were provided from the public funds of the colonies. Between 1860 and 1865, a network of roads was built into the gold regions, not only into the Cariboo (the most famous being the Cariboo Trail, completed to Barkerville in 1865) but also into the Kootenay region of southeastern British Columbia.

The impact of the roads was considerable, though not necessarily as intended. The prices of goods and provisions in the gold fields fell greatly, in many cases decreasing 70 to 90 per cent, and the lower prices no doubt prolonged the boom and helped open up some marginal claims.

Wages also fell, though not proportionately, averaging perhaps a 60 per cent decline. But by the time the roads were completed, the rush was in its autumn because of the exhaustion of placer gold and the incursion of more capital—for intensive hydraulic, sluice, and shaft mining. The number of miners in the colonies declined rapidly after 1865, from an average of around 4,300 between 1860 to 1864 to approximately 2,400 in the closing years of the decade (about 200 of these were coal miners in Nanaimo). Many of the gold miners, particularly on the lower reaches of the Fraser and in the Similkameen district, were Chinese who had emigrated from California. Unlike many of the white miners, they were predominantly wage earners, making from 50 to 70 per cent of the income of unskilled white labour. Low-wage Chinese labour was one heritage of the gold rush that was to persist, with unfortunate results, long after the boom was just a memory.

In an important sense, however, the main heritage of the heyday of placer mining was the public debt incurred, primarily for building roads but also for such things as port facilities. During the height of the boom such expenditures could be financed by the ample revenues from customs duties, land sales, mining licenses, road tolls, and a gold export tax, but all these revenue sources began to dry up after 1865. This increasing debt was a major factor in prompting the merger of the colonies of British Columbia and Vancouver Island in 1866. Still, the public debt remained at around a million and a half dollars with no immediate prospect of offsetting revenues. At the same time, the population was declining, by 30 per cent in total and by 22 per cent among the non-Indian population, between the 1861 and 1871 censuses. The cyclonic nature of placer gold had again left its havoc behind.

Nevertheless, the gold rush had produced more positive developments. In the twenty-three years (1858-80) from the arrival of the first main rush of miners to the rapid decline in production, a total of over forty-eight million dollars of placer gold was produced. This compares with under thirty million dollars in placer gold produced over the subsequent forty years to 1920.[8]

Although much of the wealth flowed out of the region to pay for imported supplies and provisions, enough was retained and spent on local output to create the beginnings of a more diversified economy. Between 1862 and 1870, agricultural production (as measured by acres under cultivation and total livestock) increased by 200 to 300 per cent. Flour mills, breweries, and distilleries also developed to meet the growing demand. Perhaps the most significant development linked to the gold rush, however, was the growth of the interior forestry industry, which was not as sensitive as other industries to the decline in placer mining after the mid-

1860's. This was because the demand for lumber for sluices and shafts increased as mining converted to more capital-intensive techniques, with hydraulic and shaft mining replacing the simpler cradle and riffle box techniques.

Nevertheless, by the second half of the 1860's it was evident that placer gold would no longer support regional economic development and the public debt acquired during the expansion phase. The merchants in Victoria, whose empire appeared to be crumbling, faced a dilemma: join the United States to get behind its tariff wall and face the competition from the Pacific Northwest, or join Canada and gain the preferential markets of the British Empire but lose the growing American market. Many merchants, particularly those with business connections in San Francisco, favoured the former, but the majority of people, including the political elite, favoured the latter. In 1871, with the promise of a Pacific railway and relief from its public debt in hand, British Columbia opted for Canada.

Placer gold remained the economic leader for another decade. In 1872, mined commodities constituted 75 per cent of exports. By 1881, this had dropped to 60 per cent, mainly because of the rise of the fishing industry, though within a couple of years coal was to replace gold as the leading mining sector.[9] Despite its economic impact in inducing linked economic development and its political impact in leading B.C. into Confederation, however, its impact on the province's social fabric appears to have been largely transitory. Placer gold was easily exploited with minimal capital, largely by independent, unskilled migrants. It required little processing, and found a ready market in the financial centres of the world. Consequently, it came and went, like the men who mined it, leaving behind little base for continuous development. Fortunately, other resource industries emerged to fill the gap, not least of which was "black gold": coal.

VANCOUVER ISLAND: THE KINGDOM OF DUNSMUIR

Though it was gold that dominated in the region through the decades of the 1860's and 1870's, coal production in the Nanaimo region continued to increase. Whereas total output from the Fort Rupert mines from 1826 to 1852 had been a mere 10,000 (long) tons, 1,840 tons were produced in the Nanaimo field in 1852, its first year, and annual production for the remainder of the decade averaged around 5,000 tons. With the 1860's, output climbed rapidly, reaching 44,005 tons in 1868. Declining slightly in 1869-70, output then entered a period of sustained expansion that did not level out until the 1890's, when tonnage averaged over 900,000 tons per year, worth around four million dollars annually.[10] By 1884, the value of coal produced in the province, all coming from the Nanaimo area, exceeded the value of total gold production. Only in the first half of the first decade of the twentieth century, when the lode mines of the southeastern interior of the province were opened up, did gold briefly regain its position as the leading mining sector in the province.

The expansion of coal mining in the Nanaimo district was marked by class and racial conflict. Three factors, geological, human, and historical, contributed to the climate of confrontation. Geologically, the coal seams were narrow, often in fractured rock, and many extended under the sea. Dangers from falling rock, methane gas, explosions, flooding, and cramped tunnels were typical of these mines. Racial tensions grew with the influx of significant numbers of low-wage Chinese workers, including those who had come to the province during the gold rush and those imported to work on the construction of the Canadian Pacific Railway (C.P.R.) in the early 1880's. But the most significant factor was the behaviour of the mine owners, particularly Robert Dunsmuir, not only in their disregard for safety conditions and the welfare of the miners, but also in their exploitation of police power and Chinese labourers in order to break any organization of miners.

In 1855, the H.B.C. had used eviction of the miners' families from company housing to break the strike prompted by "low wages, long hours, poor working conditions and inadequate housing."[11] In 1861, H.B.C. miners struck unsuccessfully again, this time against a company tax on coal containing clay. Four years later the miners were on strike once more, though the mine was now under the ownership of the Vancouver Coal Mining and Land Company. In 1871, another strike occurred, this time a protracted dispute that lasted for five months and prompted a delegation of workers to go to Victoria to seek aid.

During this pre-Confederation period, employment did not exceed around two hundred men. About half of the coal output was shipped to the San Francisco market, the remainder going to Victoria for heating and steaming. At this time, coal ranked behind gold, forest products, and fur in terms of value of exports, though by the mid-1860's the coal company had bought its own ships to shuttle coal to California.

The first big expansion in the coal-mining industry occurred after 1873 and, except for minor setbacks in 1881, 1883, and 1885, continued unabated for eighteen years. Growth did nothing to reduce labour unrest, however. In 1874 another strike broke out at the Vancouver Coal Mining colliery, but it was the Dunsmuir mines that were to become the centre of confrontation. The year 1877 was a turning point when the Wellington men struck against wage cuts, short weights, and the mandatory use of the company store. During the four-month strike, the workers formed a union, the Miners' Mutual Protective Association. Dunsmuir, who had formed his company in partnership with some naval officers, responded with imported strikebreakers. When they were persuaded to return to California, he used his military connections to dispatch a warship and the militia to Nanaimo to evict the strikers. Military action succeeded where other strikebreaking activities had failed, and this was not the last time the Dunsmuir mines were to use the militia for private strikebreaking.

Nevertheless, conflict continued, and there were numerous strikes in the 1880's and 1890's, involving the formation of several unions in a succession of unsuccessful attempts to crack the Dunsmuir empire. The 1883 strike was particularly significant in that it included the first demand for the elimination of Chinese labour in the mines, brought on by the belief that it was the presence of the Chinese that undercut wage levels. Certainly the wages paid Chinese workers were well below white wages: consistently 50 to 70 per cent of labourers' wages or approximately the level paid to boys.[12] The miners also believed that the presence of the Chinese contributed to the lack of mine safety, leading to appalling death and injury totals. By the turn of the century, the Nanaimo mines had the justly earned reputation as the most dangerous in the world, with a death rate almost double that of foreign countries and between three and four times that of mines in the British Empire.[13]

Meanwhile, Dunsmuir's empire grew. By 1883, he was able to buy out his partner's original $5,000 share for $700,000. In collaboration with American railway barons, he acquired a government grant of $750,000 and 1.9 million acres (including mineral rights) to build a seventy-mile railway on Vancouver Island. On his death in 1889, Robert Dunsmuir's empire passed to his son James, who operated it until he sold out to Mackenzie and Mann (Canadian Collieries) in 1910 for eleven million dollars. James proved no more tractable than his father in his dealings with workers.

The long economic depression of the 1890's was reflected in the stagnation of coal output and revenues, but in 1898 output and revenues again began their upward climb, hesitating only for the short-lived economic downturns of 1903 and 1908 before peaking in 1910. The pre-war depression and the massive Nanaimo miners' strike caused a major cutback in production and revenues between 1912 and 1915, before wartime demand caused an increase in both production and prices. The value of output reached a peak in 1920 of almost thirteen million dollars, though the 2.5 million tons mined that year did not quite reach the levels of 1910 and 1912, 2.8 and 2.6 million tons respectively.

The Vancouver Island mines remained the most important in the province in terms of both employment and output. In 1899, 90 per cent of coal-mine employment (3,688 persons) and 92 per cent of output was accounted for by the island collieries. The corresponding figures for 1910 were 60 per cent (4,647 persons) and 57 per cent of output; for 1920, 75 per cent (4,767 persons) and 71 per cent. In fact, the markets for coal from the coastal and the interior regions within B.C. were quite different. In 1899, 75 per cent of coast production was exported, mainly to the California market, while all of the interior production was used in the region, around one-third of it for coke production for the area's smelters. Within ten years, however, the situation was reversed. In 1910, 71 per cent of coast production was for the Canadian market compared with only 20 per cent of coal from the interior. A small proportion of coal in the coastal region was produced in mainland mines, primarily in the Nicola Valley. The trend continued so that by 1920, 75 per cent of coastal production was sold in Canada, only 30 per cent of interior coal. The low figure for the interior is slightly misleading: of the coal converted to coke (about 20 per cent of the amount of coal sold in 1910, 10 per cent in 1920) half or more was consumed in the region's smelters.

The other major difference between the two coal mining areas that contributed to the particularly bitter labour relations on the island was the use of the Chinese. Few if any Chinese, Japanese, and East Indians were used in the interior mines. This was not the case on Vancouver Island, particularly in the Dunsmuir mines. Table 1 outlines the basis of the white workers' grievances.

TABLE 1: ORIENTAL WORKERS AS A PERCENTAGE OF COAL MINE WORKERS

	1899	1910	1920
Coastal District	22.4	15.1	19.4
Dunsmuir Mines	32.9	22.6	32.9
Crow's Nest Pass Mines	0	0	0
Province	20.2	9.0	13.5

Source: *Annual Report*, B.C. Minister of Mines, 1899, 1910, and 1920.

No doubt, much of the anti-Oriental prejudice among the white miners on the coast was rooted in the fact that the Chinese were an unassimilated, largely non-English speaking minority. It is difficult to document whether in fact their lack of English literacy and their fear of deportation if they complained did contribute to the deplorable safety record in the Vancouver Island mines. On the other hand, their low wages and their use by the mine owners as strikebreakers is a matter of record.

Whatever the objective basis, anti-Orientalism became a characteristic of miners' organizations and was a powerful stimulus (along with the continuing failure of industrial action) for increasingly radical political action in the late nineteenth century. As early as 1890, two labour-backed candidates from the Nanaimo region, one a miner, were elected to the provincial legislature, though their impact on legislation was not great. More important was the election of Ralph Smith, president of the Nanaimo Miners' and Mine Labourers' Protective Association, to the provincial House of Assembly in 1898. With two other pro-labour independents, Smith held the balance of power and was able to get legislation passed which included prohibition of the employment of Chinese underground.

Continuing bitter class conflict, however, served only to radicalize the miners. In 1901, Smith, a moderate labourite and president of the Trades and Labour Congress of Canada, resigned to contest the federal election. He was replaced by James Hawthornthwaite, nominally a revolutionary socialist but in practice a successful parliamentary reformer. Again using a balance of power position in the provincial government, Hawthornthwaite was instrumental in enacting the Trade Union Act, a workers' compensation law, and the Coal Mines Regulation Act, which introduced new safety regulations to the coal mines. In 1903, he was joined by Parker Williams, a socialist miner from the neighbouring mining constituency of Newcastle; in 1905, they were able to pass legislation introducing the eight-hour day into the province's coal mines.

Despite such political accomplishments, the mine owners were continually able to thwart unionization. In 1905, the Island miners, now organized by the United Mine Workers of America (U.M.W.A.), struck to enforce compliance with the eight-hour day legislation; they won their battle for the eight-hour day but at the expense of loss of their union, in part because of the intervention of the young deputy minister of labour from Ottawa, William Lyon Mackenzie King. A mine disaster in 1909 that killed thirty-two men prompted further moves to organize miners, and two years later the Vancouver Island miners were incorporated as District 28 of the U.M.W.A. Probably the most violent labour confrontation in provincial history quickly followed, its genesis perhaps typical of the basis of the conflict endemic to the region.

In June of 1912 two miners, Isaac Portrey and Oscar Mottishaw who formed the gas committee at the Extension Mine as provided for under the Coal Mines Regulation Act, reported gas in the mine. The company, Canadian Collieries, protested, and when Mottishaw's "place" was mined out, he was not rehired. It became apparent that he was being blacklisted when he could find no employment any-where on the Island. The mine workers apparently believed that Mottishaw was being discriminated against because of the gas report, although a more likely reason was his strong union activities since there was previous evidence of harassment of the union by the company. It has been argued, in fact, that the employer was deliberately trying to provoke a strike. Earlier, Dunsmuir's interests had been bought by Mackenzie and Mann, the railway promoters, for eleven million dollars, and a stock issue floated on the company for twenty-five million. Not to prejudice a Mackenzie and Mann bond issue for railway construction on the Canadian Northern, a strike could cover the company's inability to pay dividends on the watered colliery stock.[14]

The strike lasted for two years and was marked by violence and again by the use of Chinese strikebreakers. It ended only when the militia crushed the strike, arresting the miners' leaders, in the deepening pre-war depression. Unionism again disappeared from the region, and despite the war-induced economic boom and the rapid expansion of labour organization in the province, it did not reappear until the late 1920's. The legacy of coal mining on the Island in its expansion period, therefore, was one of great personal fortunes, bitter class conflict and, most unfortunately, racism.

THE INLAND EMPIRE

Even while the Island coal mines dominated the provincial mining scene through the last decades of the nineteenth century, a whole new mining region was opening up, a region whose economic impact over the longer run was to overshadow that of the coastal collieries. This was the southeastern region comprising the West Kootenay, East Kootenay, Slocan, Boundary, and Crow's Nest Pass districts.

The origins of this interior mining industry lay in the early gold rush. In 1864-66, miners moving inland discovered gold at Wild Horse Creek and at Big Bend in the Kootenays, prompting a rush to the area. The colonial government, attempting to wrest the commerce of the region from American merchants, built a road into the interior, but the Dewdney Trail, completed in 1865, proved largely a white elephant as the gold was soon exhausted. A few miners, predominantly Chinese, continued to work the claims for a meager existence, but for the most part the Kootenays boasted little economic activity. During the 1870's, there were less than fifty electors in the region (a measure of the permanent white population) compared with around fifteen hundred miners at the peak of the boom in the mid-1860's.

There were some known deposits of silver-lead ore around Kootenay Lake. The H.B.C. had earlier used metal from these deposits to make bullets, and in 1864 a Californian named George Hearst had attempted commercial production of lead, but the isolation and the cost of transportation made the venture uneconomical and it was soon abandoned. It was almost twenty years before further attempts were made to exploit the mineral resources of the region. On the west shore of Kootenay Lake, Captain Ainsworth from San Francisco began commercial production in 1883 of the silver-lead ore (galena) and even constructed a concentrator, but transportation costs contributed to the indifferent success of the venture.

The basic problem in exploiting the mineral wealth of the region was the geography. High, rugged mountain ranges separated the north-south oriented lake and river systems. The Dewdney Trail, built to give commercial access to the area from within Canada, had long since become unusable. What limited interest there was in the area was an offshoot of the American mining industry in the mountain states—the inland empire centred on Spokane and the Columbia River system. The incentive was the American demand for precious metals to feed the money supply of an expanding economy. Gold, of course, was the primary interest, but until 1873, silver was also an official backing for the currency. Political pressure from the "silver states," however, kept interest in the metal high and prompted the U.S. Congress to pass several acts that maintained silver at artificially high prices. It was not until the presidential election of 1896, which was fought over the issue of whether silver was to be "demonetized" (made no longer official backing for the American dollar), that silver lost some of its allure. However, by this time the mining industry of the B.C. interior was well established, based not only on precious metals but also on copper.

American demand was not the only influence spurring the development of the Kootenay region. In 1885, the construction of the Canadian Pacific Railway brought prospectors who branched off north from the main line to rediscover the riches of the region. Nevertheless, the topography remained the principal barrier to development, given the relatively low-grade ore, high transportation costs, U.S. tariffs, and uncertain government policy. Still, attempts were made to exploit the mineral resources of the region. On the east shore of Kootenay Lake, American capital began operations at the Blue Bell find in 1887; the following year, over 400 tons of ore were shipped to Butte, Montana, for smelting, but large-scale operations had to await the development of more economical transportation facilities.

One alternative strategy was to erect smelting facilities at or near the mines in order to reduce the cost of shipping the low-grade ore. The other was to develop a network of transportation routes to get the ore to the existing American smelters. Both strategies were followed, but the effect was to make the whole region a tributary of the "inland empire," an extension of the American mining frontier based in Spokane.

Despite the pioneering efforts on the east and west shores of Kootenay Lake, however, the first real expansion occurred with the discovery of silver-copper ores on Toad Mountain, near Nelson, in 1886. The ore was taken, first by rawhide sled, wagon, or pack train and later by tram line, to the waterways where steam paddlewheelers carried it to smelters or rail connections in the United States.

Development from this point went in several directions. Prospectors moved west along the old Dewdney Trail to discover the rich copper-gold deposits at Rossland (Red Mountain) in 1887, then further west to the equally rich Boundary country in 1891, northwest to the silver-lead-zinc Slocan, also in 1891, and east to the East Kootenays where similar deposits were found in 1892.

At the same time, efforts were being made to improve the transportation system from the region. Speculators were active in promoting rail lines: almost fifty lines were incorporated by the turn of the century, though only eleven were ever actually built. Most of the development was aimed at improving connections with the C.P.R. mainline to the north or with the Great Northern and Northern Pacific lines south of the American border. By the 1890's, it was clear that the American route was the winner and that the commerce of the region was being captured by American merchants.

A third development was the extension of smelter facilities close to the ore supplies, to reduce the bulk and weight of the shipments and make transportation more economical. Smelters proliferated in the Kootenays and in the Boundary country at the turn of the century.

The 1890's transformed the region from isolated desertion to feverish activity. Towns grew from nothing: Kaslo's population had grown to six thousand, Nelson's to one thousand, Rossland's to several thousand, and Trail's to two thousand by the late years of the decade. As each mining area opened up, new waves of migrants flooded in, many from the American mining frontier and others from Britain, all bringing their own traditions and institutions. And not only miners came. The numerous towns that sprung up around the mines, smelters, and transportation centres required commercial and service support, and hotels, saloons, and stores proliferated. By 1901, the population of the Kootenays had risen to thirty thousand from two thousand only eleven years earlier.

The battle between the C.P.R. and the American railways for commercial control of the region was settled, almost by accident, at the turn of the century. In 1895, an American entrepreneur named F. A. Heinz had constructed a smelter at Trail, B.C. (a town named after the Dewdney Trail). He also built a narrow-gauge railway to Rossland to supply the ore. The C.P.R., anxious to capture the commerce of the region, purchased the Heinz smelter and railway line, then decided to construct a branch from its mainline in Alberta through the Crow's Nest Pass to the mining area. The C.P.R. received a massive government subsidy to construct the line; in exchange, the railway limited its rates—the famous Crow's Nest Pass rates—for transporting grain. The effect of the construction, completed in 1898, transformed the B.C. economy, for it led to the discovery of massive coal deposits in the pass. As one historian has noted:

> The integration of Crow's Nest Pass coal production and coke manufacturing with the expansion of mineral output in the Kootenay and Boundary districts was merely the first and most spectacular of the integrative effects of the Crow's Nest Pass Railway. . . . From Alberta the Kootenay drew grain and flour, livestock, meats and dairy products; from Manitoba came oats, butter, beef and pork; from Ontario, eggs and poultry. Hay, potatoes and vegetables were brought in from the Okanagan.[15]

Commercial exploitation of the coal deposits began with the incorporation of the Crow's Nest Pass Coal company in 1897; in addition to meeting the demand for steam coal by the railways, the area soon replaced Vancouver Island as a source for smelting coke. As late as 1898, mines at Comox, on Vancouver Island, shipped 32,000 tons of coke to the interior; the pass mines shipped only 361 tons. By the turn of the century, however, the Crow's Nest mines were supplying 66,000 tons, completely displacing the supply from the coast. Around one thousand coking ovens were in operation in the early years of the new century, and employment in the Crow's Nest Pass Coal Company, the dominant company in the region, approached fifteen hundred.

The spectacular growth of the hardrock mining frontier is perhaps best illustrated by the growth in the value of output. After an initial spurt in the late 1880's based on silver (a high of $105,000 of output in 1888) production declined to a low of $4,000 in 1891. From that point on, however, growth was rapid reaching over $2,000,000 by mid-decade and $10,000,000 by the end of the decade.

This growth was accompanied by a diversification in mineral production. Gold was most important, accounting for nearly one-third of lode output, while silver was now surpassed in value by lead and was rapidly being caught up to by copper. By the 1890's, copper was to surpass gold, silver, and lead in value, maintaining that dominant position throughout the following two decades (except in 1902-4 and 1910-11). By the 1920's, base metals comprised two thirds or more of the value of the interior lode mines.[16]

The transformation of the mineral base from precious to base metals was paralleled by a number of other technological and organizational changes that were to have a marked impact on the social structure of the region. The miners that flocked to the region in the 1890's had much in common with those in the earlier gold rushes. Many were independent prospectors whose goal was to stake and prove a claim before selling out. Between 1890 and 1900, over one thousand companies had been registered in the West Kootenay and Boundary districts: almost half were Canadian, 40 per cent American, and the remainder British.[17] Yet by 1901, only two hundred remained; by 1914, only thirty-five. This was a consequence of the rapid depletion of the easy-to-extract, high-grade ores. In the Kootenays, peak production in terms of value was achieved in 1901, while in the Boundary district the peak was achieved in 1912. Rising costs, falling yields, deeper shafts, and increased capitalization in the form of machinery, smelter facilities, separation and refining techniques, and power generation led to the consolidation and the domination of three companies: Consolidated Mining and Smelting Company (COMINCO), a C.P.R. subsidiary formed in 1906 and centred on the Trail smelter, and the two Boundary district giants, Granby Company, initially based on Quebec capital though later taken over by American interests, and B.C. Copper, an American-owned firm. As one observer has noted:

> In this era of creeping bigness, the three most successful consolidations were those in which the companies owned not only the mines but also the means of smelting and refining their ores. The successful combinations were those in which both horizontal and vertical consolidations were involved.[18]

The independent miner quickly gave way to the wage worker. About one-third of these workers were Americans, most of whom had worked in the mining region just across the border and were veterans of the violent class war that had erupted in those fields. Persistent conflict with the mining barons, whose opposition to unionism and whose brutality and use of police power in suppressing labour disputes was legendary, had culminated in the creation of the Western Federation of Miners (W.F.M.) in 1893. Though initially not radical, "a decade of encountering the almost total intransigence of the mine operators . . . radicalized the W.F.M.," and the union increasingly turned to direct action and meeting force with force.[19] In the first decade of the twentieth century, the W.F.M. was a prime mover in organizing opposition to the conservative American Federation of Labour and in the formation of the syndicalist Industrial Workers of the World (I.W.W.).

The American miners brought this radical heritage with them to British Columbia, but the movement was tempered considerably by factors unique to the province. One was the presence of many British miners with their heritage of more political trade unionism. Another was the important role of Canadian capital, which proved somewhat more conciliatory than its American counterpart. Also, very early the miners achieved some notable industrial and political goals that reduced conflict.

The first local of the W.F.M. was formed in 1895 at Rossland, but expansion of the group was slow until 1898, when the mine owners refused to implement the eight-hour-day legislation passed by the provincial government. The following year, four thousand West Kootenay miners struck successfully to enforce the law, and later that year thirteen locals met to form District 6 of the W.F.M. Within four years there were eighteen locals, including three coal mining locals which later split off to join with the Alberta miners as District 18 of the United Mine Workers of America.

The B.C. Trade Union Act also emerged out of the Kootenays. Its origins lay in a W.F.M. strike at Rossland in 1901 protesting company discrimination against union members. The union lost the strike and the mining companies sued the union for damages, winning the case in 1903. However, as soon as the litigation began, the labour-supported member from Rossland introduced a bill in the provincial House of Assembly to protect unions from such action. Though his particular bill was not accepted, a different version was passed, and labour achieved a considerable legislative victory.

The subsequent history of the miners' unions in the interior to the 1920's was tempestuous, mirroring the mood of the times, particularly in the great labour upheaval of 1918-20 with the rise of the One Big Union in western Canada. But the economic developments in the metal mining industry were a portent of a new era. Late in 1907 the prices of base metals collapsed, followed by wage cuts and massive layoffs (twelve hundred men in the Kootenays alone). In 1912 there was some recovery, but the major expansion was over. The mines near Rossland were largely exhausted, soon followed by the Boundary mines. Precious metals, even copper, were giving way to lead and zinc as the principal minerals, and the East Kootenay area (including Kimberley) was emerging as the major mineral source. However, the Kimberley ores were complex and low grade and it took the development of selective flotation and electrolytic refining to unlock the secret of successful extraction.

It was the demands of the First World War that gave the industry its final surge in the period. Rising prices brought a tenfold increase in zinc output, a doubling of copper output, and a 70 per cent increase in lead output over the low point of the industry in 1914. This was aided by Canadian government support to COMINCO to develop processes to separate the lead-zinc ores of Kimberley, a project which was to become the basis of the successful and long-lived COMINCO operation. For labour, however, the wartime boom was followed by decline and, after 1920, economic depression. In the metal mines and smelters, unionism disappeared. In the coal mines, it struggled on in the inhospitable climate of the 1920's when coal was in decline. By mid-decade the workers were fragmented in local organizations, and the U.M.W.A. was virtually a paper organization.

THE MINING FRONTIER TO 1920: THE LEGACY

The importance of mining to British Columbia's early development is unquestionable. Placer gold in the 1860's and 1870's, Island coal in the 1880's and 1890's, and precious and base metals from the interior, and coal from the pass area in the 1890's and 1900's provided a frontier of economic activity that helped dynamize the entire province by attracting labour and capital and providing rapidly expanding commercial, transportation, and industrial opportunities.

However, the relative importance of mining to the provincial economy declined with the growth of other export staples, first fish in the 1880's, and later lumbering, particularly as the prairie market opened up after the wheat boom. As economists have noted, "Despite the fact that there were five times as many miners in 1911 as in 1881 in British Columbia, lumbering had expanded so much more rapidly that both industries accounted for between 15,000 and 16,000 workers in the latter year."[20] Indeed, the rise of lumbering between 1881 and 1911 was spectacular, leaving lumbering on a par with mining in terms of employment; but agriculture employed about half again as many workers as lumbering or mining, and the fisheries about one-third as many as mining.

Still, mining's critical initiating role should not be downgraded, particularly its contribution to the development of the transportation infrastructure, including the first roads and trails, the harbours, and later the railways in the interior and on the Island. Mining was also a major user of lumber products, not to mention consumer goods and services in the numerous mining settlements.

Innis's characterization of staple development as "cyclonic," creating short-term feverish activity followed by a vacuum and disorder, is certainly more applicable to mining than most other staples. Except for coal, the resources quickly gave out and production moved rapidly from labour-intensive to capital-intensive methods. The boom and bust cycle and the ghost town were two legacies. So also was the COMINCO empire at Trail.

The sociopolitical legacy was no less important. The miners were arguably the most important single labour group in the province, shaping the labour movement's organization and politics. Miner-supported legislators achieved notable breakthroughs in safety legislation, including workers' compensation, hours-of-work, and trade union legislation as well as a permanent foundation for reform and socialist politics, a product of the class conflict that pervaded the underground mines throughout the period. Among the negative effects, however, were the legacy of anti-Oriental racism and the hundreds of dead and maimed victims of a brutal period of unregulated capitalism.

It is an exaggeration to claim, as Bailie-Grohman did, that gold both made and unmade British Columbia. It would not be an exaggeration, however, to claim that mining was the leading sector in the making of the province, certainly before the turn of the century if not through the entire period of the mining frontier to 1920.

NOTES

1. W. A. Bailie-Grohman, *Fifteen Years' Sport and Life in the Hunting Grounds of Western America and British Columbia*, 2nd ed. (London: H. Cox, 1907), p. 316.
2. H. Keith Ralston, "Industrial Work in a Pre-Industrial Society: the Hudson's Bay Company in Western Canada," lecture for conference entitled *Concerning Work*, Manitoba Museum of Man and Nature, 14 October 1983.
3. Paul Phillips, *No Power Greater* (Vancouver: B.C. Federation of Labour and the

Boag Foundation, 1967) p. 2; Jack Scott, *Sweat and Struggle* (Vancouver: New Star, 1974), p. 156.

4. Scott, *Sweat and Struggle*.
5. Paul Phillips, "Confederation and the Economy of British Columbia," in George Shelton (ed.), *British Columbia and Confederation* (Victoria: University of Victoria Press, 1967), p. 51.
6. Quoted in Scott, *Sweat and Struggle,* p. 159.
7. Phillips, "Confederation and the Economy of British Columbia," p. 45.
8. B.C. Minister of Mines, *Annual Report*, 1920.
9. Ibid., 1899.
10. B.C. Minister of Mines, *Annual Reports*.
11. Scott, *Sweat and Struggle,* p. 158.
12. See B.C. Minister of Mines, *Annual Reports*, 1899-1920.
13. Phillips, *No Power Greater*, pp. 8-9; Scott, *Sweat and Struggle*, pp. 149ff.
14. Phillips, *No Power Greater*, p. 56.
15. V. C. Fowke, *An Historical Analysis of the Crow's Nest Pass Agreement and Grain Rates: A Study in National Transportation Policy*, submission of the Province of Saskatchewan to the Royal Commission on Transportation (Saskatchewan: Queen's Printer, 1961), p. 33.
16. B.C. Minister of Mines, *Annual Reports*.
17. J. S. Church, "Mining Companies in the West Kootenay Boundary Regions of British Columbia, 1890-1900" (M.A. thesis, University of British Columbia, 1961), p. 235.
18. Ibid, p. 228.
19. Carlos Schwantes, *Radical Heritage* (Vancouver: Douglas & McIntyre, 1979), p. 114.
20. Richard Caves and Richard Holton, *The Canadian Economy* (Cambridge, MA: Harvard University Press, 1955), pp. 220-21.

5

Class, Ethnicity, and Conflict:
The Case of Chinese and Japanese Immigrants, 1880–1923

GILLIAN CREESE

INTRODUCTION

Studies of late nineteenth- and early twentieth-century labour history note the relatively radical character of working-class consciousness and labour organization in British Columbia compared to the rest of the country. At the same time they identify racism as a key feature of working-class activity, expressed through anti-Asian agitation.[1] The presence of ethnic cleavages and conflict within an otherwise class-conscious labour movement raises important questions about the role of class and ethnic relations in mobilizing collective consciousness and action and, especially, the relationship between class and ethnicity in ethnically segmented class societies.

This paper forms part of ongoing research into the relationship between working-class organization and ethnic conflict in British Columbia prior to 1930; it is intended to provide a framework for further research. A fruitful way to address the intersection between class and ethnicity is through an historical analysis of the "making" of the working-class and ethnic communities in the province, both as structural conditions of the social relations of production and as cultural practices and institutions consciously created to cope with, mediate, and alter relations of class oppression and ethnic subordination. The development of the class structure and of a hierarchy of ethnic relations of inequality are dual products of the historical processes of colonialism, capitalist development, and immigration policies in Canada, which combined to organize Asian immigrants into the lowest sectors of the British Columbia working class.

The following discussion of Chinese and Japanese immigration into British Columbia between 1880 and 1923 illustrates historical links between an ethnically segmented labour market, working-class organization, and ethnic solidarity. The ethnic segmentation of labour organization, expressions of racism within the Euro-Canadian labour movement, and the closure of Asian working-class ethnic communities should be understood in the context of working class divisions rooted in an ethnically segmented labour market.

CLASS, ETHNICITY AND LABOUR MARKET SEGMENTATION

The intersection of class and ethnicity can be addressed through an examination of the cultural practices of different ethnic groups within the working class. We define class as social relations to the means of production historically articulated through the processes of conflict, accommodation, struggle, and change. As E. P. Thompson writes (1963; 1978), the working class defines itself through day-to-day struggles in the labour process and throughout civil society:

> The class experience is largely determined by the productive relations into which men are born—or enter involuntarily. Class-consciousness is the way in which these experiences are handled in cultural terms: embodied in traditions, value-systems, ideas, and institutional forms (1963:10).

Cultural practices are understood as part of the material relations of social production and reproduction, not as specifically ideological phenomena. The ideas, traditions, and institutional forms embodied in socialism and trade unionism are the clearest expressions of working-class culture in capitalist societies. Our analysis is concerned with the way ethnic segmentation is reflected in working-class practices in British Columbia, since the working-out of class experiences includes handling the reality of an ethnically segmented labour market.

In the same way that working class cultural practices represent the working-out of productive relations, ethnic cultural practices are ways of handling subordinate relations within civil society as a whole. Ethnicity involves social relations of inequality that arise as persons with different national and racial origins are organized in economic and social life (Cassin and Griffith, 1981). The social organization of Chinese and Japanese ethnicity in British Columbia is characterized by social segregation—in the labour force, in residential areas, and in political, trade union, and cultural organizations—and through the simultaneous development of separate communities that tend to reproduce the characteristics defined as ethnic and legitimate the practices of racism. Like class practices, ethnic cultural practices should be understood as material and ideological sets of social relations that emerge in the working-out of unequal economic and political relations through processes of conflict, accommodation, and change.[2] We would expect to find that the working-class context of early Chinese and Japanese communities in British Columbia is reflected in the ethnic practices of those communities, just as the class practices of Euro-Canadian, Chinese, and Japanese workers tended to take an ethnically segmented form. The intersection between class and ethnicity should be understood in the context of the historical processes of colonialism, capitalist development, and immigration policies in Canada that have generated ethnic relations of inequality as a part of capitalist social relations.

Immigration policies have had a major impact on the formation of the working class in Canada as a result of the nation-state's history as a colonial-settler society. As Pentland (1981) writes, immigrants formed the raw material for the formation of a capitalist labour market in Canada beginning in the middle of the nineteenth century. Thus, Canadian immigration policies and practices occurred in the context of the labour requirements of capitalist economic development and within the British colonial heritage embedded in economic, political, and ideological structures. These two sets of historical processes, British colonialism and capitalism, have formed the focus of two different but inadequate approaches to the analysis of Canadian immigration policy and ethnic stratification.

Writers such as Porter (1965; 1979), Richmond (1970; 1978), and Hughes and Kallen (1974) identify the link between state immigration policies and ethnic inequality within the class structure as a political process: power was monopolized by the British charter group after the conquest of the French and native peoples and British racial attitudes were institutionalized into immigration policies. As Hughes and Kallen write:

> As the dominant group, English Canadians have, from the beginning, exercised control of immigration policies, responsible for determining which ethnic groups would be allowed into Canada, where they would settle, what jobs they could assume, and what ranking and social position would be accorded them within the existing system of ethnic stratification. (1974:112)

While it would be wrong to dismiss the importance of British racism and status group politics as an ideological underpinning of Canadian immigration policies, it would be equally incorrect to accept an essentially idealist causal explanation for ethnic inequality and racism in Canada. The Canadian state is fundamentally capitalist in character and not simply British in origin. Capitalist social relations form the context of state policies and class relations into which immigrants are socially organized.

A Marxist analysis of state immigration policies focuses on capitalist-class relations and the processes of accumulation. It has become common in recent years to link Canadian immigration policies with the legitimization of exploitative capitalist practices in the search for profit (Basran, 1983; Bernier, 1979; Cappon, 1975; and Li and Bolaria, 1979). Like most Marxist theorists of race and ethnicity, these authors adopt an economistic understanding of material social relations and an interventionist theory of the state, where capital dictates immigration policies and racist ideologies. In consequence, ethnic phenomena are reduced to capitalist epiphenomena. Ethnic oppression and racism, including racist immigration policies, are viewed as the direct outcome of capitalist attempts to divide the mutual interests of the working class and to prevent the development of class solidarity and effective working-class struggle through the exploitation of migrant and non-European immigrant workers (Castles and Kosack, 1972; Gorz, 1970; Leggett, 1968; Oppenheimer, 1974; Reich, 1971; 1981; and Szymanski, 1976).

The functional nature of ethnic conflict and racism for capitalist accumulation is, of course, not quite so simple. As Erik Olin Wright (1978:1390) has argued, "capitalism simultaneously undermines and reproduces racism." The processes of accumulation tend to undermine ethnic differences in the reduction of all labour costs, but the capitalist class attempts to reinforce ethnic divisions within the working class in order to reproduce its dominant class position politically. In spite of this theoretical refinement, Wright also treats ethnicity as the direct effect of capitalist employment practices and thus as secondary to class relations. While not wishing to lend credence to idealist arguments about the "primordial ties" of ethnicity, it is important to recognize that ethnic practices are not purely ideological, false consciousness, or in any way epiphenomenal to material social relations within capitalist societies. Although Marxist theorists posit the salience of racist ideas and practices within the history of European colonialism and uneven capitalist development (Cox, 1959), there is a failure to recognize that through these processes ethnic relations of inequality have become a central part of capitalist social relations in most capitalist societies and as such have real consequences at the level of political organization.

In British Columbia, the dominant (Euro-Canadian male) segment of the working class played an active role in the subordination of Asian workers in the work place and throughout civil society as part of the conflict over wages and working conditions in the province. This cannot be explained solely by the actions of the capitalist class since the working class is an active participant in its own "making." In contrast to most Marxist theorists, Edna Bonacich (1972; 1980) places labour competition at the centre of the creation of an ethnically segmented labour market. She thereby directly challenges the notion that racism within the working class is the creation of the capitalist class. According to Bonacich, the logic of capitalist accumulation seeks to drive down the price of labour, and an ethnically split labour market results from the differential resources available to various groups of workers in the struggle to improve wages and working conditions. Although employers do find ethnic cleavages functional for maintaining domination, Bonacich argues that

> the prejudices of business do not determine the price of labor, darker skinned or culturally different persons being paid less because of them. Rather, business tries to pay as little as possible for labor, regardless of ethnicity, and is held in check by the resources and motives of labor groups. Since these often vary by ethnicity, it is common to find ethnically split labor markets (1972:553).

Thus an ethnically segmented labour market results from intra-class conflict between groups of workers who have unequal economic, political, and cultural resources available to engage in the struggle for better pay and working conditions. While it is important to examine the relations between class fractions as part of the process of ethnic segmentation, Bonacich overemphasizes the role of intra-class conflict while underemphasizing the importance of the conflict between capital and labour. Perhaps most importantly, she fails to present an historical account of the emergence of dearer and cheaper groups of wage labour in the first place.[3] Bonacich's model does, however, identify the importance of differential political and economic resources for understanding the intersection of class and ethnicity within the British Columbia working class. Other theorists adopt a more historical and structural account of the formation of ethnically segmented labour markets. Edwards (1979) and Gordon, Edwards, and Reich (1982) argue that segmented labour markets emerge in the historical context of capitalist development with the formation of separate monopoly and competitive sectors, differential strategies of control in the workplace, changes in productive technology, and the differential effects of working-class struggle across economic sectors. While class struggle within the work place is taken into account, albeit in a fairly limited way, these authors completely ignore the role of the state in creating segmented labour markets (through differential immigration policies, extension of the political franchise, civil rights, and so on) and the repercussions of class struggle within state policies. As Burawoy has argued (1976), the marginal status of migrant workers is maintained largely by their relations with the state, since the absence of legal, political, and civil rights distinguishes migrants from citizens. Like contemporary migrant workers, Asian immigrants in pre-Second World War British Columbia were denied the legal and political rights of other citizens and were clearly distinguished as non-settlers, a condition which maintained the marginal status of Asians within the labour market and was reflected in the latter's exclusion from working-class political organizations.

The following discussion of ethnic conflict within the British Columbia working class will focus on the three-way conflict between employers and Euro-Canadian and Asian workers as the product of an ethnically segmented labour market. The intersection between class and ethnicity will be approached in terms of the economic, political, and cultural resources available to each group of workers in an ethnically segmented labour market formed in the context of racist immigration policies and capitalist employment practices.

ASIAN IMMIGRATION AND THE DEVELOPMENT OF AN ETHNICALLY SEGMENTED LABOUR MARKET

The demand for large quantities of cheap wage labour in British Columbia began with the construction of the Canadian Pacific Railway (C.P.R.) in the 1880's and lasted, apart from a recessionary period following the completion of the railway, through the first decade of the twentieth century (see McDonald, 1981). While skilled labour had to be imported from industrialized countries, raw (unskilled) labour could be imported more cheaply from peasant societies. Unskilled labour migrated from Ireland to central Canada in the nineteenth century and from the peasant economies of southern, eastern, and central Europe to Canada in the late nineteenth and early twentieth centuries (see Pentland, 1981). In British Columbia the demand for workers coincided with the ready availability of cheap peasant labour from China, where economic, social, and cultural conditions in the middle of the nineteenth century made emigration in search of wage labour a viable option for poor, illiterate, male peasants. Similar conditions provided a cheap source of labour from Japan beginning in the 1880's and from India around the turn of the century.[4]

Between 1881 and 1884 the Canadian Pacific Railway imported 15,000 indentured Chinese labourers to construct the British Columbia section of the railway (Canada, 1885:v). Approximately 4,000 Chinese were already in the province (most following the gold rush from California to the Fraser River), but given the extreme shortage of labour however, there was little political agitation against the Chinese prior to railway construction and the subsequent industrialization of the province (see Munro, 1971).[5] Over 9,000 Chinese immigrants remained in the province after railway construction ended, labouring in the mines, on farms, on the railway, in sawmills, salmon canneries, and as domestic servants (Canada, 1885:viii, 363-65). At the same time, the railway brought increased immigration from Europe, the United States, and central Canada resulting in direct competition between Euro-Canadian and Chinese labourers (Campbell, 1923; Cheng, 1931; Canada, 1885; and Canada, 1902). In the eighteen months between June of 1883 and November 1884, over 11,000 Euro-Canadian immigrants migrated to British Columbia (Canada, 1885:xlix). Although it is unknown what proportion of these immigrants were unskilled workers, or even how many remained in the province, this massive increase in manpower, coinciding with the decline of railway construction, resulted in considerable unemployment, competition for jobs, and anti-Chinese agitation among workers and provincial politicians. These factors were instrumental in the creation of the first *Royal Commission on Chinese Immigration* in 1885.

Competition between Euro-Canadian and Chinese workers was a direct result of capitalist employment practices: Chinese (and later Japanese and East Indian) workers earned from one-third to one-half less than unskilled Euro-Canadian workers (see Li, 1979:326-27; Ward, 1978:17; Canada, 1885; and Canada, 1902). The ability to acquire Asian workers at such low rates of pay resulted from the historically lower subsistence levels of Asian peasants; the fact that the reproduction costs of Asian labour were borne in Asia rather than in Canada; the system of contract labour to hire Asian workers; and the political inferiority accorded Asian immigrants by Canadian immigration policies. By the late nineteenth century, Euro-Canadian working-class trade union and political activity was an additional factor maintaining the relative cheapness of Asian labour in the province.

The Canadian government never considered Asians suitable settlers for Canada, but it did recognize the short-term advantages of plentiful cheap labour to build a sound economy in the west. As Avery and Neary

(1977:24-25) point out, the federal government approached Asian immigration differently from European and American immigration: "No
agents were commissioned, no promotional literature was distributed and
no plans were made for the agricultural settlement of Orientals." In a
settler colony where all non-British immigrants were accorded some
form of inferior "entrance status" (Porter, 1965), Asians shared the
unique distinction of a "non-settler" status accorded by the Canadian
government. In the *Royal Commission on Chinese and Japanese Immigration* the "non-assimilable" Asians are clearly distinguished from
"actual settlers" or "permanent citizens" of European origin. It is worth
quoting at some length from the conclusions to illustrate the racist view
of Asians encompassed in discriminatory immigration policies:

> If the end to be sought is the building up of the nation, and not the
> exploitation of these resources, the one vital interest to be secured
> above all others is an immigration of settlers of whom we may hope
> to make Canadians, in the highest and best sense of that word...
> How far do the Chinese of the labour or coolie class approach to this
> standard? They come from southern China, drawn from the poorer
> classes, reared in poverty where a few cents a day represent the earn-
> ings which must suffice for a family; accustomed to crowd together
> in small tenements or huts, close, unhealthy and filthy; with
> customs, habits and modes of life fixed and unalterable, resulting
> from an ancient and effete civilization, with no desire to conform to
> western ideas. They form, on their arrival, a community within a
> community, separate and apart, a foreign substance within, but not
> of our body politic, with no love for our laws and institutions; a
> people that will not assimilate or become an integral part of our race
> and nation. With their habits of overcrowding, and an utter disregard
> of all sanitary laws, they are a continual menace to health. From a
> moral and social point of view, living as they do without home life,
> schools or churches, and so nearly approaching a servile class, their
> effect upon the rest of the community is bad. They pay no fair pro-
> portion of the taxes of the country. They keep out immigrants who
> would become permanent citizens, and create conditions inimical to
> labour and dangerous to the industrial peace of the community where
> they come. They spend little of their earnings in the country and
> trade chiefly with their own people. They fill the places that ought to
> be occupied by permanent citizens, many of whom leave the country
> on their account. They are unfit for full citizenship, and are permitted
> to take no part in municipal or provincial government. Upon this
> point there was entire unanimity. They are not and will not become

citizens in any sense of the term as we understand it. They are so nearly allied to a servile class that they are obnoxious to a free community and dangerous to the state. . . . (Canada 1902:277-78).

All that has been said in this regard with reference to the Chinese applies with equal, if not greater force, to the Japanese . . . The consensus of opinion of the people of British Columbia is that they do not and cannot assimilate with white people, and that while in some respects they are less undesirable than the Chinese, in that they adopt more readily our habits of life and spend more of their earnings in the country, yet in all that goes to make for the permanent settlement of the country they are quite as serious a menace as the Chinese and keener competitors against the working man, and as they have more energy, push and independence, more dangerous in this regard than the Chinese (ibid.:397).

The Canadian state accorded Asian immigrants an inferior status as "non-settlers" by implementing special taxes, immigration quotas, and exclusionary laws that contributed to their marginal economic role within the labour market and their inferior political status within civil society generally. Asians were also denied the political franchise at all levels of government and were barred from some sectors of employment in British Columbia. Discriminatory immigration policies and other laws were initially premised on the national and peasant origin of Asian immigrants, and the Asians' lack of political rights reinforced their marginal economic position. Thus Asian workers were placed in a position of economic and political inferiority vis-à-vis Euro-Canadian workers: the resources used by the latter to lobby for better wages, working conditions, job security, socialist politics, and restrictive immigration policies were largely absent for Asian workers. In the context of the inferior economic and political position of Asian workers, Euro-Canadian workers began to organize to protect themselves from Asian competition. In contrast, the possibilities of successful Asian militancy in the labour scene were severely limited, and an ethnically segmented labour market was already forming at the time of the 1885 *Royal Commission on Chinese Immigration*.

Ethnic segmentation occurred in three forms: 1) segmentation by job function, with skilled labour and the more desirable unskilled jobs monopolized by Euro-Canadians while Asians performed the most menial of unskilled labour; 2) segregation within the work place, with Asians hired as groups under the authority of an Asian labour contractor separated from white workers; 3) an ethnically split wage scale, with Asians consistently paid less than Euro-Canadians for similar work. In the mining industry in 1885 Chinese labourers earned between $1.00 and $1.25 per day, while Euro-Canadian labourers earned $2.00 or more (Canada, 1885:xvi). Chinese cannery workers earned between $25.00 and $35.00 per month, while whites earned between $30.00 and $40.00 (ibid., xxv). Chinese labourers in road construction earned between $15.00 and $20.00 per month in comparison to $40.00 paid to Euro-Canadians (ibid., xl). And general labourers earned $1.25 per day if Chinese and between $2.00 and $2.50 if Euro-Canadian (ibid., p.lxxi). The contract labour system contributed to the physical segregation of white and Asian workers, to the low standard of living of the Asians, and to their relative docility within the labour market. The Asian labour contractor mediated language barriers, disciplined the workers, retained a portion of their wages, and provided food and other essentials at a profit, an arrangement that "necessarily leaves the men a good deal at the mercy of this fore-man" (Canada, 1885:81).

By the time of the 1902 *Royal Commission on Chinese and Japanese Immigration*, wage differentials had become entrenched and some suc-cessful agitation by Euro-Canadian workers had narrowed Asian employ-ment in particular areas, most notably road construction, railway em-ployment, and mining work. There were approximately 16,000 Chinese and 6,000 Japanese in the provincial labour market in 1902 (Canada, 1902:7-8, 328, 403).[6] Official records of East Indian immigration were not kept until 1904 (Cheng, 1931:138), but the number of East Indians in British Columbia in 1902 was so small that their presence was not noted in the evidence or the report of the *Commission*. Asians continued to be employed in largely unskilled, seasonal low-wage jobs. The major areas of Chinese employment were mining, the lumber industry, salmon can-ning, market-gardening, domestic service, and laundry, and tailoring businesses. A small number of Chinese in market gardening, laundry and tailoring work were petit bourgeois merchants renting farm land or busi-ness premises and employing their countrymen; but the vast majority of the Chinese engaged in these industries were employees (Canada, 1902:1-279; Cheng, 1931:194). With the exception of work in the can-ning industry, where Chinese performed semi-skilled job functions and were considered irreplaceable (at least prior to the introduction of me-chanization), Chinese labourers were unskilled and seasonally transient. The majority of Japanese in the province were engaged as fishermen, but they cannot be considered independent commodity producers, since they fished under the "attached system" and were tied to the packing com-panies that owned the boats and equipment (Knight and Koizumi, 1976). Japanese wage labourers were also employed in boat-building, in the lumber industry and, to a lesser extent, in mining (Canada, 1902:340-97).

Wage differentials between Asians and Euro-Canadian wage labourers had changed little since the 1880's. Because of the later entry of the Japanese into the provincial labour market they competed with the Chinese for jobs in lumbering and in mining, often accepting lower wages than the Chinese. However, the major difference in wages remained between Euro-Canadian and Asian workers. In the sawmills Chinese labourers earned between $1.00 and $1.50 per day, the Japanese earned between 90 cents and $1.25, and unskilled white wages started at $2.00, rising to $4.50 per day for skilled labour (ibid., pp.101-24, 360-65). Wages were similar in the logging camps, where Japanese workers averaged $1.00 per day, Chinese workers $1.25, and whites from $2.25 to $3.75 (ibid., pp.101-24). In the mining industries, Chinese labourers earned between $1.00 and $1.50 per day, unskilled Euro-Canadian labour earned between $2.50 and $3.00, while white miners earned between $3.00 and $5.00 per day (ibid., pp.72-96). Few Japanese were employed in mining, but evidence is cited of Japanese miner's helpers earning 90 cents a day (ibid., p.372). White boys received higher wages than Asians in the mines, averaging $1.50 a day as helpers (ibid.).

A major area of Chinese employment was salmon-canning, where wages were high but work lasted only six or seven weeks. The Chinese averaged $25.00 to $30.00 per month but could earn up to $75.00, while Euro-Canadian men, who served as foremen, earned an average of $75.00 to $80.00 and sometimes as much as $100 a month during the canning season. Chinese can-makers earned between $50.00 and $60.00 per month during the height of the fishing season. Although Chinese workers in the canneries were more directly in competition with native Indian workers, typically women and boys, during this period, the wages of the latter are not recorded in the 1902 Royal Commission, presumably because the commissioners were only concerned with Asian competition with white men in British Columbia (Canada, 1902:135-64). Chinese domestic servants earned between $10.00 and $30.00 per month with private families and from $25.00 to $45.00 in hotels. Since the Chinese were considered better servants, Euro-Canadian girls earned only between $12.00 and $15.00 per month in homes and do not appear to have been employed in hotels at all during this period (ibid., pp.167-71). In market-gardening and laundry and tailoring businesses, Chinese workers were employed in Chinese firms in competition with Euro-Canadian businesses employing white workers. By the turn of the twentieth century, market-gardening was dominated by the Chinese, with Chinese labourers earning $18.00 to $19.00 per month plus board on Chinese farms. On white-owned farms Chinese labourers earned $20.00 to $25.00 per month (without board) and Euro-Canadians earned $30.00 to $40.00 (ibid., pp.55-65). The Chinese also dominated the laundry business, with wages between $8.00 and $18.00 per month plus board in Chinese laundries. Automated steam laundries run by Euro-Canadians competed with Chinese labour-intensive laundries, paying their employees between $10.00 and $15.00 a week for white men and between $4.00 and $7.50 a week for white girls and women (ibid., p.175). Chinese tailors earned from $25.00 to $35.00 a month in Chinese shops, while Euro-Canadian tailors earned $12.00 per week if men and $6.00 per week if women in white tailoring shops (ibid., p.177).

The major Japanese employer was the fishing industry, with nearly 4,000 Japanese fishermen in 1901 (ibid., p.355). Fishing was the only area where remuneration was the same for Asian and Euro-Canadian workers since the price for fish did not vary between the different ethnic groups. This apparent equality was tempered by the contract system of employment and by equipment and area restrictions on Japanese fishermen that did not apply to white or native ones (Knight and Koizumi, 1976). The Japanese did not own the boats and equipment used in fishing, as white fishermen usually did, so the Japanese were tied to an agreement with specific fish-packing companies and they received only a share of the fish profits. Moreover, while packing companies dealt with white fishermen as individuals, Japanese fishermen were under contract to a Japanese labour contractor, a system that lowers the wages of individual workers (Canada, 1902:340-57). The Japanese had also begun to dominate the boat building industry by the turn of the twentieth century. In boat-building plants owned and run by Euro-Canadians, white labour earned between $3.00 and $4.00 per day for skilled labour and from $1.25 to $2.50 for boys doing the unskilled labour. The wages for Japanese workers in Japanese-owned boat-building operations are unknown, but since the Japanese undersold Euro-Canadian boat-builders by more than 50 per cent ($60.00 for a Japanese-built boat compared to $150 for a white-built boat), wages must have been comparable to or below those paid to Euro-Canadian boys (ibid., pp.357-59).

In the early period of Asian immigration the Chinese and the Japanese were almost exclusively confined to unskilled wage labour. By the mid 1920's, however, the occupational distribution and the class structure of the Asian communities were shifting. Although an estimated 80 per cent of Chinese and Japanese workers in British Columbia continued to labour for wages (see Tables 1 and 2), a significant minority of both immigrant groups had moved out of the working class and into the ranks of the petty bourgeoisie. More Chinese became involved in truck-farming and in small restaurants, laundries, and grocery stores. A significant number of Japanese became independent commodity producers in fruit- and berry-farming in the Okanagan and Fraser Valleys, while others became retail merchants (Adachi, 1976; Cheng, 1931; and Roy, 1980). This movement into commerce was directly related to successful Euro-Canadian working-class agitation to limit Japanese involvement in the fishing industry (the federal government halved the number of Japanese fishing licences in the early 1920's) and attempts to limit Asian employment in mining, railways, and public works projects (Roy, 1980). Thus, mining was no longer a major employer for the Chinese, and although over 2,000 Japanese remained fishermen (many now owning their own boats and equipment) this was only one-half of those previously engaged as fishermen (Cheng, 1931:163-97). However, the lumber industry remained an important source of employment for all Asians, absorbing one-fifth of Chinese labourers, one-third of Japanese labourers, and a full nine-tenths of the approximately one thousand East Indians in the provincial labour market in the mid-1920's (Cheng, 1931:157, 166, 197). The spread of Asian economic competition into sectors of the petit bourgeoisie had a corresponding effect on the spread of anti-Asian agitation.

TABLE 1: CHINESE OCCUPATIONS IN 1924

Occupations	*Employed Men*	*Per cent*	*Employed Women*	*Per cent*
Professional	300	1		
Factory and Mill Workers	5,500	12		
Farm Operators and Workers*	2,000	5		
Miners	700	2		
Railway and Shipping Workers	2,000	5		
Hotel and Household Servants	4,000	9	100	50
Businesses**:				
Laundries	14,000	32		
Restaurant	9,000	20		
Vegetables and Fruit	2,000	5	100	50
Others	1,700	4		
Traders with Chinese	2,500	6		
Total	43,000	101 (rounded)	200	100

Source: Cheng, 1931:196.
*Data cited by Cheng (1931:170) indicate that there were only 485 Chinese who owned or leased land in British Columbia in 1920. It is likely, therefore, that approximately three-quarters of those listed under Farm Operators and Workers were in fact farm labourers.
**Cheng lists all trade licences issued to Chinese immigrants in Vancouver, Winnipeg, Calgary, Edmonton, Toronto, and Montreal in 1924 (1931:182-83). The total number of trade licences issued that year, including such things as peddlers, hawkers, and car licences was only 2,585. It can be assumed, therefore, that the vast majority of the nearly 30,000 Chinese classified under Business (probably as many as 80 per cent) were employees rather than employers.

TABLE 2: JAPANESE OCCUPATIONS IN 1924

Occupations	*Number Employed	Per cent
Fishermen	2,500	26
Lumber and Sawmill Workers	2,733	28
Railway Workers	611	6
Fish Saltery Workers	359	4
Farm Labourers	430	4
Miners	232	2
Clerical Employees	309	3
Domestic and Hotel Employees	590	6
Miscellaneous Wage Workers	316	3
Self-employed (Gardeners, Boat Builders, Mechanics)	636	6
Farmers (Berry, Orchard, and so on)	567	6
Merchants	396	4
Professionals	106	1
Total	9,785	99(rounded)

Source: Knight and Koizumi, 1976:114-15 (compiled from information found in Cheng, 1931:197).
*The total number of employed Japanese includes 376 women, predominantly employed as domestics, fish saltery workers, farm labourers, and self-employed (Cheng, 1931:197).

"Before World War I labour organizations were in the forefront of anti-Asian agitation; by the 1920's and 1930's, farmers and retail merchants were often the most prominent objectors to the presence of Asians, their lower standard of living, and willingness to work longer and harder for lower returns than white men" (Roy, 1980:168.) The growth of ethnic businesses changed the structure of the Chinese and Japanese communities, and a growing number of Asian workers were now employed on farms and in businesses owned by other members of their ethnic communities. This trend also strengthened ethnic segmentation within the provincial labour market.

THE LABOUR MOVEMENT AND ANTI-ASIAN AGITATION

Euro-Canadian working-class organization against the Chinese first occurred in Victoria and in the Vancouver Island coal-mining districts where competition with the Chinese began in the late 1870's. The Workingman's Protective Association was formed in Victoria in 1878 to provide the mutual protection of the working class of B.C. against the great influx of Chinese; to use all legitimate means for the suppression of their immigration; to assist each other in the obtaining of employment; and to devise means for the amelioration of the condition of the working class of this Province in general (quoted in Phillips, 1967:9).

In the Vancouver Island coal mines, anti-Chinese labour demands first emerged in 1883 following claims that the inability of the Chinese to understand English caused mining accidents. After the repeated use of Chinese strikebreakers in the Dunsmuir mines, however, a general demand for the exclusion of the Chinese became a standard feature of coal-miners' labour strategy (Phillips, 1967:8; Morton, 1974:107). In the mid 1880's demands for the exclusion of Chinese formed part of the organizing drive by the Knights of Labour and contributed to its success in the province (see Phillips, 1967:14; Ward, 1978:44-46). In its submission to the 1885 Royal Commission, the Knights of Labour vigorously deplored the effect that cheap Chinese labour was having on white workers:

Chinese labor is confessedly of a low, degraded, and servile type, the inevitable result of whose employment in competition with free white labor is to lower and degrade the latter without any appreciable elevation of the former. Their standard of living is reduced to the lowest possible point, and, being without family ties, or any of those institutions which are essential to the existence and progress of our civilization, they are enabled to not only live but to grow rich on wages far below the lowest minimum at which we can possibly exist. They are thus fitted to become all too dangerous competitors in the labor market, while their docile servility, the natural outcome of centuries of grinding poverty and humble submission to a most oppressive system of government, renders them doubly dangerous as the willing tools whereby grasping and tyrannical employers grind down all labor to the lowest living point. It is for this latter reason, chiefly, that we object to the Chinese, not altogether because they accept lower wages (Canada, 1885:156).

Thus, Euro-Canadian labour opposition to the Chinese (and later the Japanese and East Indians) was based not only on the relative cheapness of Asian labour, but also on its docility, a docility which allowed employers in British Columbia to use Asian workers often and effectively to break Euro-Canadian strikes.

Since Canadian immigration policies and the allocation of inferior political status combined with employment practices to organize Asian immigrants into the lowest sectors of the provincial working class, immigration policy became a class-divided political issue in British Columbia. Capitalists who employed large numbers of Asians in mining, forestry, salmon-canning and fruit-farming industries demanded an open-door policy to supply cheap unskilled labour, while the Euro-Canadian working class led the struggle to curtail or exclude Asian immigration (Avery and Neary, 1977). Employers and employees who gave testimony at the 1885 and 1902 Royal Commissions were divided on the basis of class over the question of whether cheap Asian labour should be allowed in the country at all; however, there was a general agreement that Asians who did come should not be granted the political rights of citizenship and should not settle permanently in the country. Reflecting the general belief that Asians were "inferior" to Europeans, the 1885 *Royal Commission on Chinese Immigration* concluded that immigration must be regulated to insure that no more Chinese came to the province than were necessary for the economy. The Commission imposed a $50.00 head tax on all Chinese labourers coming to Canada, with the exception of a small number of Chinese students, merchants, and diplomats (Canada, 1885; Cheng, 1931; Ward, 1978). However, this legislation had no significant effect on reducing the number of Chinese in the province; in 1891 there were nearly 9,000 Chinese in the labour force (16.5 per cent of the non-native population), rising to nearly 15,000 by 1901 (see Ward, 1978:170).

By the 1890's the Euro-Canadian working class had broadened its anti-Asian agitation to the political sphere by running labour candidates in the provincial elections. In 1898 five labour representatives were elected to the provincial legislature, where they managed to enact legislation banning Asians from underground employment in the coal mines (Phillips, 1967:30; Schwantes, 1979:74-75). By the turn of the twentieth century over 4,500 Japanese joined the 15,000 Chinese in the provincial labour market. Labour conflict and political agitation led the federal government to raise the Chinese head tax to $500 in 1903 and to endorse Japanese immigration restrictions (Canada, 1902; Cheng, 1931). By the 1900's Euro-Canadian labour was better organized in trade unions than it had been two decades previously, and it had already enjoyed some success in electing labour candidates to the provincial legislature. The white working class, then, was in a stronger position to affect immigration policies regarding Asians. The major distinction between the 1885 and 1902 Royal Commissions, however, was the general consensus among employers that there was already an abundant supply of Asians in the province to fill the needs of cheap labour and that their immigration ought now to be drastically reduced. It should be noted about the restriction of Chinese (and later Japanese) immigrants, however, that it was Asian labourers rather than all Asians who were restricted and taxed. In addition, the massive expansion of an unskilled labour force was beginning to slow down by the turn of the century, and the restrictions on Asian immigration that began in 1902 and culminated in the mid 1920's coincided with a change in the needs of the labour market.

Restrictive legislation against the Japanese was not long in coming.[7] Riots against Asian immigration, sparked by rumours of the imminent arrival of thousands of Japanese and East Indians in Vancouver in September 1907, helped convince the Japanese government to restrict the emigration of labourers to Canada. In 1908, a "Gentleman's Agreement" was reached with Japan to limit the emigration of labourers to Canada to four hundred per year. However, this agreement allowed the wives and children of Japanese in Canada to emigrate without restriction, fostering the picture-bride system of Japanese marriages and resulting in a large number of Japanese families in British Columbia (Adachi, 1976: 85-92; Cheng, 1931:126-32). East Indian immigration was halted in 1908, with special legislation requiring potential immigrants to arrive in Canada by continuous journey from their country of origin (Cheng, 1931:139). Since there were no direct shipping routes from India to Canada, further immigration effectively ceased (Ward, 1978).

In the context of economic depression and unemployment following the First World War, and with more than 19,000 Chinese, 8,000 Japanese, and 2,000 East Indians in the provincial labour market, the Euro-Canadian working-class led a broad-based campaign to force the federal government to enact exclusionary legislation (Ward, 1978).

> Led by the V.T.L.C. (the Vancouver Trades and Labour Council), the anti-oriental campaign spread rapidly around the province. The culmination of this movement was the formation of the Asiatic Exclusion League in August of 1921 by labour, soldier and merchant groups, including six unions and the V.T.L.C., while the president and secretary of the league were prominent members of the labour council (Phillips, 1967:88).

In response to the political agitation of Euro-Canadian workers and merchants within British Columbia the Chinese Immigration Act was passed in 1923 ending further Chinese immigration; the "Gentleman's Agreement" was amended to limit Japanese labourers to 150 a year in 1923, and the picture-bride system of Japanese marriages was abolished in 1928 (Cheng, 1931:90-100, 131-36).

The role of working-class organizations in the movement to exclude Asian immigration to British Columbia was only the most successful political manifestation of anti-Asian labour agitation. Until the late 1920's the trade unions consistently refused to admit Asians into their organizations, and they applied pressure for all-white hiring policies and organized boycotts of products and retail outlets that employed Asian labour. While some socialist parties began to advocate the inclusive organization of Asians after the First World War, exclusionary labour and political organization generally remained unchallenged until the late 1920's.[8]

The Euro-Canadian working class in British Columbia marshalled its superior economic and political resources in the labour market and in the political arena for protection against cheaper Asian labour as part of the general struggle against capitalist employment practices in the province. White working-class labour organization was two-pronged: it sought protection from cheap labour competition and strikebreaking by excluding Asians, and it tried to raise its standard of living and job security through collective bargaining rights that would weaken the power of capitalists in the province. The racist content of Euro-Canadian labour organization, with its exclusionary policies and anti-Asian demands, cannot be interpreted simply as racism overshadowing class-consciousness. Ethnic conflict within the working class should be understood in the context of divisions rooted in an ethnically segmented labour market. However, exclusionary rather than inclusionary labour organization was not an automatic outcome of wage differentials in the labour market; rather, it emerged in the context of the inferior political status of the cheaper labour group that made the possibilities of successful labour militancy much more likely for Euro-Canadian workers than for Asians. The labour organizations legitimated white workers' exclusion of a group already defined as inferior by the state. Although racist attitudes about the inferiority of Asians were certainly not irrelevant to anti-Asian labour organization in British Columbia, the salience of these racist attitudes and practices should be understood within the context of social relations that ghettoized Asians economically, politically, and socially.

Paul Phillips has argued that the presence of cheaper Asian labour in British Columbia "stimulated labour political organization, militancy and class conflict" among white workers (1967:163). The radical nature of trade union and political organization documented by Phillips and others is the history of white male workers, and much of it was explicitly racist and sexist[9] in content contextualized in terms of the struggle between capital and labour in the province. The three-way conflict between capital and Euro-Canadian and Asian labour was a product of labour market segmentation and social segregation with the "non-citizen"

Asians organized into the lowest sectors of the working class. Employers paid Asians one-half to one-third less than Euro-Canadians, relegated Asians to a limited number of the least desirable jobs, hired Asians under contract rather than as individuals, physically segregated Asian and white workers on most job-sites, and frequently recruited Asians for strikebreaking purposes. These practices reflected the marginal economic and political status of Asian workers vis-à-vis those of European origin. Euro-Canadian workers handled the realities of ethnic segmentation through anti-Asian labour organization that reinforced the marginal economic and political position of Asian workers and entrenched labour market segmentation. In the short term, anti-Asian agitation strengthened Euro-Canadian labour organizations by providing a successful mobilizing focus, but in the long term it weakened the strength of labour as a whole through exclusionary rather than inclusionary labour organization. Euro-Canadian working-class organization and consciousness were ethnically fragmented and racist in form because ethnic relations of inequality were a part of capitalist social relations in British Columbia. Racism within the labour movement was not the outcome of the "social psychology of race relations" that relegated class conflict to a secondary role in British Columbia as Ward argues (1978; 1980). It was the outcome of developing, but not yet mature, working-class consciousness confronting capitalist social relations that were explicitly racist in form, producing an ethnically segmented labour market and working class.

ASIAN WORKERS, ETHNIC CLOSURE, AND
SEGMENTED LABOUR ORGANIZATION

While Euro-Canadian workers turned to exclusionary labour organization, Asian immigrants turned largely to ethnic community organization to cope with an ethnically segmented labour market and political subordination within civil society as a whole. The ethnic communities of Chinese and Japanese immigrants in British Columbia can be considered a social and economic resource. The formation of ethnic communities occurred as acts of inclusion, providing mutual aid, economic links, and sociability, and as acts of exclusion, offering self-defence against a generally hostile dominant society. The creation of ethnic communities should not be seen as the automatic outcome of traditional social and cultural practices in the homeland, especially since much ethnic practice is newly formed in the immigrant context. Rather, it should be seen as maintaining and fostering group ties based on ethnic origin. The salience of these practices in British Columbia is closely linked to the structural position of Chinese and Japanese in the labour market and civil society generally. Racism and ethnic group solidarity reinforce each other and legitimize economic and political discrimination.

Chinese and Japanese workers in British Columbia lacked not only political and economic resources, but also a history of trade union and socialist traditions and, to a large extent, a perception of permanence that characterized the success of Euro-Canadian working-class organization. Chinese and Japanese workers did engage in labour struggles and strikes against employers. But for the most part they tended to rely on ethnic solidarity rooted in common language, culture, and national origin to cope with their marginal existence in British Columbia. Ethnic community organizations and cultural practices provided Asian immigrants with some political expression. Ethnic links gave access to jobs through the ethnic labour contractors or work bosses, often providing a supply of cheap, loyal labour.[10] Social services were unavailable to them from the dominant community, but ethnic organizations provided an integrative social and cultural context that was especially important for males without a family life in British Columbia.

The Chinese and Japanese communities during this period were largely working-class communities, but they were by no means homogeneous. The internal conflicts and class cleavages within the Asian communities have been little studied. The role of labour contractors in the ethnic communities and the relationships between the presence or absence of Asian labour militancy and the system of contract labour is largely unresearched. Similarly, a small merchant population led the dominant community institutions while possessing a class position antagonistic to the ethnic workers they employed; this relationship should be investigated.[11] Although the Chinese and Japanese communities contained internal class cleavages and conflicts, the outward appearance of cohesion is based on ethnic solidarity and a common working-class position. The combined realities of a segmented labour market: working-class penury; frequent unemployment; transience; non-settler immigration status; lack of family life; residential segregation; exclusion from Euro-Canadian political, trade union, and cultural organizations; and general racism all defined the character of the early Chinese and Japanese communities. As Cho and Leigh note:

> The early Chinese community was predominantly male, unskilled, poor and persecuted. The relationships and institutions that came to typify the community reflect this; roominghouse, moneylender, gambling den, brothel, benevolent society, district association, clan association and fraternal association were ways in which the group

met its own needs and mediated with a sometimes hostile white society (1972:68).

The Chinese and Japanese workers in the labour market were cheap, primarily unskilled, seasonal wage labourers, with few women and little family life in the province;[12] these were the major forces structuring the ethnic communities in British Columbia. The major organizations in these communities, the Chinese Benevolent Association and the Canadian Japanese Association, reflected the needs of a male working-class population and the internal authority structures of relatively self-contained communities in a hostile environment.

The Chinese Benevolent Association first emerged in Victoria in 1884 in response to Chinese unemployment and penury following the end of railway construction in the province. As Sien writes, the Benevolent Association formed as "a protective association in the face of prejudice and discrimination."

> Their first task was to provide emergency relief for members of the Chinese community thrown out of work during the slump. Soup kitchens were established to feed the hungry, shelters to house the indigent and hospitals to nurse the sick (1971:215).

These functions are not unlike those performed by workingmen's protective associations in the nineteenth century. However, the Chinese Benevolent Association also acted as a political organ and a policing body in the Chinese community. Lai (1972) identifies four kinds of activities that the Benevolent Association headed: 1) organizing protests and fundraising to fight discriminatory laws and taxes in Canada; 2) fundraising for relief purposes in Canada and in China; 3) the adjudication and maintenance of peace and order within the Chinese communities; and 4) the administration of hospitals, cemeteries, schools, and other social services within the Chinese communities. In addition, district associations provided links between immigrants and their relatives in China, fraternal associations were active in politics in China, and clan associations provided social links between immigrants with common surnames (Sien, 1971:215-16). The less formal links between Chinese immigrants occurred in the rooming houses, ethnic restaurants, brothels, gambling dens, and the work place, fostering close ethnic bonds within the community.

The Canadian Japanese Association played a similar role in the Japanese community. Formed in 1897, the association "aided immigrants to find jobs and learn English, encouraged them to maintain a high moral standard and become naturalized citizens; and endeavoured generally to combat discrimination" (Adachi, 1971:222). The Japanese Consul in Canada shared a close relationship with the Canadian Japanese Association, a link which made the Canadian Japanese Association a more effective political organ in fighting discriminatory legislation than was the Chinese Benevolent Association. Like its Chinese counterpart, the Canadian Japanese Association provided essential support services for the Japanese workers: it offered second-language schools for Japanese children, policed the Japanese community, and mediated with the dominant Canadian society. In addition, locality associations provided social links for immigrants from common areas in Japan (Cheng, 1931:210-14). The less formal links in the work place, the family, ethnic restaurants, gambling dens, rooming houses, and so on formed the daily context which fostered ethnic solidarity among the Japanese.

It is clear that the Chinese and the Japanese did not recognize the commonality of their positions within the province. Each conceived of itself as distinct and separate not only from Euro-Canadian society but also from the other Asian communities. In fact, there was hostility between the Chinese and the Japanese, rooted in economic competition within British Columbia, military competition in Asia, and Japanese ideologies of racial superiority (Adachi, 1976:40). The category "Oriental" was a Euro-Canadian construct overlooking differences between Asian groups in favour of their similar position within the labour market and civil society. Labour competition and the processes of ethnic closure within the Asian communities resulted in the lack of co-operation in the struggle to redress legal and labour market discrimination. Ethnic solidarity strengthened the cleavages between the Chinese and the Japanese as well as between Asians as a group and Euro-Canadians.

While Asian immigrants did not recognize the commonality of their positions as minority ethnic groups, there is clear evidence that they did recognize their commonality as workers. Asian workers did take an active part in labour conflict in the province, although less often than Euro-Canadian workers and often in an unorganized form. When Asian workers did form trade unions, moreover, these were ethnically segregated. Chinese, Japanese, and East Indian workers struck by themselves and in conjunction with Euro-Canadians in the fishing industry, the lumber industry, and to a much lesser extent, the mining industry. By the end of the First World War, both the Chinese and the Japanese had begun to form their own labour unions.

The history of Asian strikes in the fishing industry began with Chinese cannery workers' strikes in 1881 and 1889 and with the involvement of Japanese fishermen in the 1893 Fraser River strike (Knight and Koizumi,

1976:105-6). Japanese fishermen on the Fraser River organized themselves into the Japanese Fishermen's Benevolent Society in 1900 and engaged in strikes alongside the Euro-Canadian Fishermen's Protective and Benevolent Association and native Indian fishermen in 1900, 1901, 1904, 1913 and 1925 (Knight and Koizumi:105-7). In the mining industry, Chinese and Japanese workers were involved in the 1903 Cumberland strike, and in the initial stages of the long 1912-14 Vancouver Island strikes (Bennett, 1935:118; Knight and Koizumi, 1976:108). According to Bennett (1935:115-20), the Western Federation of Miners was the first trade union in British Columbia to attempt to organize Asians during the 1903 C. P. R. strike. They had little success, though, since the absence of unified labour organization weakened the strikes in fishing and mining, with employers often able to exploit the weaker economic resources of the Asian participants, forcing them back to work after a short period of time.

 • The first recorded strike by Asians in the lumber industry occurred in January of 1903, when one hundred Japanese struck a New Westminster saw mill (see Canada. Labour Gazette: February 1903:601). During the First World War Asians became extremely active in labour conflicts in the lumber industry, and because of the labour shortage, they were often successful in their demands. The Chinese formed the Chinese Canadian Labour Union (later the Chinese Workers' Union) in 1916, an organization that was involved in some strikes in the shingle mills but was more concerned with educational activities within the Chinese community (*Chinese Times*, 1917-21). In 1919 the Chinese Shingle Workers' Union of Canada was formed specifically to support Chinese union organization in that industry. The Chinese were involved in a series of strikes in shingle mills throughout British Columbia between 1917 and 1921. In 1917 and 1918 these strikes were for wage increases, shorter hours, and occasionally wage parity with Euro-Canadian workers in the mills; beginning in 1919 the strikes were against wage reduction in the shingle mills during the post-war recession (*Chinese Times*, 1917-21; Canada. Department of Labour, Strikes and Lockout Files, 1917-21). Many of the strikes in the shingle mills during this period involved Japanese, East Indian, and Euro-Canadian workers in conjunction with the Chinese, who formed a majority. The Shingle Weavers Union organized many of the white strikes in the shingle mills, while the Lumber Workers Industrial Union organized Euro-Canadians in the sawmills.

In 1920, after a successful strike in a sawmill, the Japanese in the lumber industry organized the Japanese Camp and Mill Workers Union (first called the Japanese Labour Union) to co-ordinate Japanese involvement in strikes in the lumber industry. The union was open to all Japanese workers in the province and sought affiliation with the Euro-Canadian trade union movement to integrate Japanese workers into the mainstream. In 1927, the Vancouver Trades and Labour Council finally ended its exclusionary policy and admitted the Japanese Camp and Mill Workers Union as full trade union members (Knight and Koizumi, 1976:38-57, 113). In the mid 1920's the Japanese Camp and Mill Workers Union had sixteen hundred members, but its membership was scattered throughout the province and thus the organization was weak. Ryuichi Yoshida, an activist in the union from its formation, summarizes the problems that confronted a Japanese union that was isolated from the general trade union movement:

> The practical problem was that the Labour Union didn't increase in membership. It was not possible to strengthen the Labour Union because we could not achieve any gains in wages and conditions. Our union, consisting of just some Japanese workers, was too small to achieve any improvements in work conditions and pay. We were too scattered. Without the cooperation of the white unions we could achieve nothing. The white unions were organized by occupations but they did not accept Japanese members usually. Because of that the Labour Union included Japanese workers of all occupations. But our activity was not related to everyday work questions. The fishermen had their own organizations and they did not join the Labour Union, except as individuals. Those who had socialist views or who supported the labour movement from moral reasons were our only continuous supporters (in Knight and Koizumi, 1976:54-55).

With groups of workers organized in different bodies on the basis of ethnic origin, employers were often able to pit one group of strikers against another or to bring in strikebreakers from a different ethnic group. Nor were the strikebreakers always Asian. In April 1921, eighty Japanese workers struck at a Vancouver sawmill against a reduction in wages; they were replaced by white men at a high rate of pay (Canada. Department of Labour, Strikes and Lockout Files, Volume 324 Strike 31). In October 1929, forty Chinese shingle packers struck a New Westminster shingle mill against a wage reduction and were replaced by white girls; several years previously, the Chinese men had been used to replace white male workers during an unsuccessful strike (Canada. Department of Labour, Strikes and Lockout Files, Volume 344 Strike 103). Although ethnic segmentation and gender segmentation within the trade union movement weakened all workers, it naturally weakened most those workers whose social and economic position was the most marginal. Given the reality of an ethnically segmented labour market, lack of political rights, and the superior resources available to Euro-Canadian labour organizations in the province (particularly when much white labour organization explicitly included anti-Asian demands) Asian workers often resorted to the economic, political, and social links afforded by their ethnic communities rather than organizing within the work place to improve the condition of their lives in British Columbia.

CONCLUSION

This overview of working-class organization and ethnic conflict in British Columbia between 1880 and 1923 illustrates the fruitfulness of approaching working-class and ethnic community formation as historical processes "made" by working out social relations of production through cultural practices and institutions. The intersection between class practices and ethnic practices occurred in the context of ethnic segmentation as part of capital-wage labour relations in the province. The working class experienced an ethnically segmented labour market and handled it in different ways. Ethnic segmentation was reflected in working-class practices, with Euro-Canadian, Chinese, and Japanese workers engaging in ethnically separate forms of labour organization. Joint working-class action involving Euro-Canadian and Asian workers did occur, particularly after the First World War when Asians played a more active role in provincial labour conflicts, but its success was often hampered by ethnic segmentation.

The formation of an ethnically segmented labour market and a politically segmented working class in British Columbia was a complex historical process. Differential employment practices were essential for the formation of a segmented labour market, but they occurred in the broader context of social relations. The historical conditions of labour migration, uneven capitalist development, racist Canadian immigration policies, the exclusionary practices of the white working class, the formation of ghettoized ethnic communities, and racist ideologies generated by and legitimating these practices all contributed to and were facilitated by the creation and maintenance of an ethnically segmented labour market in the province. Ethnic conflict within the working class occurred not merely as the outcome of wage differences between dearer Euro-Canadian and cheaper Asian workers but also in the context of the inferior political status accorded Asians by the Canadian state. This status made the success of labour militancy much less likely for Asians than for Euro-Canadians, and legitimated the white workers' exclusion of a group already defined as inferior by the state and civil society. Asian immigration became a major organizing focus for Euro-Canadian workers in British Columbia, fostering class-conscious political intervention. The focus of the political intervention and much of the labour organization in the workplace was anti-Asian, yet it was contextualized, quite consciously, in terms of the struggle between capital and labour in the province. Racism within the labour movement was a product of developing, but not yet mature, working-class consciousness confronting explicitly racist capitalist social relations.

Asian immigrants' lack of political resources and settler immigration status reinforced their economic position in the labour market and fostered ethnic community organization as a means of coping with and mediating conditions in the province. Ethnic institutions provided economic links in the wage labour market and in ethnic business, a means of political expression against discriminatory laws in Canada, social services not provided by the dominant society, and an integrative social and cultural milieu closed to the racist dominant society. The working-class nature of the Asian immigrant experience in British Columbia was reflected in the cultural practices and institutions within the Chinese and Japanese communities and in their involvement in labour conflicts throughout the province. Asian involvement in strikes and trade union organizations was limited not only by their lack of political and economic resources but also by the exclusionary nature of the Euro-Canadian labour movement. Successful Asian labour organization was only possible under two circumstances: 1) a shortage of unskilled labour such as occurred during the First World War; and 2) Asian inclusion within the mainstream trade union movement, which did not occur before the 1930's. In the absence of inclusive labour organization, ethnic conflict within the labour movement persisted, ethnic solidarity within the Asian communities was enhanced, and racism within the dominant society deepened.

NOTES

*An earlier version of this paper was presented at the annual meeting of the Canadian Sociology and Anthropology Association in Vancouver in June 1983. I would like to thank Don Black, Wallace Clement, Dennis Olsen, Daiva Stasiulis, Frank Vallee, and Rennie Warburton for providing valuable comments and criticisms on earlier drafts.

1. For a discussion of working class radicalism in British Columbia, see Bercuson (1977), Pentland (1979), Phillips (1967, 1973), McCormack (1977), and Schwantes (1979). For discussions of anti-Asian racism within the working class, see Pentland (1979), Phillips (1967, 1981), Roy (1976, 1980), and Ward (1978, 1980).
2. References to ethnicity throughout this paper refer to ethnic groups or communities as distinct sociological phenomena and not to the more general ethnic categories of descent (see Hughes and Kallen, 1974). In its broadest sense ethnicity is used as the generic term for relations of domination and subordination between groups defined socially as sharing a common ancestry based on perceived biological (racial) and/or cultural criteria (see Cox, 1959; Bonacich, 1972, 1980; and Hughes and Kallen, 1974).
3. I would like to thank Daiva Stasiulis for this formulation of the weaknesses in Bonacich's model of an ethnically split labour market.
4. East Indian immigrants have not been included for discussion in this paper although the framework used to discuss the Chinese and the Japanese could also be fruitfully applied to an analysis of Indian immigration to British Columbia during this period.
5. The provincial legislature did enact legislation against the Chinese in the 1870's. In 1874 Chinese were disenfranchised from provincial elections; in 1878 they were barred from public works; and in 1878 and again in 1884 special taxes against the Chinese were passed and later declared *ultra vires* by the British Columbia supreme court. However, evidence suggests that these actions were spearheaded by a few provincial politicians as part of a struggle with Ottawa and did not result from any widespread political agitation in the province (see Cheng, 1931; Munro, 1971; and Ward, 1978).
6. There are less than 100 "other Asians" recorded in British Columbia in the 1901 census. Although the precise number of East Indians is not known prior to 1904, over 5,000 East Indians arrived in British Columbia between 1904 and 1908. Many either moved on to the United States or returned to India, because by 1911 the census records just over 2,000 East Indians in the province. By the 1920's, only 1,000 East Indian workers remained in British Columbia (see Cheng, 1931:138; and Ward, 1978:170-71).
7. The "problem" of Japanese immigration was dealt with more diplomatically than Chinese immigration because Japan was a world military and trading power with whom it was important to maintain cordial relations, while China was divided and weak under colonial rule (see Adachi, 1976; Lyman, 1968).
8. Research on the exclusionary practices of Vancouver trade unions during this time was undertaken as part of my Ph.D. dissertation, "Working Class Politics, Racism and Sexism: The Making of a Politically Divided Working Class in British Columbia, 1900-1939," Department of Sociology and Anthropology, Carleton University, 1986. Sources for this information are found in the minutes of the Vancouver Trades and Labour Council, records of union locals, and the labour newspapers of the period, particularly the *British Columbia Federationist*, the *British Columbia Labour News*, and the *Labour Statesman*.
9. Recent research in British Columbia has pointed out the sex-blind nature of traditional labour history and has begun to document the sexist nature of trade union activity within the working class (see Campbell, 1979, 1980; Rosenthal, 1979; and Bernard, 1982).
10. Bonacich and Modell (1980) document the role that economic factors played in forming and maintaining ethnic solidarity in the American Japanese community. Their work suggests several lines of investigation that could be followed in British Columbia, particularly the relationship between the use of cheap Asian labour and the success of ethnic business enterprises and the relationship between "middlemen minorities" and the dominant society.

11. See Modell (1969) for an interesting study of class conflict and ethnic solidarity in the Japanese fruit industry in Los Angeles.
12. Family life did not exist for the Chinese in Canada. In 1925, there was only one adult woman to every thirty-eight adult men, with the majority either prostitutes or wives of wealthy merchants. On the other hand, by 1920 the sex ratio among the Japanese was one adult woman for every two adult men, while the ratio of children to adults was also one to two (Cheng, 1931:205-6). This growing importance of Japanese families had an impact on the tendency for the Japanese to begin to adopt a more permanent and future-oriented perspective, while the Chinese tended to maintain a temporary orientation in British Columbia.

REFERENCES

Adachi, Ken. 1971.
"The Japanese." In John Norris (ed.), *Strangers Entertained: A History of Ethnic Groups of British Columbia*. Vancouver: Evergreen Press Ltd.
—1976 *The Enemy that Never Was: A History of the Japanese Canadians*. Toronto: McClelland and Stewart.
Avery Donald. 1979.
'Dangerous Foreigners': European Immigrant Workers and Labour Radicalism in Canada, 1896-1932. Toronto: McClelland and Stewart.
Avery, Donald and Peter Neary. 1977.
"Laurier, Borden and a White British Columbia." *Journal of Canadian Studies* 12, no.4 (Summer):24-34.
Basran, Gurcharn S. 1983.
"Canadian Immigration Policy and Theories of Racism." In Peter S. Li and B. Singh Bolaria (eds.), *Racial Minorities in Multicultural Canada*. Toronto: Garamond Press: pp.3-13.
Bennett, William. 1937.
Builders of British Columbia. Vancouver: Broadway Printers.
Bercuson, D. J. 1977.
"Labour Radicalism and the Western Industrial Frontier: 1897-1919." *Canadian Historical Review* 58, no. 2 (June):154-75.
Bernard, Elaine. 1982.
The Long Distance Feeling. A History of the Telecommunications Workers' Union. Vancouver: New Star Books.
Bernier, Bernard. 1979.
"Classes sociales et idéologie raciste dans les colonies de peuplement." In Danielle Juteau Lee (ed.), *Frontières ethniques en devenir*. Ottawa: University of Ottawa Press.
Bonacich, Edna. 1972.
"A Theory of Ethnic Antagonism: The Split Labour Market." *American Sociological Review* 37 (October):547-559.
—1973 "A Theory of Middlemen Minorities." *American Sociological Review* 38 (October):583-594.
Bonacich, Edna and John Modell. 1980.
The Economic Basis of Ethnic Solidarity: Small Business in the Japanese American Community. Berkeley: University of California Press.
Burawoy, M. 1976.
"The Functions and Reproduction of Migrant Labor: Comparative Material from

Southern Africa and the United States." *American Journal of Sociology* 81 (March):1050-87.

Campbell, Marie. 1979.
"Unlocking Women's Experience: A Method for Using Historical Sources." *Our Generation* 13, no. 3 (Summer):11-15.

— 1980 "Sexism in British Columbia Trade Unions, 1900-1920." In Barbara Latham and Cathy Kerr (eds.), *In Her Own Right: Selected Essays on Women's History in B.C.* Victoria: Camosun College.

Campbell, Persia Crawford. 1923.
Chinese Coolie Emigration to Countries within the British Empire. New York: Negro Universities Press, reprint 1969.

Canada. 1885.
Report of the Royal Commission on Chinese Immigration. Sessional Papers No. 54a. Ottawa: King's Printer.

Canada. 1902.
Report of the Royal Commission on Chinese and Japanese Immigration. Sessional Papers No. 54. Ottawa: King's Printer.

Canada
Department of Labour. Strikes and Lockouts Files. Ottawa: Public Archives of Canada.

Canada
Labour Gazette: The Journal of the Department of Labour.

Cappon, Paul. 1975.
"The Green Paper: Immigration as a Tool of Profit." *Canadian Ethnic Studies* 7, no. 1 (May):50-54.

Cassin, Marguerite A. and Alison I. Griffith. 1981.
"Class and Ethnicity: Producing the Difference that Counts." *Canadian Ethnic Studies* 13, no. 1:109-29.

Castles, Stephen and Godula Kosack. 1972.
"The Function of Labour Immigration in Western European Capitalism." *New Left Review* (May-June):3-21.

Chan, Anthony B. 1983.
Gold Mountain. Vancouver: New Star Books.

Cheng, Tien-Fang. 1931.
Oriental Immigration in Canada. Shanghai: Commercial Press.

Chinese Times. 1917-21.
Translations. Chinese Canadian Project. Special Collections, University of British Columbia, Vancouver.

Cho, George and Roger Leigh. 1972.
"Patterns of Residence of the Chinese in Vancouver." In Julian V. Minghi (ed.), *Peoples of the Living Land: Geography of Cultural Diversity in British Columbia.* Vancouver: Tantalus Research Ltd.

Cox, Oliver C. 1959.
Caste, Class and Race. New York: Monthly Review Press.

Creese, Gillian. 1986.
Working Class Politics, Racism and Sexism: The Making of a Politically Divided Working Class in Vancouver, 1900-1939. Ph.D. dissertation, Carleton University.

Edwards, Richard. 1979.
Contested Terrain: The Transformation of the Workplace in the Twentieth Century. New York: Basic Books.

Gordon, David M., Richard Edwards and Michael Reich. 1982.
Segmented Work, Divided Workers: The Historical Transformation of Labor in the United States. Cambridge, MA: Cambridge University Press.

Gorz, André. 1970.
"Immigrant Labour." *New Left Review* 61 (May-June):28-30.

Hughes, David and Evelyn Kallen. 1974.
   The Anatomy of Racism: Canadian Dimensions. Montreal: Harvest House.
Kallen, Evelyn. 1982.
   Ethnicity and Human Rights in Canada. Toronto: Gage.
Knight, Rolf and Maya Koizumi. 1976.
   A Man of Our Times: The Life-History of a Japanese-Canadian Fisherman. Vancouver: New Star.
Lai, Chuen-Yan David. 1972.
   "The Chinese Consolidated Benevolent Association in Victoria: Its Origins and Functions." *B.C. Studies* 15 (February):53-67.
Leggett, J. 1968.
   Class, Race and Labour: Working Class Consciousness in Detroit. New York: Oxford University Press.
Li, Peter S. 1979.
   "A Historical Approach to Ethnic Stratification: The Case of the Chinese in Canada." *The Canadian Review of Sociology and Anthropology* 16, no. 3 (August):320-332.
Li, Peter S. and B. Singh Bolaria. 1979.
   "Canadian Immigration Policy and Assimilation Theory." In John Allan Fry (ed.), *Economy, Class and Social Reality*. Toronto: Butterworth.
Lyman, Stanford M. 1968.
   "Contrasts in the community organization of Chinese and Japanese in North America." *Canadian Review of Sociology and Anthropology* 5, no. 2 (May):51-67.
McCormack, A. Ross. 1977.
   Reformers, Rebels and Revolutionaries: The Western Canadian Radical Movement 1899-1919. Toronto: University of Toronto Press.
McDonald, Robert A.J. 1981.
   "Victoria, Vancouver and the Economic Development of British Columbia, 1886-1914." In W. Peter Ward and Robert A. J. Mcdonald (eds.), *British Columbia: Historical Readings*. Vancouver: Douglas & McIntyre Ltd.
Modell, John. 1969.
   "Class or Ethnic Solidarity: The Japanese American Company Union." *Pacific Historical Review* 38 (May):193-206.
Morton, James. 1974.
   In the Sea of Sterile Mountains: The Chinese in British Columbia. Vancouver: J.J. Douglas.
Munro, John A. 1971.
   "British Columbia and the 'Chinese Evil': Canada's First Anti-Asiatic Immigration Law." *Journal of Canadian Studies* 6 (November):42-51.
Oppenheimer, Martin. 1974.
   "The Sub-proletariat: Dark Skins and Dirty Work." *Insurgent Sociologist* 4, no. 2 (Winter):7-20.
Pentland, H. Clare. 1979.
   "The Western Canadian Labour Movement, 1897-1919." *Canadian Journal of Political and Social Theory* 3, no. 2 (Spring-Summer):53-78.
   1981 *Labour and Capital in Canada 1750-1860*. Toronto: James Lorimer.
Phillips, Paul. 1967.
   No Power Greater: A Century of Labour in B.C. Vancouver: B.C. Federation of Labour and the Boag Foundation.
— 1973 "The National Policy and the Development of the Western Canadian Labour Movement." In A. W. Rasporich and H. C. Klassen (eds.), *Prairie Perspectives 2: Selected Papers of the Western Canadian Studies Conferences, 1970, 1971*. Toronto: Holt, Rinehart and Winston.
— 1981 "Identifying the Enemy: Racism: Regionalism, and Segmentation in the B.C. Labour Movement." Unpublished paper.

Porter, John. 1965.
The Vertical Mosaic. Toronto: University of Toronto Press.
—1979 *The Measure of Canadian Society: Education, Equality and Opportunity*. Toronto: Gage.
Reich, Michael. 1971.
"The Economics of Racism." In David Gordon (ed.), *Problems in Political Economy*. Lexington, Mass.: Heath.
—1981 *Racial Inequality: A Political-Economic Analysis*. Princeton: Princeton University Press.
Richmond, Anthony. 1970.
"Immigration and Pluralism in Canada." In W. E. Mann (ed.), *Social and Cultural Change in Canada*, Vol. 1. Toronto: Copp Clark.
—1978 "Immigration, Population, and the Canadian Future." In Daniel Glenday et al. (eds.), *Modernization and the Canadian State*. Toronto: Macmillan Co. of Canada Ltd.
Rosenthal, S. 1979.
"Union Maids: Organized Women Workers in Vancouver, 1900-1915." *B.C. Studies* 41 (Spring):36-55.
Roy, Patricia E. 1976.
"The Oriental 'Menace' in British Columbia." In J. Friesen and H. K. Ralston (eds.), *Historical Essays on British Columbia*. Toronto: McClelland & Stewart.
—1980 "British Columbia's Fear of Asians, 1900-1950." *Histoire Sociale/Social History* 13, no. 25 (May):161-72.
Schwantes, Carlos A. 1979.
Radical Heritage: Labour, Socialism and Reform in Washington and British Columbia, 1885-1917. Seattle: University of Washington Press.
Sien, Foon. 1971.
"The Chinese." In John Norris (ed.), *Strangers Entertained: A History of the Ethnic Groups of British Columbia*. Vancouver: Evergreen Press.
Szymanski, Albert. 1976.
"Racism and Sexism as Functional Substitutes in the Labour Market." *Sociological Quarterly* 17 (Winter):65-73.
Thompson, E. P. 1963.
The Making of the English Working Class. London: Harmondsworth.
Ward, W. Peter. 1978.
White Canada Forever: Popular Attitudes and Public Policy Towards Orientals in British Columbia. Montreal: McGill-Queen's University Press.
1980 "Class and Race in the Social Structure of British Columbia, 1870-1939." *B.C. Studies*, 45 (Spring):17-35.
Wright, E.O. 1979.
Class, Crisis and the State. London: Verso.

6

Relations of Production and Collective Action in the Salmon Fishery, 1900–1925

JAMES CONLEY

Between 1900 and 1925, the salmon fishing industry in British Columbia changed significantly. Salmon canning became more mechanized, more concentrated in ownership, and more diversified in the species of salmon packed. The technology of salmon fishing was transformed as motor boats, seines, and trolls supplanted sails, oars, and gill nets. The location of fishing and canning expanded from its original concentration on the Fraser River to new centres on the northern coast and on the west coast of Vancouver Island. And the fishing labour force changed as more fishermen owned their boats and gear and as Japanese fishermen grew into the largest racial group and then suffered drastic reductions through licence restriction.

Existing scholarly work on the salmon fishing industry from 1900 to 1925 has concentrated on its economic history, on technological development, on industrial relations, and on racial relations.[1] While it remains enormously indebted to previous studies, the present paper seeks to go beyond them by examining changes in the salmon fishing industry from the perspective of conflicts between salmon fishermen and canners, and among salmon fishermen themselves. The main lines of the argument to be pursued here are indicated in the excerpt reproduced below from the 17 July 1917 *Proceedings* of a Special Fisheries Commission chaired by Sanford Evans.[2]

> A: Andrew Johnson . . . We had a strike here, I suppose you have heard.
> Q: Sanford Evans . . . What was the strike about?

A: It was to get a raise of pay of course.

Q: In the price paid per fish?

A: Yes, in the price paid per fish. We were striking for 25 cents. We came here for 20 cents. They met us half way and offered us 22½ cents, which they settled the strike for on the Skeena River . . . we decided to take that compromise of 22½ cents.

Q: Why did you ask 25 cents?

A: Well, I believe that 25 cents is justifiable . . . I don't know if the canners can afford to pay it or not, but certainly it isn't too much money for the fishermen.

Q: That will largely depend, will it not, on how the prices of the cannery products are set?

A: Yes.

Q: We are not in a position to determine how that might be, but if, for example, the canners had to sell the bulk of their product in the British market, and they had as competitors, either the United States, Siberia and some Japanese fish and if our canners therefore could not determine the price, but it is determined by competition, the price they can afford to pay for fish will be influenced by that. Are you prepared to take all those things into consideration, or do you say that you simply like 25 cents and therefore strike for it?

A: You can understand that a workingman strikes for a living wage, and that is all. He is barred, through lack of opportunity of ever getting the market conditions on the finished product. All he has anything to do with in any relation whatever, is his two hands . . . the last sack of flour I bought was $4.15. The market price for salmon has raised very largely. All commodities have a pretty high price, and the commodity of labour has not reached a terribly high price yet. Of course it has quite an increase. We have from 15 cents last year to 22½ cents this year. Personally I have no objections to the way things have gone. We should do very well this year.

In his questioning of Andrew Johnson, a fisherman and photographer, Evans tried to show that the dependence of salmon canners on a competitive international market for their product limited the price they could afford to pay fishermen for their fish. This was just one of three critical conditions that constrained the operation and profitability of salmon canning companies in B.C., forcing canners to adopt the strategies examined in the first part of this paper.

Like Evans, Johnson was concerned with "the price paid per fish" when fishermen sold their catches to canners. But as the secretary of the

Rivers Inlet Fishermen's Union, Johnson considered that price in terms of "a living wage" relative to the price of other commodities. In other words, salmon fishermen had to make a living as simple commodity producers or as wage workers, a point of view examined in the second part of this paper. The different "cycles of social reproduction" of wage workers and fishermen provided the basis for the mobilization of different groups of fishermen around common interests when their reproductive cycles were undermined by the accumulation strategies of canners.

Evans and Johnson discussed the price of raw salmon in the context of a strike of salmon fishermen against canneries at Rivers Inlet and the Skeena River barely two weeks earlier. Evans's over-riding concern for canner profits and Johnson's concern for a living wage illustrates the source of conflict between canners and fishermen, which was manifested in numerous strikes and other forms of collective action by fishermen between 1900 and 1925. In the final section of this paper the pattern of that collective action is analysed.

SALMON CANNING:
THE CONTRADICTIONS OF CAPITAL ACCUMULATION

Most of the salmon caught in British Columbia after 1900 were canned. Because sockeye salmon was the most important species for canning, the salmon fishing industry in B.C. revolved around the six to eight weeks when they migrated from the Pacific Ocean to their principal spawning grounds in the Fraser River system in the south and in the Nass, Skeena, and Rivers Inlet systems in the north. As the sockeye were depleted and as new markets were developed, other species of Pacific salmon—the spring, pink (or humpback), coho, and chum (or dog) —became increasingly important to the canning industry.

Anticipating the case that salmon canners would make before his commission, Sanford Evans pointed out to Andrew Johnson that the actions of salmon canners towards fishermen were constrained by forces largely beyond their control. Two of those conditions were discussed by Evans and his fellow commissioners in their final report: competition with American canners, and substantial problems of overcapacity. To these should be added a third that Evans did not mention: the problem of securing a seasonal labour force. The obstacles to profitable operation that each of these conditions presented led salmon canners in B.C. to evolve a number of individual policies and collective strategies which directly impinged on salmon fishermen's social reproduction.

The first problem faced by B.C. canners was competition with American producers for export markets and for their raw material, salmon. The price of canned salmon on the world market was set primarily by American production costs and secondarily by supply and demand. Canadian canners were highly dependent on export markets: three-quarters of Canadian canned salmon was exported, principally to the United Kingdom. In contrast, American producers sold nearly three-quarters of their pack domestically. B.C. canners were at a further competitive disadvantage because their production costs were higher than those of American packers. The latter were free to use low-cost, capital-intensive methods of catching fish, such as traps and purse seines, but canners in B.C. were initially limited by fishery regulations to the more labour-intensive gill net method.[3] Even when traps and seines were allowed in the province, American canners still had the advantages of operating larger plants, processing larger packs, and selling to a large, protected domestic market. The position of canners in B.C. in competition for export markets compelled them to try to reduce production costs.

As well as competing with American canners for export markets, canners in the Fraser River district competed with them for salmon catches. Puget Sound canners were able to capture salmon before they reached Canadian waters, seriously depleting stocks in the Fraser River and reducing the catches of fishermen there. In addition, canners from Washington were able to pay higher prices than B.C. canners for fish caught by B.C. fishermen, and they would do so when Puget Sound catches were poor.[4] To counter this competition, canners in B.C. sought international agreements for conservation or tried to deprive American canners of Canadian fish either by catching them before they reached American waters or by preventing Canadian fishermen from exporting their catches.

A second major problem facing B.C. canners was overcapacity. Because of both the nature of the resource being processed and trends in capital accumulation in the industry, fixed capital lay idle or was used below capacity most of the year. Salmon canners processed a raw material whose supply was largely uncontrollable. Until 1913, when the big run was virtually wiped out by a rockslide at Hell's Gate, the supply of sockeye on the Fraser varied widely in a four-year cycle; many canneries did not even open in the poor years. There was not such a marked cycle in the north, but everywhere the season was short, and the run of salmon could vary from a very few to an overwhelming number in a few days. Simply in order to handle the large runs, canners had to invest heavily in buildings, canning equipment, scows, tenders, boats, and nets that lay idle for most of the year and were used well below capacity for much of the season.

A tendency to overcapacity was also inherent in capital accumulation in salmon canning. New canneries were continually being established, either as speculative, often underfinanced, investments, or as attempts by existing companies to strengthen their position against competitors. Canneries also became more mechanized early in the period to overcome production bottlenecks and to reduce the need for increasingly expensive, skilled Chinese labour. By 1916, overcapacity was so pronounced that all the cannery machinery on the Fraser, running to capacity, could have packed the forty-eight-day season's catch in twenty hours. To maintain profit levels, canners had to limit investments in fishing and canning.[5]

The need for a large seasonal labour force for fishing and canning operations was the third problem facing salmon canners in B.C. According to Gregory and Barnes, "the key factor in the salmon industry is control over supply."[6] In B.C. at this time, the supply of salmon available to a cannery depended mainly on the number and productivity of fishermen delivering fish to it. Consequently, as the number of canneries grew, and their capacity increased, the number of fishermen also rose. In the face of natural limits to salmon stocks in a given area, the introduction of more fishermen eventually led to overfishing, smaller catches per boat, and competition with other employers to recruit fishermen. Over the years canners expressed alarm at shortages of labour owing to the existence of better-paying jobs in railway construction, logging, sawmills, and even spring salmon trolling.[7] For each canner, the solution to the problem was to attach a dependable, productive fishing force to his cannery.

The policies of individual canners led to contradictions within the industry as a whole, which were felt in particular by old established cannery companies. In 1910, H. O. Bell-Irving stated their position:

> Every increase in the number of canneries has been regularly followed by an increase in the number of boats, and a proportionate decrease in the number of fish caught per boat, and a decrease in the pack per cannery. This has resulted greatly to the disadvantage of the older concerns who originally started the business . . . Their operating expenses have been increased, and their pack reduced by more than half. The capacity of their canneries is in many instances already far larger than is necessary; year by year they have gradually seen their business cut down by new concerns.[8]

But the increasing number of canneries and fishermen only worsened problems of high production costs, overcapacity, and labour supply; the strategic implication for canners was to find ways to limit the number of canneries and fishermen.

In order to compete with American packers for salmon catches and markets, and to deal with problems of overcapacity and seasonal labour force requirements, canners evolved a number of policies. Some measures could be taken by individual canners, but those most important for fishermen required that canners act in concert, often in order to demand government regulations that would protect their collective interests. These policies can be summarized in two main categories: monopoly strategies, and strategies that directly shaped the relations of production.

"Monopoly strategies" encompassed efforts by canners to act in concert to regulate the salmon industry in their own interests. Monopoly strategies were adopted primarily to counteract the overcapacity promoted by competition among canneries and to lower production costs by controlling the price paid to fishermen for salmon. The two principal monopoly strategies were the formation of cannery combines to set prices and the imposition of state regulations to limit the number of canneries and fishermen.

Cannery associations were formed in B.C. to set a uniform price for raw salmon, in order to prevent fishermen from profiting from competition among canners.[9] According to W. D. Burdis, secretary of all the B.C. canners' associations from 1901 to 1923, they were formed primarily to set "the price to be paid for fish and the price to be paid for Chinese labour." The price per fish was set by the association before the season began; canners in the association were expected not to go above that price. Price-fixing attempts were not entirely successful, however. One or two canneries failed to join the association every year, and the price often rose in unexpectedly poor years as everyone scrambled to get salmon supplies.[10]

The associations' monopoly on the purchase of salmon was also threatened in the south by competition from U.S. buyers and throughout the province by cold storage companies, fresh fish dealers, and other processors. Beginning in 1894, the challenge from American buyers was partly controlled by various prohibitions on the export of salmon for canning or other processing. In general, whenever U.S. competition for B.C. fishermen's salmon catches increased canners agitated for export prohibitions.[11] Competition from other buyers in Canada was countered as much as possible through informal agreements with fishermen to deliver their catches to particular canneries, backed up if necessary by the state, as in the system of attached licences in the north. Cannery com-

panies also diversified into other forms of processing, such as cold
storage, and competed with other buyers on their own ground. For
salmon fishermen, the consequence of this first monopoly strategy was
that they could rarely get higher prices by selling to the highest bidder,
although they did attempt to prevent canners from closing off that alternative. Consequently, their main avenue for collective action was in
strikes against the canners' association.

The existing canners also tried to prevent the entry of new canneries
into the industry and to limit the number of boats and fishermen. Most of
these efforts were directed at the state, seeking regulations to limit the
number of canneries in the name of conservation. The most successful of
these efforts was the boat rating system established in the north, which
limited the number of boats a cannery could fish and even distributed Indian, Japanese, and white fishermen proportionately to each cannery.
Boat ratings began as voluntary arrangements among canners in 1902,
1905, and 1908, but they kept breaking down as the construction of new
canneries led to renewed competition for fishermen. Following an appeal
from the older firms after the breakdown of the last voluntary agreement,
boat rating was made part of the fishery regulations for the north, accompanied by the "attach" system that licenced fishermen to fish for particular canneries. Overcapacity and labour supply problems were temporarily
arrested by the boat rating system, and fish prices were kept lower in the
north than on the Fraser. The system started to break down again in 1913
as new canneries were allowed on an *ad hoc* basis and as unattached licences were given to white settlers. However, it still served to give canners considerably more monopoly power over fishermen in the north than
in the south. The boat rating system even affected fishermen in the south
because it enabled canners to prevent technological change in the north,
thereby limiting the mobility of southern fishermen.[12]

The second category of strategies adopted by canners consisted of
measures to shape the technical and social relations of production in
salmon fishing. "Technical" relations refer to the means of production
and how they are used to catch salmon; "social" relations are the relations of economic ownership and control under which that work is performed.

Salmon canners in B.C. made two main collective efforts to shape
technical relations of production in salmon fishing: demanding to be allowed to adopt trap nets and purse seines, and preventing the use of
motor boats for gill netting in the north. Traps and seines were prohibited
by fishery regulations after 1894, but following the fishermen's strikes
on the Fraser in 1900 and 1901, canners increasingly pressured the federal government for permission to use them. They claimed that only with

traps and seines could they compete successfully with low-cost American producers and be immune from high price demands from fishermen. In 1904 the government gave in, over fishermen's protests, but traps and seines still did not become the dominant methods of production, mainly because of technical limitations and the large expense involved compared to gill netting.[13]

The other main area of technological change in salmon fishing between 1900 and 1925 was the introduction of motor boats for gill netting. Small gasoline motors were first used for gill netting on the Fraser River in 1906, and they appeared in the north in 1909 and 1910 under individual ownership. In the winter of 1910-11, the plans of at least two northern canneries to employ motor boats on a large scale became known. This was regarded as a threat by most canners because motor boats would only worsen the problems of overfishing and overcapacity that were inherent in capital accumulation in the canning industry. Fishermen with motor boats could go farther afield, make more drifts, and get an increased catch. If one cannery supplied its fishermen with motor boats, all would have to be provided with them if each cannery were to maintain its share of the catch. Yet, "[if] every boat was operated by power, so that all would be on an equality, we contend that the difference in the total catch as compared to the old methods would have but an inappreciable effect," according to H. Doyle. Unless the catch were increased, motor boats would only increase canners' costs of production and overcapacity. The established canners avoided this by persuading the federal government to prohibit motor boats for gill netting in northern waters from 1911 to 1923.[14] Their success was not solely the result of their political influence. Because of the social relations of production in the north, most fishermen there also opposed motor boats.

The configuration of the social relations of production in B.C. salmon fishing, formed under the influence of canners' problems of overcapacity, labour supply, and competition, was a combination of simple commodity production and wage labour. Ideally, simple commodity production would be the solution to canners' overcapacity in fishing equipment, since the fisherman would own the equipment, bear all the risks of fishing and sell his catch to the canner. Simple commodity production is rarely that simple, however, and fishermen who owned their means of production were often heavily and chronically in debt to canners for their boats and nets and for advances to buy food and supplies. The real advantage for canners was that, on the Fraser River at least, a growing corps of simple commodity producer fishermen provided a stable and productive seasonal fishing labour force. They fished year in and year out for the entire salmon season, so they were present when the runs were small, and as they were fishing for themselves, they were also intensive and productive fishermen.[15]

In the sparsely settled north, there was little opportunity for the kind of year-round small boat fishery that made simple commodity production possible in the south, so the fishing labour force required by canners was provided by fishermen working under the shares system. Shares fishermen also provided additional labour on the Fraser when runs were heavy. The cannery supplied the boat, net, and other gear and received in turn one-third of the proceeds of the catch: the rest was divided between the net man and the boat puller (if there was one). As a form of piece wage, the shares system encouraged intensive fishing efforts by fishermen in a situation where direct supervision by cannery management was practically impossible. Canners also kept a record of fishermen's catches and gave the best equipment to the most productive fishermen. This practice had the effect of giving preference to Japanese fishermen, who were generally the most productive, and left white and Indian fishermen with a chronic grievance that was a source of collective action.[16]

Each strategy used by canners affected the interests of fishermen, creating issues that could result in conflict. In order to see how canner strategies were transformed into fishermen's collective action, however, the social relations of production must be examined from the point of view of fishermen.

CYCLES OF REPRODUCTION IN SALMON FISHING

The social and technical relations of production in salmon fishing formed part of the workers' cycles of social reproduction, a concept derived from Marx's analysis of the circulation of capital. In that circulation, the capitalist exchanges money for means of production and labour power and combines them in the production process. The commodities produced there are then sold, realizing the value created in production, and the money received is used to resume the process on the same or an expanded scale. Similarly, in the cycle of reproduction of labour, the wage worker, who by definition does not own means of production, exchanges labour power for wages and enters the capitalist production process. Wages are used to buy articles of consumption, and their consumption renews the worker's labour power to be sold again, beginning the cycle anew. Finally, in the reproduction of simple commodity production, the producer, who by definition owns the means of production, produces commodities using his or her own labour. Proceeds from the sale of the commodities are used for consumption and to maintain or expand ownership of the means of production, allowing the cycle to begin again.

Each cycle of social reproduction is a series of social practices—in the labour and commodity markets, in production, and in consumption—through which a set of social relations is continually recreated and transformed. Each cycle is unified by the overall objective: for the capitalist, profit and capital accumulation; for the wage labourer, consumption at a certain culturally defined level; for the simple commodity producer, consumption and continued ownership of means of production. Understood in this way, the concept of cycles of social reproduction can be used first to distinguish between wage workers and simple commodity producers as different classes of fishermen, and second to locate differences within those classes.[17]

Class differences among salmon fishermen can be identified by situating the immediate relations of production in the fishery within the annual cycles of social reproduction of the fishermen. The reason behind this was aptly stated by a cannery manager named R. J. Ker. Complaining that fishermen wanted to live the whole year from the proceeds of a summer's sockeye salmon fishing, he pronounced: "The days of their big six weeks money has gone by, just [as] have the days of big cannery profits."[18] The objectives of simple commodity producers and wage workers could not be met simply by salmon fishing, and the men who fished in the summer supported themselves the rest of the year through subsistence production, wage labour, or simple commodity production. Wage worker and simple commodity producer fishermen can be distinguished by the different roles which salmon fishing played in their annual cycles of reproduction. The distinction is not always easily drawn, especially since workers were often moving from one cycle to another, but its broad contours can be discerned from the information available.

Differences within each class of salmon fishermen were also significant for their collective action. These differences can be located at the level of the concrete social practices at each phase of the wage labour and simple commodity cycles of reproduction. In particular, there were characteristic differences among white, Indian, and Japanese fishermen which can be interpreted in their socioeconomic context as differences in consumption, labour market, commodity market, and production practices.

WAGE LABOUR CYCLE OF REPRODUCTION

A wage labour cycle of social reproduction characterized fishermen who fished on shares for canneries during the sockeye run, then returned to wage work in other occupations. Large numbers of men flocked to the Fraser River during the peak of the sockeye run. In 1902, for example, six to eight hundred fishermen fished only during the three weeks between 26 July and 16 August when the run was heaviest.[19] Other fishermen on the Fraser and in the north fished for much or all of the salmon season, then were employed in other industries which needed labour in the winter. Japanese worker-fishermen in particular combined work in the forest industry with salmon fishing, returning from fishing in the north to work in sawmills and shingle bolt camps around Vancouver. For many Indians, salmon fishing was part of a cycle of seasonal migratory labour that included berry and hop-picking and logging in the winter. For white fishermen, the employment possibilities in the off-season were greater: temporary fishermen were mechanics, labourers, longshoremen, miners, loggers, butchers, barbers, and clerks.[20]

The economic rationale behind summertime fishing by wage workers was to make more money in a short time than they could in other occupations. "Just making wages" summed up disappointed expectations:

> This year I think the average fisherman, if he made wages that would be all.
> Q: What do you call wages?
> A: I am just speaking of the going wages in the country. Anything from $80 to $90 clear of expenses.[21]

Fishing was often not good enough to earn "wages" however, and fishermen regulated their participation in the salmon fishery according to the expected size of the run, the price offered by the canners, and the wages in other jobs. For example, dissatisfaction with the sliding scale of prices offered by canners on the Fraser River, and the existence of "sure and profitable" employment at shingle bolt camps, kept hundreds of Japanese workers away from salmon fishing in 1902. In other years employers of Japanese in the vicinity of Vancouver raised their wages in the summer in order to keep them on the job.[22] Similarly, Indian fishermen acted as if their labour power was a commodity to be sold at the best price: they generally travelled to the river where they expected to make the best money; if better paying jobs in railway construction or logging were available, the number of Indians fishing declined.[23] In some years there were shortages of fishermen because of better pay or steadier work elsewhere; in other years, especially in the early 1900's, there were labour shortages in other jobs because men had gone fishing.[24]

Whether they fished for the whole season or for the height of the sockeye run only, wage worker fishermen did so using cannery gear. Anyone who fished for only a few weeks simply could not afford to own a boat and net, and if he was only selling to canneries anyway, there was little advantage in owning equipment.[25] For some, fishing on shares for the salmon season and working for a wage the rest of the year were undoubtedly steps towards saving enough to buy a boat and net, that is, toward simple commodity production. It is impossible to say how many made this transition, although the rising levels of gear ownership on the Fraser River during this period indicate that the number may have been substantial. Despite this, it remains possible to speak of a class distinction between fishermen whose immediate relations of production and cycle of reproduction were working class on the one hand and simple commodity producer fishermen on the other.

SIMPLE COMMODITY CYCLE OF REPRODUCTION

Simple commodity producer salmon fishermen were those fishermen who owned and worked their own boats, nets and other gear. A simple commodity cycle of social reproduction is one where the producer's ownership of the means of production and his or her capacity to use them is maintained or expanded. In addition to salmon fishing, this kind of cycle could involve wage labour in fishing or other occupations; other forms of simple commodity production such as trapping, hand logging, or farming; and full-time fishing on a simple commodity production basis. The latter was the most important cycle of reproduction, and those who engaged in it, owning their means of production and fishing year-round, were known as "bona fide fishermen."[26]

The number of fishermen owning their boats, nets, and other gear increased outside the northern district throughout the period from 1900 to 1925.[27] Legal ownership of their means of production did not eliminate simple producer fishermen's dependence on canners, however: they were often in debt to canners for boats, nets, or advances; many lived in company-owned houses; many were tied by contracts to deliver salmon to a particular cannery; virtually all were subordinated to the monopoly of canners as buyers of both sockeye and other species of salmon. Under these conditions, were simple commodity producers really any different from wage worker fishermen who fished with cannery gear? Did their legal ownership of the means of production correspond to any effective economic ownership, that is, "the power to assign the means of production to given uses and so to dispose of the products obtained?"[28]

The main difference between simple commodity producer fishermen and those who did not own their boats and nets was that the former were not restricted to fishing for the canneries. During the period examined here, other markets opened up. By 1905, considerable numbers of fishermen on the Fraser were fishing for spring salmon, mostly for the fresh market, and in the fall as many as one thousand boats caught dog salmon to sell to salteries for export to Japan and cohoes to be frozen for export to Europe. In 1908, white and Japanese fishermen were fishing for herring, cod, and spring salmon in the off-season. After 1906, the mosquito fleet of gas-engined Columbia River boats became increasingly mobile, and the development of trolling after 1912 gave fishermen on the Fraser River a chance to escape the direct domination of canners. In 1918 and 1919, hundreds of Japanese fishermen left the Fraser in their motor boats to troll off the west coast of Vancouver Island, and their success led white and Indian fishermen to follow.[29]

Fishermen who owned their means of production were never entirely independent of canners, however; they still needed them as a market for sockeye. As cannery and other processing companies became more diversified, the independence the fishermen did possess decreased. Still, simple commodity producer fishermen's ownership of their means of production gave them more power than wage worker fishermen to decide how to use those means of reproduction and how to dispose of the product.

In the literature on the relationship of simple commodity producers to capitalism, it is often suggested that this dependence distorts or "truncates" simple commodity production.[30] That is, either simple commodity producers are unable or must go to extraordinary lengths to reproduce themselves economically. If this thesis is correct, then we should expect to find that simple commodity producer fishermen experienced persistent difficulties in maintaining economic ownership of their boats and gear.

Trollers were one category of salmon fishermen who had little difficulty in reproducing themselves as simple commodity producers during this period. Skilled trollers were reportedly able to start one year with a row-boat, or with an advance from a canner or fish buyer for a motor boat, and earn enough in a season to buy a motor boat the next year. The other gear needed for trolling—lines and lures—was comparatively cheap, and troll-caught fish fetched better prices because of their superior condition.[31]

Most fishermen remained gill netters however, and they faced more problems in reproducing themselves as simple commodity producers. For example, Japanese fishermen were reported to be living year round in tiny quarters, often in small cabins on their boats, in order to save for bigger boats. Only by foregoing the value of their labour power and living at a level of subsistence which most workers in B.C. would not accept, and by accepting the assistance provided by the Japanese community, could they pursue the expanded reproduction of their simple commodity production.[32]

There is little information bearing directly on the ability of simple commodity producers on the Fraser River to reproduce their ownership of their means of production, but there are many indications that chronic indebtedness was common. Speaking in opposition to the proposal to allow motor boats in the north in 1917, one Japanese fisherman referred to the experience of Japanese fishermen on the Fraser: "I stay at Steveston ten years ago and everybody make some money, but now, all the time they use motor boats and they can't make any money. . . . Cost money to fix up, get new nets, all the time in debt to canneries."[33]

The source of the problem did not lie solely in the use of the more expensive motor boats; the depletion of the river and the increasing cost of nets also played a role. Furthermore, the prohibition after 1911 on motor boats in the north and the system of attached licences there prevented Fraser River fishermen from taking advantage of the mobility provided by motor boats to fish in the productive northern waters. At hearings of the commissions investigating the motor boat and other issues in 1917 and 1922, it was repeatedly stated that simple commodity producer fishermen, as well as other fishermen who owned their boats and nets, wanted to use their gas boats to fish for sockeye in the north. For example, A. G. Harvey, representing "100 odd" fishermen from Vancouver, Nanaimo, and Malcolm Island who fished at Rivers Inlet and the Nass River, stated:

> Most of us have small boats. During the best part of our fishing we have to lay these boats up. . . . At Sointula these people have $62,000 invested in Gas Boats and Engines and during the best part of the season the investment has to lie idle.[34]

To reproduce themselves as simple commodity producers, fishermen had to use their equipment in a variety of fisheries and areas, and were prevented by the prohibition on motor boats in the north.

Canners in the north generally supported the motor boat prohibition, as did the majority of fishermen there, who felt that they could not afford to buy boats for themselves and feared that if canners undertook the expense they would pay fishermen less for their fish. Most of the fishermen who opposed motor boats in the north were wage workers in both their immediate relations of production and in their cycles of reproduction.[35] The support of canners and wage-worker fishermen in the north for a measure that restricted a simple commodity cycle of reproduction strongly suggests that capitalist relations of production with a temporary, migrant labour force constituted the principal obstacle to that cycle. It also suggests that the interests of simple commodity producer and working-class fishermen were opposed.

In effect, the temporary labour force of working class fishermen was a reserve army of labour for canneries.[36] They were generally available to fill the fluctuating needs of canners for fishermen, depending on the expected size of the run of salmon, and they were a cheap source of labour. The last point is not immediately apparent, since all fishermen were paid the same price, minus the share taken by canners when they employed men on shares, but some speculation on how the price of raw salmon was determined supports that conclusion. On the one hand, the upper limit of prices was set by what canners could afford to pay and still operate at a profit. Although they always claimed to be paying that limit, their virtual monopoly and strong organization in the north makes their claim unlikely. On the other hand, the lower limit on fish prices was determined by the canneries' need to attract a productive and reliable working-class labour force. To attract workers, they had to pay enough so that if the run was successful there was the prospect of earning more by fishing than in alternative occupations. It is unlikely that the latter amount would need to be sufficiently high to pay the costs of production and reproduction of simple commodity producer fishermen. In short, the existence of a reserve army of working class fishermen lowered the price paid to simple commodity producer fishermen.

Full-time, simple commodity producer fishermen were aware of the relationship between the temporary working-class fishermen and the price they received for fish. For example, in 1902 the Grand Lodge of the B.C. Fishermen's Union based its price demands in part on how many "woodsmen-fishermen" were expected to leave the logging camps to fish. In 1905, G. W. West, a Fraser River fisherman, denounced working-class fishermen: "Us practical fishermen is killed by the drygoods clerks and counter-jumpers that goes fishing. They just does it for a holiday." When a man has his own gear, he continued, "then he can go to the cannery and ask for a reasonable price. . . . There are plenty of us without them and we're men that can get a living if we get a fair chance."[37] Simple commodity producer fishermen were consequently in a difficult position, since in addition to the threat to their reproduction posed by working-class fishermen, they were also threatened by competition from traps and seines and weakened by competition among themselves for catches. These conditions shaped fishermen's collective action.

SALMON FISHERMEN'S COLLECTIVE ACTION, 1900-1925

> Re strike, or cessation of work by Fraser River salmon gill net fisher-
> men recently, it cannot be described in the stereotyped lexicon of or-
> dinary labour disputes. These men are not employees, they own their
> own boats and gear and are known as independent operators,
> mostly.[38]

Collective action is defined by Tilly as people "acting together in pursuit of common interests." Consideration of salmon fishermen's collective action in this paper is limited to that which is contentious: that is, to
that in which claims or demands are made which, if realized, would affect the interests of some other parties. Contentious collective action thus
denotes events such as strikes, demonstrations, and petitions.[39]

The analysis of relations of production in salmon fishing in the first
two sections of this paper helps us to understand how the common interests of different groups of salmon fishermen were formed in opposition
to those of canners or other fishermen, and how they were able (or unable) to act collectively upon them. Fishermen's collective action was in
large part a response to canner strategies which interfered with their reproduction cycles; in turn those cycles shaped fishermen's definition of
their interests, and their capacity to mobilize for collective action.

On the one hand, competition with low-cost producers in an international market, idle fixed capital, and labour supply problems have been
shown to lie behind canners' monopolization and relations of production
strategies. On the other hand, the analysis of reproduction cycles of
salmon fishermen has shown a division of interests between simple commodity producer and working-class fishermen. The pattern of collective
action that resulted was a combination of demands directly opposed to
cannery strategies and attempts by fishermen themselves to monopolize
fishing opportunities. A brief overview of major instances of contentious
action between 1900 and 1925, concentrating on action by Fraser River
fishermen, will demonstrate this pattern.

From 1900 to 1903, collective action by fishermen on the Fraser River
was dominated by the annual strikes of sockeye gill netters over the price
of salmon. This issue followed directly from canners' monopoly strategy
of keeping down costs of production by depressing the price paid to
fishermen. The price issue also followed from the tendency of capital accumulation in canning, which led to increasing numbers of salmon
fishermen as canneries added more boats. As a result, the catches of individual boats declined and fishermen needed higher prices to realize "a
living wage." Fishermen on the Fraser River felt pressure from both

these sources in the early 1900's. The number of fishermen on the river had risen rapidly from the mid-1890's, as had the number of canneries, and the 1900 strike followed closely upon the formation of the Fraser River Canners' Association.[40] Both the 1900 and 1902 strikes were against association attempts to keep prices down by adjusting them to the size of the sockeye run. In 1900, when fishermen demanded a flat minimum price for the season, canners offered a maximum price, which would be lowered when the run became heavy. They were more interested in regulating price competition among themselves than in bargaining with the fishermen. The fishermen struck, and succeeded in winning a minimum price, although not the one originally demanded. In 1902, canners tried to keep production costs in line with prospective prices of the canned product by proposing a sliding scale in which the final price paid fishermen would be inversely related to the size of the total pack. Dissatisfied fishermen struck again.

In comparison with subsequent strikes, the first four strikes on the Fraser River were large: about 7,000 strikers in 1900, 8,000 in 1901, over 1,000 in 1902, and 5,000 to 6,000 in 1903. With the exception of 1902, virtually all the fishermen on the river were involved each year, mobilized through their organizations, the British Columbia Fishermen's Union (B.C.F.U.) and the Japanese Fishermen's Benevolent Society. Racial divisions weakened the fishermen in each strike, however. In 1900, 1901, and 1903, Japanese fishermen capitulated to the canners before the others; in 1902, the B.C.F.U. gave in to the canners in order to avoid "the disastrous results of our former strikes." In every case, militia or police intervention on behalf of canners prevented the strikers from using the system of union patrol boats started in the 1900 strike to stop others from returning to work.[41]

The New Westminster fishermen who formed the sole remaining local of the B.C.F.U. after 1903 considered the 1900 and 1901 strikes "disastrous." The feeling must have been general, for there were no more strikes of sockeye salmon fishermen until 1913 (although there were small strikes of spring salmon fishermen in 1902 and 1907). The 1913 strike, over a ten cent price reduction in August, was led by Japanese fishermen, who by this time were the largest and best organized racial group on the river. In a new development, the 5,000 or so Japanese, Indian, and white fishermen were joined on strike by 1,200 Indian and Japanese women working in the canneries. The strike was limited to the lower river, and fishermen from New Westminster and vicinity continued to fish at the reduced price. After two days most of the Japanese fishermen started fishing when several canners outside the canners' association began to pay the price demanded, and the strike collapsed. Once again the Japanese were blamed for deserting the others.[42] Another lull in strike activity followed, until several hundred spring salmon fishermen struck against a price reduction in May 1925. The same September, a strike of about 1,000 pink and chum fishermen against the canneries was settled when Japanese salteries agreed to take all chums at a price the fishermen found satisfactory, and the canneries were shut out altogether.[43]

Strikes were instances of collective action by salmon fishermen in response to the efforts of canners to control production costs by limiting the price paid for gill-netted salmon. Another canner strategy for lowering production costs was the adoption of other methods of fishing, such as traps and purse seines. Canners hoped and fishermen feared that traps would be very successful in catching sockeye, and they were a major issue between 1900 and 1904. The B.C.F.U. urgently petitioned the federal government not to allow traps, because they "will totally destroy the means we fishermen have of earning a living." After the canners won permission for traps in 1904, fishermen pressed for their strict regulation. They later urged the abolition of purse seines when these became a threat to catches.[44]

At the same time as they proposed limitations on the use of gear such as traps and seines, fishermen opposed proposals emanating from canners that would limit gill-netting operations. Fishermen from New Westminster and upriver in particular opposed proposals for closure of the Fraser above the New Westminster bridge, for limits on the depth of gill nets, for annual close seasons at the end of August, and for complete closure of the river as a conservation measure in 1906, 1908, and 1910. They also fought an embargo on the export of raw salmon through which Fraser River canners tried to prevent American competition for B.C. fish. In general, gill netters sought to defend what they considered their right to catch salmon and do with them as they pleased, against canners' attempts to restrict that right.[45]

Some groups of fishermen also asserted a right to fish to the exclusion of other groups of fishermen. Simple commodity producer fishermen sometimes tried to exclude working-class fishermen, whose role as a reserve of labour for canners reduced catches and prices. For example, in 1902, 1905, and 1917, New Westminster fishermen asked to have licences limited to Indians and bona fide fishermen owning their own gear, in order to protect them against the competition of those who fished for only a few weeks a year.[46] Most of the time, however, conflict was on racial lines, as white and Indian fishermen sought to exclude Japanese fishermen from B.C.

Complaints against Japanese fishermen were voiced by white and Indian fishermen at every commission relating to the province's salmon industry. They were accused of unfair and illegal fishing practices, of fraudulently obtaining fishing licences, and of being favoured by the canners. Their early capitulation in strikes was an additional source of friction. Although the issue had come up in a small way before, collective action to restrict Japanese participation in the salmon fishery did not begin in earnest until 1914; the agitation was started not by fishermen, but by New Westminster businessmen.[47] M. Monk, a fish dealer and canner, first raised the alarm at the Fisheries Committee of the Board of Trade. He described plans by a lower-river cannery to locate Japanese fishermen on scows above the New Westminster bridge in order to secure the privilege of "between bridge" licences, which were intended to provide settlers with a source of cash income. The Board of Trade, whose members found white and Indian, but not Japanese, fishermen a good source of business, sponsored mass meetings against the "invasion." At the second of these, the representative of the New Westminster Trades and Labour Council persuaded the fishermen in attendance to form a permanent organization to press for the elimination of Japanese fishermen from the river. The resulting organization, the Fraser River Fishermen's Protective Association, had as its objective "the preservation of the fishing rights of the Fraser River for the benefit of the white and Indian fishermen, and the elimination of Asiatics from the River and the Gulf of Georgia." Immediate demands were that no licences be granted to Japanese fishermen above the New Westminster bridge, that the number of licences on the Fraser be limited, and that white and Indian fishermen be issued licences first. The activities of and support for the association were centred among the simple commodity producer fishermen in New Westminster and the farmer-fishermen upriver; and it also received support from city and town councils in the Fraser Valley, the New Westminster Trades and Labour Council, the Retail Merchants Association, and other bodies.[48]

Agitation for the elimination of Japanese from the salmon fishery largely died out during the First World War, as hostilities were directed elsewhere and as white and Indian fishermen joined the armed forces. By 1918, however, a new element entered the situation, when thousands of demobilized soldiers arrived in Vancouver at the same time as the economy started to slide into post-war depression. Veterans pressed for special fishing privileges, which they were given in 1919, with 30 per cent of gill net licences in the north reserved for them. They continued to press for special consideration, and with white fishermen also lobbying for the elimination of Japanese fishermen, the federal government began to restrict the number of licences available to others than whites or Indians.[49] By 1922, the issue had been decided. In the words of the commissioners who toured the province that year,

> The question we have to consider . . . is not whether Oriental licences should be reduced in number, but what percentage of reduction should be decided upon in order to bring about the displacement of Orientals by white fishermen in the shortest possible time without disrupting the industry.

The commission proceeded to recommend a 40 per cent reduction in licences. Further reductions were made in the years following, over the protests of canners and Japanese fishermen, until stopped by Supreme Court and Privy Council judgments in 1928 and 1929. The 1922 commission also recommended that the prohibition on motor boats in the north be ended, so white simple commodity producers won a dual victory: their most effective competitors were reduced in number, and the restriction on mobility which had hindered their reproduction was eliminated.[50]

H. K. Ralston has suggested that strike militancy among Fraser River fishermen declined after the big strikes of the early 1900's because new channels for political action were opened, through which fishermen could express their grievances.[51] The evidence of fishermen's collective action on the Fraser between 1900 and 1925 supports that view. It also shows that the fishermen best able to make use of political channels were the simple commodity producer fishermen living in New Westminster and the fishermen-farmers living on the shores of the Fraser River. The strikes of 1900 to 1903 were regarded by them as failures; faced with legislative changes that would threaten their livelihoods, they reacted in the only way open to them, by petitioning and lobbying the federal government. They could hardly strike against legislative changes, especially those such as the elimination of the prohibition on traps, which were designed to make strikes ineffective by providing an alternative supply of fish for canneries. To strike for political purposes would not have won the support of the wage worker fishermen who fished just for the season, since their main objective was to make big money in a short time. Furthermore, the time for action was not just the salmon season but year round, since the rhythms of political activity were not those of the salmon fishery.

The timing of political activity relative to the salmon season also helps explain why the full-time fishermen of New Westminster and vicinity dominated the collective action of salmon fishermen on the Fraser after 1903. These fishermen had a solidarity, provided by settled residence and common occupation, which wage worker fishermen scattered around the province could not maintain. For that reason, simple commodity producer fishermen constituted a sufficiently important local political force for their collective action to be facilitated and legitimated by organizations and people such as the Board of Trade, city council, the local member of parliament and others. While the white wage worker fishermen of Vancouver and the lower Fraser River could count on the support of the Vancouver Trades and Labour Council in the early years of the B.C.F.U., they did not have the same political resources as the New Westminster fishermen and lacked the opportunity to respond collectively to canner strategies.[52]

Although they did not have the same barriers to mobilization as white working-class fishermen, Indian and Japanese fishermen also faced obstacles to collective action. Because of their strong band organization, Indian fishermen did not lack solidarity, but because they were subordinated to a paternalistic relationship with the federal government, they lacked the political resources to achieve much through collective action.[53] Yet paternalism, and the solidarity they displayed with white fishermen during strikes, did make for an alliance between white and Indian fishermen against canners and the Japanese.

Like Indian fishermen, the Japanese had solidarity within their community, but they laboured under several disadvantages in turning that solidarity into collective action. Early in the 1900's, Japanese fishermen were heavily dependent on fishing for their livelihood. If they missed much of the sockeye run they faced the prospect of a winter of destitution: thus their speedy capitulation to canners in strikes. As they became less dependent on salmon fishing, they became more militant, but even then they were dependent on the house bosses who acted as intermediaries between them and the canners and who were not expected to welcome a strike. Still, strikes were the main form of collective action engaged in by Japanese fishermen, because the alternative of political action was largely closed off: they had no vote, and racist ideologies ensured that they would get little political support for their interests from outside their own community. Indeed, when they did turn to political action to defend themselves against licence restriction, their appeals went unheeded.[54]

The pattern of collective action and mobilization by Fraser River salmon fishermen between 1900 and 1925 exhibits two general types. Until 1914, when white fishermen started to organize and campaign actively for the elimination of Japanese from the salmon fishery, their collective action was primarily reactive. That is, the collective actions of fishermen were mostly occasioned by direct challenges to their interests on the part of canners, following strategies of monopolization and of the transformation of relations of production. Tilly defines reactive collective action as "group efforts to reassert established claims when someone else challenges or violates them." Fishermen were mobilized to act collectively when canners tried to change fishery regulations: when these became known or when commissions arrived in B.C. to investigate, mass meetings were held, resolutions passed, petitions organized, letters sent to Ottawa, and representatives dispatched to hearings. Fishermen did not generally take the offensive and "assert group claims which [had] not previously been exercised"; they certainly did not try to change the structure of ownership and control in the industry. Instead, to continue with Tilly's classification of claims made in collective action, they were preoccupied with competitive actions which "lay claim to resources also claimed by other groups which the actor defines as rivals, competitors, or at least as participants in the same context."[55] Japanese and working-class fishermen were both seen as competitors of white simple commodity producer fishermen on the Fraser. It was in the interests of simple commodity producers to have the number of fishermen limited, since the tendency of capital accumulation in salmon canning led to increased numbers of fishermen and thus lower catches for each boat. It is not surprising to find that competitive collective actions by white or Indian simple commodity producer fishermen turned from working-class fishermen to Japanese fishermen. Firstly, they were the most effective competitors in the salmon and other fisheries. Secondly, there was little ideological support for excluding working-class fishermen, but the definition of Japanese fishermen as the problem could mobilize support from broad sectors of B.C. society. Therefore attempts to exclude working-class fishermen failed but efforts to exclude Japanese fishermen finally succeeded.

This analysis of collective action by fishermen on the Fraser River has revealed the general pattern of interests and the social base for mobilization. In the north, the pattern was similar. Most collective action was reactive, in response to canner initiatives, until anti-Japanese action grew after the First World War. The north became the centre of strike activity after 1903, with at least eight strikes, reflecting the increasing importance of fishing in the north and the decline of strike militancy on the Fraser. The strikes were usually small, based on a single racial group: Indians or Japanese on the Skeena and Nass, whites at Rivers Inlet.[56]

The pattern of ethnic and racial mobilization was followed in other forms of collective action. The difficulties experienced by Andrew Johnson in union organization at Rivers Inlet indicate the reasons:

last year we had a meeting and tried to organize amongst ourselves, some of the fishermen. It fell through for various reasons. You can understand that with only six weeks job here, and so many different nationalities, perfect strangers coming on there every year, it is almost impossible to form an organization of any kind; but this year we succeeded very well, and practically all the white fishermen have now united into the organization.[57]

With a short season and "perfect strangers coming on there every year" the only social basis for organization lay in the pre-existing solidarities of fishermen, which were usually racial or ethnic. Indian and Japanese fishermen acted under the same constraints as in the south, and the main social base for mobilization among the whites lay in fishermen resident in the district, like the Finns of Malcolm Island, who also had a strong ethnic and ideological basis for solidarity. This was similar to the Fraser where, among white fishermen, the most coherent social basis for collective action was the full-time simple commodity producer fishermen of New Westminster and vicinity.

CONCLUSION

The development of salmon fishing in B.C. between 1900 and 1925 has been understood in terms of the accumulation of cannery capital and the cycles of social reproduction of fishermen. Analysis of the relations of production from the point of view of canners showed how capital accumulation followed a contradictory path that kept the fishing industry in a chronic state of near-crisis. Competition with low-cost American producers, overcapacity, and labour force recruitment were problems that generated canner strategies to monopolize the fishing industry and to transform the relations of production in fishing. Analysis of the cycles of social reproduction of salmon fishermen showed that they were disrupted by the strategies of canners, and that working-class and simple commodity producer fishermen had different interests. These two analyses were combined to interpret the pattern of collective action by fishermen. On the one hand, most fishermen's collective action was a response to threats to their livelihood from canner strategies; that which was not directed against the canners was directed against other fishermen in an effort to escape the effects of canner stategies. On the other hand, the reproduction cycles of different groups of fishermen were the bases for their different responses to those strategies: in part they responded differently because their interests were different; in part because their solidarity and political resources differed. Those considerations were used to explain the central role played in fishermen's collective action by white simple commodity producers and to understand why their action eventually took the direction of seeking the exclusion of Japanese fishermen.

Some important questions about the development of salmon fishing and salmon fishermen's collective action in B.C. between 1900 and 1925 remain to be answered, however. For example, more research into the exact relationship between fishermen and canners is needed. What were the obligations of shares fishermen to canners? How much debt was there between simple commodity producers and canners, and what did this relationship mean for the reproduction cycles of the fishermen? This topic could be investigated through the correspondence, diaries, and records of cannery companies. The same sources would also provide more information about the strategies canners adopted to deal with the industry's accumulation problems.

There also needs to be more research into the concrete reproduction cycles of the different racial groups in salmon fishing. What was the relationship between Japanese house bosses and the fishermen under them, and how did that affect their reproduction cycles and their mobilization for collective action? How was the participation of Indians in salmon fishing organized, and what were the relationships among Indian fishermen, Indian leaders, Indian agents, and canners? What was the relationship between wage labour, simple commodity production, and subsistence production for Indian fishermen?

This paper has only scratched the surface of fishermen's collective action, especially in the north. More information on who engaged in collective action and what their demands were could be obtained from the voluminous correspondence of the federal fisheries department, the records of cannery companies, and contemporary newspapers.

NOTES

This is a revised version of a paper originally presented at the 1982 meetings of the Canadian Sociology and Anthropology Association in Ottawa. For comments on earlier drafts, I would like to thank Gertrud Neuwirth and John Myles. The research was supported by a Social Sciences and Humanities Research Council Doctoral Fellowship.

1. W. A. Carrothers, *The British Columbia Fisheries* (Toronto: University of Toronto Press, 1941); David J. Reid, "Company Mergers in the Fraser River Salmon Canning Industry, 1885-1902," *Canadian Historical Review* 56 (1975):282-302; L.

Anders Sandberg, "A Study of Canadian Political Economy: A Critical Review and the Case of the British Columbia Salmon Canning Industry, 1870-1914" (M.A. thesis, University of Victoria, 1979); Duncan A. Stacey, "Technological Change in the Fraser River Salmon Canning Industry, 1871-1912" (M.A. thesis, University of British Columbia, 1977); Duncan A. Stacey, *Sockeye and Tinplate: Technological Change in the Fraser River Canning Industry, 1871-1912* (Victoria: British Columbia Provincial Museum, Heritage Record No. 15, 1982); Percy Gladstone and Stuart Jamieson, "Unionism in the Fishing Industry of British Columbia," *Canadian Journal of Economics and Political Science* 16 (1950):146-71; Percy Gladstone, "Industrial Disputes in the Commercial Fisheries of British Columbia" (M.A. thesis, University of British Columbia, 1959); H. Keith Ralston, "The 1900 Strike of Fraser River Sockeye Salmon Fishermen" (M.A. thesis, University of British Columbia, 1965); Ken Adachi, *The Enemy that Never Was* (Toronto: McClelland and Stewart, 1976); W. Peter Ward, *White Canada Forever: Popular Attitudes and Public Policy Toward Orientals in British Columbia* (Montreal: McGill-Queen's University Press, 1978).

2. Canada, Commission to Enquire into and Report on Certain Matters in Connection with Fishing and Canning Industries in District No. 2, British Columbia, *Transcript of Proceedings* (Ottawa, 1917). Located in Fisheries and Oceans Library, Ottawa. Hereafter referred to as Canada, *Proceedings*, 1917.

3. For descriptions of the principal fishing methods, see J. N. Cobb, *Pacific Salmon Fisheries*, 4th ed. Appendix 13 to the Report of the Commissioner of Fisheries for 1930, Bureau of Fisheries Document 1092 (Washington: United States Government Printing Office, 1930); Stacey, "Technological Change," and *Sockeye and Tinplate*, and Duncan A. Stacey, "The Block and the Drum: The Revolution in Seining," *The Fisherman*, 12 December 1980, pp. 17-21; Rolf Knight and Maya Koizumi, *A Man of Our Times: The Life History of a Japanese Canadian Fisherman* (Vancouver: New Star Books, 1976), pp. 22-24. Comparisons of Canadian and American costs are found in H. G. Doyle to A. G. Kittson, 1 February 1902, quoted in Leslie J. Ross, *Richmond, Child of the Fraser* (Richmond: Richmond '79 Centennial Society, 1979), p. 120; Canada *Procceedings*, 1917, pp. 1339, 1346; Canada, Special Fishery Commission, *Report* 1917 (Ottawa: King's Printer, 1918), pp. 15-18 (hereafter referred to as Canada, *Report*, 1917); Public Archives of Canada (PAC), Fisheries Records, RG 23, Vol. 1223, file 726-34-4 [3], Gosse-Millerd to E. Lapointe, 8 January 1923.

4. Vancouver *Province*, 3 February 1911, p. 1; Canada, Fisheries Branch, *Annual Report*, 1915-16, p. 244; Canada, *Report*, 1917, p. 37; Canada, Parliament, House of Commons Select Standing Committee on Marine and Fisheries, *Official Report of Evidence taken by the Marine and Fisheries Committee of the House of Commons, Canada, respecting Fisheries of British Columbia* (Ottawa: King's Printer, 1922), pp. 62-63.

5. Homer E. Gregory and Kathleen Barnes, *North Pacific Fisheries with Special Reference to Alaska Salmon* (San Francisco: American Council Institute of Pacific Relations, 1939); Stacey, *Sockeye and Tinplate*; Canada, *Report*, 1917, pp. 11-15; Canada, *Proceedings*, 1917, exhibit 52.

6. Gregory and Barnes, *North Pacific Fisheries*, p. 116.

7. See for example *Province*, 14 July 1910, p. 8; 18 July 1910, p. 8; 21 June 1917, p. 2; *Canadian Fisherman*, June 1918, p. 803; Vancouver *Sun*, 6 June 1918, p. 2.

8. Canada, Dominion-British Columbia Boat-Rating Commission, *Report and Recommendations, with Appendix* (PAC, RG 23, Volume 80, file 6, part 6, 1910), p. 27. (Hereafter referred to as Canada, *Report*, 1910.) See also similar comments by other canners in Canada, British Columbia Fisheries Commission, *Evidence Submitted to a Dominion Fishery Commission Known as the British Columbia Fisheries Commission 1905-6 Including Proceedings of an International Fisheries Conference Held at Seattle, Washington* (Victoria: Times Printing and Publishing,

1905-6), p. 278. (Hereafter referred to as Canada, *Evidence*, 1905-6.) See also Canada, *Proceedings*, 1917, pp. 203-4, 1584-85.

9. The amalgamation of cannery companies, such as the formation of B.C. Packers, had similar objectives, plus reducing the number of plants in operation. See Ross, *Richmond, Child of the Fraser*, p. 120; Reid, "Company Mergers in the Fraser River Salmon Canning Industry," Gregory and Barnes, *North Pacific Fisheries*, pps. 98, 120-24.

10. Canada, *Proceedings*, 1917, pp. 110, 113.

11. Ibid., pp. 11-13; *Province*, 24 January 1917, p. 7; 7 May 1919, p. 15; *Pacific Fisherman*, June 1919, p. 44; *Canadian Fisherman*, March 1920, pp. 57-58.

12. Canada, *Proceedings*, 1917, p. 833. The history of boat ratings in the north can be reconstructed from Canada, *Report*, 1910; PAC, RG 23, Volume 80, file 6, part 5A; Canada, *Proceedings*, 1917, pp. 2-9; Canada, *Report*, 1917, pp. 30-31.

13. PAC, RG 23, Vol. 131, file 222, part 2, W. D. Burdis to Hon. R. Prefontaine, 13 July 1903 (plus other correspondence from canners in the same file); *Province*, 13 April 1905, p. 15; Sandberg, *A Study of Canadian Political Economy*; Canada; Fisheries Branch, *Annual Report*, 1905, p. 33 and *Annual Report* 1906, p. 216; Stacey, "The Block and the Drum," and Stacey, *Sockeye and Tinplate*.

14. Stacey, *Sockeye and Tinplate*; *Province*, 7 December 1910; PAC, RG 23, Vol. 80, file 6, part 6, D.M. Moore to A. Johnson, 27 January 1911, W. D. Burdis to L. P. Brodeur, 7 February 1911, H. Doyle to L. P. Brodeur, 25 February 1911; Canada, *Proceedings*, 1917, pp. 167, 1128-29; Canada, Commission to Investigate Fisheries Conditions in British Columbia, 1922, *B.C. Fisheries Commission Report and Recommendations* (Ottawa: King's Printer, 1923), pp. 8-9. Hereafter referred to as Canada, *Report*, 1922.

15. See Jacques Chevalier, "There Is Nothing Simple About Simple Commodity Production," *Studies in Political Economy* 7 (1982):89-124, on the complexity of simple commodity production. A variety of sources show increasing ownership of gear by fishermen: Canada, British Columbia Salmon Commission, *Record of Proceedings* (PAC, RG 23, Vol. 336, file 2918, part 3; hereafter referred to as Canada, *Proceedings*, 1902), session 12, J. A. Russell, "Relative Interests of Fishermen on the Fraser River as of Sept. 20, 1901"; Provincial Archives of British Columbia (PABC), Attorney-General Papers, GR 429, Box 11, file 3, W. D. Burdis to C. Campbell, 25 July 1904; *Province*, 3 February 1911, p. 2, 25 August 1916, p. 4; *Canadian Fisherman*, June 1914, pp. 185-86, February 1918, p. 612, August 1920, p. 183; Canada, British Columbia Fisheries Commission, *Evidence (Taken in British Columbia)* (PAC, RG 23, Vol. 1233, file, 726-34-4 [1], Vol. 1234, file 726-34-4 [2] (hereafter referred to as Canada, *Evidence*, 1922): New Westminster, 7 September, W. E. Maiden.

16. Henry Doyle, "Excerpts from the Diaries of Henry Doyle: An Early Canner's Account of Salmon Strikes and Profit," *The Fisherman*, 11 December 1981, p. 28; George A. Rounsefell and George B. Kelez, *The Salmon and Salmon Fisheries of Swiftsure Bank, Puget Sound and the Fraser River*. Department of Commerce, Bureau of Fisheries Bulletin No. 27 (Washington: Government Printing Office, 1938), p. 707; *Province*, 6 December 1905, p. 2; Canada, *Proceedings*, 1917, pp. 1108-9.

17. The concept of cycle of social reproduction owes its origins to work on the life cycle of households in simple commodity production agriculture by Harriet Friedmann, "Simple Commodity Production and Wage Labour in the American Plains," *Journal of Peasant Studies* 6 (1978):71-100 and to an unpublished paper by M. Lebowitz, "The One-Sidedness of *Capital*," but neither author is to blame for the uses to which their ideas have been turned.

18. Canada, *Proceedings*, 1902, session 12.

19. British Columbia, Report of the Fisheries Commissioner, 1902, *British Columbia, Sessional Papers*, 1903, p. G10. Some were part of the "large number" of fisher-

men who came from the north when the runs ended there, but a substantial proportion must have been local workers getting a respite from wage labour. See *Province*, 4 August 1902, p. 1.

20.   Knight and Koizumi, *A Man of Our Times*, pp. 24-51; Daphne Marlatt (ed.),
Steveston Recollected: A Japanese Canadian History (Victoria: PABC, 1975), p.
24; Charles H. Young and Helen R. Y. Reid, *The Japanese Canadians* (Toronto:
University of Toronto Press, 1939), pp. 46-47; Canada, *Proceedings*, 1902, Session 16, McKuni; Canada, *Proceedings*, 1917, pp. 498, 502, 639-40, 761-62, 982,
992. Regarding Indians, see *Province*, 2 September 1903, p. 9; Canada, *Proceedings*, 1917, p. 1030; Rolf Knight, *Indians at Work: An Informal History of Native
Indian Labour in British Columbia, 1858-1930* (Vancouver: New Star, 1978). Regarding whites, see *British Columbia Federationist*, 7 November 1913, p. 4; PAC,
RG 23, Vol. 81, file 6, part 7, "Deputation of Canners Received by the Honou-
rable the Attorney-General, Parliament Buildings, Victoria," 29 October 1912.

21.   Knight and Koizumi, *A Man of our Times*, p. 26; Canada, *Proceedings*, 1917, p.
992; Canada, *Evidence*, 1922: Port Essington, 19 August, C. J. Fox; Prince
Rupert, 14 August, R. Hanna; *Labour Gazette* 5 (September 1904), p. 254; *Province*, 19 August 1909, p. 1.

22.   *Labour Gazette* 3, p. 64; *Province*, 3 and 10 July 1902; 14 July 1910, p. 8.

23.   *Province*, 4 June 1903, p. 1; 20 June 1906; Canada, *Evidence*, 1905-6, pp. 275-80,
388-90, 423-25; Canada, *Report*, 1910, p. 408; *Canadian Fisherman*, August
1917, p. 334; Knight, *Indians at Work*.

24.   *Province*, 20 September 1909, p. 1; 18 July 1910, p. 8; 17 July 1901, p. 7; 22 July
1903, p. 9; 8 August 1905, p. 1; Canada, *Proceedings*, 1917, pp. 639-40; *Canadian Fisherman*, August 1917, p. 334; *Labour Gazette* 4 (August 1903), p. 127.

25.   Canada, *Proceedings*, 1917, pp. 300-2; Canada, *Evidence*, 1922: Port Essington,
19 August, T.H. Davidson.

26.   For definitions and examples of "bona fide fishermen," see Canada, *Proceedings*,
1902, session 3, Demes; session 4, P. Wylie; session 5, Gonzales; session 8, G.
Mackie; Canada, *Evidence*, 1905-6, pp. 151, 308-10; Canada, *Proceedings*, 1917,
pp. 270-72, 1402-6.

27.   See note 14 above.

28.   Nicos Poulantzas, *Classes in Contemporary Capitalism* (London: New Left Books,
1975), p. 18.

29.   *Labour Gazette* 5 (March 1905), p. 970; *Province*, 13 November 1905, pp. 4, 12;
22 September 1908, p. 7; 7 November 1908, p. 5; Vancouver *Sun*, 12 June 1918,
p. 2; *Pacific Fisherman*, August 1919, p. 24; PAC, RG 23, Vol. 1233, file 726-34-
4 [3], "Memorandum Presented to the Fisheries Commission of the Dominion
Government of Canada by the Steveston Fishermen's Benevolent Society, Vancouver, B.C., September 1922."

30.   See for example R. James Sacouman, "Semi-Proletarianization and Rural Underdevelopment in the Maritimes," *Canadian Review of Sociology and Anthropology* 17 (1980):232-45.

31.   Canada *Proceedings*, 1917, p. 751, Canada, Fisheries Branch, *Annual Report*,
1916-17, p. 231.

32.   *Province*, 21 March 1908, p. 4; *Sun*, 25 March 1912, p. 15.

33.   Canada, *Proceedings*, 1917, p. 377, see also pp. 310-11, 501.

34.   Canada, *Evidence*, 1922: Vancouver, 9 September, A. G. Harvey; Canada, Parliament, House of Commons Select Standing Committee on Marine and Fisheries, *Official Report of Evidence* taken by the Marine and Fisheries Committee of the
House of Commons, Canada, respecting Fisheries of British Columbia (Ottawa:
King's Printer, 1922), p. 30; Canada, *Proceedings*, 1917, pp. 9, 510, 516, 838-39.

35.   Canada, *Evidence*, 1922: Port Essington, 19 August, T. H. Davidson; Canada, *Report*, 1922, p. 9; PAC, RG 23, Vol. 1233, file 726-34-4 [3], "Evidence of No. 2
District Fishermen's Association."

36. See Karl Marx, *Capital: A Critical Analysis of Capitalist Production*. Vol. 1 (Moscow: Progress Publishers, n.d.), Chapter 25, sections 3-4, on the concept of a reserve army of labour.
37. *Province*, 5 July 1902, p. 1; Canada, *Evidence*, 1905-6, p. 149. For similar comments see Canada, *Proceedings*, 1902, session 11, W. Cassidy; Canada, *Proceedings*, 1917, pp. 1542-43; Canada, *Evidence*, 1922: Rivers Inlet, 23 August, G.S. McTavish.
38. PAC, Department of Labour, RG 27, Vol. 335, file 25 (80), W.E. Maiden to Deputy Minister of Labour, 14 October 1925.
39. Charles Tilly, *From Mobilization to Revolution* (Reading, PA: Addison-Wesley, 1978), p. 7; Louise A. Tilly and Charles Tilly (eds.), *Class Conflict and Collective Action* (Beverly Hills: Sage Publications, 1981), p. 49.
40. Rounsefell and Kelez, *The Salmon and Salmon Fisheries*, p. 706; Canada, Fisheries Branch, *Annual Report*, 1925-26, p. 68; Ralston, "The 1900 Strike," pp. 95-96.
41. For the 1900 strike, see Ralston, "The 1900 Strike." For the 1901 strike, see *Province*, 2, 5, 8, 9, 10, 15, and 19 July 1901, p. 1. For the 1902 strike, see *Province*, 14, 16, 18, 19, 21, 22, and 24 July 1902, p. 1; Vancouver *Independent*, 12 and 19 July 1902. For the 1903 strike, see *Province*, 6, 13, and 14 July 1903, p. 1; New Westminster *Weekly Columbian*, 21 July 1903, p. 9; *Labour Gazette* 4 (August 1903), p. 126.
42. *Province*, 3 July 1913, p. 15; 4 August 1913, pp. 1, 4; 5 August 1913, p. 20, 6 August 1913, p. 15; Vancouver *News-Advertiser*, 5 August 1913, p. 1; *Sun*, 5 August 1913, p. 2.
43. PAC, RG 27, Vol. 334, file 25 (41) and Vol. 335, file 25 (80); PAC, RG 23, Vol. 891, file 721-3-18 (2), J. A. Motherwell to W. A. Found, 18 May 1925.
44. PAC, RG 23, Vol. 131, file 222, part 1, C. Durham to Hon. L. P. Brodeur, 1 October 1900; see also *Independent*, 3 May 1902; *News-Advertiser* 14 February 1903, p. 6, 17 February 1903, p. 6; Canada, *Proceedings*, 1902, session 4, Anderson, session 7, Cross, session 8, G. Mackie, R. Mackie; Canada, *Evidence*, 1905-6, pp. 68-76; Canada, *Proceedings*, 1917, p. 1512; *Province*, 16 February 1910, p. 2; 15 April 1918, p. 13.
45. PAC, RG 23, Vol. 79, file 6, part 2, C. B. Sword to E. E. Prince, 28 February 1900; ibid., "Abstract of Minutes of Meeting of Fraser River Fishermen," in C. B. Sword to Department of Marine and Fisheries, 7 February 1904; PAC, RG 23, Vol. 364, file 3214, "Recommendations of the B.C. Fishermen's Union Committee," 17 April 1909; *Province*, 9 January 1905, p. 1; 22 August 1908, p. 1; 16 February 1910.
46. Canada, *Proceedings*, 1902, session 8, G. Mackie; *Province*, 4 November 1905, p. 4, 6 November 1905, p. 2, 22 November 1905, p. 13; Canada, *Proceedings*, 1917, pp. 1537, 1543.
47. *Province*, 14 September 1910, p. 2; 4 May 1912, p. 13; 16 October 1913, p. 7; New Westminster *British Columbian*, 20 September 1910, p. 20.
48. *British Columbia Federationist*, 3 April 1914, p. 7; 17 April 1914, p. 5; 24 April 1914, p. 2; 1 May 1914, p. 2; 8 May 1914, p. 2; 22 May 1914, p. 2; *British Columbian*, 7 April 1914, p. 11; 28 April 1914, p. 1; 30 June 1914, p. 10; 7 July 1914, p. 1; 14 July 1914, p. 18; *Province*, 20 April 1914, p. 18; 6 June 1914, p. 6; *News-Advertiser*, 16 June 1914, p. 7; PAC, RG 23, Vol. 81, file 6, part 8, "Minutes of Meeting of Fraser River Fishermen's Protective Association and B.C. Canners' Association in Vancouver, June 24, 1914."
49. *Province*, 20 April 1918, p. 3, 28 August 1918, p. 17, 17 June 1919, p. 32; *Pacific Fisherman*, June 1919, p. 44; PAC, RG 23, Vol. 931, file 721-4-67 (21); *Canadian Fisherman*, January 1920, p. 18.
50. Canada, *Report*, 1922, pp. 8-13; Ward, *White Canada Forever*, pp. 122-23; Adachi, *The Enemy that Never Was*, pp. 105-6.

51. Ralston, "The 1900 Strike," pp. 174-75.
52. For examples, see *News-Advertiser*, 14 February 1903, p. 6, 17 February 1903, p. 6; PAC RG 23, Vol. 131, file 222, part 2, "L. B. Lusby to Minister of Marine and Fisheries, 24 April 1903, W. A. Duncan to Hon. J. Sutherland, 30 April 1903, R. MacPherson to Hon. R. Prefontaine, 28 March 1904; PAC, RG 23, Vol. 365, file 3214, part 2, C. Wade to Minister of Fisheries, 19 February 1910.
53. See, for example, the hostile reaction of the 1922 commissioners to Indian claims based on aboriginal rights, Canada, *Evidence*, 1922: Prince Rupert, 15 August, C. Perry; Nanaimo, 29 August, A. Paul.
54. See, for example, PAC, RG 23, Vol. 1233, file 7264-34-4 [3], "Memorandum...by Steveston Fishermen's Benevolent Society, Vancouver, B.C., September, 1922."
55. Tilly, *From Mobilization to Revolution*, pp. 145-47.
56. *Province*, 13 June 1904, p. 1; 2 July 1904, p. 1; 31 May 1907, p. 15; 3 July 1922; Vancouver *World*, 4 July 1922; *Sun*, 15 July 1922; PAC, RG 23, Vol. 891, file 721-3-18 [2]; PAC, RG 27, Vol. 329, file 22 (62), Vol. 333, file 24 (41).
57. Canada, *Proceedings*, 1917, pp. 304-5.

REFERENCES

Adachi, Ken. 1976.
   The Enemy that Never Was. Toronto: McClelland and Stewart.
Canada, Royal Commission on Chinese and Japanese Immigration. 1902.
   Report. Sessional Paper No. 54, 1902.
Canada, British Columbia Salmon Commission. 1902.
   Record of Proceedings. PAC RG 23 Vol. 336, file 2918, part III.
Canada, British Columbia Fisheries Commission. 1905-6.
   Evidence Submitted to a Dominion Fishery Commission known as The British Columbia Fisheries Commission 1905-6 including Proceedings of an International Fisheries Conference held at Seattle, Washington. Victoria: Times Printing and Publishing (in PAC RG 23, Vol. 335, file 2918, part I).
Canada, Dominion British Columbia Fisheries Commission. 1905-7. 1908.
   Report and Recommendations with Addenda and Appendices. Ottawa: Government Printing Bureau.
Canada, Dominion-British Columbia Boat-Rating Commission. 1910.
   Report and Recommendations, with Appendix. PAC RG 23, Vol. 80, file 6, part 6.
Canada, Commission to Enquire into and Report on Certain Matters in Connection with Fishing and Canning Industries in District No. 2, British Columbia. 1917.
   Transcript of Proceedings (in Fisheries and Oceans Library, Ottawa).
Canada, Special Fishery Commission, 1917. 1918.
   Report. Ottawa: King's Printer.
Canada, British Columbia Fisheries Commission. 1922.
   Evidence (Taken in British Columbia). PAC RG 23 Vol. 1233 file 726-34-4 (1), Vol. 1234 file 726-34-4 (II).
Canada, Commission to Investigate Fisheries Conditions in British Columbia, 1922. 1923.
   B.C. Fisheries Commission Report and Recommendations. Ottawa: King's Printer.
Canada, Parliament, House of Commons Select Standing Committee on Marine and Fisheries. 1922.
   Official Report of Evidence taken by the Marine and Fisheries Committee of the

House of Commons, Canada, respecting Fisheries of British Columbia. Ottawa: King's Printer.
Chevalier, Jacques. 1982.
"There Is Nothing Simple About Simple Commodity Production." *Studies in Political Economy* 7: 89 -124.
Carrothers, W. A. 1941.
The British Columbia Fisheries. Toronto: University of Toronto Press.
Cobb, J. N. 1930.
Pacific Salmon Fisheries, Fourth Edition. Appendix XIII to the Report of the Commissioner of Fisheries for 1930. Bureau of Fisheries Document 1092. Washington: United States Government Printing Office.
Doyle, Henry. 1981.
"Excerpts from the Diaries of Henry Doyle: An Early Canner's Account of Salmon Strikes and Profit." *The Fisherman* (Vancouver), 11 Dec., 1981.
Friedmann, Harriet. 1978.
"Simple Commodity Production and Wage Labour in the American Plains." *Journal of Peasant Studies* 6: 71 -100.
Gladstone, Percy. 1959.
Industrial Disputes in the Commercial Fisheries of British Columbia. M.A. thesis, University of British Columbia.
Gladstone, Percy, and Stuart Jamieson. 1950.
"Unionism in the Fishing Industry of British Columbia." *Canadian Journal of Economics and Political Science* 16: 146-71.
Gregory, Homer E. and Kathleen Barnes. 1939.
North Pacific Fisheries with Special Reference to Alaska Salmon. San Francisco: American Council Institute of Pacific Relations.
Knight, Rolf. 1978.
Indians at work: An Informal History of Native Indian Labour in British Columbia 1858-1930. Vancouver: New Star Books.
Knight, Rolf, and Maya Koizumi. 1976.
A Man of Our Times: The Life History of a Japanese Canadian Fisherman. Vancouver: New Star Books.
Marlatt, Daphne, ed. 1975.
Steveston Recollected: A Japanese Canadian History. Victoria: Provincial Archives of British Columbia.
Marx, Karl. n.d.
Capital: A Critical Analysis of Capitalist Production, Vol. 1. Moscow: Progress Publishers.
Poulantzas, Nicos. 1975.
Classes in Contemporary Capitalism. London: New Left Books.
Ralston, H. Keith. 1965.
The 1900 Strike of Fraser River Sockeye Salmon Fishermen. M.A. thesis, University of British Columbia.
Reid, David J. 1975.
"Company Mergers in the Fraser River Salmon Canning Industry, 1885-1902." *Canadian Historical Review* 56: 282-302.
Ross, Leslie J. 1979.
Richmond, Child of the Fraser. Richmond: Richmond '79 Centennial Society.
Rounsefell, George A. and George B. Kelez. 1938.
The Salmon and Salmon Fisheries of Swiftsure Bank, Puget Sound and the Fraser River. Washington: Government Printing Office (Dept. of Commerce, Bureau of Fisheries Bulletin No. 27).
Sacouman, R. James. 1980.
"Semi-Proletarianization and Rural Underdevelopment in the Maritimes." *Canadian Review of Sociology and Anthropology* 17: 232-45.

Sandberg, L. Anders. 1979.
A Study of Canadian Political Economy: A Critical Review and the Case of the British Columbia Salmon Canning Industry, 1870-1914. M.A. thesis, University of Victoria.
Stacey, Duncan A. 1977.
Technological Change in the Fraser River Salmon Canning Industry, 1871-1912. M.A. thesis, University of British Columbia.
—1980. "The Block and the Drum: the Revolution in Seining." *The Fisherman*, Dec. 12, 1980: 17-21.
—1982. *Sockeye and Tinplate: Technological Change in the Fraser River Canning Industry 1871 -1912*. Victoria: British Columbia Provincial Museum, Heritage Record No. 15.
Tilly, Charles. 1978.
From Mobilization to Revolution. Reading: Addison-Wesley.
Tilly, Louise A. and Charles Tilly, eds. 1981.
Class Conflict and Collective Action. Beverly Hills: Sage Publications.
Ward, W. Peter. 1978.
White Canada Forever: Popular Attitudes and Public Policy Toward Orientals in British Columbia. Montreal: McGill-Queen's University Press.
Young, Charles H. and Helen R. Y. Reid. 1939.
The Japanese Canadians. Toronto: University of Toronto Press.

7

Workers, Class, and Industrial Conflict in New Westminster, 1900–1930

ALLEN SEAGER

INTRODUCTION

It was a tense morning outside the gates of New Westminster's Broder Canning Company on 7 July 1926. Three hundred workers, who considered themselves "fortunate to earn $1 a day" under prevailing piece-rates, were out on strike for higher pay. But no union was involved, and the seemingly spontaneous job action by the all female "cannery girls" might better be described as a work place protest than as a formal strike or lockout under the terms of reference of the federal department of labour whose files record the incident.[1] One-third of the strikers were Japanese; the majority were drawn from the English-speaking, francophone, and Italian communities; the committee women who negotiated on their behalf included Ethel Mead, Grace Saul, M. Murray, Violet Murray, Priscilla Stewart, Mrs. Green, V. Croteau, Therese Therien, S. Pare, and B. Marcellini. The rebellion proved short-lived, ending with summary dismissal of the ringleaders and a return-to-work by the rank and file; the "Japs" were among the last holdouts in the one-day strike. The next evening, however, the "cannery girls" won a gesture of sympathy from New Westminster city council; it appeared that Mayor Annandale had been successful in securing the reinstatement of the fired workers from a publicly chastized Mr. Broder.[2] Though not a large event in B.C. labour history, one may rest assured that the tale would be told and retold over three hundred supper tables in the Royal City that summer.

Traditional generalizations about working-class experience and class formation in British Columbia history are recognized as increasingly inadequate. Oblivious to the strong trend towards urbanization in the Far West during the twentieth century, political economists have painted a quite misleading portrait of the region's working class as a "resource proletariat."[3] Studies focusing on "western radicalism" leave little room for microanalysis, while the silences and stereotypes on such crucial issues as race and gender have been noted.[4] One is loathe, however, to criticize the literature for its institutional bias—so little is actually known about the emergence and development of working-class institutions in British Columbia.[5]

What follows is a study of workers, class, and industrial conflict in a small but diverse urban setting prior to the Great Depression. As a means to establishing an empirical basis for new, more complex syntheses of class formation in British Columbia, we examine the local socioeconomic context of New Westminster from 1900 to 1930, and the trade union movement, contours of labour unrest, and patterns of labour voting in the community. New Westminster is broadly representative of major themes in the urban working-class experience in British Columbia: the early establishment of a working-class presence, class conflict, and the rise of political differentiation and identification (perhaps the most important "test" of class).[6] These processes, however, were structured and limited by specific economic, social, and cultural factors.

NEW WESTMINSTER: AN INDUSTRIAL COMMUNITY

New Westminster is one of the oldest white settlements in western Canada. Its "official" history naturally revolves around the romance of nineteenth-century colonization and the "Royal City's" apex of regional commercial and political power between the 1860's and the 1890's.[7] However, this version of its local history ignores the far more significant evolution of the then fading mainland metropolis into a small-scale but viable industrial community between the 1890's and the 1920's. In 1910-11, one out of every ten New Westminster residents (men, women, and children) was employed in manufacturing—1,238 workers engaged in twenty-four different enterprises having an average capitalization of $160,000.[8] Capital goods produced in industrial New Westminster included marine equipment and vessels, logging machinery, and railway rolling stock: "the first [and among the last] cars to be manufactured in British Columbia."[9] Undoubtedly more important from the perspective of employment was a range of economic activity related to the processing of goods drawn from the agricultural and resource-extractive hinterland:

the manufacture of boxes and cans, beer and vinegar, fish and food products, and especially lumber and shingles. Industrial New Westminster was built on a foundation of sawdust.[10]

During the late nineteenth and early twentieth century, New Westminster's business class was instrumental in laying out the infrastructure of industry and commerce: publicly owned electric power, federally sponsored port facilities, and a series of vital railway and river connections.[11] Between 1901 and 1911, the great expectations of the industrial community's "magnetic" attractions were met in full; the city's population increased by over 100 per cent, from 6,500 to 13,000. However, demographic growth in the decade 1911-21 was barely perceptible, and the 1920's saw only modest expansion. Like the rest of western Canada, New Westminster would largely be left behind by the "New Economic Era" of the 1920's. In the 1930's, it gradually fell into the orbit — as a very junior satellite — of the region's most dynamic urban centre, the city of Vancouver.[12]

Industrial prosperity in the years 1900-1930 was uneven. The impact of the recessions of 1907-8, 1913-15 and 1920-24 — each crisis deeper than the one before — was marked and long-term.[13] A healthy shift of New Westminster's economic locus from forest products to engineering occurred between 1916 and 1919, as a result of wartime contracts let to a local shipyard, B.C. Construction and Engineering, by the Imperial Munitions Board (I.M.B.). The I.M.B.'s "war socialism" proved temporary, however, and fears for the future were well-grounded.[14] The economic stabilization of the latter 1920's was similarly based on two external factors: the modernization of the port of New Westminster, thanks to Ottawa's patronage, and a dramatic upsurge in foreign demand for B.C.'s sawn lumber.[15] But New Westminster was ill-prepared for the collapse of international commodity markets and the Canadian economic system between 1929 and 1934 and would suffer accordingly.

The one survey of New Westminster's social structure which covers the period under review is the returns from the 1931 census of occupations (Appendix 7). These data are problematic in light of the extraordinary percentage of "labourers" enumerated in the census: one-fifth of the total workforce of 5,518 males and 1,319 females, both employed and unemployed. Such labourers were undoubtedly unskilled workers employed in local industries (except for a small number of agricultural labourers). But they were not classed by economic sector, only by socioeconomic status. There are also excellent reasons to believe that the census category of "labourer" in British Columbia was in part a racial category into which low-status Asian immigrants were habitually structured, literally as well as figuratively.[16]

What is clear from the census is that New Westminster did not share the social or occupational homogeneity usually associated with industrial communities—mine towns or mill towns—in British Columbia. Moreover, New Westminster, like Vancouver or Victoria, had a substantial middle-class population. Over four hundred census categories in 1931 included scores of occupational groups, like shopkeepers, self-employed professionals, managers, and even foremen, that must be excluded from any strict definition of "the working class." Such groups made up one-fifth of the local labour force in 1931 and have not been included in Appendix 7.

The remaining three-fifths of the workforce (who were neither labourers nor members of non-working-class occupational groups) can be fitted into twenty-five recognizable categories of employment, proceeding from the often arbitrary distinctions of the census-takers. Only a handful of these categories accounted for more than 2 per cent of the entire work force. Various branches of the transportation industry accounted for about 10 per cent and of manufacturing about 13 per cent; the latter group would have been much larger were it not for the huge number of labourers. In this *bloc* of wage and salary earners were many white-collar workers, semi-professionals, and others who would not have identified themselves with the working classes in 1931. Teachers, nurses, clerical, and sales personnel made up 18 per cent of the total work force, including the majority of the city's working women.

Thus, about two-thirds of the labour force in New Westminster were blue-collar workers—a significant fact in an era when trade unionism was almost synonymous with blue-collar unionism, or when working-class parties made overtly proletarian appeals. The success or failure of such movements must be measured in terms of their actual constituency not abstract statistical entities such as "the non-agricultural work force" or "the electorate."[17]

Moreover, a substantial part of New Westminster's working class was comprised of Asian immigrant workers normally excluded from the trade union movement and certainly cast outside the pale of the officially sanctioned body politic.[18] Members of three racial minorities—Chinese, Japanese, and East Indians—made up an important segment of the population: from 7 to 14 per cent between 1901 and 1931. The economic life of these communities centred around forest-related industries, including the giant Fraser Mills, located just east of the city.[19] The overall contribution of so-called "Orientals" to B.C.'s forest industries is an unwritten chapter in provincial history, but one which leaps off the pages of contemporary documents. As late as 1923, after Oriental exclusion had become effective public policy, 39 per cent of all sawmill workers and 54 per cent of all shingle mill workers in B.C. were Asian immigrants.[20] The local correspondent to the *Labour Gazette* reported in 1915 that: "with the exception of the Fraser Mills, which employs about half the staff white men [*sic*] Orientals are in the majority."[21] A 1931 payroll from Fraser Mills indicates that one-quarter of its work force were Chinese, Japanese, and East Indian.[22] Cries of "Chinamen, manning the wheels of industry while white workers, many of them born in this country, are jobless and almost penniless," were heard from New Westminster on the morrow of the 1929 stock market crash. But at least one local shingle mill operator had been displacing "Chinamen" with even cheaper female white and Japanese labour in 1929. Chaotic labour markets in the non-union lumber industry were accurately described as a human "scrap heap" of exploitation.[23]

In this context, it is easy to conclude that racial cleavage was as important as class conflict; yet this conclusion would be profoundly misleading. In the first instance, the very fact of institutionalized racism meant that most workers—white or Oriental—were never actually engaged in ethnically based competition in the labour market. The economic activities of non-white workers were, at least by 1900, carefully circumscribed, even in the lumber trade. For example, as an official inquiry into the shingle industry disapprovingly noted: "white men and boys . . . now refuse to do 'Chinese work'. The Chinese, however, have become expert packers and at present this branch of industry is practically controlled by them."[24] In a rigidly segmented labour market, it remained to be seen what avenues existed, for example, in the shingle industry, for the emergence of *blocs* of white and non-white labour, each with their own set of grievances and demands against the mill owners. As we shall see, the more common experience in industrial New Westminster was not racial conflict but working-class struggle, often buttressed by the solidarity of non-white immigrant workers.

TRADE UNIONS IN NEW WESTMINSTER

Which labour institutions flourished, and which foundered, in New Westminster? The local trade union movement had a respectable pedigree by western Canadian standards even in 1900. During the last quarter of the nineteenth century, city workers figured prominently in such pioneering organizations of B.C. labour as the Workingmen's Protective Association, the Knights of Labor, the British Columbia Federated Labour Congress, the B.C. Shipwrights and Caulkers' Association, and the Fraser River Benevolent Association. The latter organizations were still active on the local labour scene in 1901, by which time international craft unionism dominated B.C. labour.[25]

In New Westminster, as elsewhere in B.C., international unions tended towards a more pragmatic and flexible approach to jurisdictional matters than was laid down in the official credo of the American Federation of Labor (A.F.L). Vancouver-based Local 213 of the International Brotherhood of Electrical Workers (I.B.E.W.) organized across craft lines in the telephone industry at the turn of the century, and its New Westminster members included female telephone operators.[26] The most successful of A.F.L.-affiliated unions in the city, also organized at the turn of the century, was New Westminster Division 134 of the Amalgamated Association of Street and Electric Railway Workers, representing all employees of the B.C. Electric Railway Company. Much less successful was the United Brotherhood of Railway Employees (American Labor Union), a general transport union that failed to gain a foothold in the Lower Mainland during its dramatic strike in 1903.[27]

The first international union to establish a branch in New Westminster was actually the British-based Amalgamated Society of Carpenters and Joiners, created in 1890. Although the New Westminster local continued to function throughout the period under review (finally as an affiliate of the All-Canadian Congress of Labour in the 1920's), the union is most notable for its pioneering attempt to organize across craft lines in the woodworking industry. During the 1890's, these building tradesmen undertook the creation in the mills of a sub-local called the Factory and Sawmill Machine Hands' Union; it held the membership of workers at Royal City Mill in 1894-95.[28]

In 1903, enthusiastic public meetings were held in New Westminster in support of a second attempt to organize in the saw and shingle mills, this time by an A.F.L.-chartered Woodworkers' Union.[29] Connections between this fledgling organization and the Socialist party were evident: the socialist lawyer J. Edward Bird acted as its spokesman at the 1903 Royal Commission on Industrial Disputes in British Columbia. Bird was a well-known advocate of civil rights for Asian-immigrant workers, but in 1903, his major concerns lay elsewhere.[30] As the strikers faced certain defeat by the united employers, he commented:

> It would appear that a combination of employers has been made [in the woodworking industry] for the purpose of meeting and resisting every demand of labour . . . It is difficult to see what the future will be if [such combinations] are made for the purpose of coercing employees, irrespective of questions of right or wrong.[31]

This uncertain future was seemingly forecast in a series of violent strikes in the Puget Sound saw and shingle mills after 1907.[32] Out of the movement in the American Northwest would emerge two new factors in the woodworking industry: the A.F.L.-chartered industrial union, the International Union of Shingle Weavers, Sawmill Workers and Woodsmen, and revolutionary industrial unionism embodied in the Industrial Workers of the World (I.W.W.). Both the Shingle Weavers and the I.W.W. were to affect, directly and indirectly, New Westminster's labour scene. New Westminster Local 28 of the Shingle Weavers was formed in 1912, representing a core group of American immigrants in local mills. In 1917, Local 28 spearheaded a strike and campaign for the eight-hour day in the Lower Mainland which, though as unsuccessful as all previous attempts to establish collective bargaining in the province, underlined once more the potential for militant unionism in the work force. At one meeting held in New Westminster, members of the Chinese Labour Benevolent Association attended *en masse,* and the leaders of the two organizations made a public pact of mutual assistance.[33] Although the Shingle Weavers' Union disbanded after the 1917 campaign, the cause of the "American agitators" was taken up again in 1919 by a most unlikely group. In March 1919, a strike of 1,200 shingle mill workers took place in New Westminster and other B.C. centres in response to wage rollbacks by members of the B.C. Shingle Agency. The strike was organized by "Oriental labourers" (the Chinese) whose leaders, based in the ethnic community, not the B.C. Federation of Labour, negotiated an acceptable compromise.[34]

By mid-1919, the various strands of labour protest in the lumber and woodworking industries in British Columbia—including agitation by skilled workers in the mills, I.W.W.-inspired strikes in the logging camps, and the communal solidarity of Asian-immigrant workers—had begun to merge. Under the leadership of indigenous radicals, the newly-formed Lumber Workers Industrial Union (L.W.I.U.) set out to forge the one big union in wood. Provincial secretary Ernest Winch reported in June 1919: "our membership totals a few over 8,000 including . . . Japanese, Chinese and Hindoo [sic]."[35] In 1920, there was talk of a renewed drive for the eight-hour day,[36] and the opening of an L.W.I.U. hall in New Westminster.[37] The "first" Lumber Workers Industrial Union, however, melted away in the face of the post-war recession, to re-emerge under communist leadership at the end of the 1920's.

Looking at the contours of the general trade union movement in New Westminster, however, we find that the ephemeral organizations of lumber workers played only a minor role in buttressing the numerical strength of the unions between 1900 and 1930. Twenty-one local unions had a combined membership of 1,015 in 1913, at the height of the pre-war boom. Union membership declined to just over 400 in 1915, as a measure of the vulnerability of all craft and other unions to economic conditions at this time.[38] But the militant wartime labour movement enrolled as many as 1,000 new members. New Westminster's Trades and Labour Council boasted 1,380 members among its affiliates in 1918. These numbers are impressive by any standard, but even more interesting are the data on trade union membership in New Westminster during the 1920's—the supposed nadir of organized labour strength and class conflict in British Columbia and Canada.[39]

The open shop drive of the early 1920's had its effect in restructuring and diminishing the considerable power of local trade unions. Among its casualties were unions of letter carriers, musicians, meat packers, and telephone workers. At least half of New Westminster's local unions simply disappeared between 1918 and 1923. Even the 87 members of the New Westminster Teachers' Association (never counted as a trade union in official statistics) felt the lash of the anti-labour climate of the era and were forced out on strike in 1921.[40] In 1923, the New Westminster Trades and Labour Council, with a membership estimated at a mere 250, voted to disband and merge its meagre forces with those of the Vancouver council.

However, the virtual collapse of the A.F.L.-affiliated unions in the early 1920's cannot be interpreted as the downfall of organized labour. In 1925, New Westminster unions reported a membership of 1,270, and in 1928 of 1,514. In 1929 and 1930, reported membership reached the suspiciously large figure of 3,000, which probably included the regional membership of the New Westminster-based B.C. Fishermen's Benevolent Association. The increased union membership of the decade is nonetheless remarkable; although a union-by-union breakdown is not available, it appears that independent organizations such as the fishermen's were primarily responsible. Another such organization was the New Westminster Waterfront Workers' Association, capitalizing on the extension of port facilities and the dramatic increase in deep sea sailings (from a mere thirteen in 1921 to nearly two hundred in 1928).[41] With the significant exception of the lumber workers' organizations, New Westminster labour seemed to be in a state of healthy recuperation at the end of the 1920's, with active locals of retail clerks, painters and decorators, journeymen barbers, machinists, railway workers, and building tradesmen. Finally, there was the Working Women's Association, an independent feminist organization that was one of the legacies of the radical upsurge of 1918-19.

INDUSTRIAL CONFLICT IN NEW WESTMINSTER

The 1919 General Strike

New Westminster workers and trade union leaders gained a small measure of national attention in June 1919, when, in the midst of the nation-wide "Labour Revolt," the city's Trades and Labour Council authorized a General Strike in support of the demands of the Winnipeg and Vancouver strikers.[42] Some locals had already walked out; others had passed resolutions to strike "if force was used" in Winnipeg. The New Westminster General Strike idled 537 workers, according to official Labour Department calculations.

However, this number is a far from accurate reflection of the depth of labour unrest in the community in 1919. Of key importance in undercutting the power of the strike movement was the shutdown of the local shipyards, throwing some five hundred union members out of work in the winter of 1918-19. In April 1919, the remaining members of the Shipyard Labourers' Union voted 98 to 5 in favour of affiliation with the One Big Union (O.B.U.)—a purely symbolic act, but the shipyards would undoubtedly have been tied up by the General Strike in June.[43] Equally significant in calculating the actual number of strikers in 1919 was the role of the lumber workers' organizations. Operating Engineers' Local 620 was, at that time, the only established trade union organization in the woodworking sector, and it represented only 20 of the 537 "strikers." Local 620 had also voted in favour of affiliation to the O.B.U. (in effect, voting to merge with the strongly O.B.U. Lumber Workers Industrial Union). When the operating engineers closed down a half-dozen sawmills in support of the General Strike, other workers followed suit. The New Westminster *British Columbian* reported that "many Chinese millworkers have quit, having been organized by two Chinese organizers paid by the loggers' union [L.W.I.U.]."[44]

The militant action by New Westminster labour in 1919 surprised many knowledgeable observers, because the community's most influential labour leaders were far from the "rampant, red revolutionaries" who dominated the O.B.U. While the B.C. Federation of Labour, District 18 of the United Mine Workers, the Lumber Workers Industrial Union, and even the Vancouver Trades and Labour Council seemed to fall under the sway of "Bolshevik" elements, the "Westminster men" cut an independent and moderate path. The local trades council was clearly dominated by two individuals of moderate persuasion: R. A. Stoney, leader of the Typographical Union and former provincial labour federation executive, and William Yates, president of Division 134 of the transit workers' union. Each of their unions had voted down the O.B.U., and both opposed the General Strike on principle. The most prominent advocate of the General Strike in New Westminster in 1919 was Tom Barnard, a trades council delegate from a tiny engineers' union, whose real power base lay outside the ranks of organized labour. A former sergeant in the Canadian Expeditionary Forces, Barnard was the president of New Westminster's Great War Veterans' Association; his militant perspective stemmed as much from the trenches as from the work place.

On 21 June 1919, William Yates addressed the only public meeting held in New Westminster about the strike. "More and more," he was reported to have said, "the realization is growing that there is a class war — a war in which there is no discharge." The ultimate decision to participate in the General Strike remained in the hands of the local unions; those who joined included: the Butcher Workers (at the Burns' Meat plant); "hello girls" who were members of I.B.E.W.-213; metal trades workers at Heaps' Engineering and the Westminster Foundries; railway shop workers at the Canadian Northern Port Mann yards; Division 134; carpenters; brewery workers; cigar makers; and lumber workers. The public service unions — civic employees and firefighters — and others did not strike (see Appendix 3). Organized fishermen could offer only moral support, extended by trades council delegate "comrade" W. E. Maiden; the same was true of the Working Women's Association, headed by Mrs. Tom Barnard.[45]

The New Westminster General Strike was a sympathetic walkout that ended with the conclusion of the events in the larger cities. It did not last long enough, nor did it become closely enough entwined with local grievances, to escalate into any kind of "class war." But it was a notable moment of working-class mobilization that had no small impact on local politics.

Strikes and Lockouts, 1901-1929

Counting the 1919 strike as one dispute, there were at least forty-eight strikes and lockouts recorded in New Westminster between 1901 and 1929. The number of disputes registered in the federal Department of Labour's Strikes and Lockouts files is actually higher, owing to that department's tendency to include under "New Westminster" anything that smelled of fish or sawdust but could not be filed elsewhere in the far western province. Like the 1919 walkout, these officially recorded strikes were confined to private sector employers, but they were widely scattered across the economy. Many strikes, walkouts, or turnouts did not involve the ordering of formal relationships between union and management. Rather, they were part of a theatre of confrontation and accommodation at the work place, like the Broder Cannery strike of 1926. On the other hand, there were many trade unions in New Westminster that engaged in collective bargaining with varying degrees of success but did not embroil themselves in industrial disputes. On the whole, New Westminster labour leaders like Stoney or Yates would have endorsed the old Chartist maxim on strikes: "the next best thing to keeping out of a scrape is, when in, to get out of it."[46] Thus, the record of strikes and lockouts in New Westminster is incomplete.

The majority of industrial disputes in New Westminster occurred in the lumber industry, in transportation, the metal trades, and the fishery (Table 1).

TABLE 1: STRIKES AND LOCKOUTS IN NEW WESTMINSTER, 1901-29*

Economic Sector	Excluding June 1919	Including June 1919
Lumber	11	14
Transport	11	13
The fishery	8	8
Metal trades**	5	7
Building trades	4	5
Food, drink, tobacco	4	7
Telecommunications	2	3

*A chronological listing of these disputes is given below in Appendices 1-3.
**Including shipyard disputes, 1917-18.

Unlike the politically inspired walkout in 1919, the primary issues in these disputes were economic. Twenty-three of thirty-nine industrial disputes (excluding the General Strike itself, and the fishery, whose conflict always involved bargaining over fish prices) were primarily fought over wages. Ten disputes raised thornier issues of union recognition or security (the right to hire and fire), for example, while in five instances, workers sought reduced hours. As often as not, workers succeeded in gaining all or part of their objectives. On the other hand, failure in a strike or lockout could mean dire consequences for the people involved. Like the 1919 strike, the larger patterns of industrial unrest in the community must be placed against the backdrop of prevailing social and economic conditions.

It is possible to organize industrial conflict in New Westminster chronologically. Between 1901 and 1907, the trade unions took the offensive in British Columbia and elsewhere in Canada: close to half (46 per cent) of all local disputes recorded in New Westminster from 1900 to 1930 took place in this half-decade. The years 1908-16, marked by two major recessions and a general marshalling of employer resistance to labour demands, saw only three disputes. But there were ten strikes or lockouts from 1917 to 1920: years of acknowledged crisis in Canadian class relations. Moreover, despite an evident decline in militancy among fishermen (none of the ten disputes engaged the fishery), the key struggles of this period were shared by New Westminster workers and their counterparts elsewhere in the region. These strikes of shipyard, transit, and lumber workers provide a tangible explanation for the fact that the labour movement would even contemplate the prospect of a General Strike in 1919. The last period under discussion, from 1921 to 1929, witnessed a return to localism. Only the disastrous longshore strike of 1923 and the nearly ruinous moulders' strike of 1926 brought together New Westminster workers with similar people outside the city. The most salient fact about this period, however, is that it saw only a diminished level of class conflict, not an abandonment of the class struggle by capital and labour. The data from New Westminster, and from Vancouver (which experienced at least forty-two strikes and lockouts in the same years), show that the conventional portrait of the 1920's in labour history has been overdrawn.

In summary, at least twenty-three different labour organizations confronted twenty-seven different employers in New Westminster in strikes or lockouts in the years 1901-29 (see Appendices 4-5). Trade unions were clearly not involved, however, in roughly one-third of all disputes. As if to refute the notion that union agitation was the "cause" of industrial unrest, unorganized workers often tied up production in conflicts over wages and conditions. At Fraser Mills in 1909, for example, "two hundred Hindoos [sic] ... went on strike ... this being the first labour trouble the Orientals have figured in since their arrival in the country. Their grievance is that their leader [the labour contractor], Udah Ram, has not been paying them their wages for some time past. ... Udah Ram is a Brahmin, and because of his high caste the workers decline to do him violence."[48] Similarly, in 1903, Japanese mill workers had struck the Brunette Lumber Company to secure the *reinstatement* of their foreman —highlighting the ambiguous role played by the ethnic straw boss in B.C. industry.[49]

The record in New Westminster shows that traditional emphasis on the "tractibility" of Asian immigrant workers, and their alleged role as strikebreakers, has been seriously misplaced.[50] In the context of the struggles that surrounded the birth of the Lumber Workers Industrial Union, radical labour spokesmen freely admitted that the Chinese were better organized than any other group on the shop floor of the saw and shingle mills. The One Big Union celebrated the awakening of the "long despised, poorly paid, and docile [Oriental] mill workers," while capital's spokesmen in 1919 denounced Asian immigrant militancy in exactly the same terms as they did "dangerous foreigners" from continental Europe.[51] Perhaps the last word on the question should be given to New Westminster fishermen's leader W. E. Maiden, writing his report to the Department of Labour on the 1925 salmon gillnetters' protest: "Re strike, or cessation of work . . . it cannot be described in the stereotyped lexicon of ordinary labour disputes. . . . Whites and Japs, organized and unorganized, quit operating. It was a spontaneous performance."[52]

LABOUR POLITICS IN NEW WESTMINSTER, 1900-1933

In the more modern context, New Westminster is known as part of the heartland of British Columbia's social democratic labour movement. In eleven consecutive provincial elections held between 1952 and 1983 in New Westminster's legislative district (the only one in the province to conform with municipal boundaries), the Co-operative Commonwealth Federation (C.C.F.) and its successor, the New Democratic Party (N.D.P.), held the reins to local power. In 1985, New Westminster was represented by social democrats at both the provincial and federal level. Its mayor, an officer of the carpenters' union, also claimed social democratic affiliations. New Westminster's first social democratic legislator, "Ray" Eddie, was a former officer of the International Woodworkers of America: the union that, with Communist help, finally broke the open shop in the woodworking industry in 1942-46.[53] Another former woodworker, and grandson of early craft union leader R. A. Stoney, represented I.W.A. Local 1-357 and the rest of New Westminster labour in the highest councils of social democracy: as president of the provincial N.D.P.[54] New Westminster workers have been important architects of British Columbia's ideologically polarized politics in the twentieth century. All of this is special cause for reflection upon the role of the working class and its political institutions in New Westminster's past.

Social democrats in British Columbia, however, disarm themselves with an historical mythology that assigns an exaggerated significance to the C.C.F. in the 1930's. One academic has said, "the left was only a marginal force in British Columbia before the great depression."[55] In New Westminster, however, the left was a force to be reckoned with long before the founding of the C.C.F. in 1932. The C.C.F. itself did not substantially alter the balance of forces in the community during the 1930's, achieving neither political leadership over a united labour movement nor an "enlargement" of an already existing political constituency until the 1940's. In part, its failure in the 1930's was a measure of the relative success of the rival Communist party, whose cadres were well entrenched during the depression decade in unions representing lumber workers, dock workers, and fishermen, and in an active movement of resident unemployed (the New Westminster Unemployed Workers' Association, organized in 1930-31).[56]

The history of New Westminster socialism extends back into the 1890's, with the founding of local branches of both the Socialist Labor Party and the Canadian Socialist League, and publication of a short-lived socialist newspaper, the *Pathfinder*.[57] Will MacClain, a machinist and fishermen's union organizer, was nominated to stand as the first socialist candidate for the Canadian parliament in 1900 in New Westminster, although his name did not appear on the ballot.[58] The Socialist Party of Canada (S.P.C.) finally placed its candidate in the lists during the provincial elections of 1907; 11 per cent of New Westminster's electors voted for the S.P.C.'s "one plank platform"—Abolition of Wage Slavery—in 1907. Two years later, the New Westminster Trades and Labour Council (T.L.C.) saw a heated debate over political affiliations, which sowed "the seeds of dissension . . . setting brother against brother, craft against craft," as Socialists, Labourites, Grits, Tories, and Prohibitionists "struggled for the beliefs."[59] For the 1909 provincial elections, the class-conscious socialists withdrew in favour of the T.L.C.-endorsed Labour candidate, Walter Dodd, a street railwayman and future Labour alderman. The presence of a straight labour candidate made no difference in the equation of class politics in New Westminster, as Dodd did no better than to corral the existing socialist constituency and 10 per cent of the vote.[60]

It was the war time and post-war experience that produced the most lasting realignment in local politics, with elections in 1920 (provincial) and 1921 (federal) proving a watershed. In 1920, W. J. Sloan was chosen as a Soldier-Labour candidate for the legislature, supported by delegates from the Great War Veterans' Association, the Fishermen's Protective Association, Division 134 of the transit workers' union, civic employees, and postal workers. His campaign garnered over one-third of the votes and came perilously close to victory in an apparently staunch Liberal bastion.[61] In 1921, veteran S.P.C.-er R. P. Pettipiece contested the federal riding of New Westminster on a Labour ticket, winning 25 per cent of the city-wide vote and actually capturing seven city polls. Of this campaign, clearly the project of the local left, Pettipiece commented: "we had no money, little organization, and only evening work of volunteers. Despite this handicap we rolled up a vote which cannot be ignored and will be increased."[62]

The 1920's would be a decade of discord and disappointment for political activists in New Westminster and British Columbia, as the Federated Labour Party, the Canadian Labour Party (C.L.P.), and the Independent Labour Party all attempted to forge a viable coalition of labour and socialist forces in the province. In 1924, a C.L.P. candidate in New Westminster polled only 17 per cent of the provincial vote, while the fourth party Progressives stole another 14 per cent.[63] But the face of local politics had been permanently altered. In 1933, the first standard bearer of the C.C.F. in New Westminster, Dan McGrath, did recapture that quarter of the electorate that had been mobilized by post-war radicalism. Significantly, the C.C.F. in New Westminster seemed unconcerned with the goal of winning middle-class converts; the party was more worried about being outflanked by the Communists on the left. During the 1933 campaign, McGrath dismissed the difference between himself and United Front candidate Tom Douglas, a Coquitlam alderman, as "one of method, rather than objective" and declared that there was "no limit" to how far the C.C.F. would go in implementing its radical Regina programme.[64] Anchored in its working-class milieu, social democracy in New Westminster would have to await the expansion of the trade union movement during the Second World War, the decline of Communist influence, and the demise of the Liberal populism of provincial premier T. D. Pattullo before registering new gains. But would the subsequent successes of the social democratic movement in New Westminster have been possible without the existence and formation of a solid socialist and labour constituency in the years from 1900 to 1930? The answer must be an unqualified no.

CONCLUSION

A survey of class relationships and class formation in New Westminster between 1900 and 1930 is a useful corrective to B.C. labour historiography, with its traditional emphasis on radical responses to the peculiar circumstances of the resource "frontier." The findings also challenge the "revisionist" model of B.C. class relationships in this period put forward by Ward. He has understated the influence of both urban trade unionism and working-class politics while ignoring the central question of class conflict at the work place, which, in New Westminster at least, extended beyond the ranks of the organized work force. At the same time, Ward has overstated and misinterpreted the issue of racial segmentation in the work force. In New Westminster, the "Oriental Question" was a management problem of labour indiscipline: Asian immigrant workers were, in fact, involved in a disproportionately large number of strikes. Trade unions were mainly, but not exclusively, confined to the ranks of skilled, white, male workers. As shown by the events of 1919, however, the trade unions were by no means a "coopted" layer of the working class. An anonymous craft worker during the 1926 moulders' strike expressed the basic credo of an emerging class and movement: "Our objective must be and shall remain 100 per cent organization of ourselves... 100 per cent class consciousness in all the trades. Our objective must [be] the emancipation of man from the thraldom of his own making."[65]

NOTES

*I should like to thank my colleague Bryan Palmer for his commentary on this project.

1. Public Archives of Canada (PAC), Department of Labour, RG27, Strikes and Lockouts file, Vol. 337, file 37.
2. "Cannery Girls Make Appeal to City Council," New Westminster *British Columbian*, 7 July 1926.
3. Daniel Drache, "The Formation and Fragmentation of the Canadian Working Class: 1820-1920," *Studies in Political Economy*, 15 (Fall 1984):43-90. As early as 1911, less than one-fifth of British Columbia's total work force was engaged in primary production of the staple commodities of "rocks" (minerals and coal), logs, and fish. An additional 12 per cent was found in agriculture. By 1931, an astonishing 35 per cent of the entire population of the province was living in the city of Vancouver, Canada's fifth largest manufacturing centre.
4. See the narrow focus of the two contributions in labour history found in W. Peter Ward and Robert A. J. McDonald (eds.), *British Columbia: Historical Readings* (Vancouver: Douglas and McIntyre, 1981): David Jay Bercuson, "Labour Radicalism and the Western Industrial Frontier, 1897-1919," and A. Ross McCormack, "The Industrial Workers of the World in Western Canada, 1905-1914." See also W. Peter Ward, "Class and Race in the Social Structure of British Columbia, 1870-1939," *B.C. Studies*, 45 (Spring 1980):17-35, printed in Ward and McDonald, *Historical Readings*, 581-99; and Rennie Warburton, "Race and Class in British Columbia: A comment," *B.C. Studies*, 49 (Spring 1981):79-85.
5. One survey, now badly outdated, is Paul Phillips, *No Power Greater: A Century of Labour in B.C.* (Vancouver: B.C. Federation of Labour and the Boag Foundation, 1967); the only extensive history of a B.C. trade union is Elaine Bernard, *The Long Distance Feeling: A History of the Telecommunications Workers Union* (Vancouver, 1982).
6. Gerald Friesen, *The Canadian Prairies: A History* (Toronto, 1984), p. 287.
7. Barry Mather, *New Westminster: The Royal City* (Vancouver, 1958); Margaret Ormsby, *British Columbia: A History* (Toronto, 1958), pp. 176-80 *passim*.
8. *Canada, Census of Manufactures* (1916), p.186.

9. *Labour Gazette*, 3 (1902-3): 600. For detailed reports on local industrial progress, see also *Labour Gazette* 4 (1903-4): 883, 5 (1904-5): 351, 6 (1905-6): 515-16.
10. G. W. Taylor, *Timber: A History of the Forest Industry in British Columbia* (Vancouver, 1975), pp. 40-43.
11. G. W. Taylor, *Builders of British Columbia: An Industrial History* (Vancouver, 1982), pp. 131-34.
12. Ibid. Between 1901 and 1931, the population of New Westminster increased by 169 per cent. That of Vancouver (including the previously unincorporated suburbs of South Vancouver and Point Grey) increased by nearly 800 per cent. The former metropolis of New Westminster had a population equal to 22 per cent of Vancouver's in 1901; by 1931 the figure was 7 per cent.
13. For useful insights into the business cycle of boom and bust in New Westminster, see Jacqueline Gresko and Richard Howard (eds.), *Fraser Port: Freightway to the Pacific* (Vancouver, 1986), which arrived too late to be incorporated into this research.
14. "Shipyards Laying Off Nearly All Men," *British Columbian*, 5 June 1919; see also Marine Retirees' Association, *A History of Shipbuilding in British Columbia* (Vancouver, 1977), Chapter 7.
15. W. A. MacIntosh, *The Economic Background to Dominion-Provincial Relations* (Toronto, 1964), pp. 90-94; Jacqueline Gresko, "The Fraser River Harbour Commission, 1888-1979," unpublished manuscript, courtesy of the author.
16. Research into the only available manuscript census for B.C. (1881) suggests that the habit of categorizing Asian immigrants as "labourers"—without specifying occupational sectors— began early and was of course reinforced by language barriers.
17. Ward, "Class and Race in the Social Structure of British Columbia," is notable for a total lack of attention to social structure from a sociologist's point of view.
18. Patricia E. Roy, "Citizens without Votes: East Asians in British Columbia, 1872-1947," in Jorgen Dahile and Tissa Fernando (eds.), *Ethnicity, Power and Politics in Canada* (Toronto, 1981), pp. 151-71.
19. Donald MacKay, *Empire of Wood: The MacMillan Bloedel Story* (Vancouver, 1982), p.18.
20. Survey published in the *Port Alberni News*, 3 January 1923, cited in Gordon Hak, "On the Fringes: Capital and Labour in the Forest Economies of the Port Alberni and Prince George Districts, 1910-1939" (unpublished manuscript).
21. *Labour Gazette* 15 (1914-15):918
22. Jeanne Williams, "Ethnicity and Class Conflict at Fraser Mills-Maillardville: The Strike of 1931" (M.A. thesis, Simon Fraser University, 1982):37.
23. H. A. Townsend, "Chinese Again Fill Places of White Workers," *Vancouver, Labor Statesman*, 22 November 1929; "Women Fill Jobs of Striking Chinese Scabs," ibid., 25 October 1929.
24. "Report of the Royal Commission on Chinese and Japanese Immigration," *Labour Gazette* 2 (1901-2):605.
25. W. Peter Ward, *White Canada Forever: Popular Attitudes and Public Policy Towards Orientals in B.C.* (Montreal, 1978), pp. 34-36; Jonathan Garlock, *Guide to the Local Assemblies of the Knights of Labor* (Westport, CN, 1982), p.556; Eugene Forsey, *Trade Unions in Canada 1812-1902* (Toronto, 1981), p.426.
26. Bernard, *The Long Distance Feeling*, Chapters 1-4; Ian MacDonald, "The United Brotherhood of Electrical Workers—Local 213," paper presented at the Pacific Northwest Labor History Association Annual Conference, Vancouver, 15-17 June 1984.
27. Patricia E. Roy, "The B.C. Electric Railway and its Street Railway Employees: Paternalism in Labour Relations," *B.C. Studies* 16 (Winter 1972-3): 3-24 Hugh Tuck, "The United Brotherhood of Railway Employees in Western Canada, 1898-1905," *Labour/Le travailleur*, 11 (Spring 1983): 63-88.
28. Forsey, *Trade Unions in Canada*, p.193; see also the report on local activities of the Amalgamated Carpenters and Joiners in the *Victoria Colonist*, 7 May 1890.

29. "Woodworkers Meet at New Westminster," Vancouver, *Western Clarion*, 16 May 1903.
30. See Hugh Johnston, *The Voyage of the 'Komagata Maru'* (Delhi, 1979), pp. 62-65.
31. Canada, *Sessional Papers*, 1904, no. 36a, transcript, Royal Commission on Industrial Disputes in the Province of British Columbia (1903), pp. 805-8.
32. See Norman Clark, *Milltown: A Social History of Everett, Washington* (Seattle, 1971); Harvey O'Connor, *Revolution in Seattle: A Memoir* (New York, 1964).
33. "Shingle Mills Closed Down," *British Columbian*, 23 July 1917; PAC, Department of Labour, RG 27, Strikes and Lockouts File, Vol. 306, file 43, William Yates to Department, 13 August 1917.
34. Ibid., Vol. 310, file 27, Frank Nash, Shingle Agency, to Department, 27 March 1919; "Shingle Mills to Reopen Soon," *Columbian*, 9 April 1919.
35. Dorothy Steeves, *Compassionate Rebel: Ernest Winch and the Growth of Socialism in Western Canada* (Vancouver, 1960), p.53. Local activists frankly admitted that "the Chinese were better organized than the whites," Vancouver *British Columbia Federationist*, 17 October 1919.
36. For surveys of forest-industry industrial relations see Myrtle Bergren, *Tough Timber: The Loggers of British Columbia—Their Story* (Toronto, 1967) and Jerry Lembcke, "The International Woodworkers of America in British Columbia, 1942-1951," *Labour/Le travailleur* 6 (Autumn 1980):113-48.
37. See "Lively Debate in New Westminster," British Columbia *Federationist*, 9 May 1919; "New Wage Scale for Mill Workers," ibid., 16 March 1920; "Will Ballot on 44 Hour Week," ibid., 30 April 1920.
38. These data are drawn from the official statistical review of Canadian trade unions published annually after 1911 as *The Report on Labour Organizations in Canada*.
39. See Ian Angus, *Canadian Bolsheviks: The Early Years of the Communist Party of Canada* (Montreal, 1981), pp. 133-36; Irving Abella, *The Canadian Labour Movement, 1902-1960* Booklet 28 (Ottawa: Canadian Historical Association, 1975), p. 15; Stuart Jamieson, *Times of Trouble: Labour Unrest and Industrial Conflict in Canada, 1900-1966* (Ottawa, 1971), pp. 192-213; Phillips, *No Power Greater*, pp. 185-200.
40. "School Board Rejects Offer of Citizens Who Seek to Resolve Conflict," *British Columbian*, 13 December 1921; F. Henry Johnson, *A History of Public Education in British Columbia* (Vancouver, 1964), pp. 241-2.
41. "City's Deal in Terminals Discussed," *British Columbian*, 1 November 1934.
42. See Gregory S. Kealey, "1919: The Canadian Labour Revolt," *Labour/Le travail*, 13 (Spring 1984):11-44; Allen Seager, "Nineteen Nineteen: Year of Revolt," *Journal of the West*, 23, no. 4 (1984):40-47.
43. University of British Columbia, Special Collections, One Big Union Papers, file 213.
44. PAC, Department of Labour, RG 27, Strikes and Lockouts File, Vol 315, file 221, clipping from the *British Columbian*, 21 June 1919.
45. Yates quoted in the *British Columbian*, 21 June 1919. The keynote speaker at the New Westminster strike rally was Vancouver socialist John Harrington, who elicited "much laughter and good-humoured sallies from members of the audience [of] about two hundred people, including a fair sprinkling of women." Other press reports on the New Westminster events include "Royal City not striking," Vancouver *Province*, 12 June 1919, "Typos Reject One Big Union," *British Columbian*, 1 May 1919, and "Returned Men Discuss Unrest," ibid., 16 June, 1919. For the Barnards see Steeves, *The Compassionate Rebel*, p.41.
46. Feargus O'Connor in the *Northern Star*, 6 January 1864; for a penetrating insight into this mentality see E. P. Thompson, "The Peculiarities of the English," in Thompson, *The Poverty of Theory and Other Essays* (London, 1978), pp. 245-302.
47. PAC, Department of Labour, RG 27, Strikes and Lockouts File, vol. 296, file 3113, D. J. Stewart to F. A. Acland, 27 February 1909.

48. *Labour Gazette*, 2 (1902-3): 626; for a contemporary insight into the role of "Boss Chinaman" see Francis Herring, *Among the People of British Columbia: Red, White, Yellow and Brown* (London, 1903), pp. 272-73.
49. Ward, *White Canada Forever*, pp. 17-18. Ward does note the "occasional strike" by Chinese workers but gives no examples.
50. "Mill Workers Now Demand 8 Hour Day," *British Columbia Federationist*, 16 April 1920; see also PAC, Naval Service of Canada, RG24, vol. 3985, 1055-2-21, file 1, General Officer Commanding, R.N.W. M.P. (Victoria) to Adjutant-General, Ottawa, 13 June 1919; Donald Avery, *"Dangerous Foreigners": European Immigrant Workers and Labour Radicalism in Canada, 1896-1932* (Toronto, 1979).
51. PAC, Department of Labour, RG27, Strikes and Lockouts File, Vol. 335, file 80, W. E. Maiden to F. E. Harrison, 14 October 1925; for background see Harry Keith Ralston, "The 1900 Strike of Fraser River Sockeye Salmon Fishermen" (M.A. thesis, University of British Columbia, 1965): 125, passim; Rolf Knight and Maya Koizuma, *A Man of Our Times: The Life History of a Japanese Canadian Fisherman* (Vancouver, 1976).
52. Daisy Webster, *Growth of the NDP in British Columbia: Eighty-One Political Biographies* (Vancouver, n.d.), pp. 23-24; Lembcke, "The International Woodworkers in British Columbia." John McRae Eddie, benefitting from disciplined C.I.O. union backing and the extraordinary political circumstances in British Columbia in 1952, defeated Liberal leader Bjorn (Boss) Johnson that year with a mere 30 per cent of first choice ballots, increased to 37 per cent in 1953. Defeated C.C.F. candidates in 1945 and 1949 had polled exactly 39 per cent of the votes in New Westminster, while in 1942 the combined total for C.C.F. and labour candidates in the riding was 36.5 per cent.
53. I am indebted to Gerry Stoney for additional information on some of the personalities involved in the history of labour and the C.C.F.-N.D.P. in New Westminster.
54. Ward, "Class and Race in the Social Structure of British Columbia," p.24.
55. In 1933, the communists' 2 per cent of the vote in New Westminster seemed marginal in comparison to the C.C.F.'s 26 per cent. In 1937, political schisms on the left were more than evidenced by a three-way split in the "labour" vote: 17 per cent C.C.F., 7 per cent communist, and 1 per cent Independent Labour (see also note 52 above).
56. G. Weston Wrigley, "Socialism in Canada," *International Socialist Review*, 1 May 1901, 687; Carlos A. Schwantes, *Radical Heritage: Labor, Socialism and Reform in Washington and British Columbia, 1885-1917* (Vancouver, 1979), p. 83; Ross Alfred Johnson, "No Compromise—No Political Trading: The Marxian Socialist Tradition in British Columbia" (Ph.D. diss., University of British Columbia, 1975): 55.
57. Thomas Robert Loosmore, "The British Columbia Labour Movement and Political Action, 1879-1906" (M.A. thesis, University of British Columbia, 1954):109-10, 137-39.
58. "Are Aroused about Politics," *Columbian*, 20 November 1909.
59. *Canadian Parliamentary Guide*, Ottawa, 1910, p.429.
60. Ibid., 1921, p.496; *Province*, 28 October 1920, courtesy of Elizabeth Lees.
61. "Says Campaign Is Just Opened," *British Columbian*, 10 December 1921; Canada, *Sessional Paper*, 1922, no. 13, "Report of the Chief Returning Officer' [1921 General Elections], pp. 399-400.
62. Martin Robin, *The Rush for Spoils: The Company Province, 1871-1933* (Toronto, 1972), p.213; Walter Young, "Ideology, Personality and the Origins of the C.C.F. in British Columbia," in John Norris and Margaret Prang (eds.), *Personality and History in British Columbia: Essays in Honour of Margaret Ormsby* (Vancouver, 1977), pp. 140-43.

63. "Candidates in City Address War Veterans," *British Columbian*, 28 October 1933.
64. Ward, "Class and Race in the Social Structure of British Columbia."
65. "A Molder's Scribe," *Labor Statesman*, 13 August 1926.

APPENDIX 1

STRIKES AND LOCKOUTS (INDUSTRIAL) IN NEW WESTMINSTER, 1901-30

Year	Dates	No. of workers'	Trade/ occupation	Cause/ grievance	Resolution
1901	16 March	25	shingle weavers	wages	strikers left
1901	9-10 Sept.	9	deck hands	wages	increase in wages
1901	13 Sept.		longshoremen	"refusal to work with Americans"	not clear
1902	28 Nov.- 12 Dec.	50	telephone workers I.B.E.W.*	pay; union security	demands met
1903	15-16 Jan.	150	mill workers (Japanese)	discharge of foremen	demands met
1903	9 Feb.	10	deck hands	wages	demands met
1903	3 March	15	C.P.R. clerks U.B.R.E.*	union recognition	strike failed
1903	28 May- 14 July	57	mill workers A.F.L.*	nine-hour day	strike failed
1906	27 Feb.- June	54	telephone workers I.B.E.W.*	contract for telephone operators	strike failed
1906	24-26 Dec.	18	metal workers I.A.M.	wages	increase in wages
1907	24 Feb.	100	mill workers ("Hindus") (at Fraser Mills)	wages	not clear
1907	1 April	10	carpenters AC&J	eight-hour day	strikers replaced
1907	9-11 April	8	deck hands	wages	increase in wages
1907	10 April	8	deck hands (C.P.R.)	wages	strikers replaced
1907	1 May	6	deck hands	wages	increase in wages
1907	24 June- 5 July	12	moulders I.M.U.	wages	increase in wages
1907	7 Sept.	10	deck hands (C.P.R.)	wages	strikers replaced
1907	1-23 Oct.	40	lumber handlers	increase in hours	demand granted

SUBTOTAL, 1901-10: 18

Year	Dates	No. of workers'	Trade/ occupation	Cause/ grievance	Resolution
1911	1-17 May		bakery workers Bakers*	eight-hour day closed shop	contract signed
1917	2-5 Feb.	56	iron workers Boiler-makers*	wages	increase in wages
1917	13-21 June	150	transit workers Div. 134*+	wages	increase in wages
1917	17 July		mill workers Shingle weavers*	union shop	strike failed

Year	Dates	No. of workers	Trade/ occupation	Cause/ grievance	Resolution
1918	24 May- 4 June	250	shipyard workers Several*	eight-hour days wages	demands met
1918	1 June- 11 July	205	transit workers Div. 134*+	eight-hour day wages	demands met
1919	6 March- 10 April		mill workers ("Orientals")*	wage cut	wages reinstated
1919	June (various dates)		10 trades T.L.C. and others*	—General Strike— (see Appendix 3)	
1920	7-11 April	75	mill workers O.B.U.	wages	increase in wages
1920	3 May-	7	bakery workers Bakers*	union shop	strike failed
1920	3-10 May		bricklayers Bricklayers	wages	increase in wages

SUBTOTAL, 1911-20: 11

Year	Dates	No. of workers	Trade/ occupation	Cause/ grievance	Resolution
1921	1-8 Jan	100	mill workers O.B.U.(?)	wage cut	strike failed
1921	2 Feb.- 2 March	25	brewery workers Brewery Workers	firing of member	financial settlement
1922	20 July- 22 Aug.	14	carpenters C&J	wages	demands not met
1923	8 Oct.- Dec.	35	longshoremen I.L.A.*	5 cent bonus	strike failed
1925	3 March	20	mill workers	wages	strikers fired
1926	1 April- 15 Aug.	13	moulders I.M.U.	wages	demands not met
1926	21 May-	6	mill engineers B.O.E.	wages	strikers fired/left
1926	6 July	200	food workers	wages	ringleaders fired
1928	21 Nov.- 4 Dec.	33	pile drivers C&J	employment of non-members	demand was met
1929	25 Oct.-		mill workers (Chinese)	rents	strikers fired/left
1929	15 Nov.-	60	mill workers Local	wages	strike failed

SUBTOTAL, 1921-30: 11

Sources: PAC, Public Records, RG 27, Department of Labour, Strikes and Lockouts Files, vols. 296 (1907) to 344 (1929); *Labour Gazette* (monthly), vols. 1 to 7 (1900-1907).

*Indicates that the strike or lockout was part of a trade dispute involving union workers at New Westminster and Vancouver.

+Division 134, Amalgamated Association of Street and Electric Railway Employees. For labour organizations abbreviated above, see Appendix 4, below.

APPENDIX 2
FISHERIES DISPUTES REPORTED OUT OF NEW WESTMINSTER INVOLVING LOCAL MEN, 1901-30

Year	Dates	Species	Name of Union	No. of people involved
1901	1-20 July	salmon	B.C. Fishermen's Union	5,000
1901	25 September	salmon	B.C. Fishermen's Union	
1903	1-15 July	salmon	B.C. Fishermen's Union	4,100
1907	22-29 June	salmon	B.C. Fishermen's Union	125
1912	1 Nov.-29 March	halibut	Seattle-based union	3 NW boats
1913	3-5 August	salmon	various	2,000
1925	11-18 May	salmon	Fishermen's Prot. Assn.	1,000
1925	21-18 Sept.	salmon	Fishermen's Prot. Assn.	630

APPENDIX 3
"GENERAL AND SYMPATHETIC STRIKES" AT NEW WESTMINSTER JUNE 1919

Trade/Occupation	Nos.	Date Commenced	Called off
Telephone workers	26	3–4 June	mid-July (some not rehired)
Meat packers	80	3–4 June	24 June (some not rehired)
Moulders (Heaps Engineering)		3–4 June	24 June
Railway shops	80	18 June	24 June
Transit workers	280	18 June	24 June
Machinists	10	28 June	24 June
Engineers, sawmills	20	20 June	24 June
Carpenters	10	20 June	24 June
Cigar makers	6	20 June	24 June
Brewery workers	25	20 June	24 June

Note: Barbers, Typographers, Civic Employees, Retail Clerks, Teamsters, and Postal Workers were reported as not participating in the strike. PAC, RG 27, vol. 315, file 221, clippings and memoranda.

APPENDIX 4
PARTIAL LIST OF UNIONS INVOLVED IN TRADE AND FISHERY DISPUTES IN
NEW WESTMINSTER, 1901-29

Amalgamated Association of Street and Electric Railway Employees (Division 134)
Amalgamated Society of Carpenters and Joiners, No. 1 (A.C.&J.)
American Federation of Labor, chartered mill workers' local (A.F.L.)
B.C. Fishermen's Union, Lodge No. 1
B.C. Fishermen's Protective Association, N.W.
Brotherhood of Railway Carmen
Brotherhood of Maintenance-of-Way and Shop Labourers, Local 1734
Brotherhood of Steam and Operating Engineers (B.O.E.)
Cigarmakers' International Union, Local 486
International Union of Bakery and Confectionary Workers (Bakers)
International Brotherhood of Electrical Workers, Local 213 (I.B.E.W.)
International Association of Machinists, Lodge No. 151 (I.A.M.)
International Moulders' Union (I.M.U.)
International Union of Shingle Weavers, Sawmill Workers and Woodsmen, Local 28
    (Shingle Weavers)
International Longshoremen's Association (I.L.A.)
International Union of Meat Cutters and Packinghouse Workers
International Union of Bricklayers and Helpers (Bricklayers)
The One Big Union; Engineers and Lumber Workers' Units (O.B.U.)
The Trades and Labour Council (T.L.C.) New Westminster
Shipwrights and Caulkers' Association
"Shingle Weavers' Union of Vancouver and Vicinity" (Local)
United Brotherhood of Carpenters and Joiners (C&J)
United Brotherhood of Railway Employees (U.B.R.E.)
Total No.: 23

APPENDIX 5
PARTIAL LIST OF EMPLOYERS INVOLVED IN TRADE DISPUTES IN NEW
WESTMINSTER 1901-29

B.C. Box Factory
B.C. Construction and Engineering
B.C. Electric Railway
B.C. Shipping Federation
B.C. Telephone
Beaches Mills
Burns Meat
Brunette Lumber Company/Brunette
    (Shingle) Mills
Canadian Northern Railway
Canadian Pacific Railway
Dominion Construction
Dominion Shingle Mills
Grant's Bakery

Great Northern Railway
Heaps Engineering
Lulu Island Lumber Products
New Westminster Foundries Ltd.
Royal City Planing Mills
Schaake Machine Works
Schull Lumber and Shingle
Shelley's Bakery
Small and Bucklin Lumber Company
Western Steamboat Company
Westminster Brewery
Westminster Iron Works
Westminster Mill Company
Vulcan Iron Works

Total: 27

APPENDIX 6
ETHNIC/NATIONAL BACKGROUND OF THE POPULATION, NEW
WESTMINSTER, 1901-31

Census year	Population	Per cent British	Per cent Asian*	Per cent Other**
1901	6,499	75	14	11
1911	13,199	71.5	8	20.5
1921	14,495	81	8	11
1931	17,524	78.5	7	14.5

*Ethnic breakdown available for 1911 only, as follows: Chinese 609,
Japanese 367, "Hindu" 74.

**Ethnic breakdown (major groups) for 1931, as follows: "Scandinavians"881,
French/French Canadian/Belgian 332, Germans 288, Czechs/Slovaks/"Austrians"
106, Italians 181, Finns 148, Dutch 100, Russians 91, Poles 69, Ukrainians 30,
Jews 20.

Source: Dominion Census Reports, 1901, 1911, 1921, 1931.

APPENDIX 7
MAJOR OCCUPATIONS IN THE WORK FORCE, NEW WESTMINSTER, 1931

Trade/occupation	Males	Females	Total	Per cent of workforce
Labourers	1,305	34	1,339	19.5
Clerks	222	275	497	7.5
Building trades	444		444	6.5
Metal trades	356		356	5
Sales	244	110	354	5
Mill trades	243	7	250	3.5
Domestic servants	19	189	208	3
Nurses		183	183	2.5
Teachers	58	124	182	2.5
Railway/street railway workers	174		174	2.5
Manufacturing: food, leather, tobacco	134	16	150	2
Teamsters/truck drivers	143		143	2
Warehouse workers	111	21	132	2
Light and power workers	117		117	1.5
Longshoremen	114		114	1.5
Janitors/housekeepers	57	49	106	1.5
Loggers/miners	96		96	1.5
Seamen/deckhands	92		92	1.5
Telephone/telegraph workers	25	41	66	1
Fishermen	63		63	1
Garment workers	40	23	63	1
Firemen/police	61		61	1
Laundry workers	18	34	52	less than 1
"Public service officers"	41		41	
Postal workers	21		21	
Printers	20		20	
Subtotal (27 trades)	4,217	1,107	5,324	78
Total work force (including professionals, self-employed, foremen, owners and managers, and others)	5,518	1,319	6,837	

Source: as calculated from data on occupations in New Westminster, Dominion Census,
1931, vol. 7, pp. 276-87.

8

Class and Community in
the Fraser Mills Strike, 1931

JEANNE MEYERS

During the Great Depression, Canadian workers faced a series of assaults on their wages and working conditions. Threatened by shrinking markets and narrowing profit margins, Canadian employers moved to reduce labour costs. When the Canadian Western Lumber Company (C.W.L.C.) at Fraser Mills, B.C., attempted to follow the pattern of wage cuts being set throughout the Canadian economy, the millworkers went on strike. For some of the men, the proposed cut would have been the sixth in eighteen months. The labour protest by the millworkers and their families lasted for two-and-one-half months and ended in success.

The success of the 1931 strike stands in contrast to the generally weak performance of organized labour during the early 1930's. Why did the Fraser Mills strikers succeed, while workers in other Lower Mainland sawmills achieved far less in their struggles with management? The answer is multifaceted. Union leadership certainly played a role. The strike was led by the militant Lumber Workers' Industrial Union (L.W.I.U), an affiliate of the Workers' Unity League (W.U.L.). During the 1930's, the W.U.L. was one of the most dynamic labour organizations in Canada. Yet the real strength of the protest, and the reason it eventually succeeded, can be found in features internal to the community.

The worker community of Maillardville/Fraser Mills, originally a company town, was remarkably stable and socially cohesive. The marriage of communist organizational talent and the internal features of the community would give the strike action a firm foundation. The work force's extraordinary cohesion was largely the result of a persistent, tightly bonded community of French-Canadian workers, originally imported by the C.W.L.C. in 1909 and 1910 to replace its Asian workers. By 1931, the millworkers at Fraser Mills had developed a well-defined associational network which not only facilitated organization prior to the strike but also ensured its success once the strike was under way. The objective of this paper, drawn from a larger study, is twofold: to present an overview of the 1931 strike, which has an important place in the history of unionization in B.C.'s forest industry, and to consider the relationship between labour protest and the community from which it emerged.

The C.W.L.C. operation at Fraser Mills was one of the largest sawmills in the Pacific Northwest and was one arm of an industrial giant with extensive holdings that included lumberyards, railways, and logging operations. In 1907, the Fraser Mills sawmill, previously owned by Lester David, was taken over by an investment syndicate headed by A. D. McRae of Winnipeg and Senator P. Jansen of Nebraska, both of whom had access to considerable economic and political resources.

McRae and Jansen began a reorganization completed in 1910 with the formation of the C.W.L.C., a company which would become a leading agent in the developing forest industry of British Columbia. With the reorganization of capital interests, Lester David, former manager of Fraser River Sawmills, withdrew from the company in a flurry of writs. By 1910, the company's officers included such prominent entrepreneurs as W. MacKenzie, D. D. Mann and D. B. Hanna of the Canadian Northern Railway Company; R. M. Horne-Payne, President of the British Columbia Electric Railway; A. R. Davidson of the Saskatchewan Lane company; and James D. McCormack, Manager of the Columbia River Lumber Company at Golden, B.C. McRae served the C.W.L.C. as vice-president and general manager under the presidency of Andrew D. Davidson, while Senator Jansen sat on the board of directors. Ed Swift of the Chicago meat-packing firm was a major shareholder.[1]

The resources of the men at the helm of the C.W.L.C. were obviously substantial. With a capitalization of $10,000,000, the C.W.L.C. undertook revisions to Fraser Mills and purchased extensive timber limits, 150,000 acres of largely Crown lands, on both Vancouver Island and the B.C. mainland.[2] The timber limits were extended until, according to Ormsby, "they became the largest in the world,"[3] and the mill "could compare with the world's largest mills."[4]

Improvements, at a cost of over $500,000, not only increased the productive capacity of the mill but also expanded the services available to the resident work force. With 450 acres of land obtained to build a town dependent on the mill,[5] Fraser Mills now offered a store, community hall, post office, and railway station with resident agent. The residence of a former manager served as a hospital, and a New Westminster doctor was in daily attendance. Millworkers paid for such services in the traditional manner of a company town: a hospital fee was levied directly through the payroll office, as were any charges made at the general store, rent payments, or payments for lots and building supplies. By 1908, about twenty homes had been built for employees, serviced with electricity supplied by the mill. The managers' residences were set off somewhat from the millsite along the northern perimeter of Fraser Mills.[6] As the New Westminster *British Columbian* reported:

> Far up the hill north of the town and opening on to the Pitt River Road is the magnificent residence built by the company for the manager, Mr. Rogers and his family. It is an ideal home practically constructed and furnished in excellent taste under the supervision of Mrs. Rogers, who has not overlooked a cosy den for the master of the house.[7]

Clustered close to the mill, and meriting a starker description, were a "colony of bunk houses, Hindu homes, Japanese houses, and separate quarters for the white men."[8]

By 1910, French-Canadian lumber workers had been brought to Fraser Mills by the company; they were experienced and stable millhands, who appeared to be ideal employees. The French Canadians purchased lots immediately adjacent to the Fraser Mills townsite, and the community known as Maillardville began taking shape. These workers did indeed prove to be highly persistent and a steady source of labour for the C.W.L.C. For the francophone community at Maillardville, as well as for the ethnically mixed population of the Fraser Mills townsite, the mill was the focal point of every family's life.

Author G. W. Taylor has referred to Fraser Mills as a "model industrial village,"[9] and business and community leaders considered it a showcase. The nature of the community was described in the 1912 "Report to the Directors of the Canadian Western Lumber Company":

> Your company gives very careful consideration to the welfare of its employee. Modern homes are provided... provisions and supplies are sold at a normal advance over cost, all with a view of making the living expenses of our employees less than elsewhere in the Province. These advances, together with the steady employment assured by the continuous operation of your mills, the pleasant surroundings under which your employees work and with all the community spirit

developed at Fraser Mills—not only attracts to us and gives us the privilege of selecting the best men, but makes it easy for us to retain them . . . We have no labour troubles, a general feeling of content prevails among the employees.[10]

But the company was not motivated by altruism. By supplying housing and services, or making property available to its employees, the C.W.L.C. encouraged the dependence of the men and their families on the mill. The company reached into all facets of daily life, operating a clubhouse and community centre as well as organizing the Circle F dancing club and baseball team to fill their employees' leisure hours. The company had tight control over their employees' buying power: a company store was widely favoured by employees because of the community's geographic isolation and the need to buy on credit toward the end of the month.

In the early years, relations between the company and its employees were marked by symbolic gestures implying co-operation between capital and labour. At Christmas every married man would be given a turkey; in return the men would present gifts to the general manager, who, according to the *British Columbian*, "was gratified to know that such a feeling of harmony existed between him and his men."[11] Yet this "model industrial village" with its "feeling of harmony" would not long enjoy such organic unity. By 1931, labour relations had deteriorated sharply and workers and management stood polarized.

The workers at Fraser Mills in 1931 were drawn from twenty different national/ethnic groups, although some groups were represented only marginally. Table 1 categorizes the work force by country of origin. Some further distinctions can be made, as with English and French Canadians. English Canadians made up 22 per cent of the Fraser Mills work force; French Canadians accounted for 18 per cent of the millworkers, the second largest group. Despite the claims of the C.W.L.C. in 1909 that French Canadians would displace all Oriental workers at the mill, they did not. The continuing practice of using imported contract labour meant that a sizeable number of Japanese, Chinese, and East Indian workers were employed at Fraser Mills. Asian labour accounted for 150 of the millworkers in 1931, just over 20 per cent. Scandinavian workers, many of whom also came to the mill under contract, accounted for a sizeable percentage of the total work force: Norwegians made up almost 8 per cent, while Finnish and Swedish workers each accounted for 5 per cent. The British, at 13 per cent, and the Americans, at 3-1/2 per cent, were the other national groups well represented.

TABLE 1: WORK FORCE BY NATIONAL ORIGIN, 1931

	Number	% of total	% of Caucasians	% of Orientals, East Indians
French Canadian	121	18.0	24.1	0.0
English Canadian	145	22.2	28.9	0.0
Chinese	66	10.1	0.0	43.7
Japanese	56	8.5	0.0	37.0
Norwegian	51	7.8	10.2	0.0
English	45	6.8	9.0	0.0
Finnish	31	4.7	6.2	0.0
Swedish	31	4.7	6.2	0.0
East Indian	29	4.4	0.0	19.2
Scottish	19	2.9	3.8	0.0
American	17	2.6	3.4	0.0
Other	40	6.1	8.0	0.0
Unknown	2	.3	.4	0.0
	653	100.0	100.0	100.0

Apart from a breakdown by nationality, the work force can also be described in more general terms. The workers were predominantly young to middle-aged men: 63 per cent were under forty years of age. Many were married and household heads (53 per cent). Others were married but separated, with their wives and families overseas. With relatively stable employment histories at Fraser Mills — twenty-two men had been at the mill over eleven years and 57 per cent had been at the mill at least five years — many of the men had roots in the community. A kinship network also helped bond the millworkers. Between 35 and 40 per cent of the men had at least one relative working in the mill and probably more, if relatives by marriage could be identified. Yet another cohesive force existed in the high degree of residential concentration among millworkers. Indeed, co-residence of the workers was common. In any event, 66 per cent of the work force lived in either Fraser Mills or nearby Maillardville. For the most part, skill-level could not divide this work force; it was predominantly semi- or unskilled (82 per cent). Further ethnic/national divisions among the workers were offset by structural integration in the work place. Although there was divisive potential in the ethnic diversification of the work force, it was offset by patterns of persistence, residential concentration, and social levelling that characterized life at Fraser Mills/Maillardville. In 1931, these workers proved themselves to be effective fighters: all fought to maintain decent living standards, and many fought for the Red Flag.

The union which would challenge the company in 1931 was directly affiliated to the Communist Party of Canada (C.P.C). When the Lumber

Workers' Industrial Union began reorganizing in B.C. in 1928, its leadership included militants who had been active in the lumber workers' union during the O.B.U. years and early 1920's. In 1928, B.C.'s L.W.I.U. leaders turned to the Lumber and Agricultural Workers' Industrial Union centred in Northern Ontario for organizational assistance.[12] The Ontario Lumber Workers' Union was closely tied to the Communist Party through the Trade Union Educational League. After the Workers' Unity League was created as a labour central for Canadian trade unions, the Lumber Workers' Industrial Union immediately affiliated and embarked on an organizational drive which realized a clear success at Fraser Mills in the fall of 1931.

The 1931 Fraser Mills strike has not received much attention from historians; there has been some tendency to dismiss it as simply a symptom of communist agitation. J. R. Stewart notes that "some of the leading spirits in the strike were outsiders and one or two were quite candid about their Communist background."[13] While there were outsiders involved who had connections to the C.P.C., it is impossible to overlook the degree of support enjoyed by the L.W.I.U. at Fraser Mills. In fact, at Fraser Mills, 50 per cent of the employees had a union card prior to the first day of the strike. Over the duration of the strike this number grew to 461, or more than 70 per cent. Obviously the L.W.I.U. had achieved a wide base of support at Fraser Mills well before the strike began.[14]

This solid support base was a function of deteriorating labour standards. The years from 1921 to 1929 had provided the men with relatively stable incomes, but 1930 and 1931 brought an assault on the men's wages.[15] The payroll records provide hourly wage rates as well as annual earnings for the men at Fraser Mills: Table 2 gives an indication of the hourly wage rates being received by Caucasian workers. The mean hourly wage for white males of 34-1/2 cents is actually higher than most would have received. The curves were skewed by extremes on the top end of the range, and the median $ .314 and mode $ .313 give a much better indication of typical hourly wages. Wages had declined for the men who had worked at Fraser Mills from 1927 to 1931, or even 1921 to 1931 (Table 2). The early 1920's were not a time of economic buoyancy, but even then wages averaged substantially higher than in 1931. Wages did not begin dropping until early 1930; there were five major cuts between January 1930 and September 1931, and some men's wages were cut up to six times during that twenty-month period. Approximately one-third of a man's wages were withdrawn, a few cents at a time, until the going rate at the mill had fallen to 31 cents for married men, 27 cents for single men and twenty cents for Asians.

TABLE 2: HOURLY WAGES FOR CAUCASIAN WORKERS, 1921-31

	1921	1927	1931
Mean	$.417	$.488	$.344
Median	$.351	$.449	$.314
Mode	$.35	$.40	$.313
Range	$.20–$1.08	$.25–$1.25	$.185–$.84
Standard deviation	$.161	$.135	$.085

TABLE 3: INCOME DISTRIBUTION BY PERCENTAGE, 1921-31

Annual Income (Dollars)	1921	1923	1925	1927	1929	1930	1931
1– 399	0.0	0.8.	0.6	1.2	0.6	0.5	1.4
400– 499	2.3	0.0	0.6	1.2	0.8	1.4	12.2
500– 599	3.4	1.7	2.4	3.2	1.7	1.0	31.7
600– 699	1.1	0.0	1.8	1.2	3.4	3.8	16.7
700– 799	8.0	0.0	5.4	5.6	2.5	11.9	9.3
800– 899	10.2	5.0	7.2	9.7	9.3	16.2	10.6
900– 999	13.6	10.8	18.7	16.5	18.6	22.1	5.4
1000– 1099	9.1	11.7	6.6	10.9	13.8	8.8	3.8
1100– 1199	6.8	10.0	7.8	8.1	8.5	5.2	2.7
1200– 1299	12.5	6.7	6.0	5.6	5.4	4.3	1.1
1300– 1399	6.8	6.7	8.4	3.6	4.2	7.1	0.7
1400– 1499	6.8	10.0	4.8	5.6	5.1	4.3	0.9
1500– 1999	10.2	25.0	21.1	19.8	18.9	9.3	1.8
2000– 2999	6.8	8.3	6.0	6.0	4.8	3.6	1.4
3000– 3999	1.1	1.7	1.8	1.2	1.1	0.5	0.0
4000– 4999	0.0	0.0	0.0	0.0	0.0	0.0	0.0
5000– 5999	1.1	0.8	0.6	0.4	0.0	0.0	0.0
6000– 9999	0.0	0.8	0.0	0.0	0.6	0.2	0.2
Over 10000	0.0	0.0	0.0	0.0	0.6	0.0	0.0
	100.0	100.0	100.0	100.0	100.0	100.0	100.0
Mean	$1,268	$1,525	$1,327	$1,262	$1,343	$1,105	$739
Median	$1,117	$1,350	$1,166	$1,107	$1,085	$ 959	$616
Standard deviation	$ 670	$1,007	$ 634	$ 594	$1,084	$ 483	$397

In terms of annual earnings, the figures are even more dramatic. In 1931, 45 per cent of the work force earned less than $600 for a year's work (Table 3). Even had the men not been on strike for two and a half months, the average still would have been well below income levels reached in 1930.[16] The median is perhaps more useful a figure than the mean; by 1931, more than 50 per cent of the men earned less than $615.00, compared to $959.37 in 1930 and $1,085.00 in 1929. While prices were indeed falling during these years, they did not fall 30 per cent between 1929 and 1931—wages did. In fact, the *Labour Gazette* of February 1931 provides figures on the cost of living in Canada from 1913 to 1932 which show that retail prices began to drop in mid-1930. By September 1931, prices had dropped approximately 20 per cent. Prices for housing, fuel, and utilities dropped only slightly, although food costs dipped sharply. Nonetheless, the loss in real income is most definite. [17]

With $9.10 a week in basic food costs, the average family would have spent $473.20 each year; housing costs also added to basic expenditures. Thirty-four per cent of the Caucasian employees lived in the townsite, as did almost all of the 152 Chinese, Japanese, and East Indian workers. Some of the Caucasian workers living in Fraser Mills owned their own homes, but the vast majority rented from the company. Rents in the townsite ran from $8.00 to $11.00 per month on average; rents outside the townsite commonly ranged from $12.00 to $22.00. [18] Housing advertised in the *British Columbian* was available at anywhere from $10.00 to $30.00 per month, with most rents falling between $15.00 and $20.00. Rooms or suites ran from $8.00 to $20.00 per a month, while room and board could run as high as $28.00. [19] Estimating on a monthly basis, using median wage figures derived from Table 2, a man with a wife and three children would have a monthly income of approximately $64.00. Of that amount, the family could spend $39.43 on food, leaving $25.30 for housing costs, fuel, light, clothing, and miscellaneous expenses. Even a family renting from the C.W.L.C. at $8.00 a month, which was abnormally low, would have seen over 73 per cent of the household head's wages go for basic costs — food and shelter. For a family living outside the townsite, paying perhaps $15.00 monthly rent, as much as 85 or 90 per cent of a man's income could be taken up by mere subsistence costs. [20]

On 14 September 1931, the L.W.I.U. called its Fraser Mills membership to a meeting in the parish hall; 266 men met to determine a course of action in the face of further wage cuts and the company's dismissal of men refusing to work overtime. Demands were set and the question of possible strike action came to a vote with 181 in favour and 81 opposed. The demands set forth included a 10 per cent increase on all wages; time-and-a-half for overtime; an upward adjustment in the rate for shingles; and a closed shop for union men. The following day, two delegates approached Mackin, the general manager, to present the demands. On 16 September, the secretary recorded in the minutes of the Strike Committee that Mackin "simply said no." [21]

A second meeting on the evening of 16 September upheld the earlier decision to back the demands with strike action; the vote was 251 to 71. [22] Both union membership and the list of demands were growing. The number of men voting under the leadership of the L.W.I.U. had risen to 322 (or 50 per cent) of the Fraser Mills men in just two days. Additional demands included an end to wage discrimination between single and married men, as well as a further request for upward adjustment in the rate of shingles.[23] The L.W.I.U. also called for reinstatement of men fired earlier for refusing to work overtime.

A picket line went up at the mill the next morning, bringing operations to a standstill. Although the picket line may have grown in the telling over the years, it was clearly immense. The line was reinforced by 150 members of the National Unemployed Workingmen's Association (N.U.W.A.), many of whom were unemployed loggers living in Vancouver, as well as by non-union men who had arrived at the mill unaware of the union's activity.[24] Harold Pritchett, chairman of the Strike Committee, recalls that some of the organizational work took place on the line.[25] The plant superintendent estimated the strength of the line at 650 men. Other estimates range from 350 to 1,000.

The scene at the mill carried the threat of violence, but the strikers were not an undisciplined mob. The L.W.I.U. quickly formed a 31-man Strike Committee, then organized picket squads. When outbreaks of violence did occur, the Strike Committee and picket captains showed considerable control and restraint, and the first day of the strike passed in relative calm.

Tensions began escalating the following day, with the picket line standing at four to five hundred men, monitored by thirty-eight provincial police and six Mounties. With confrontation imminent, the provincial police responded swiftly to the municipality's request for assistance.[26]

The company, fearing its property threatened, had the grounds patrolled by an armed "Special Watch," comprised of foremen and superintendents.[27] With machine guns mounted at the entrance to the mill, and police in constant surveillance, violence would be met with violence —thus an uneasy truce prevailed.[28]

The third day of the strike brought action from provincial authorities. According to the *British Columbian* of 19 September 1931, "John Doe" warrants had been issued for the arrest of men alleged to be ringleaders of the previous days' events. Mounted city police from Vancouver, directed by W. L. R. Dunwody, assistant commissioner of the British Columbia Provincial Police,[29] drove demonstrators away from the mill entrance, arresting ten men: "Police had picked the men among the crowd whom they wished to arrest, and the whole procedure was methodically arranged... Officers walked into the crowd and picked up the men they wanted."[30]

Of the ten men arrested, only two were on the Strike Committee; however at least four, and perhaps six, were millworkers. Four of those arrested were from Vancouver, with addresses in Gastown (the center of N.U.W.A. activities); they were likely N.U.W.A. members. One of the arrested men had been active in the heyday of the One Big Union (O.B.U.)[31] All ten were charged with unlawful assembly, and two faced additional charges of assaulting a constable. The first charge was later reworded and finally dismissed and the two men charged with assault received a two-day jail sentence.[32] The city police remained on the scene, and later in the day R.C.M.P. arrived to help disperse the crowd which had regathered at the mill entrance. As the *Unemployed Worker*, the N.U.W.A. press, put it, "Bingham's bloody Cossacks" had been sent to "club workers back on the job."[33]

While strikers struggled to hold positions on the picket line, the union's negotiators engaged in a head-on battle with Mackin. Negotiations were aggravated by the L.W.I.U.'s attempts, generally unsuccessful, to extend the strike to four other mills in the area.[34] The activities of the L.W.I.U. not only agitated Mackin but also prompted a committee of lumbermen to seek assistance from the provincial government. On 13 October, a committee including Mackin, H. R. McMillan, A. Flavelle, F. E. Harrison and twenty other lumbermen met with the provincial cabinet. The Conservative, business-conscious government of Premier S. F. Tolmie issued a warning to labour agitators:

> Industry in this province is going to be protected to the fullest extent of the law. We have assured the lumbermen that when men want to work they are not prevented from doing so by any intimidation or otherwise. The lumbermen assure us that their troubles lately have been due to agitators and Communists and they have given us detailed facts on various difficulties they have had in labour matters to support this contention.[35]

Small wonder the scene at the picket line continued to be tense. Attorney-General R. W. Pooley declared that the full resources of the province, backed by the federal government, would be available to enable men to work. "British Columbia," said Mr. Pooley, "did not intend to stand for the fomentation of industrial disputes in its mills and plants by imported radicals."[36] Most of the radicals, however, were not "imported" but came from the mills and logging camps of British Columbia.

The L.W.I.U. recognized the need for industry-wide organization in the face of the consolidation of interests by B.C. lumbermen. If other mills in the area had gone out, the strikers' demands would have been strengthened. And the Strike Committee shared the L.W.I.U.'s commitment to industry-wide organization. A statement made by George Lamont, L.W.I.U. president, before a meeting of the New Westminster Trades and Labour Council, illustrates this intent rather succinctly:

> In a short time 40,000 lumber and logging employees in B.C. will be organized in one union . . . the lumber workers will enlist all trade unions in their cause to secure improved living conditions from the lumbermen. We intend to fight the Fraser Mills company and the Federated Timber Mills of B.C. not on the basis of communism but on the basis of bread and butter.[37]

However, other mills continued to produce lumber for the C.W.L.C.[38] With relations between Mackin and the union strained, negotiations followed an inconsistent course. Three weeks of inertia would follow.

The C.W.L.C. finally made a move during the first week in October. The company's new attitude of conciliation came in the wake of the enforced closure of the Comox Logging company, (a C.W.L.C subsidiary), which employed three hundred men and supplied lumber to Fraser Mills.[39] With two operations threatened, the company proved more willing to bargain. In response to a federal Department of Labour report on a 2 October meeting with Tom Bradley and the Strike Committee, Mackin stated that he was prepared to make a substantial offer, subject to the approval of J. D. McCormack, vice president of the C.W.L.C. The offer included restoration of an earlier wage cut; an increase in the rate paid for shingles; willingness to meet with an employees' committee (although not formally with the L.W.I.U.), and a guarantee of no discrimination against union men.[40]

The offer, while less than the union sought, was not unreasonable in its immediate concessions. In making the offer, Mackin stipulated that it be put to a vote by secret ballot under the direction of Mayor Gray of New Westminster, Reeves McDonald of Coquitlam, and Pritchard of Burnaby. Ballots would be sent by mail to every man on the payroll. Reaction to the offer was mixed among the Strike Committee: union organizer Bradley opposed it strenuously, arguing against both the offer and the voting method. Not only did the offer dismiss the union's role, but it was also inadequate in its failure to address many outstanding grievances: "the dismissal of certain foremen, the elimination of payment of rent for some Orientals and the reinstatement of certain men . . . dismissed two months before the strike."[41] Nonetheless, Bradley and the Strike Committee agreed to present the offer at the next union meeting. They did so, but hardly impartially. After hearing Bradley and a Communist leader identified only as Finley "ridicule the proposal" and denounce Gray, McDonald, Pritchard, Bell, and Harrison as "tools of the capitalists," all 389 men at the meeting voted to reject the company's offer.[42]

Harrison and Mackin felt that, if permitted to vote without outside influence, the men would accept the offer.[43] Their decision to go ahead with a registered vote by ballot proved them wrong. The vote, held 16 October, received a dismal turnout. It would be another forty days before the strike would end. During that time a non-union Employees' Committee would enter into negotiations; composed of men with union ties, the committee would eventually divorce itself from the L.W.I.U. The final vote to end the strike and accept the C.W.L.C.'s terms would be held in two halls, one for union men, and one for non-union.

The offer accepted on 20 November had originally been made on 6 October 1931. It was not modified in the slightest. Only voting procedures had been relaxed. Why had it not been accepted earlier? The answer seems fairly obvious. The company would have concluded the strike through settlement with the non-union committee. Yet the majority of the men were not willing to allow the C.W.L.C. to circumvent the union. Although the company would brook no part of the original demand for union recognition and a closed shop, a union of the men was a fact which Mackin could not negate; in the end, he could only ignore it.

Although the *Labour Gazette* of November 1931 considered the strike a compromise, the concessions won by the strikers were substantial. In the context of the early depression, all gains made by labour are noteworthy. Any analysis of the 1931 strike must address the following questions: why did labour organization succeed at Fraser Mills when it failed elsewhere in the region, and to what extent was the community radicalized? In taking on the C.W.L.C., the union initially seemed no match for its opponent. Yet the strike was remarkably successful, particularly in view of the many forces working against it. The reason is threefold: firstly, with wages falling faster and farther than prices, the material conditions were ripe; secondly, the leadership core of the union proved both effective administrators and skilled politicians in their own right; and finally, the community of Fraser Mills/Maillardville exhibited characteristics conducive to both organization and protest.

Since the Lumber Workers Industrial Union had tried organizing elsewhere with little success, the features internal to this particular community and work force must be considered.[44] Fraser Mills/Maillardville was still somewhat isolated geographically in 1931. Most of those who lived there were working class, and most worked for a single employer; thus, the employees came into daily contact with each other both on and off the job. As indicated above, the millworkers and community members were linked by a strong kinship network in addition to a high degree of residential and occupational contact. While there is no doubt that ethnic or national origin played a large role in determining social relationships, it is equally clear that it did not place insurmountable barriers between the workers at Fraser Mills. There were points of contact which mitigated against intra-class conflict. The majority of workers were semi- or unskilled, earning similar, declining wages bi-monthly. The men, many of whom were young and married with roots in the community, vented their frustrations through strike action. The network born of residential, familial, and class bonds sustained communal survival during the long strike.

While Maillardville was not a company town in the strict sense of the word, Fraser Mills most certainly was, and the municipal line separating the two was of little consequence. Management and workers formed two distinct social groups early in the community's history. There is no evidence of any spontaneous social interaction between them, although frequently managers and their families lived in the community. It may be that managers and foremen frequented the social gatherings of millworkers and their families, but the reverse is most unlikely. No workers' names appear on the lists of those taking part in "fishing and picnic excursions" held in the community's early years.[45] Although foremen joined mill managers for "social evenings," other millworkers did not.[46] And few of the millworkers' wives would have had time to join the Fraser Mills Ladies Alpine Club for hiking expeditions, even had an invitation been extended.[47]

The working class had different social outlets. Often co-ordinated by the company or the church, the men and their families gathered for dances, games, picnics, and sports events. As well, the family and neighbourhood ties of the millworkers afforded plenty of opportunity for "social evenings" of their own.[48] Religious organizations such as the Knights of Columbus, the League of the Blessed Heart, la Confrerie du Tres Saint Sacrement, and the Ladies of Ste. Anne were also part of the associational framework, at least for the Catholic workers.[49] Although managers and foremen lived in the same community, social distance was great. A vast discrepancy in wealth was obvious, and it underlay the social relationships which developed. Visible symbols of the economic and social polarization could be found in the large gracious homes of the mill managers, some of which still stand today. These homes stood in sharp contrast to the squalid "Hindu Homes" and rows of workers' cottages found in Fraser Mills, or the modest homes of the French Canadians in Maillardville.

At Fraser Mills, the social cohesiveness of the working class allowed a

clear expression of collective identity. Community members pooled resources and "articulated the identity of their interests"[50] through their
actions during the strike. The behaviour of the millworkers presupposes
certain values and attitudes indicative of collective, not individualistic
interests. If considered in context, political content can be easily seen.
Throughout the long strike, the men and women of the community
worked together to ensure their mutual welfare. Although French Canadians took the lead, the entire community was involved in building a support system. Polarization of interests—"the company wouldn't give in
and the men wouldn't give in"—cemented working-class bonds.[51]

Numerous measures were undertaken to ensure the community's survival. A relief kitchen, run by the wives and mothers of strikers, supplied
meals to single men. On the second day of the strike, a relief committee
was elected to begin the task of keeping the kitchen operating and to provide food and fuel to families. This group included many members of the
Strike Committee, as well as representatives from the Japanese and
Chinese communities. A "Bumming Committee" of three was designated, with two centres set up to receive donations, one in Maillardville
and one at the National Unemployed Working Men's Association headquarters in Gastown, which also served as headquarters for the union.[52]
Food, donated by a variety of associations and communities as well as by
local merchants, brought relief to many families. Skills and services were
traded. Whether repairing shoes, cutting hair, keeping wood supplied,
organizing fund-raisers, or soliciting donations on the street corner, the
community pitched in.

Women as well as men played an active role in maintaining services
and morale. The Woman's Labour League claimed a membership of
ninety, "all in favor of a good, long fight."[53] Women, predominantly
but not exclusively French-Canadian, ran the relief kitchen (with the help
of two kitchen boys), addressed meetings, organized petitions in aid of
the arrested men, and served on the bumming committees. They also attended the picket line and demonstrated, with their children, in support
of the strikers. The *British Columbian* reports a demonstration held 25
September outside the Coquitlam municipal hall: "While provincial police mounted guard on the hall, a crowd gathered on the lawn, the boule-
vard and across the road. Fifty children of school age, marching two
abreast, were brought from Millside school, led by a determined looking
lady with a stout stick."[54]

This demonstration would end peacefully, but on other occasions
women became involved in direct confrontations with police.[55] The
women's support was indispensable and a strong indication of unity,
community of interest, and determination. Backing for the strike came

from other sources as well. Representatives of the Asian workers not only sat on the Relief Committee but also were instrumental in securing donations. Vegetables donated by the Japanese farmhands of Hammond municipality stretched out food supplies. The Asian workers also set up bumming committees which enabled them to make direct cash contributions to the relief fund.

Relief funds, which often ran dangerously low, were bolstered by sports events, concerts, and dances, all organized by the strikers. An amateur show troupe performed in aid of the men and their families. Some financial assistance came from the New Westminster Trades and Labour Council, and the organized fishermen donated part of their catch for strike relief. Area residents donated generously to rummage sales held to generate strike funds, and some actively solicited funds even though they did not work for the C.W.L.C. and had no connection with the L.W.I.U.[56] The money raised kept the relief kitchen running for a month and a half until it finally closed on 5 November, about two weeks before the strike ended. Through early November almost two hundred families continued receiving direct relief supplies which, while barely adequate, improved a desperate situation. Many of the fund-raising techniques first used during the strike were employed again during the ensuing depression years, indicating that community response was more than just an isolated reaction to a specific situation. Those individuals who were instrumental in co-ordinating relief work continued their activities for the Unemployed Movement in the early 1930's.[57]

That the worker community was willing to fight for its interests was itself a political statement. Yet there are further indications of radicalization within the community. The French-Canadian community serves as an illustration. During the strike, the parish priest, Father Teck, tried to intervene directly to send the men back to work. In his endeavours to redirect his spiritual charges, Father Teck used a variety of tactics; in his 28 September sermon, for example, he spoke out against "communists and radical revenge"[58] while sending up a "priere pour la bonne fin" to the labour dispute.[59] This censure, widely interpreted as a denouncement of the union, created tension in the rank and file. Nonetheless they stayed off the job. Father Teck then moved from general condemnations to specific threats. If the men did not surrender their union cards they could not receive absolution in the confessional. Members of the Strike Committee approached the priest at a neighbouring parish, and for a time residents of Fraser Mills/Maillardville attended Sunday mass in New Westminster.

The adherence of the French Canadians to Catholicism did not deter them from militant action, however. These French Canadians were in transition. While still tied to the church, they were undergoing a realignment of loyalties and readjustment of values. In addition to the general pressures of assimilation, the French Canadians, particularly the second-generation millworkers, found a new cultural source to be the mill floor, seeing the associations formed in the work place just as fundamental to their lives as those developed through the church. In the midst of their cultural redefinition, the assault on their standard of living in the early 1930's was the catalyst which prompted French Canadians to start thinking and acting like a class, rather than simply a parish.[60]

Many of the strike leaders developed a well-defined class analysis and voiced their critique of capitalism in no uncertain terms, even though they chose to downplay revolutionary ideology. Some of them became members of the C.P.C. after the strike.[61] The local section of the C.P.C. claimed between thirty and forty members,[62] and meetings were attended by prominent members of the community.[63] The Unemployed Movement remained active in the community as well, but the community as a whole showed more support for the democratic socialism of the Independent Labour Party and, later, the Co-operative Commonwealth Federation (C.C.F.). In fact, the strength traditionally enjoyed by the Liberal Party in the community shifted to the C.C.F.[64]

The political experience of the workers at Fraser Mills and their response to the early depression were conditioned by a variety of factors. The initial impetus to organize, derived from falling living standards, was facilitated by the social cohesion developed within the context of a company town. This collective response and the bitterness engendered by the strike served to radicalize the community. Social protest did not end with the strike settlement, and throughout the 1930's the church and company continued working to hold protest in check. Yet, amidst these tensions, labour protest continued quietly but persistently, finding political expression in the Unemployed Movement, in limited support for the C.P.C., and in the more widespread adherence of the community to the democratic socialism of the C.C.F.

Despite scattered victories, the 1920's were lean years for labour, and the early 1930's were even worse. Not until the latter half of the decade, and the emergence of the C.I.O. did the labour movement begin to regain lost ground. During the first years of the depression, the Workers' Unity League was the only labour organization on the move: its organizers could be found in the textile mills of Quebec, the coal fields of Alberta, the garment factories of Toronto, Winnipeg, and Montreal, and the lumber camps and sawmills of British Columbia. The gains made for the working class by the W.U.L. are often overlooked, diminished by the tragedy of Estevan and overshadowed by the fratricidal struggles precipitated by the red unionists.

The contribution of the working class should not be ignored, however. As has been shown, the workers at Fraser Mills did not achieve large wage increases, their union was not recognized, and many of their demands were never seriously considered. Yet the downward spiral of wages stopped. Community residents recall that the 1931 strike not only improved company policy towards its work force, but it also brought an end to what one resident called "nationalism," referring to ethnically or nationally provoked antagonism. The communist role in achieving these ends must be acknowledged.

While the revolutionary leadership of the W.U.L. and the C.P.C. doubtless had more far-reaching objectives, the strike was successful for it as well as for the workers. As at Cowansville, Quebec the same year, the C.P.C. had made no inroads among workers until the strike. Addressing practical rather than theoretical issues, the W.U.L. organizers were met enthusiastically by the workers. Labour unrest was a fact at Fraser Mills before the L.W.I.U. appeared on the scene, but it required a coherent outlet, and the L.W.I.U. offered an institutional structure capable of focusing that unrest. The C.P.C., on the other hand, managed to secure a presence in a major industrial plant (not to mention the church choir!).

The 1931 strike is of significance to labour historians for a number of reasons. It shows the response of a segment of the working class to the exigencies of the economic depression, and it is the history of action by the working class and of reaction by the repressive forces of church, state, and capital interests. But the 1931 organization of men at Fraser Mills is also part of the wider history of organization in the lumber industry. As the first strike in a B.C sawmill to derive support along industrial rather than craft lines—support which strengthened labour's hand—the strike was clearly a step forward for labour in British Columbia. The 1931 Fraser Mills strike would be followed by further organizational efforts which signalled that organizer Bradley's prediction of industrywide organization would be fulfilled. Indeed, Harold Pritchett, chairman of the Strike Committee at Fraser Mills in 1931, would become the founding president of the International Woodworkers of America just six years later.

NOTES

1. J. Stewart, "Early Days at Fraser Mills" (n.p., n.d.) 23; and Margaret Ormsby, *British Columbia: A History* (Toronto: Macmillan, 1976), p.376.
2. Stewart, "Early Days," p.27.
3. Ormsby, *British Columbia,* p.357.
4. Stewart, "Early Days," p.15.
5. New Westminster *British Columbian,* 20 June 1908.
6. The community formally became Fraser Mills in 1913 but took the name some years earlier.
7. *British Columbian,* 20 June 1908.
8. Stewart, "Early Days," p.17.
9. G. W. Taylor, *Timber* (Vancouver: J. J. Douglas, 1975), p.93.
10. Crown Zellerbach Limited, Private Collection, "Report to the Directors of the Canadian Western Lumber Company," Financial Statement, Canadian Western Lumber Company, 1912. Crown Zellerbach acquired the records of the C.W.L.C. in its 1953 takeover of the company. The collection includes payroll, personnel, and municipal records of Fraser Mills. All C.W.L.C. and Fraser Mills records cited are in this collection.
11. An expanded discussion of the work force and its characteristics on the eve of the strike can be found in Jeanne Meyers Williams, "Ethnicity and Class Conflict in Fraser Mills/Maillardville: The Strike of 1931" (M.A. thesis, Simon Fraser University, 1982), Chapter 2.
12. The Lumber and Agricultural Workers' Industrial Union changed its name to Lumber Workers' Industrial Union in 1932. L.W.I.U. will be used to refer to the union during both periods.
13. J. R. Stewart, "French-Canadian Settlement in British Columbia" (M.A. thesis, University of British Columbia, 1956), p. 67.
14. University of British Columbia Library, Special Collections, I.W.A./Pritchett Collection, Minutes of the Strike Committee, files 10-11, 10-12. As the minutes of the Strike Committee serve as a base reference for the account of the strike, they will be cited only when quoted directly.
15. See Williams, "Ethnicity and Class Conflict in Fraser Mills/Maillardville," Chapter 3.
16. For example, a man earning $600.00 in 1931 might have earned as much as $757.00 had the mill not been shut down for two-and-a-half months and had the company not kept reducing wages below the levels reached by September 1931. It is probable that the men would have seen further wage cuts, which were the company's solution to slumping markets. The above figure is derived from the following formula: $600/9.5 = 63.15 \times 12 = 757, where $600 is actual earnings in 1931, 9.5 the number of months worked, $63.15 the average monthly income, and $757 projected by multiplying average monthly income by twelve months. If this formula is applied to the figures in Table 2, close to half the men would have earned less than $757 in 1931, a $200 drop over 1930 earnings.
17. Canada, Department of Labour, *Labour Gazette, 1932* (Ottawa: F. A. Acland, 1933), p.231.
18. As an example, a six-room house with modern conveniences would rent for $18.00 or more. *Labour Gazette, 1931,* p.1145.
19. *British Columbian,* September 1931. The classified ads were surveyed to estimate rental costs outside the townsite at the time of the strike.
20. As Terry Copp points out in *The Anatomy of Poverty: The Condition of the Working Class in Montreal, 1900-1929* (Toronto: McClelland & Stewart, 1974), p.31, the modern Statistics Canada definition of poverty—"any family spending more than 70 per cent of total income on food, clothing and shelter"—places the majority of

the population which he studied below the poverty line. Certainly the majority of Fraser Mills workers were in similar circumstances.

21. Minutes of the Strike Committee, 14 September 1931.
22. Vancouver *Daily Province,* 17 September 1931.
23. The new demands included a raise of two cents per thousand for No. 1 shingles and twelve cents per thousand for No. 2 shingles.
24. Hercules Lamoureux, a labourer at the mill, stated: "I didn't even know there was a Lumber Workers' Union. I had not heard of it until the morning I went to work." By the afternoon he was on the Strike Committee. Vancouver Oral History Project, Vancouver, B.C., 25 April 1972.
25. Interview with Harold Pritchett by Clay Perry, 30 October 1978, I.W.A., Regional Council 1.
26. Crown Zellerbach Limited, Correspondence, Municipal Records, Fraser Mills.
27. Interview with Harold Pritchett by Clay Perry, 27 October 1978, I.W.A., Regional Council 1.
28. Minutes of the Strike Committee, 24 September 1931; and author's interview with Leo Canuel, 14 August 1981.
29. *Daily Province,* 19 September 1931.
30. *British Columbian,* 19 September 1931.
31. Canuel interview, 14 August 1981; and Leo Canuel, written submission, I.W.A., Regional Council 1.
32. *British Columbian,* 25 September 1931.
33. *Unemployed Worker,* 19 September 1931.
34. *British Columbian,* 23, 24, 29, 30 September and 7, 8 October 1931.
35. Ibid., 13 October 1931.
36. Ibid., 13 October 1931.
37. Ibid., 22 October 1931.
38. Ibid., 30 September 1931.
39. F. E. Harrison to Ward, 8 October 1931, Public Archives of Canada, Department of Labour, RG27, Strikes and Lockouts File, Fraser Mills, 1931. Unless otherwise cited all correspondence is from this source.
40. Ibid., 6, 7 October 1931.
41. Ibid., 7 October 1931.
42. Ibid., 14 October 1931; and Minutes of the Strike Committee, 9 October 1931.
43. Harrison to Ward, 7 October 1931.
44. See Williams, "Ethnicity and Class Conflict at Fraser Mills/Maillardville," Chapter 2.
45. *British Columbian,* 31 July 1911.
46. Ibid., 2 April 1907.
47. Ibid., 1 May 1911.
48. Canuel interview, 14 August 1981.
49. S.F.U. Archives, RG91, Parish Records, Notre Dame de Lourdes, Scrapbooks and Photos, Annual Report to the Vancouver Archdiocese, 1931, and Father Teck's Notebook, November 1929 to December 1934.
50. To borrow a phrase from E. P. Thompson.
51. Interview with Arthur Laverdure, Vancouver Oral History Project, 25 April 1972.
52. Undated letter, Arne Johnson to Myrtle Bergren, I.W.A., Regional Council 1.
53. Minutes of the Strike Committee, 1 October 1931.
54. *British Columbian,* 25 September 1931.
55. Canuel interview, 14 August 1981, and Minutes of the Strike Committee, 18 October 1931.
56. Such instances are recorded throughout the Minutes of the Strike Committee.
57. Canuel interview, 14 August 1981.
58. Minutes of the Strike Committee, 28 September 1931.

59. S.F.U. Archives, RG91, Parish Records, Notre Dame de Lourdes, Father Teck's Notebook, 27 September 1931.
60. Gregory Baum points out that, during the 1930's, Catholics protested the existing social order in a variety of ways. Some lent their support to the C.C.F. As Baum puts it, these "non-conformist Catholics ... demonstrated diversity within the Catholic Church even in a period when great stress was put on conformity." See Gregory Baum, *Catholics and Canadian Socialism* (Toronto: Lorimer and Company, 1980), p.8.
61. Canuel interview, 14 August 1981; and interview by Clay Perry with Harold Pritchett, 23 October 1981, I.W.A., Regional Council No. 1.
62. Canuel interview, 18 August 1981; Pritchett interview, 23 October 1981. Oddly enough, Father Teck's annual report of 1933 stated that thirty-five of his parishioners were negligent in their religious duties. S.F.U. Archives, RG91, Parish Records, Notre Dame de Lourdes, Annual Report to the Vancouver Diocese, 1933.
63. Canuel interview, 18 August 1981; and Pritchett interview, 23 October 1981.
64. In the 1933 provincial election in B.C., the C.C.F. candidate for the Dewdney electoral district received strong support, although he was defeated. (*British Columbian*, 3 November 1933). Two years later, C. G. MacNeil, the C.C.F. candidate running federally would be elected with the help of the voters of Fraser Mills/Maillardville. (*British Columbian*, 15 October 1935). See also Stewart, "French-Canadian Settlement," p.143.

9

Ethnicity and Class
in the Farm Labour Process

ALAN DUTTON
and
CYNTHIA CORNISH

INTRODUCTION

There are an estimated 20,000 seasonal farm workers in British Columbia. The majority are recent immigrants from the Punjab region of India,
and they constitute the bulk of the labour force which is required to hand-
harvest fruits, vegetables, and berry crops in the Fraser Valley. Because
seasonal farm labour is excluded from minimum wage laws, health and
safety regulations, and other labour standards legislation, East Indian
farm workers suffer some of the worst working conditions in Canada.

There have been few attempts to explain this kind of discrimination
and disadvantage in the province.[1] The few studies which address the issue of Asian-Euro-Canadian relations and labour market segmentation
tend to reduce the problem to one of culture or to the economic benefits
of racism and cheap labour for Anglo-Canadians. For example, Ward
argues that in the past Asian immigrants suffered racial prejudice,
hostility, and discrimination because Anglo-Canadians feared that Asian
ethnic groups posed a threat to European cultural institutions, traditions,
and values (Ward, 1978; 1980). On the other hand, Li (1979) argues that
the root cause of ethnic antagonisms, racial prejudice, and job discrimination does not lie in culture, but in the utilitarian interest of Europeans
in cheap Asian labour. Li maintains that Asian labour was created as a
separate category through job segregation and that this benefited virtually
all Europeans, including workers, politicians, and employers.

However, neither culturalist nor economistic explanations provide an
adequate framework for understanding ethnic relations in the farm labour

process. In fact, local labour unions, the B.C. Federation of Labour, and the Canadian Labour Council as well as community groups and social activists have provided funding and support to organize a farm-workers' union, despite the supposed importance of cultural differences or the alleged economic interests of Anglo-Canadian workers in exploiting Asian workers. In contrast, and regardless of ethnic origin, labour contractors and farm owners have strongly opposed the formation of a union to protect farm workers.

This broad-based support and the opposition it has elicited indicate the importance of viewing the social organization of agricultural production not from the perspective of ethnic relations, but from the point of view of contradictory class interests in the development and expansion of the capitalist mode of production (Dutton, 1984; Miles and Spounley, 1985). In this view, workers must sell their labour in order to survive while capitalists attempt to maximize profits at the expense of workers' incomes. Thus, minimum wage laws, health and safety protections, unemployment insurance payments, and Workers' Compensation are opposed by capital because they directly affect profit margins. Workers, on the other hand, have sought legislative protections to improve both working conditions and wage-rates. Since a pool of cheap labour is a threat to organized labour, it is in its interests to help the unorganized form unions to raise wage levels.[2] The following analysis of ethnicity in the farm labour process uses this perspective to explain the legislation governing working conditions, health and safety regulations, and the attempts to organize a Canadian farm workers' union.

REGULATING FARM LABOUR

The farm labour process in British Columbia is essentially an anachronism in modern state capitalism. Farm workers are used as stoop labour to hand-harvest fruits, berries, and vegetables at below the minimum wage for up to twelve hours a day, seven days a week.

Workers are recruited by two methods: through provincial employment bureaus and by the contract labour system. In the former case, the federal government provides funds for farm labour pools where workers are advised of grower requirements. In the latter, labour contractors directly exploit their connections with ethnic communities to recruit labour for farm owners. The vast majority of farm workers are recruited by this method.

Workers are transported to farms in open trucks which are often overcrowded and unsafe. Women, children, and men are forced to hang onto ropes attached to the front of the cab as trucks navigate the roads to farms. This method of transporting workers has resulted in a number of serious accidents. Yet, despite highway traffic laws to regulate transportation, the conveyance of farm workers is rarely policed (Johnson, 1974).

There is also a lack of policing of health and safety on the job. It has been argued that this lack of policing is directly responsible for the high farm-accident rate.[3] In addition, there are constant horror stories of workers being directly sprayed with chemicals and being forced to work in newly sprayed, or "wet," fields (Sandborn, 1981; Labonte, 1982). According to one recent survey, workers experienced a high level of exposure to pesticides regardless of job type or crop. It is often stated that regulation of pesticide use on private land is unnecessary given that most growers follow the recommended guidelines of the Ministry of Agriculture pertaining to safety and health. The reality, we find, is quite the opposite. In a recent study eight out of ten of those surveyed *regularly* suffer from direct contact (on skin or clothing) with pesticides and almost one-fifth often breathe pesticide fumes while working. The rest reported working in fields which had been sprayed recently (Abbotsford Community Services, 1982).

Moreover, while most workers in B.C. are protected by Workers' Compensation and by strict regulation of health and safety standards, these do not apply to farm workers. The Workers' Compensation Board (W.C.B.) was established with two objectives in mind. The first was to provide no-fault insurance to employees injured during the course of their work and to compensate workers for the income lost as a result of injury. The second objective of the W.C.B. was to ensure safety in the work place through both research and a programme of accident prevention. This has benefited most workers since they have been able to receive compensation without having to resort to the long and costly process of suing employers for damages. This does not apply to farm workers. While they are forced to work in a dangerous industry with exposure to noxious chemicals and back strain, they are not provided with the same health and safety protections afforded to other workers.

In addition, farm owners do not provide farm workers the hygienic facilities which they are supposedly compelled by law to provide. The lack of basic facilities ranges from toilets to drinking water. More serious neglect involves the lack of adequate housing for migrant workers. While the Industrial Camp Regulations (part of the *Health Act*) govern housing for workers in isolated environments, these have not been enforced (B.C. Human Rights Commission, 1983). An inquiry surveying living conditions for farm workers found that the barns, chicken coops and tents in which workers were forced to stay were like "Nazi concentration camps" and unfit for human habitation (ibid.). Other serious consequences of the failure to administer the legislation involve the spraying of living areas with pesticides.

To compound this, farm workers are not given the same protections as other workers under the *Employment Standards Act* (1981). This act consolidates earlier legislation governing hours of work, child labour laws, termination of employment, and holidays. As with the legislation governing minimum conditions of work, the new act is supposed to set the minimum standards for *all* workers in the province. Yet the regulations which govern the administration of the act specifically exclude farm workers historically employed on a piece-work basis to hand-harvest fruit, vegetables and berry crops from its major provisions and set separate piece-rates for each type of crop harvested.

Farm workers have also been denied the right to unionize. This was finally corrected in 1975. The New Democratic Party government appointed a Select Standing Committee on Labour and Justice which toured the province in order to solicit opinions on reforms to labour legislation affecting both domestic and farm workers. Ironically, the first farm workers to take advantage of the inclusion of farm work under the British Columbia Labour Code were a group of university and college students employed on a 38,000 acre farm unit owned by South Peace Farms, a joint venture of two U.S.-based corporations. To date this is still one of the few organized farms in the province.

A third piece of legislation which discriminates against farm workers is the federal Unemployment Insurance Act (U.I.C.). Regulation 16 of the act stipulates that employees must work more than twenty-two consecutive days in any one establishment in order to have that period counted towards benefits. However, since farm workers usually work for shorter periods on many farms over the growing season, this stipulation is rarely met. As a result, the majority of farm workers are seldom able to qualify for U.I.C. despite having worked for the required total number of weeks.

In short, farm workers face a wide range of legislative "omissions," making their work not only difficult and dirty but also dangerous. These conditons have helped to maintain an ethnically segmented labour market in which labour is cheap and expendable. This, of course, is profitable for farm owners, many of whom have a short-term interest in excluding farm work from provincial and federal labour and safety legislation.

The N.D.P., community workers, and the Canadian Farm Workers Union argue that it makes no moral or legal sense to discriminate against farm workers by not providing them with the same protections afforded to workers in other industries. This systematic discrimination does, however, make economic sense when viewed in terms of the growth of corporate farming in British Columbia. This trend is discussed in the following section.

CONCENTRATION AND CENTRALIZATION OF
AGRICULTURAL PRODUCTION

Over the past two decades there has been a dramatic reorganization of agricultural production in B.C. This is evident in terms of farm size and the distribution of farm revenue. For example, between 1950 and 1981 the number of farm units decreased from 26,406 to 20,012 units. This represents a loss of nearly one-quarter of B.C. farms. Yet land in agricultural production has actually increased by 17 per cent over the same period. These figures point to concentration in the agricultural industry which is resulting in fewer but larger farm units (see Table 1).

The concentration of production is also evident in terms of the distribution of cash sales. In 1981, agriculture cash sales amounted to just under eight hundred million dollars. Yet only 19.7 per cent of B.C. farms—fewer than 4,000—accounted for 87 per cent of all cash sales —nine-tenths of production. More than one-half of all cash sales was produced in one area: the Fraser Valley—the main region in which seasonal farm labour is used. This, it may be argued, amounts to a high degree of centralization and concentration of agricultural production (see Mullan, 1974; Malcolmson, n.d.).

At the same time as the number of farms has decreased, the number of paid farm workers has increased dramatically, replacing family farm and owner-operator labour. For example, between 1953 and 1977 the percentage of paid farm workers doubled. As a result, nearly half of all farm work is performed by paid workers as opposed to unpaid family or owner-operator labour. Many of the paid workers in the agricultural labour force are seasonal workers. While estimates vary, during the peak harvest period from July to September, there may be as many as 20,000 paid workers employed at the same time to harvest produce. In contrast, the winter months may see as few as 4,000 paid workers employed (Department of Agriculture, 1974; Sharma, 1983).

This same trend to paid farm labour is also evident in the agricultural industry across Canada. In 1953, for example, paid farm workers formed 13.2 per cent of the Canadian farm-labour force but by 1977 they comprised 31 per cent. The per cent of unpaid family workers declined over the same period from 21.4 per cent of the agricultural labour force to

17.98 percent (Table 2). Statistics compiled by Mullan (1974) and Malcolmson (n.d.) reveal a close association between the larger, more productive units and the use of paid farm workers. In 1971, for example, 40
per cent of the province's farms reported using paid labour. Of these
farms, 17 per cent had cash sales over $35,000, but employed 60 per cent
of all paid labour. While it is difficult to compare 1971 with later years
because of the effects of inflation and the classification of farms by cash
sales, statistics for 1981 show that 87 per cent of that labour was accounted for by farms with sales in excess of $25,000.

These figures refute the notion that farm labour is spread evenly
throughout the agricultural industry and that, by implication, higher farm
labour costs would necessarily drive the small family farm out of business. In fact, it could be argued that cheap farm labour gives a special
and unwarranted advantage to corporate agriculture. As an American
farmers' organization testified to the United States Congress: "If cheap
labour was not available to the corporate-type farming operations, we believe the family-type farmers could compete on a more favourable basis
with the corporate operators" (cited in Canadian Farm Workers' Union,
1981).

Yet large growers have apparently convinced the B.C. government
that cheap labour benefits the whole industry. As a result, the government has consistently refused to implement long-awaited reforms to legislation because of the argument that increased costs would drive farmers
out of the market in the face of cheaper California produce (B.C. Select
Standing Committee on Labour and Justice, 1975; Farm Workers' Organizing Committee, 1980). Indeed, draconian measures have been taken
to preserve an essentially pre-industrial (though not pre-capitalist) labour
process for corporate growers. It is no surprise, given B.C.'s long history
of racism, that those most affected by the absence of state regulation are
members of minority ethnic groups dependent on seasonal work.

Large numbers of workers from so-called third world countries were
made available to the labour market as the Canadian economy began to
expand in the 1950's and 1960's. Changes in the immigration policy resulted in a marked shift in the ethnic composition of the immigrant labour
force. In fact, between 1973 and 1977 one-half of the immigrants to B.C.
came from Asia and Japan (Stanton, 1980).

Because of the industrial nature of the expanding Canadian economy,
however, the general emphasis of Canadian immigration policy encouraged skilled technical and professional workers to immigrate. This
policy had a number of consequences for "sending" and "receiving"
countries. First, it created a 'brain' drain in under-developed nations.
Second, it siphoned off a portion of the surplus population, providing a

safety-valve by exporting those who might have had high expectations and who may been have been prone to express discontent. Finally, it alleviated the costs to the Canadian state of training the indigenous population to meet the needs of technological change.

Nonetheless, despite the general emphasis on skilled labour which arose in the 1960's, both federal and provincial governments once again recognized farm owners' demands for cheap farm labour. This view was expressed in 1974 by the Minister of Human Resources, Norman Levi, who said:

> I do have, as indeed the rest of the government does, a very real concern about making available a pool of labour to the farming industry. I accept that while we have numbers of employable people on welfare in British Columbia, we have to develop mechanisms to make available pools of labour at times when they are needed by the farming industry (Levi, 1974).

The same year, when opening a Canada Farm Labour Pool office in Red Deer, Alberta, the federal Minister of Manpower and Immigration, Robert Andras, stated that the federal government was prepared to allow temporary or "guest" workers to enter Canada to perform the work which Canadians were "unwilling to do." In Andras's words:

> There will be circumstances when workers other than Canadians or landed immigrants will be required to bolster the agricultural work force for a temporary period. If Canadians or landed immigrants are not available or unwilling to do the work, and if employers are prepared to provide adequate wages and working conditions, my department will admit the necessary numbers of offshore workers through approved programs, in the first instance. If these are inadequate to meet the demands, the necessary off-shore workers will be permitted entry provided employers meet certain minimum wage and working requirements (Andras, 1974).

However, in B.C. sufficient immigration was made available so that offshore workers were not generally required. A recent survey of farm workers in the major fruit, vegetable, and berry growing areas reveals that 55 per cent of paid farm workers do not speak English even as a second language and 58 per cent do not read English. Of those interviewed, 61 per cent reported Punjabi as their first language and 29 per cent reported French (Abbotsford Community Services, 1982). While the percentage of other minority ethnic groups is not given in the Abbotsford study, there are significant numbers of Chinese in the agricultural area south of the city of Vancouver and native people on Vancouver Island and in central and northern B.C. The mix of minority groups is confirmed by Malcolmson's (n.d.) study of farm work (see also Sharma, 1983). Relying on the *Food Commission Report*, Malcolmson maintains that approximately 70 per cent of farm workers in the Fraser Valley, the main area of farm employment, are of East Indian descent while many of the remainder in the valley were of Chinese extraction.

The special problems faced by recent immigrants, such as language difficulties, lack of familiarity with the Canadian legal system, and so on have made this fraction of the working class especially susceptible to exploitation at the hands of growers and labour contractors. Fortunately, a broad-based community response has arisen to combat the conditions which the majority of farm workers face. The support for farm workers' rights is examined below.

THE CANADIAN FARM WORKERS' UNION

In the spring of 1979 the Farmworkers Organizing Committee (F.W.O.C.) was formed to address the need for legislative reform, the unionization of farm workers, and the development of community support for farm workers' issues. The role of organized labour in the struggle against exploitation from both growers and contractors was recognized in the early stages of the farm worker's union movement. In the words of the F.W.O.C.:

> the support of the working class movement is very important. The farm workers are after all a part of the work force contributing through their hard labour to the well-being of the economy and of people. Their struggle for the democratic rights of trade union and legal protection are part of the whole working class struggles, and it is only with the support of the whole working class that they can advance their cause. The F.W.O.C. hopes that their support will continue to come in even greater measure (F.W.O.C., n.d., 9).

The F.W.O.C. clearly recognized that the struggle of farm workers must be consciously linked to the wider struggles between labour and capital in the province, rather than minorities versus Anglo-Canadians. Indeed, the use of cheap minority labour has "split" the working class in the past, and these divisions have weakened the working-class struggle (Sharma, 1983; Dutton, 1984). From the point of view of farm workers, this division has resulted in the maintenance of an anachronistic labour process and ethnically segmented labour force to service it. According to the farmworkers' committee:

> The use of this so-called "cheap labour" services the interests of the bosses and hurts the interests of the working class as a whole because it maintains areas of extraordinary exploitation and splits the working class.
>
> The ideology of racism is built on this split. The owners of factories and farms want cheap labour and a weak working class which will not be able to make too many demands. For this reason they bring and exploit immigrant workers, try to use their insecurity against the interests of the established working class, and stimulate hostility and suspicion between the two sections of the working class with racist ideas like: "Immigrant workers take away jobs from Canadian workers." Obviously, to the extent that workers are turned against themselves, they are made weak in their common struggle against their exploiters (F.W.O.C., n.d., ll).

Since 1979, the F.W.O.C. has become the Canadian Farm Workers Union (C.F.U.) and has established funding through ethnic communities and trade unions, including the Canadian Labour Congress, the British Columbia Federation of Labour, and other union locals. Support has also been provided by individuals and church organizations. Yet, organizing farm workers has been very difficult, and only three locals have been established to date. The first union contract was at Bell Farms with the average wage rate raised to $8.65 per hour in 1983. A second contract was signed with Fraser Valley Frosted Foods in 1982, raising the average wage rate to $7.58. Finally, a third contract exists with Reimer Nurseries Ltd., establishing an average wage rate of $9.18 per hour. This represents a substantial improvement over the older wage-rates (Sharma, 1983).

A contract was also signed with Jensen Mushroom Farm, but the union was decertified after the farm was closed by a fifteen-month strike and the union failed to retain the necessary union support from newly hired workers. Labour relations at Bell Farms have also been problematic. In February 1983, the farm sold approximately 240 of its 280 acres. When the Canadian Farm Workers' Union applied for successor status, whereby the new owners would have to bargain with the union, the Labour Relations Board ruled against the C.F.U. The union is currently appealing the decision.

The C. F. U. has also concentrated its efforts on improving conditions on the farms by pursuing statutory recognition and protection. Protecting workers from legislative discrimination would significantly improve the conditions on the farms. As a result, with the support of other unions, the C.F.U. has attempted to force the government to include farm workers under the provisions of the Employment Standards Act, and have applied for a writ against the government to have it enforce the "compulsory" regulations for farm workers which are part of the Workers' Compensation Act.

The organizing attempts by the union have been hampered by a number of factors including the seasonal work force which is reconstituted each summer for the harvest season. Many workers are also recent immigrants and are not familiar with their rights or with the English language.[4] In addition, corporate farms in B.C. are quite small, compared with the larger agribusiness farms in California. As a result, the transient work force is smaller and thus more difficult to organize.

Farm workers are also drawn from ethnic communities which have not as yet developed the kind of political mobilization needed to bargain effectively with the government. In addition, C.F.U.'s efforts have also been hampered by the lack of the kind of sustained community support which assisted in the organization of Chicano and Mexican farm workers in California in the late 1960's and early 1970's (Jenkins and Perrow, 1977). There, community action groups, unions, and churches developed public awareness which finally resulted in a successful boycott against growers. This boycott forced growers to recognize the union. The same level of public support is needed in British Columbia.

But the main impediment to the organization of farm workers lies with the growers, who clearly recognize that union recognition would lead to higher wages and therefore higher costs. As a result, growers have petitioned the state to leave the farm-labour process in their hands. Although this preserves social injustice, the growers have continued to be successful in their efforts to retain legislative discrimination against farm workers, largely because of their well-organized political constituency which holds the balance of power especially in small rural ridings. This farm lobby has, therefore, been the main instrument affecting farm-worker rights and the lack of protections.

The current economic situation and the concentrated attack on unions means that support will be difficult to mobilize. The problem now is to overcome the ideology of neo-conservatism and the growing public antipathy to unions as the Social Credit government plays union against non-union workers and the economic crisis continues to deepen. If this wider public support is not mobilized more effectively, if the current economic recession forces Anglo-Canadians to compete for farm work, and if the liberal-democratic state's "safety net" is replaced by laissez-faire capitalism and workers are phased off both unemployment insurance and welfare, ethnic antagonisms may soon erupt.

CONCLUSION: ETHNICITY AND CLASS

The persistence of ethnically segmented labour markets and ethnic divisions in Canada and other industrialized nations has convinced many sociologists, social historians, and anthropologists that ethnicity, or the identification with a cultural group, is "primordial," or ontologically rooted. On this basis it has been assumed *a priori* that the socioeconomic conditions in which groups come together are, at best, merely secondary to cultural considerations (Geertz, 1963; Gordon, 1964; Ward, 1978). However, as the case of farm workers in B.C. makes clear, not all "ethnic relations" can be reduced to cultural differences. Instead, ethnic relations must be located within the context of fundamental socioeconomic processes; these conditions, that is, the development and expansion of the capitalist mode of production and contradictory class interests, must be taken seriously in any attempt to explain ethnic relations, something which current mainstream perspectives fail to recognize or achieve. As a result, many mainstream perspectives have tended to reify cultures, treating each cultural group as homogenous with discrete and separate interests. As Wolf points out:

> The habit of treating named entities such as Iroquois, Greece, Persia, the United States ('Asians,' 'whites,' etc.) as fixed entities opposed to one another by stable internal architecture and external boundaries interferes with our ability to understand their mutual encounter and confrontation. In fact, this tendency has made it difficult to understand all such encounters and confrontations . . . We seem to have taken a wrong turn in our understanding at some critical point in the past, a false choice that bedevils our thinking in the present (Wolf, 1982:7).

In the case of farm workers, mainstream perspectives fail to explain the alliances which have been formed within the working class against growers and the state. Nor do they explain the articulation of the interests of East Indian and Chinese-Canadian labour contractors and growers with other "White" capitalists, rather than the agricultural labour force. Minority ethnic relations in the farm labour process cannot, therefore, be reduced to "ethnic" phenomena; they are part of a wider set of social relations inextricably connected with the contradictions inherent in the capitalist mode of production.

It is clear from the analysis of social relations presented here that it is not cultural differences between social groups that lead to ethnic antagonisms or the supposed utilitarian benefits of cheap minority labour, but rather the sociopolitical and economic relations into which these groups are placed together in a profit-motivated labour process which is constituted in a dialectical manner by contradictory class interests and class struggle. Using this focus helps to penetrate the ideology of mainstream approaches to ethnic relations and provides a more comprehensive understanding of the factors which produce and reproduce ethnic relations.

TABLE 1: FARM UNIT SIZE IN BRITISH COLUMBIA, 1931-1981

Total No. of Farms	1931	1941	1951	1961	1966	1971	1981
	26,079	23,394	26,406	19,934	19,085	18,400	20,010
Farms	Percentage						
1-50 acres	60	60	65	60	58	57	N/A
51-299 acres	30	29	23	24	23	23	N/A
300+ acres	10%	12	12	16	19	20	N/A
Total acreage in farms (thousands)	3,541	4,033	4,702	4,506	5,292	5,823	6,053
Percentage of total land area in farms	1.5	1.8	2.0	2.0	2.3	2.6	2.7

*Figures may not add to 100 because of rounding.
Sources: Statistics Canada, British Columbia Agriculture, 1971 and 1981; Mullan, 1974.

TABLE 2: PAID WORKERS IN THE CANADIAN FARM LABOUR FORCE

	Total Employment (thousands)				
	1953	1963	1973	1974	1977
Canada	858	649	467	473	468
Atlantic Provinces	56	34	20	22	18
Quebec	203	124	88	84	72
Ontario	220	172	122	120	128
Prairies	358	300	216	226	227
British Columbia	21	18	21	21	21
	Paid Workers				
	1953	1963	1973	1974	1977
Canada	113	103	96	97	145
Atlantic Provinces	9	8	7	9	n/a
Quebec	19	19	16	15	22
Ontario	38	37	34	32	50
Prairies	42	31	31	34	54
British Columbia	5	8	8	9	10
	Paid Workers as a Percentage of Total Employment				
	1953	1963	1973	1974	1977
Canada	13.2	15.9	20.6	20.5	31.0
Atlantic Provinces	16.1	23.5	35.0	40.9	n/a
Quebec	9.4	15.3	18.2	17.8	30.6
Ontario	17.3	21.5	27.9	26.7	39.1
Prairies	11.7	10.3	14.4	15.0	23.8
British Columbia	23.8	44.4	38.1	42.8	47.6

Sources: Statistics Canada, The Labour Force, 71-001; B.C. Select Standing Committee on Agriculture, 1979.

TABLE 3: FARM LABOUR AND CASH SALES

SALES $	$0–2,500	$2,500–$9,999	$10,000–$24,999	$25,000+	Total
Cash wages paid	1,703,989	3,211,600	5,943,766	90,276,300	101,135,636
Weeks paid labour	10,077	21,086	32,651	420,351	484,165
Percentage of paid labour	.02	.04	.07	.87	1.00
No. of census farms reporting	895	1,783	1,367	3,959	7,904
Percentage of all farms	.11	.23	.17	.50	.39

Sources: Statistics Canada, 1981 Census of Agriculture, B.C.

NOTES

1. For a critical review of the literature on Asian-European relations, see Roy (1979) and Dutton (1984; 1986; 1987).
2. See Dutton (1984; 1987) for a discussion of the alternatives available to workers.
3. Between 1976 and 1980 there were at least sixty-five deaths in British Columbia resulting from farm-related accidents (Sandborn, 1981).
4. This is why the C.F.U. sponsors language workshops and attempts to inform workers of their legal rights.

REFERENCES

Abbotsford Community Services. 1982.
Agricultural Pesticides and Health Survey Results Project, Abbotsford, B.C., October.
Andras, R. 1974.
Public Address, Red Deer, Alberta. Beveridge, Karl and Conde, Carole. 1982.
Canadian Farmworkers Union. "The Effects of an Automated Agribusiness on Workers' Lives are often Hidden." In *Fuse*. Toronto: Anton's Publishing.
Bonacich, Edna. 1972.
"A Theory of Ethnic Antagonism: The Split Labour Market." *American Sociological Review* 37:5 (Oct.):547-559.
British Columbia Government, Ministry of Labour. 1980.
Employment Standards Act, Chapter 10. (replacing R.S. 1979, c. 107). Victoria: Queen's Printer.
—1981. *Employment Standards Act Regulation*. Reg., 37/81, Victoria: Queen's Printer.
—1981. *The New Employment Standard Farm and Domestic Workers: Your Rights and Benefits*. Victoria: Agency Press.
British Columbia Human Rights Commission. 1983.
"What This Country Did to Us, It Did to Itself." *Report*. Vancouver, B.C.
British Columbia Select Standing Committee on Agriculture. 1979.
The Impact of Labour on the British Columbia Food Industry. Richmond, B.C. Phase 3 Research Report.
British Columbia Select Standing Committee on Labour and Justice. 1975.
Brief. Victoria, B.C.
Bronson, H. E. 1972.
"Continentalism and Canadian Agriculture." In Gary Teeple (ed.), *Capitalism and the National Question in Canada*. Toronto: University of Toronto Press.
Canadian Farmworker's Union. (1981)
Newsletter. Burnaby, B.C. 1981. Brief to J. Heinrich, Ministry of Labour.
Canadian Federation of Agriculture. 1974.
Labour Standards. National Office Report 41010-2, July.
Clarke, John. 1977.
"Unionization of Farmworkers: B.C. Sets a Significant Precedent." *Labour Gazette*, 77:260-61, June.
Creese, Gillian. 1988.
"Immigration Policy and the Formation of Class, Ethnicity, and Ethnic Conflict in British Columbia: Chinese and Japanese Immigrants, 1871-1923." Ch. 5, herein.
Department of Agriculture. 1974.
"How Much Agricultural Labour Is Hired?" Unpublished report.

Dutton, Alan. 1984.
"Capitalism, the State and Minority Ethnic Relations in British Columbia." M.A. thesis, University of Victoria.
— 1987. "Ethnic Antagonisms: The Case of Asian-European Immigrants in B.C.," ms, Simon Fraser University, Department of Sociology and Anthropology.
— 1987a. "Theories of Asian-European Conflict in B.C.: Three Generations of Studies," ms, Simon Fraser University, Department of Sociology and Anthropology.
Farm Workers Organizing Committee. (n.d.).
Support B.C. Farmworkers. Burnaby, B.C.
— 1980. "Concerning Legislative Recommendation on Matters that Affect B.C. Farmworkers." Brief presented to Hon. Jack Heinrich, Vancouver, B.C., February.
Geertz, Clifford. 1963.
"The Integrated Revolution: Primordial Sentiments and Civil Politics in New States." In Clifford Geertz (ed.), *Old Societies and New States*. New York: Free Press of Glencoe.
Godley, Elizabeth. 1980.
"Death of Children Blamed on Lack of Daycare Facilities." *Vancouver Sun*, 25 August, p. F8.
Gordon, Milton M. 1964.
Assimilation in American Life. New York: Oxford University Press.
Hume, Stephen. 1983.
"Canada's 'Quiet Racism' Hurts Workers." Victoria *Times-Colonist*, 17 February, pp. A1-A2.
Jenkins, J. Craig and Perrow, Charles. 1977.
"Insurgency of the Powerless: Farmworkers' Movements (1946-1973)." *American Sociological Review* 42, (April):249-68.
Johnson, Eva. 1974.
"Backbreaking Work at $1.40 Per Hour." *Vancouver Sun*, 18 June, p. A4.
Labonte, Ronald. 1982.
"Racism and Labour: The Struggle of British Columbia's Farmworkers." *Canadian Forum* (June-July):9–11.
Labour Advocacy and Research Association. 1979.
Taken for Granted: The Legal Rights of Farm and Domestic Workers. Vancouver. Legal Services of B.C.
Leiber, Gary L. 1973.
"Labour-Management Relations in Agriculture: The Need for Meaningful Collective Bargaining." *American University Law Review* 23:145-82.
Levi, Norman. 1974.
Letter to the British Columbia Federation of Agriculture (private correspondence)
Li, Peter S. 1979. "An Historical Approach to Ethnic Stratification: The Case of Chinese in Canada, 1858-1930." *Canadian Review of Sociology and Anthropology* 16:320-32.
Lipton, Charles. 1967.
The Trade Union Movement of Canada 1827-1959. Toronto: N.C. Press Ltd.
Malcolmson, John. (n.d.).
The Political Economy of Farmworkers' Unionization in B.C.. Burnaby: Simon Fraser University.
Miles, R. and P. Spounley. 1985.
"The Political Economy of Labour Migration: An Alternative to the Sociology of Race and Ethnic Relations in New Zealand." *Australia and New Zealand Journal of Sociology* 21:1:3-25.
Mullan, A. E. 1974.
"Workmen's Compensation and Agricultural Workers." *Preliminary Study*. Vancouver: Workers Compensation Board of B.C., unpublished.

Pfeffer, Max J. 1980.
    "The Labor Process and Corporate Agriculture: Mexican Workers in California." *Insurgent Sociologist* 10, no. 2 (Fall):25-44.
Roy, Patricia. 1979.
    "White Canada Forever: Two Generations of Studies." *Canadian Ethnic Studies* 11, no. 2:97-109.
Sandborn, Calvin. 1981.
    "Equality for Farmworkers—A Question of Social Conscience." Submission to the Legislative Caucus of the Provincial New Democratic Party.
—1982. "The Racist History of Present Laws that Discriminate Against Farmworkers." Brief presented to the B.C. Human Rights Commission.
Sharma, Hari. 1983.
    "Race and Class in British Columbia—The Case of B.C.'s Farmworkers." *South Asia bulletin* 3, no. 1 (Spring):53-69.
Stanton, Patrick. 1980.
    "A Historical Review of Immigration to British Columbia." *Labour Research Bulletin* (February):15-20.
—1980. "B.C. Immigration in the Post-War Period, Patterns and Characteristics." *Labour Research Bulletin* (June):12-20. Victoria: Queen's Printer.
Statistics Canada. 1973.
    1971 Census of Canada, Agriculture: British Columbia. Catalogue 96-711, Vol. 4, Part 3, Ottawa.
    1978. *1976 Census of Canada, Agriculture: British Columbia.* Catalogue 96-810, Bulletin 13-4, Ottawa.
    1981. *Census of Canada, Agriculture: British Columbia.* Catalogue 96-911. Ottawa.
Terry, James. 1980.
    "The Political Economy of Migrant Farm Labor, Immigration, Mechanization and Unionization in the Midwest." *The Insurgent Sociologist* (Spring):63-75.
Vancouver *Sun*. 1984.
    "Literacy a Crusade [for East Indian Farmworkers]," 9 January, p. A3.
    1983. "Only Farmers' Urged for Agency," 19 March, p. A9.
    1983. "Down on the Farm," 19 March.
Victoria *Times-Colonist*. 1974.
    "Farm Labour Probe Exploitation Stuns MLA," 3 November.
    1984. "English Lessons Mean Freedom for Farmworkers," 10 January.
Warburton, Rennie. 1981.
    "Race and Class in British Columbia: A Comment." *B.C. Studies* 49 (Spring):79-85.
Ward, Peter. 1978.
    White Canada Forever: Popular Attitudes and Public Policy Towards Orientals in British Columbia. Montreal: McGill-Queen's University Press.
—1980. "Class and Race in the Social Structure of British Columbia, 1870-1939." *B.C. Studies* 45 (Spring):17-35.
    1981. "Race and Class in British Columbia: A Reply." *B.C. Studies* 50 (Summer):52.
Wolf, Eric. 1982.
    Europe and the People Without History. Berkeley & Los Angeles: University of California Press.

10

Public Policy, Capital, and Labour
in the Forest Industry

M. PATRICIA MARCHAK

When I was conducting interviews for *Green Gold*[1] in the still affluent late 1970's, I found myself waiting on a float one day for a small plane to take a group of seasoned loggers and myself out of a logging camp half-way up Williston Lake. The loggers were discussing their fear of small planes. I expressed some surprise: I had watched them over several days driving machines in conditions that were dangerous, and the accident rate in that camp was admitted by all to be "gawd-awful high." As well, these were the same fellows who trotted out bravado statements about what the straw boss could do if he violated their notions of acceptable authority.

But they were frightened, and perhaps because at that moment they felt vulnerable, they talked about other fears in their lives that they had not mentioned during interviews; fears for their young wives and small children who spent snow-bound winters in trailer camps; about frequent layoffs; about accidents and mortgages on their trucks and skidders. As the plane glided in to the float, one logger said to me: "I appreciate your caring about us guys. A lot of people treat us like bums. I'd really like it if you'd tell our side of the story."

A few years later an International Woodworkers of America survey indicated that 40 per cent of all loggers in B.C. were laid off. The rate in 1982, at the bottom of the recession, was 54.1 per cent. In the sawmills, between 28 per cent of workers in the interior of the province and 30 per cent at the coast were laid off. Nearly 60 per cent of workers in the shake and shingle sector were unemployed.[2] The levels of unemployment were greater than those loggers on the float could have anticipated in 1977.

Between the two periods, much had changed in this industry.

In this article, I will outline the public policy context within which forest firms have harvested trees in British Columbia and describe the firms and the labour force in the 1950-79 period. The recession, as far as this industry is concerned, is not over at the time of my writing (June 1987). There continue to be long-term problems, and there is no prospect that industry employment rates of the 1970's will ever again be attained in British Columbia. The changes of the 1980's are discussed in a concluding section, together with proposals put forward by diverse affected groups for reform of the industry.

THE POLICY CONTEXT

The modern forest industry took its bearings from the Sloan Commissions of 1945 and 1956.[3] The impetus for the first Sloan investigation was probably the popularity of demands by the C.C.F., the opposition party then in the provincial legislature, for nationalization of the industry, together with demands from the larger companies for long-term guarantees of resource supplies. A Royal Commission was struck to investigate the situation and advise the government about policy options.

Chief Justice Sloan's reports argued in favour of a sustained yield policy and harvesting quotas. He noted that at the current rate of tree removal and with the failure to replant adequately, the province would eventually have a severe timber shortage. The governments of the period (a Liberal-Conservative coalition; then, after 1952, Social Credit) chose to interpret this as an argument in favour of oligopolistic control. They argued that large, integrated companies would be the best harvesters of the resource because they have long-term horizons.

In consequence, small firms were gradually phased out, either through rules regarding bidding for timber-cutting rights or through the establishment of new technical standards in sawmills which they could not implement because they lacked capital. Many were bought out by larger companies. The number of independent sawmill firms dropped from over two thousand in the immediate post-war period to under one thousand by the early 1960's and to just over three hundred by 1978.[4] Logging which had been done by the sawmill companies or small, local contractors became impossible: independent loggers could not gain access to timber. By the 1970's virtually all logging companies were either subsidiaries or on contract to a few large companies.

On the eve of the second Sloan Commission Report, the provincial harvest was 9.4 million cunits (100 cubic feet of wood). On the eve of the Pearse Commission investigation, twenty years later in 1974, it was 21.2 million cunits. In 1954, the ten largest companies controlled 37.2 per cent of the yield; in 1974, they controlled 54.5 per cent.[5]

The Pearse Commission was appointed by a New Democratic Party (N.D.P.) government (briefly in power from 1972 to 1975), but the report was given to a Social Credit government in 1976. Pearse raised many questions about the large companies. He suggested, for example, that their size made them inefficient: the efficiencies of scale realized in pulpmill operations were not similarly realized in sawmills and logging operations, nor in the total, integrated complexes that now ran the industry.[6]

There was, he argued, no genuine log market at the coast and a limited market in the interior of the province. The stumpage (resource rent) charged by the government was based on the "market value" of logs, but with such limited competition in the market this was meaningless, and there were considerable grounds for believing that the stumpage was unnecessarily low.[7] The market had been eroded by the integration of the industry: large companies controlled the timber, their logging operations cut it, their sawmills and pulpmills manufactured it, and small, independent manufacturing companies were effectively blocked from obtaining supplies. The stumpage rates were, in consequence, essentially determined by the firms themselves, going through the artificial process of charging their own subsidiaries for purchases from other subsidiaries. At best, the large companies engaged in swaps in order to obtain specific timber supplies in each region and avoid transportation costs.

Not within the Pearse Commission mandate, but of considerable importance to the provincial economy, was the problem of staples dependence associated with the forest industry. In 1978, B.C. exported 79 per cent of B.C.'s lumber, 30 per cent of its pulp, and 83 per cent of its newsprint to the United States. Japan obtained nine per cent of its lumber and 17 per cent of its pulp.[8] In addition, the province exported a small but valuable proportion of its timber products in the form of logs and pulpwood chips to the United States and Japan where parent companies of firms located in B.C. or other firms in those countries processed it into newsprint and other paper products.

These are not advanced manufactured products. B.C. produced scarcely any quality coated papers (Canada as a whole produced not more than five per cent of the North American total).[9] As noted by a writer for the Science Council of Canada in the early 1970s:

we are the world's largest exporter of pulp and paper, but we import much of our fine paper and virtually all of the highly sophisticated paper, such as backing for photographic film and dielectric papers for use in electronic components.[10]

Though the industry requires chemicals for pulp, and transportation equipment for logging, most of these materials were imported. As well, B.C. imported 52 per cent of its consumer items from the United States, and 24 per cent from Japan.[11]

Secondary industries unrelated to forestry were also underdeveloped. Of the province's total exports in 1980, the semi-processed forest products together with refined aluminum, lead, and zinc, comprised 69.5 per cent; coal, natural gas, copper and molybedenum, and crude oil comprised 20.6 per cent.[12] As these figures show, B.C. relied on the export of raw and semi-processed materials for its economic health. This kind of economy is known as a "staples" economy, and such economies tend to be highly vulnerable to boom and bust cycles, dependent always on markets elsewhere for their unprocessed materials.[13]

With forestry as the mainstay of the provincial economy, the apparent means of diversifying the base and reducing the vulnerability would have been to charge high resource rents for timber while markets were strong and to apply these to the development of wood products industries; or attach requirements to companies receiving harvesting rights that they create value-added manufacturing industries. The British Columbia government took neither of these routes over the post-war period.

The problem was not a lack of control over the timber. Large companies obtained harvesting rights to the resource, and only 5 per cent of forest lands remained outside crown ownership. There was strong public opinion in favour of public ownership, but also the private companies had no objection to the public bearing costs of forest maintenance, while their fortunes were made in the processing. Insecurity of tenure and crown monopoly over the resource and conditions of its extraction were offset by the long-term harvesting rights which effectively guaranteed a continuing supply of the raw materials for large mills. Clearly this was the intent of the 1978 government legislation regarding tenures, as stated by the minister of forests when he introduced the most recent Forest Act:

> neither the Royal Commissioner nor this government proposes drastic revisions of the existing system. Some self-interest groups have clamoured for wholesale redistribution of timber rights. Again, neither this government nor the Royal Commission recommended this nor is there any valid reason to do so. The objective is to achieve good management through tenure security and not to impede good

management through chaotic disruption of employment, communities or investment security.[14]

The new legislation offered no solutions to the problems noted by Pearse. Sustained yield concepts were ignored, and allowable cuts for the companies were to be determined as much by reference to the crown's social policies and the needs of existing mills as to any biological criteria. Twenty-five-year harvesting tenures were augmented by ten-year preliminary periods during which time the licensee could opt for extensions, and except for minimal provisions to enable farmers to cut woodlots and small firms to bid on small area timber supplies, the new Forest Act clearly favoured a continuation of control by the few large companies.[15]

This control might have been acceptable if the combination of crown lands, large companies, and the stumpage fees had resulted in a conserved and perpetually regenerated forest. But the long-term horizons notwithstanding, most replanting on public lands was inadequate both in quantity and quality. From 1980 onward, public commentary and studies made this painfully clear.[16] Even when seedlings were planted, the essential silviculture that nurtures the young trees, thins out the stands, and treats the soils was insufficient. The Forest Service could not take responsibility for replanting or overseeing company stands. With the low resource rents from which the Service is financed, it was chronically short of funds to do its job. As well, it was impossible for the Service to plan long-term reforestation projects because it simply could not obtain guaranteed funding for them. The "Green Gold" gradually dwindled.

The implication of the minister's approach was that only those groups which proposed a redistribution of timber rights were acting in their self-interest. But the continuation of a system which allowed a few companies to control the timber was obviously in the interests of those few companies. The government argued that the interests of the companies were the interests of the citizens, but the over-cutting, the failure to reforest, the over-investment in mill capacities and lack of investment in secondary industries were hardly in the interests of B.C. citizens.

There are two plausible explanations: 1) that members of the government shared the interests of the investors, and therefore acted in their own interests when helping investors to make profits; 2) that whether or not members of the government shared the interests of investors, the structure of capitalism is such that they were obliged to support investor interests.

The most powerful support for the first argument would be a demonstration that individual members of governments throughout the post-war period themselves had investments in these or linked companies or some other powerful incentive to co-operate with the companies. Such evidence is not available, though some individual members of some of these governments have had investments of this sort. In the main, members of the provincial government in B.C. (unlike those at the federal level) are rarely members of the corporate elite before or after their political careers; they are rarely educated at the "best" schools and universities. In fact, their most common characteristic is that they have been small businessmen prior to entry into politics, and the second most common feature is that they are not university graduates. In these respects they are like much of the electorate in an essentially "frontier" and economically underdeveloped society.

The second (but weaker) form of support for the first argument would be to demonstrate that members of government share a worldview—an ideology—which supports the interests of these companies. That is easily provided in the form of public statements, speeches in the legislature (of which the excerpt above is typical), and policies of the governing parties over the entire post-war period except for the three years during which a social democratic party was in power. Nor would these members deny that they share such a worldview: they call it "free enterprise," even if the reality is oligopsonistic control of raw materials and oligopolistic control of markets. Members of the Social Credit government have repeated many, many times that in their view private capital should not be hindered by government in its pursuit of profit. At the same time, they have made it clear that government should provide enabling legislation, infrastructure, and raw materials for the private sector. So the ideology is no secret, and for that reason I will not provide pages of citations to demonstrate it.

The alternative argument is that liberal democratic governments in capitalistic countries are embedded in the economic fabric in such a way that even if the members of any particular government wished to deny the demands of large-scale capital, they are unable to fundamentally alter the structure. Offe, for example, has argued that because these governments ultimately depend on taxation and taxing powers ultimately depend on continuing accumulation by private capital, they are structurally constrained to allocate resources and intervene on behalf of capital.[17]

Since no B.C. government has attempted to alter the structure, there is no test case here. However, one may consider specific kinds of changes that a government might attempt and speculate about the chances of their success. Would it be possible, for example, for a government of British Columbia to have obliged international companies to invest in manufacturing capacity in the province instead of using B.C. resources for the manufacturing plants elsewhere? Would it be possible for a government to abrogate unilaterally timber-cutting contracts with the large companies in order to diversify the ownership pattern? Would it be possible to insist that machinery, chemicals, and other inputs be purchased from B.C. firms and to invest public funds in the start-up costs for such firms? Would it be possible to increase the stumpage rates so that reforestation could be undertaken?

We do not know the answer to these questions, but we do know that when a New Democratic Party government attempted to diversify timber-cutting tenure ownership on a modest scale, it incurred considerable opposition; that when, in other industries, it attempted to increase the rents paid to government for minerals and to reduce the profits earned by private insurance companies, it involuntarily created a liaison between mining and insurance firms which financed the opposition party and orchestrated a public campaign against the government.[18] The abrogation of contracts would involve such extensive litigation that a government would soon "go under" fighting court cases. An increase in stumpage rates might be expected to have similar effects to the increase in mining royalties. On this evidence, we might conclude that governments with different ideological persuasions are severely constrained in what they can do and that their chances of remaining in power are greatly reduced when they offend monied interests.

However, we cannot conclude that the outcome is pre-determined. Governments elsewhere have limited the power of private capital exclusively to extract resources and have initiated successful implementation of diversified industries. Norway and Sweden, neither enjoying natural advantages of location for manufacturing industries and both having rich forest resources, developed secondary industry through government initiatives beginning in the late nineteenth century.[19] Thus, a more temperate conclusion would be that while the constraints imposed by private investors and investment patterns in the global economy are hurdles for small regional economies, they are not necessarily insuperable. The pattern of development in British Columbia may not have been inevitable, but it became inevitable when none of the major participants—capital, government, and labour—sought the tougher path of diversification.

COMPANIES[20]

Most of the large companies in B.C. before 1980 also operated in the United States or Japan. In forestry, Weyerhaeuser, Scott Paper,

Champion International (Weldwood in Canada), International Paper (half owner of Tahsis at Gold River), Columbia Cellulose, owner of mills at Port Edward and holder of the large tree farm licence #1 in the Nass Valley until their purchase by B.C. Resources Investment Corporation (B.C.R.I.C.), and Crown Zellerbach were huge companies on the international scale, all owned in the United States. B.C. Forest Products was co-owned by Scott and Mead, both continental companies of the United States, together with the Alberta Energy Corporation and Noranda. International Telephone and Telegraph owned the Rayonier mills in B.C. and Quebec.

MacMillan Bloedel (M.B.), the largest company, had dispersed ownership, the largest shareholder being Canadian Pacific Investments (C.P.I.). C.P.I. was ousted in 1981 by Noranda, which added the company to its already extensive holdings in Canada and the United States, but simultaneously gave up its shares in B.C. Forest Products because of an anti-combines suit lodged against the company in the United States. Noranda was subsequently taken over by the Bronfmann interests (Toronto); Bronfmann also purchased shares in the Scott Paper parent company. The minority shareholder in M.B., Olympia and York, owned by the Reichmann family of Toronto, also had shares in firms elsewhere including the major company, Abitibi-Price. Canadian Pacific continued to own Pacific Logging and other forest companies elsewhere.

Enzo-Gutzeit Osakeyhtio of Finland co-owned Eurocan Pulp and Paper at Kitimat with West Fraser of the United States, West Fraser at that time also owning shares in Abitibi Price. The East Asiatic Company (Europe) held half of the shares in Tahsis. Japanese companies, likewise, had much larger concerns than their holdings in B.C., which included half-ownership in three pulpmills and shares of several sawmills. The major companies were Daishawa Marubeni, which shared ownership of the Cariboo Pulp and Paper Company with Weldwood; and Mitsubishi and Honshu Paper, which together held half the shares in Crestbrook Pulp and Paper.

Of the major companies, only Canadian Forest Products (C.F.P.) (privately held by the Prentice and Bentley families) and the crown corporation (B.C.R.I.C.) were formally owned by B.C. investors. C.F.P. held all shares in the Prince George Pulp and Paper Company and majority shares in Intercontinental Pulp. Minority shares in that company were held by Feldmuehle of Germany. B.C.R.I.C., created as a crown corporation under the New Democratic Party government of 1972-75, purchased the Ocean Falls mill previously owned by Crown Zellerbach and the Port Edward mills previously owned by Columbia Cellulose.

These companies were either newcomers who took over and combined smaller firms in the late 1940's and 1950's or were amalgamations of previous firms. The two largest companies, M.B. and Crown Zellerbach, together with Canadian Pacific, held most of the remaining private forest lands originally given to railway companies, or sold outright before the first forest legislation in 1912.

Crown Zellerbach and MacMillan Bloedel operations were situated mainly on the west coast. I.T.T. (Rayonier) purchased mills also situated on the coast and Vancouver Island. In the post-war period, the interior woodlands became more accessible, especially after the development of the Peace River dam project and the opening of the northeastern sector of the province. B.C. Forest Products and Canadian Forest Products established pulp mills in the Prince George and northeast regions. Weyerhaeuser situated its pulpmill in the central interior, and other firms moved to the southeast.

In addition to the large companies, there were both subsidiaries and independent middle-sized companies with sawmills throughout the interior and northern sectors of the province. These mills sold woodchips to the major mills, and low grade lumber to the eastern seaboard of the United States.

Throughout this period, pulp, newsprint, and dimensional lumber were sold to U.S. markets tariff-free. The market seemed insatiable, and U.S. softwood producers (many of whom also operated in Canada) had no fear of competition since they were able to sell all they produced. Finished wood products, however, encountered tariffs at the border. This was a major disincentive to diversification and development of more end products from Canadian wood.

LABOUR

Workers in the forest industries have never been noted for docility. The early history speaks of harsh struggles against rapacious employers for both wages and safe working and living conditions.[21]

During the early 1930's, wood-workers became members of the Workers' Unity League, organized by the communist Workers' Party of Canada. When the party disbanded the League in 1935, a still-militant leadership sought affiliation with the American Congress of Industrial Organizations. While coping with internal strife and a predominantly non-communist membership, the leaders of the Canadian union had to cope with the war and post-war anti-communism in the United States. At the 1940 convention, held in the United States and not open to the Canadian president because he was a communist, the Congress proposal to exclude communists from membership was narrowly defeated.[22]

However, non-communists obtained control of the B.C. Federation of Labour in 1948. Accusing the Congress of "red-baiting" and pointing to the numerous occasions on which the international body had appointed organizers against the leadership in Canada, and to the fact that Canadians were not permitted to attend international meetings in the United States, the International Woodworkers of America (I.W.A.) executive created the Woodworkers Industrial Union of Canada but failed to establish an independent national union. After 1948, the Canadian I.W.A. was effectively integrated with its American counterpart, though unlike most Canadian components of international unions based in the United States, the Canadian I.W.A. members were not in a minority position. With fully half of the total membership, they retained autonomy and equality within the larger organization.

For an international union such as the I.W.A., the underlying rationale for integration of workers in different countries was that they shared the same class situation.[23] The I.W.A. argued that despite Canada's relative underdevelopment, Canadian components of international unions, including the I.W.A., act with reference to class in a continental economy rather than with reference to regional or national priorities. Thus, the unions might mount a campaign against Reagan's monetarist policies, which equally harm labour on both sides of the border; but refrain from arguing a case for the purpose of strengthening specifically Canadian control of national resources.

The two Canadian pulpworkers' unions, the Pulp, Paper, and Woodworkers of Canada (P.P.W.C.) and the Canadian Paperworkers Union (C.P.U.), each with about 6,000 members in the late 1970's, were national bodies. Both were breakaways from American parents. The B.C.-based P.P.W.C. was established in 1963 after a split in the American Pulp, Sulphite union following charges of corruption being laid against union officers. The larger C.P.U. representing mainly central Canadian pulpworkers, split with the United Paperworkers International Union in 1975. The P.P.W.C. was overtly nationalistic, arguing for Canadian and regional control within the union. Locals have greater power to determine their actions than is possible within a continental union, and this has frequently led to conflict between the I.W.A.and P.P.W.C., where locals of the pulp union refused to accept outcomes agreed to by the I.W.A.[24] Despite its more nationalist stance, the P.P.W.C. and as well the C.P.U. took no part in the 1978 debate on forest policy, and specifically took no stand against ownership in the industry at that time.

During the 1978 debates on forest policy in the provincial legislature, the I.W.A. took the position that continuing allocation of timber licences to a few integrated, large firms was to be preferred over more dispersed licensing policies. The large companies were perceived to be more stable, better able to pay high wages, more safety-conscious, and better employers overall as compared to smaller companies. In the view of the union, there was no realistic alternative to continued oligopsony control of the timber-harvesting rights and increasing concentration of ownership over the entire industry. They felt reforms should include a better-financed and more professional forestry service to supervise the practices of the large corporations, more public investment in reforestation and silviculture, and the employment of more workers in the replanting process.[25]

Thus while the unions, during this period, were prepared to engage in strong bargaining, they were not prepared to oppose the structure of the industry as it existed at that time or government legislation designed to perpetuate the dominance of a few large, vertically integrated firms. To understand this position, it is helpful to consider the working conditions in the three major sectors of the industry.

Pulp Sector

From the 1950's to the 1970's pulpmills produced pulp and newsprint for a steady market with standardized prices and long-term contracts with buyers. The ten new mills (for a total of twenty-four) constructed during that period were automated, eliminating many floor-level jobs for relatively unskilled workers. Many workers in automated mills must be literate in order to read computer data; they are recruited from schools and universities and trained within the plants. A second group of workers are tradesmen who service the expensive machinery; they were in short supply throughout this period, and pulpmills competed for them with other industries. The machinery is expensive, paying for itself only if operating continuously; downtime caused by inexperienced workers or inadequate supplies of tradesmen would be costly. Consequently, at a time when markets were strong, managements needed a steady and committed work force. They sought this through payment of high wages, fringe benefits, guaranteed housing in company towns, promotion policies, and in-plant training programmes.

These developments led to a rise in the number of hourly workers in pulping from 7,630 to 13,073, a percentage increase of 71.3 per cent, while overall production volume increased by 122.9 per cent. Salaried workers increased from 1,602 in 1973 to 5,800 in 1978, a change of 192 per cent.[26]

Sawmill Sector

In contrast to pulpmills, sawmills during this period were mostly mechanized, though a few of the newer ones had more advanced automated components. These mills employed a large labour force with skills possessed by numerous workers in B.C. Training for a large proportion of jobs was minimal. While sawmills also required tradesmen, these were a smaller proportion of the total, and the machinery, if shut down, was not as high an operational risk as for pulpmills. Markets have always been more variable, subject in high degree to interest rates in the United States which determine the number of new housing starts. Employment practices reflect these variable markets and labour demands, with sharp fluctuations from year to year and occasional prolonged lay-offs.

In the same period marked by expansion of pulpmills, the number of sawmills declined from 967 (1961) to 330 (1978), and while production volume increased by 123 per cent, production workers increased by only 41.7 per cent (from 22,599 to 32,032). Salaried workers increased by 22.2 per cent to a total of 4,472.[27] The difference between production volume and employment increases is explicable in terms of the centralization of large mills and phasing out of smaller ones. Of particular note in the historical data is a sharp drop in the number of man-hours worked during the 1974-75 period when, with the "energy crisis", the industry had an eighteen-month recessionary period.

Logging Sector

Logging, still in the main conducted with small and mobile machinery, is not like either the mechanized sawmills or the automated pulpmills. Its products are sold on internal markets to its "parent" firms, and its "markets" fluctuate according to their demands. Prior to the 1950's, logging demanded heavy physical labour and the top jobs, those of fellers and bunchers, required a high degree of skill, experience, and agility. Over the post-war period, an increasing number of jobs have involved machinery—caterpillers, tractors, skidders, loaders, and yarding equipment of various kinds—which most male workers in the general labour force can handle (women could handle them as well, but fewer women have had the opportunity to learn the skills). An ever smaller proportion of the labour requires the specialized skills of the faller, bucker, or other experienced woodsman. The larger part of the labour force is therefore "semi-skilled." Because of the variable markets, machinery that can be shut down without excessive loss, and labour requirements that can usually be met from the general labour pool, logging companies will dismiss workers during a market slump.

In order to obtain the logging force without incurring long-term obligations, forestry companies contract out half of all logging. The major contractors in turn employ owner-operators who own their machinery (trucks, small loading and hauling equipment) and who work on piece rates for specific tasks. The contractors are not independent, since they have no ownership rights to the timber, but they shoulder the risks of over-capitalization, soft markets, and employment. In this way, the major employer is directly responsible for only half of the labour force, which is employed on hourly wage rates. Whether in contracting firms or on hourly wages, the logging labour force experiences frequent lay-offs, and employment levels vary directly with ups and downs in timber demands from sawmills and pulpmills.

Production volume in logging increased 80.1 per cent in the 1963-78 period, but the increase in number of hourly workers was only 29.9 per cent. The increase in salaried workers from 1,805 to 2,904 in this period (60.9%) is large partly because the base was small, and the increase includes the transformation of logging firm owners into contractors and supervisors.[28] As for sawmill workers, there was a sharp decrease in man-hours worked during the 1974-75 slump.

Increasing use of machinery in the woodlands operations, especially in interior operations where flat land facilitates the use of harvesters, has steadily decreased the number of workers required for logging. Thus while a third more workers overall were paid wages by 1978, their production was vastly greater than in 1963.

DISCUSSION

Given such variability of employment, one may wonder why workers would choose to take jobs in sawmills and logging; and wonder even more how employers can be sure that a labour supply will remain available in their region through a lay-off.

An initial explanation is that choices of occupation are rarely made as if all possible outcomes were available. Family income, parents' occupations, regional location, cultural background, and quality of public education are among the variables that limit choices; even limit awareness of choices. In the *Green Gold* sample survey, we discovered that where fathers had been loggers at the time sons in our interview sample had entered the labour force, 47 per cent of the sons became loggers. Where fathers had been sawmill workers at that time, 25 per cent of sons became sawmill workers; where fathers were pulpmill workers, 38 per cent became pulpworkers. Of the sons who entered employment other than that of their fathers, a majority of those whose fathers were logger and sawmill workers entered forest-related work elsewhere, agricultural work, mining, construction, or transportation work. The findings support the hypothesis that class origins, as measured by father's occupation, were more influential in determining occupational entry points (and subsequent work patterns as well) than education levels. Regional location was another important conditioning factor in occupational patterns.[29]

Another explanation is simply that there are few alternatives. A staples economy such as that in British Columbia provides a limited range of possibilities for employment, and hinterland regions provide limited access to college and university training or manufacturing employment. When its staples industries are not operating, workers have little choice but to wait out a slump on unemployment insurance.

The third explanation is the relatively high wage return. Compared to workers in the same jobs in the Atlantic, Quebec, and American industries, forest workers in British Columbia received high wages. Because forestry was the major industry and employed a tenth of the total labour force, these high wages, and similar wages in the construction industry and mining, established the pattern for other wages in B.C. This led to a large labour supply, among other things, because the wages attracted migrants from other provinces, especially from agricultural regions of Quebec and the Atlantic region.

The wages were obtained through collective bargaining, not firm by firm but between regional councils of employers and regional units of the I.W.A. and two pulpworker unions. The I.W.A., because of its size, was the major negotiator. As long as the markets stayed buoyant, companies had a positive incentive to accept higher wage costs as the price of uninterrupted production. The companies may have had another reason for accepting wage costs. Copithorne argued that the stumpage formula permitted employers to deduct some portion of increases in wage costs from resource rents.[30] Both the companies and the I.W.A. argue that this is an inaccurate representation of the case, but the matter remains open to further debate. Wages were cited as an offsetting cost of production for Canadian companies otherwise blessed with low resource rents by the United States Senate International Trade Commission in its report on Canadian competition in lumber markets in 1982. By their estimation, Canadian wage costs averaged 12 per cent above those in the United States.[31]

When there is a large reserve labour force, high unemployment, a lack of alternatives, and high wages, employed workers are reluctant to consider alternative ways of organizing an economy. With the exception of logging contractors, they do not own any of the means of production and are fully subordinated to corporate organization; contractors without access to timber are equally dependent.

In addition, the past history of the industry is a constant reminder of even less secure and poorly paid working conditions. During the more competitive phase of the industry and up to the early 1950's, small companies were frequently "cut and run" operations, leaving in their wake unpaid and poorly paid workers. Their operations were often unsafe and conditions were insecure. Corporate capitalism may de-skill workers, create mass-production lines that are intrinsically boring, diminish the area of personal control, and oblige workers to develop a transient pattern of existence.[32] Nonetheless, it provides work, fringe benefits, and the possibility for labour organization which the earlier companies did not provide.

In this context, then, the unions supported their corporate employers over the allocation of forest harvesting rights. Moreover, their determination to stay at the top of the wage scales for production workers had a depressant effect on manufacturing industries. These, unlike the resource industries, have no elasticity in costs of supplies. Whatever the benefits of the low stumpage rates for forest companies, these do not extend to independent companies producing furniture, prefabricated houses, or the many other wood-based consumer products. Yet the high wages in the economy, led by the forest and construction workers' wages, would have to be met by such producers, hindering the manufacturing process. In fact, the I.W.A. recognized the potential for lowering overall wage settlements if wood-products manufacturing by small and non-uinionized companies were established;[33] it opposed changes in forestry legislation that might lead to diversification of the industry at the price of reduced overall wages.

THE CRISIS OF THE 1980'S

The apparent advantages of corporate employers turned out to be less permanent than the workers imagined. And as became clearer in the late 1970's and 1980's, the practice of "cut and run" was by no means peculiar to small "gypo" operations. While much of the capitalist world underwent a severe recession in 1982 and emerged from it (though not unscathed), the recession in British Columbia began in 1981 and continued on through the middle of the decade.

Shutdowns in sawmills and in pulpmills affected the communities dependent on their employment and the many equipment supplier, service, and retail dealers connected to the industry. As well, not all the lay-offs were temporary. At Port Alberni, for example, MacMillan Bloedel warned its employees that following the recession there would be a 30 per cent reduction in the total labour force rehired. The reasons included termination of positions which were already redundant and those which would become redundant following technological changes to be implemented while plants were shut down.

All companies in B.C. suffered financial troubles during the early 1980's. Canadian Forest Products began trading on the public markets because of its internal difficulties. B.C.R.I.C. declined precipitously and quietly ceased to be a major company in B.C. MacMillan Bloedel had a long slide downward through the first half of the 1980's, though by 1986 it was again showing profits.

Five large American companies withdrew between 1975 and 1987. The exodus began with Columbia Cellulose, which sold its properties to the Crown in 1975. Rayonier sold its antiquated mills and timber rights to three firms dominated by B.C. Forest Products under the umbrella title, Western Forest Products. Later, Mead sold B.C.F.P. shares to financial companies which subsequently sold them to Fletcher Challenge of New Zealand. Fletcher Challenge also purchased the major remaining Canadian holdings of Crown Zellerbach. International Paper (U.S.) sold its half of the Tahsis (Gold River) mill to Canadian Pacific Investments.[34]

In each case there were internal explanations: Rayonier, for example, had a cash flow problem because of investments in Quebec and apparently sold its B.C. holdings as part of its solution. Crown Zellerbach apparently had similar cash-flow problems. B.C. Forest Products had overextended on its purchases of both Rayonier and Crown Zellerbach properties, and Western Forest Products was, according to financial analysts, in serious financial difficulty by 1982. These developments explain why a continental company begins to cut back its operations, but one still has to explain why the chosen region for cut-backs would be the B.C. softwood operations.

Among the causes of this prolonged downturn are world overcapacity and overproduction of pulp and newsprint together with new technologies and resource supplies for paper production and changing technologies and markets for wood. Complicating the situation for B.C. producers are new countervailing duties and other barriers to sales in the United States.

Overcapacity and Overproduction

Without counting new suppliers based on hardwood resources, there already was, by 1980, too much pulp produced for existing world markets. In Canada the overcapacity had been created in part by federal and provincial government subsidies throughout the 1970's. In addition to production intentionally created, several countries found themselves with resources that could not be used if not processed and sold immediately. Most particularly, West Germany discovered that parts of the Black Forest had been so harmed by acid rain that the trees were dying; much of their production in the 1980's, in consequence, is tied to a resource they cannot conserve for better markets. In British Columbia, some part of current production also involves decadent timber that will not stand alive far into the future.

New Technologies and Sources for Paper Production

Softwoods have always dominated the market for paper production because they have long, tough fibres. But during the 1970's, pulping technologies changed, and it became possible to produce increasingly higher quality papers from various pine species and from hardwoods. Pines grown in thirty-year cycles, in contrast to the fifty-to-one-hundred-year cycles required for commercial softwoods, were being planted and harvested in New Zealand, Australia, South Africa, and the southern United States in the 1970's. These claimed a share of the pulp market. In the 1980's, with further technological development of pulp-mill machinery, it became possible to transform eucalyptus trees, grown in seven-year cycles, into high grade paper.

The eucalyptus trees are now being harvested in Brazil, Africa, Portugal, and Spain. They require less land space, and thus lower land and operating costs, than softwoods. They are easier to harvest, and their short growing period permits investors to gain returns on their capital much more rapidly and more frequently. Their share of the global kraft paper market went up from 4 per cent in 1976 to 27 per cent in 1984.[35] Thus in addition to overcapacity in conventional softwood paper production, there is now a wholly new industry competing for the same markets.

Technological Change in Wood Products Production

Automated laser sawmills are able to produce more variable runs and cuts than conventional, mechanized mills. They do not depend on efficiencies of scale in the same degree as the mass production mills of the post-war period. They can be operated with a much smaller work force. Companies with investments tied up in the older mills are operating at a disadvantage in markets increasingly penetrated by the products of automated mills, and naturally they are seeking means of phasing out the old mills, and constructing new ones.

Countervailing Duties and Export Taxes

With declining world and domestic market shares, lumber and cedar shake- and shingle-producers in the United States began agitating for countervailing duties against the products of Canadian competitors. An initial investigation in 1982 failed to support their argument that Canadian production was subsidized through low stumpage. The U.S. Senate at that time concluded that while Canadian resource rents were, indeed, well below similar resource costs in the United States, this did not, technically, constitute a subsidy.[36] However, in 1986 they reconsidered the problem, and finally imposed duties on cedar shakes and shingles, then on dimensional lumber. The duty on lumber was waived when the Canadian government imposed an export tax on wood products shipped to the United States, thus achieving for the American producers roughly the same result (and from Canada's point of view, a slightly better result because the tax stayed in Canada whereas the countervailing duties would have gone to the United States).

This development may oblige small companies in the shake and shingle business to drop out. It will reduce the profits for large lumber producers, especially in the interior of B.C. because it is these mills, producing low-grade lumber, which are most affected by U.S. competition in the American market. It is not clear at the moment of writing whether the duties will extend to pulp products: logically they should since pulp is produced from the same forests at the same stumpage rates. The full impact cannot be assessed but we could reasonably assume that it will involve reduced employment in British Columbia.

Among the fall-outs from the countervailing duty wars and the more general recession throughout the Pacific Northwestern regions of both Canada and the United States has been the division of the International Woodworkers of America. The Canadian section has withdrawn, and talks are moving forward toward integration with workers in the pulp sectors. The reported membership of the I.W.A. was about approximately 33,000 by 1985, a dramatic drop since 1979.

A Staples Economy: Is There a Solution?

Two questions relevant to the history discussed in this paper are: would the depression in B.C. have been equally devastating had the economy been more diversified? and is there an exit from the "staples trap" at this point?

The answer to the first question has to be "no," since clearly not all industries are equally affected by a recession even if all are affected to some degree. The more diversified the economic base in a region, the more unevenly distributed are the effects of a recession. While workers in the most affected industries would still lose their employment, others would retain theirs and contribute to the overall viability of the regional economy. This was in fact demonstrated in a study by Byron, through comparison of employment statistics of towns with differing degrees of dependence on the forest industry. The town most dependent was most affected by a downturn, a result scarcely surprising but curiously ignored when single-industry towns are being planned.[37] Sustained yield principles, while important for the long-term nurturance of the resource, will not in themselves provide employment stability, since employment in the resource industries is a function not of forest resources but of markets.

The creation of a more diversified and self-sufficient economy in the post-war period would at the least have required the extraction of much higher resource rents and the application of these toward the development of viable secondary industries as well as adequate reforestation. Given the high market demand over those years, it is probable that forest companies would have accepted higher stumpage rates. It is also probable that higher rates and a stumpage formula which reduced the exemptions would have reduced employers' willingness to meet union wage demands, so that overall wages in the industry would not have risen as rapidly or as high as they did. Possibly lower wages in the leading sector of the economy would have removed one of the disincentives to manufacturers establishing plants in B.C.

But even with the build-up of government revenues and a deliberate industrial strategy, B.C. would have continued to have a resource-based and export-oriented economy as long as its industrial units were large, international resource companies. While such units might pay adequate rents if the resource had good markets, the companies would not have eagerly moved into more diverse investments within B.C. where the domestic market is small, export tariffs are inhibiting, and other costs of manufacturing higher than in the United States, central Canada, Japan, and Europe. The industrial units most capable of providing the diversified base are not large companies competing on a mass production and mass consumption market: they are small, domestic companies producing a small range of more specialized goods for both domestic and world markets.

The industry and some members of the government have argued that the forest industry would flourish if the forest lands were privatized. They claim that then the private owners would plant more trees and care for them. But there are strong arguments against this proposal.

To begin with, there would be no resource rents into the future. Eventually softwoods will gain new value for specialized users. Companies will be competing for much scarcer raw materials. If the land is sold now, necessarily at depression prices, B.C. would lose the growth in value that will occur in the 1990's and after that.

Secondly, there is no incentive at all for these companies to diversify our economy, and investments would not go into further manufacturing of wood products. The companies which have had long-term tenures in the past have not invested in advanced manufacturing, and private ownership would facilitate the process of using B.C. woods as inputs for manufacturing units outside B.C. Future governments would have no leverage in persuading them to do otherwise.

A second proposal made by some members of the N.D.P. is to bring the manufacturing sector as well as the land under public control. The argument in favour of this is that it might permit the government to manage the forest in the social interest and develop secondary industry from revenues.

The arguments against government monopolies in general are applicable to forestry. There is a tendency for large monopolistic units, whether private or public, to discourage open debate, to keep extraction and utilization rates either secret or not fully disclosed, to treat labour as a commodity, and to develop huge mass-production units which inevitably waste much of the resource.

In addition to the very real problems of an enormous, bureaucratic state, there is the question of where public monies are best spent. If they are spent on takeovers of existing large companies, the cost would be prohibitive. There would then be relatively little capital for development of the manufacturing sector and diversification of the overall economy.

A third proposal has emerged within several of the forest communities themselves and has become part of the N.D.P. policy on forests. It is to increase community participation in ownership of tree farm licences and in resource management decisions. Licences could be allocated in future to community-based organizations on stipulated conditions of harvesting, wood utilization, reforestation, and manufacturing. The organizations could be managed by community personnel with elected boards of directors accountable to the communities affected.[38] This plan would be viable if a marketing board were established to seek out world markets for specialized wood products produced by community firms which would be too small in themselves to maintain sales organizations.

Efficiencies of scale are not explanations for the dependence on large companies. Pearse argued that in the lumber sector small firms are actually more efficient than large ones and that the large resource firms had passed the point of maximum efficiency. The contracting system in logging is based on the recognition that smaller logging firms are more efficient than large company camps. Briefs to the Commission indicated the extent of wastage involved in clear-cut logging would have provided the resource suitable for more specialized manufacturing. The only sector which appears to require large units (but not necessarily integrated companies) is pulping. But the product of most of the mills is an intermediate product, used in the manufacture of paper elsewhere, so that B.C. receives much less in returns on the resource than is justified by the arrangements which give these production companies such extensive harvesting rights.

A strategy to encourage smaller production units and more selective resource harvesting processes would not in itself have avoided the impact of the recession, but it would surely have reduced its extent. Had the strategy been in place early in the 1950's, it would have permitted the development of linked production sectors—in machinery suitable for smaller mills, paints and finishes for the wooden goods produced, a publishing business based on more affordable high-grade papers, and so forth. None of these businesses would have provided enormous profits to investors, but neither would they have required enormous capital investments, harvesting schedules, and markets to justify the inputs.

Such a strategy is still possible for the future. It would require a government to remove timber rights in excess of genuine requirements for existing mills and thus decrease the capacity to hoard timber. It would also require the establishment of rules to encourage the development of a genuine log market at the coast, with all timber being up for sale rather than moved through integrated units of the same few large companies and artificially priced by them. It would require a stumpage rate based on genuine log values to begin with and then with built-in incentives for further manufacturing and better utilization standards. Companies wishing to exit rather than meet these conditions could be informed that there would be no automatic transfer of timber licences to new companies which buy out their facilities. The resource rights instead would revert to the Crown to be transferred to local community businesses. Perhaps exiting companies should be subjected to an audit, and if it turns out that they are leaving behind them forests that have no future, they would be charged with the cost of regeneration. This could be written into future contracts.

Workers in all sectors of the industry have suffered so greatly throughout the early 1980's that their struggle is no longer for higher wages but simply for employment. As the industry strives to recover markets, companies are moving toward smaller and more automated mills because it is clear that the heyday of mass production is past. In these circumstances, workers may well be more open than in the past to greater public involvement in resource policy direction, more community control over production and investment, and smaller units which manufacture more end products. A cut in wages would be much less painful if the *quid pro quo* were more community control for the very communities in which the workers live.

NOTES

1. Patricia Marchak, *Green Gold: The Forest Industry in British Columbia* (Vancouver: University of British Columbia Press, 1983).
2. International Woodworkers of America, *Forest Industry Direct Unemployment in Western Canada as of November 1, 1982.* 1982.
3. Royal Commission on the Forest Resources of British Columbia, Gordon M. Sloan, Commissioner. *Report of the Royal Commission, 1945* (Victoria: King's Printer, 1945); and Royal Commission on the Forest Resources of British Columbia. Gordon M. Sloan, Commissioner, *The Forest Resources of British Columbia, 1956.* 2 vols. (Victoria: Queen's Printer, 1957).
4. Statistics Canada, *Sawmills and Planing Mills*, Cat. No. 25-202 and special runs by Vancouver Office.
5. Peter Pearse, *Timber Rights and Forest Policy in British Columbia*, Report of the Royal Commission on Forest Resources (Victoria: Queen's Printer, 1976), 1, pp. 22-48.
6. Ibid. pp. 60-62.
7. Ibid. pp. 296-301; see also British Columbia, *Task Force on Crown Timber Disposal*, 2d Report (Victoria: Queen's Printer, 1974), pp. 167-68.
8. Government of British Columbia, Ministry of Finance, *British Columbia Financial and Economic Review*, 39th ed. (Victoria: Queen's Printer, 1979), Table 42.
9. Pulp and Paper, *North American Industry Factbook, 1980-81* (San Francisco: Miller Freeman, 1981).
10. Pierre Bourgault, *Innovation and the Structure of Canadian Industry* (Ottawa: Science Council of Canada, 1972), p. 52.

11. B.C. Government, Ministry of Industry and Small Business, *B.C. Economic Activity 1980*, 1981:12-14.
12. Government of British Columbia, Ministry of Industry and Small Business Development, *British Columbia Economic Activity 1980, Review and Outlook*, 1981, pp. 12-14.
13. Theories about economies dependent on staples include: W. A. MacIntosh, "Economic Factors in Canadian History," *The Canadian Historical Review*, 4(1), 1923: 12-25; Harold Innis, *The Fur Trade in Canada* (Toronto: University of Toronto Press (1930) 1954; and Mel Watkins, "A Staples Theory of Economic Growth," *Canadian Journal of Economics and Political Science* 29(2) (May, 1963):141-58; and "The Staples Theory Revisited," *Journal of Canadian Studies* 12(5), (Winter, 1980):83-95.
14. Minister of Lands and Forests, Tom Waterland, in Province of British Columbia, 34rd session, 31st Parliament, *Official Report of the Debates of the Legislative Assembly* (Hansard), 4 (5) (14 June 1978):2311.
15. British Columbia, *Forest Act*, 1978.
16. In 1980 both the Provincial and Federal governments expressed fears of deforestation. Emergency measures were announced by the B.C. government though the measures did not result in reforestation, and by 1983 reforestation funds were diverted to other areas. The Professional Foresters Association reported large reductions in government spending in 1984.
17. Claus Offe, "The Theory of the Capitalist State and the Problem of Policy Formation," in *Stress and Contradiction in Modern Capitalism, Public Policy and the Theory of the State*, edited by L.N. Lindberg, et al. (Lexington, Mass.: D.C. Heath, 1984):125-44.
18. See Raymond W. Payne, "Corporate Power, Interest Groups and the Development of Mining Policy in British Columbia, 1972-77," *B.C. Studies*, No. 54 (Summer, 1982):3-37; Philip Resnick, "Social Democracy in Power: The Case of British Columbia," *B.C. Studies*, No. 34 (Summer, 1977):3-20; Alan Artibise, "'A Worthy, If Unlikely, Enterprise': The Labour Relations Board and the Evolution of Labour Policy and Practice in British Columbia, 1973-1980," *B.C. Studies*, no. 56 (Winter, 1982-83):3-43.
19. See for extended discussion, Gordon Laxer "The Social Origins of Canada's Branch Economy, 1837-1914" (Ph.D. diss. University of Toronto, 1981), Chapter 5.
20. Company histories are described in *Green Gold*, chapter 4. Changes since that time are taken from newspaper and industry publication reports.
21. An account is given in Myrtle Bergren, *Tough Timber: The Loggers of British Columbia - Their Story*, 2d ed. (Toronto: Progress Books, 1967).
22. Irving Martin Abella, *Nationalism, Communism, and Canadian Labour* (Toronto: University of Toronto Press, 1973).
23. This and following observations are based on the I.W.A. publications and memoranda, and most particularly on interview data obtained from Clay Perry, Legislative Director and Executive Assistant, I.W.A. Quotations are given in Marchak, *Green Gold*.
24. Information about P.P.W.C. obtained through interview with Angus McPhee, bargaining agent for the P.P.W.C. in 1978.
25. International Woodworkers of America. "A Guide to Forest Policy," 1980.
26. Percentages were computed from raw data in Statistics Canada *Pulpmills. Principal Statistics*, catalogue 36-204. Annual.
27. *Sawmills. Principal Statistics*, catalogue 35-204. Annual.
28. *Logging. Principal Statistics*, catalogue 25-201. Annual.
29. Full data reported in Marchak, *Green Gold*, Table 5.5, p. 135 and accompanying text.

30. Laurence Copithorne, "Natural Resources and Regional Disparities: A Skeptical View," *Canadian Public Policy*, 5 no. 2 (Spring, 1979):181-94. Averages for weekly earnings in B.C. industries for this period ranked construction workers in first place, followed by logging and mining workers. All manufacturing groups combined followed (this incudes not only pulp and paper workers but also mineral processing and miscellaneous others). Workers in trades and services fell well below all of these groups (Statistics Canada, *Employment Earnings and Hours*, catalogues 72-002 and 72-517 (weekly, monthly and occasional publications). Incomes for a sample of workers in the three sectors in 1977 are given in detail in Marchak, *Green Gold*.

31. United States International Trade Commission, Report to the Senate Committee on Finance on Investigation No. 332-134, under Section 332 of the Tariff Act of 1930, *Conditions Relating to the Importation of Softwood Lumber Into the United States*, April 1982, Washington.

32. Detailed job descriptions and also workers' own perceptions of them are given in Marchak, *Green Gold*, chapters 9 and 10.

33. Personal correspondence and discussion with Clay Perry, Legislative Assistant, I.W.A., Vancouver.

34. Financial Post Corporation Service, 1981; Richardson Securities of Canada, *Investment Thinking*, November, 1981; Company reports, 1981-86.

35. Hay-Roe's PaperTree Letter. November, 1985. Vancouver.

36. U.S. International Trade Commission, op. cit.

37. Ronald Neil Byron, "Community Stability and Economic Development: the Role of Forest Policy in the North Central Interior of British Columbia" (M.B.A. thesis, University of British Columbia, 1976). See also, R. N. Byron, "Community Stability and Forestry Policy in British Columbia," *Canadian Journal of Forestry Research* 8(1978):61-66.

38. Slocan Valley Community Forest Management Project, *Final Report*, 1975.

11

Workers' Control at B.C. Telephone: The Shape of Things to Come?

ELAINE BERNARD

In 1969, when workers at B.C. Telephone were threatening to take their first strike action in fifty years, a company negotiator confided to the federal conciliation officer that the company did not fear a strike. Management was confident that it could maintain operations throughout a strike; it also knew that "no telephone union [had] ever won a strike" even though strikes in the industry lasted "on an average seventy days."[1] The 1969 strike lasted just over a month. Management personnel assured the continued operation of the telephone network throughout the strike, and for much of the public the strike was a brief news story or a slight inconvenience, if any.

Telephone workers' strikes fit into a general model of "utility" strikes. Utilities are for the most part highly automated, the service provided has been viewed as essential, and the company has tended to have a monopoly over the provision of service. Workers in other industries have the power to stop production and the creation of profit simply by laying down their tools, but utility workers lack this crucial economic leverage on their employer. In these highly automated industries, a strike does not usually stop the delivery of service nor does it interrupt the company's collection of revenues. Rarely does a customer refuse to pay a utility bill simply because the work force is on strike. While there may be a noticeable decline in service, a relatively small management force working as strikebreakers can nevertheless keep the production functioning. With a majority of the work force on strike or locked out, the company saves millions of dollars a week in workers' wages. As monopolies, most utilities do not even risk a loss of customers because of declining service.

A frequent tactic used by unions confronting a monopoly utility has been to try to bring public pressure to bear on the company. But this approach is seldom successful, as the public is generally indifferent to strikes while it is still receiving service. Worse still, because strikebreaking management personnel are seen as delivering the service to the public, it is the striking or locked out workers who come under increasing pressure to settle the dispute.

One of the most innovative utility strikes in recent times was the 1981 province-wide five-day occupation of the B.C. Telephone exchanges. Arising out of a stalemate in the 1980 contract negotiations at B.C. Telephone, the occupation of telephone exchanges marked a radical departure in industrial dispute resolution, both for British Columbia and the telephone industry. The occupation resulted, for a short time, in the operation of a privately owned utility under workers' control, which showed observers how things could be at the telephone company if the workers were in control. But the significance of the 1981 occupation goes beyond its radical or militant character and lies in the recognition that many of the underlying features leading to the workers' occupation are appearing in other industries.

This paper examines the 1981 occupation, with particular emphasis on the circumstances which led the workers to take this dramatic action, why it succeeded, and some of the changes in the labour process initiated by the workers during the occupation. Finally, it looks at those causes of occupation which are common to most automating industries.

The 1981 occupation at B.C. Telephone was a direct product of a decade-long battle between workers and management on issues of technological change. The 1970's had heralded the computer age at B.C. Telephone, and throughout this decade microelectronic equipment rapidly replaced electromechanical devices. Technological change affected workers in all areas of the telecommunications industry.

In the traffic area, computerized long-distance switchboards, the Traffic Service Position System (T.S.P.S.), eliminated much of the work of long-distance operators, deskilling the operator while at the same time eliminating much of the variety and personal satisfaction traditionally associated with long-distance operating. With the automation of directory assistance, operators in this area completely lost control over their pace of work. Calls were automatically fed to the operators, who were subjected to constant electronic monitoring.[2]

In the craft areas, the change from electromechanical to electronic switching required far less routine maintenance, also resulting in an overall deskilling of the work force. As well, electronic switching made it possible for the company to transfer a number of craft workers' tasks to lower-paid clerical workers. The remaining craft workers increasingly became "card pullers," using automatic diagnostic systems to identify malfunctioning integrated circuits or boards.[3]

Computers, electronically based record and accounting systems, and data banks were used in clerical work. Clerical workers using computer terminals fell under a new work regime where the computer programme controlled the operator's work, creating a rigid and often frustrating dialogue between operator and machine in which the machine had the final say. In clerical areas not immediately subjected to automation, new "decision trees"—modelled on the rigid yes/no flow chart logic of computers—were established. Most workers recognized that decision trees—which detailed every step in decision-making—were paving the way for the eventual transfer of even the most limited decision-making to the computer system.[4]

While automation of the telephone company had not reached the stage of the fully automated electronic office by the late 1970's, most of the workers at B.C. Telephone had much to be concerned about. They knew that the ultimate outcome of the automation programme would be the integration of office record systems with the electronic switching computers of the central office. Eventually a subscriber would be able to telephone a service representative and place an order for service, and the entire process would be completed by a single employee while the customer waited on the line.[5]

The central concern of the workers facing this massive technological change was job security. Automation meant that fewer workers, with less training, could maintain and operate the telephone network. While the company argued that jobs would be secure because of the overall growth in the telecommunication and information field, the workers did not believe it. In many workers' minds was the experience of the earlier dial conversion. With this change, the work force had grown while the new system was being installed, tested, and integrated. But this growth was both temporary and deceiving. As often happens in any massive technological change, the new system of dial telephones and automatic (electromechanical) exchanges operated in parallel with the old manual system for a short time during the conversion. But once a majority of the exchanges had been changed over to the new system, the manual parallel system disappeared, and with it went hundreds of jobs.

An additional major concern with technological change was the continuing loss of collective bargaining strength by the union. Even as early as 1969, the company had sufficient supervisory staff, non-bargaining unit workers, and professional employees to provide a powerful strike-breaking force which could maintain the network during a strike. The new wave of automation would make the job of strikebreaking even easier.

The decade preceding the occupation saw constant conflict between the union and company over issues such as contracting out of work, changes in work methods and organization, the transfer of tasks from one component to another within the bargaining unit, attempts to transfer bargaining unit work to non-bargaining unit personnel, reclassification of jobs, and the opening of Phonemart stores. All these issues were rooted in the workers' growing concern for job security and the weakening of their union. In their quest for job security, the workers found themselves fighting a defensive battle to preserve their jobs and their work, a battle which brought the union into conflict with the company's view of management rights. To the company, choices of equipment, the organization of labour in the work place, and decisions on the nature of work not explicitly covered by the contract were the sole concern of management. It follows from such a view that changes in work and equipment, regardless of the consequences for labour, were the sole right of management.[6]

In the 1977-78 lockout which preceded the occupation, the central issues were management rights and contracting out. Using the restrained bargaining climate accompanying the federal government's wage and price control legislation, the company demanded the elimination of the powerful contracting-out clause and the inclusion of a management rights clause in the new collective agreement. The contracting-out clause in the expired agreement was an exclusive clause explicitly listing thirty jobs which the company was permitted to contract out. Any additional contracting out required the company to negotiate with the union. With the increased use of computers at B.C. Telephone, management wanted to get rid of this restrictive clause in order to make possible the contracting out of repairs and maintenance of computers as non-bargaining unit work. The restrictive clause which the company sought to dump, however, assured that the union members would continue to service and be retrained in the use of the new equipment, thereby constituting an essential component of the work force's job security.

With the breakdown of negotiations in July 1977, the union took a successful strike vote. Recognizing the difficulty of applying pressure on the company through a full strike, the union opted for selective one-day walkouts. The company countered the union strategy of rotating strikes with rotating lockouts. By the end of November 1977, the entire unionized work force, approximately 10,000 workers, were on the streets, staying out until February 1978. The new collective agreement which settled this dispute included 1) the retention of most of the old wording to the contracting-out clause, 2) the addition of a special union-company contracting-out and technological change committee, and 3) a guarantee by the company that regular employees with two or more years seniority would not lose their jobs as a result of technological change.

In spite of agreement on a new contract, the 1977-78 lockout ended with a great deal of bitterness, and the usually routine signing of a back-to-work agreement prolonged the lockout for a week. As a requirement for returning to work, the company demanded that each employee sign a statement guaranteeing no more job action and assuring his or her willingness to work alongside management personnel. As well, the company informed the union that they would call employees back to work at their discretion over a nine-day period. The union refused to accept this back-to-work agreement and the company remained adamant that the individual employee guarantees were a prerequisite to any return to work. The union decided to break the deadlock and force an end to the lockout by publicly announcing that all employees would be returning to work on Monday, 13 February, whether a back-to-work agreement was signed or not. The prospect of thousands of workers returning to work and congregating outside B.C. Telephone buildings around the province brought sufficient pressure on the company that a non-discriminatory return-to-work agreement acceptable to the union was signed.[7]

This dramatic ending to the 1977-78 lockout did not bode well for hopes of labour peace and job security at B.C. Telephone. The union had viewed the lockout as a defensive struggle fought for its very existence. In the wake of the dispute, the atmosphere at B.C. Telephone remained tense, with most workers recognizing that the settlement was simply a pause before the next round in the labour war.

The union and company began bargaining talks toward a new agreement in the fall of 1979, but little progress had been made by the contract expiry date of January 1980. The union recognized that it was in for another long, hard battle and suspected that the company felt that the three-month lockout in 1977-78 had sapped the union's strength. From this position of weakness the union was driven to seek new tactics in order to apply pressure on the company for settlement.

The union developed a strategy of economic pressure through selective job action; it also sought to rally public pressure to force the company to maintain and improve service and prevent a lockout of workers which might further reduce service. The key to the public campaign was the union's intervention in the 1980 B.C. Telephone rate increase hearings of the federal regulatory body, the Canadian Radio-Television Commission (C.R.T.C.).

In this remarkable set of hearings, the longest in the C.R.T.C.'s history (forty-one days), the union opposed the company's rate increase application on the grounds that any increase should be contingent on an improvement in service. The union argued that the company's massive automation campaign was not designed to improve service but rather to create an outlet for the sale of G.T.E. (B.C. Telephone's parent company) equipment, with telephone subscribers in British Columbia footing the bill through higher rates. The union opposed the company's centralization plans, including the proposed office closures which were estimated to eliminate 850 jobs from small communities around the province and millions of dollars from the local economies. Union witnesses testified time and again that the company was reducing the quality of service to customers while at the same time driving up the rates of telephone service.[8]

The union members contributed testimony that no other group could— an insider's view on the operation of the company. In aligning with consumer and community groups in opposition to the company's requested rate increase, the telephone workers played the invaluable role of expert witnesses. They were experts in the telecommunications industry, and the C.R.T.C. intervention helped consolidate this consciousness. As well, the hearings gave the union a public forum to argue that the company, not the workers, was responsible for inadequate service and high telephone rates. The union was taking the offensive by publicly challenging management's plan for the future of the telephone network. Workers had left the traditional industrial relations terrain of the wage and benefit package and were raising the issue of the company's use of new technology, demanding that the company justify its programme.

On the economic front, the union had started its "Super Service" campaign early in 1980, a form of work-to-rule where workers followed company regulations to the letter, resulting in production sinking to all time lows. With the company's rejection of a conciliation report, the union escalated its job action. Starting 22 September 1980, 530 craft workers in Special Services, one of the company's most lucrative sectors, reported to work but refused all assignments except emergency repair work. The selective strike was aimed at B.C. Telephone's money-making areas, including its major business accounts; it did not affect the vast majority of telephone subscribers.

The striking workers reported to work and then "sat in" in the coffee rooms, garages, or spare rooms in the compounds. They played basketball and volleyball in the parking lots when the weather was pleasant, or stayed indoors and watched video movies or played cards, chess, or checkers in bad weather. There were no pickets because the purpose of the selective strike was to place economic pressure on the company while leaving the majority of employees on the job. As the striking workers were carrying on the battle for the whole union, they were paid 70 per cent of their gross wage from the union's strike fund. To help fund the selective strike, the more than 10,000 employees remaining on the job were asked to contribute $13.00 a week to the strike fund.

Within weeks, the selective strike produced a significant backlog in construction and switchboard installation and repair. The company began sending out supervisors to replace the striking employees. The union responded by following the supervisors to the job sites with flying picket squads. As supervisors left the B.C. Telephone buildings, they were followed through streets by union pickets. As a result of the union flying squads, most companies with an organized work force decided to wait until the end of the dispute rather than risk a picket and a shutdown of their job site.

In early November, the company obtained an injunction against the union's flying pickets, limiting pickets to two per building entrance. At the beginning of December, the company was granted a variance in the original injunction. The new wording of the court order allowed the company to expel the 530 sit-in strikers from company property throughout the province. It prohibited the union "from trespassing on any premises owned, leased or therewise in the possession of the Plaintiff in the province of British Columbia by sitting in and refusing to leave such premises within ten minutes of being told by the Plaintiff to leave and not return until notified by the Plaintiff." With the expulsion from company property of the 530 strikers and the new wording of the injunction, the company appeared to be preparing for a lockout.[9]

Early in 1981, negotiations started again with the aid of a federal mediator, but by the middle of the month they had broken off. A week later the company initiated a campaign of selective suspensions. Starting in mid-January, the company suspended a few hundred workers a week. The union, having paid the original 530 strikers 70 per cent of their gross wage, continued the policy for the additional workers put on the streets through the escalating suspensions.

The union's tactic of a selective strike had been calculated to soften the employer by shutting down some of B.C. Telephone's most lucrative services. But as the company was well aware, the selective strike also took a toll on the union, with the growing ranks of locked-out employees draining the union's dwindling strike fund, eventually leaving the union with no money and with all of its members locked out. As well, the company avoided the unfavourable publicity which would accompany a mass lockout, by only locking out a few hundred workers at a time through suspensions for the duration of the dispute.

By the end of January 1981, close to 1,000 workers were off the job. On 29 January, the C.R.T.C. brought down its decision granting the company its rate increase with the warning that a "minimum acceptable level of service quality" had to be reached by the end of 1981 or the Commission would take "action appropriate to the response of the company."[10]

There was a general feeling among the workers that, now that the company had received all that it asked for from the C.R.T.C., a total lockout was imminent. The union's strategy, unchanged since September, was starting to falter in face of the company's selective lockouts. In closed sessions of convention in January, the union had brainstormed on various actions which could be taken in face of a lockout, including a possible union occupation of B.C. Telephone buildings. The union's strike co-ordinator had asked local strike captains to discretely poll their members and ascertain whether they would be willing to stay on the job in case of a company attempt at a full-scale lockout. Since December the union, for the most part, was reacting to company initiative.

The union quickly recaptured the initiative in the next week. Just before quitting time on Tuesday, 3 February, twenty-one maintenance workers in Nanaimo and eight in Duncan were suspended for "going slow." In response to the suspension, which the workers interpreted to be a prelude to a full lockout in Nanaimo, the switchmen gathered in the lunchroom of the company's headquarters on Fitzwilliam Street and, after consultation with the union office in Burnaby, occupied the telephone building. The occupiers secured the doors and posted groups of union members at the main entrance. The door committee asked for union cards and checked the identification of personnel seeking admission into the building. Management personnel were allowed to remain in the building but were relegated to a suite of offices on the ground floor. Workers replaced all supervisors and the occupiers took over responsibility for the continued staffing of the boards and maintaining the switching equipment. From late afternoon well into the evening, shop stewards phoned workers at home and set up shift schedules to cover the boards twenty-four hours a day, and to provide security staff for the buildings.

By evening, reinforcements started to arrive with sleeping bags, snacks, and provisions for a long stay. The unionists vowed to stay in the buildings "until we get our contract." Defending their action, the occupiers explained, "if we leave, we feel the public will get inferior service from the supervisory personnel, who are not trained to operate the equipment properly." A local union official told reporters "we're just your common or garden switchmen, and when people, ordinary people, get desperate enough to take a building over things are getting pretty desperate." In reply to the company's claim that the switchmen had not been producing, the union spokesperson explained, "when you've been sixteen months without a contract you're not exactly a star performer. . . . Morale has been very low and hasn't been getting any better." He charged that the company had been keeping "everyone in a state of turmoil and upset," with people becoming "more and more frustrated."[11]

The occupation brought about a complete change in atmosphere in the Nanaimo telephone building. Grinning faces from people enjoying their jobs could be seen everywhere. A make-shift banner announcing "Under New Management, T.W.U." was hung from the microwave tower on top of the Fitzwilliam Street building. Smaller door signs proclaimed "B.C. Tel, Now 100% Canadian Owned." The union encouraged operators to give the best service. Operating boards were fully staffed. Experienced operators taught clerical and craftworkers the rudiments of operating, and many worked full shifts on the boards. "It's almost been a carnival since we took over," commented an occupant. "People are glad to be free of supervisors." As word of the occupation spread throughout the province, B.C. Telephone workers called the Nanaimo office with messages of support and encouragement. More than one B.C. Telephone office took up a collection and sent the occupiers money to send out for pizzas.

In spite of the jovial atmosphere in Nanaimo, there was increased tension in every other centre in the province. The union recognized that it was in a critical situation. Over two months before, the company had received an injunction which specifically prohibited sit-ins. While the union saw its action as a defensive move aimed at preventing a company lockout, few thought that the courts would side with the union. The union executive met all day Wednesday to discuss a course of action, and two union officers were sent to Nanaimo to view the occupation firsthand and to bring a report back to the executive.

In the other telephone offices throughout the province, workers spent Wednesday discussing the Nanaimo action, asking themselves: if a request came from the union office for a province-wide occupation, would I participate? Nanaimo provided a valuable example. Newspaper articles and television news items from Nanaimo showed that the occupation was peaceful and the workers were enjoying themselves. Initial reaction of the public and press was not unfavourable. As well, the news reports clearly showed that the action was not a desperate act of an isolated minority. The occupiers in Nanaimo were as diverse a group of telephone workers as existed in any other centre in the province. A union member in Nanaimo hit a common chord when he stated, "we're not playing snakes and ladders here. I've got a wife and kids. I need to get a decent living out of this company and I'm going to put my job on the line for it."

On Thursday morning, 5 February, the union extended the occupation throughout the province, calling telephone workers in the province, with instructions to take over service. By noon, the occupation had swept the province. The union president defended the workers' takeover of B.C. Telephone offices explaining that in response to "provocations" and a company "attempt to force a lockout" the workers had decided to "maintain the telephone service . . . staying on the job and providing basic telephone service." The union was careful in its statements to use defensive wording, referring to its action as "staffing the offices for essential services."[12]

As with Nanaimo, the occupied exchanges across the province were quickly transformed. Supervisors were asked either to leave the buildings or to remain in designated areas. Most management personnel opted to go home. Supervisors, police, or reporters wishing to inspect the buildings were granted entry and accompanied on their tours by union members. There were two main assignments in each building: securing entrances in order to restrict access to the buildings and assure that the union stayed in control, and staffing the operating boards. Strike leaders in many areas stayed the full five days in the buildings, but the vast majority of workers came and left the buildings according to organized schedules.

The union executive set out some general rules of conduct in the occupied buildings. Most importantly, they decided that "there is to be no damage and no violence." The union's position in face of a possible police attempt to expel the occupiers was to urge members to resist passively by sitting or lying down, forcing the police to remove each worker bodily. Workers held meetings in most occupied buildings and worked out shifts, assignments, and "occupation rules."

With the workers in control, the regimentation demanded by the company in the work place was abandoned. Operators were no longer required to place a flag on the supervisor's desk when going to the washroom. Breaks were taken when required, and no one was reprimanded for taking too long with a subscriber. If workers found that calls were building up, they recruited more operator volunteers and trained them on the operating equipment. Operators varied their responses from the rigid mechanical replies demanded by the company; in some areas operators agreed to answer directory assistance inquiries with "T.W.U. directory assistance" or "B.C. Tel, under workers control." Workers rotated their jobs, helping to alleviate the monotony. Many workers took tours of the buildings and were introduced to jobs and tasks which they had heard about through their long years with the telephone company but had only the vaguest idea about. For many, it was the first time in all their years with the company that they had seen other areas in the buildings. In a number of buildings operator lounges and coffee rooms were transformed into child care centres.

But the key difference was the atmosphere of co-operation and responsibility. Craft and clerical workers gained new respect for the operators and greater sympathy for the stress in their job. More than one craftworker abandoned operating after only a few hours, in disbelief that anyone could work under such conditions for seven hours a day. For the first time in many years, telephone workers began to feel proud of the work they did. They were still able to assert some control and authority, but it was limited because pace and structure of work were dictated by the machinery. Most felt a tremendous relief from the feeling of being constantly monitored.

The five days during which the union occupied the telephone exchanges had an excited quality about them. In most areas of the world, the seizure of the telephone exchanges by workers constitutes the first act of a revolution. While B.C. Telephone characterized the occupation as "anarchy," most saw it as a further escalation of a longstanding labour dispute. By seizing the telephone buildings the union had gone beyond the normal bounds of collective bargaining, but the union members felt that their inability to have any effect on the telephone company through traditional tactics made the occupation necessary.

A unique set of circumstances combined to allow the union to win public sympathy in this dispute. The drawn out C.R.T.C. rate hearings had brought B.C. Telephone under public fire. In the highly publicized hearings, British Columbians were constantly reminded of the company's large profits and arrogant management. As the telephone workers argued that the company's rate increase was not merited and criticized the company's quality of service, there was little public sympathy left for the company.

When the company refused to sign the conciliation report, it was widely condemned for deteriorating labour relations. The union's occupation was a peaceful and disciplined action, which saw the continuation of basic telephone service for the public. For many, it was a novelty, with subscribers being able to chat with operators. By continuing to staff operating services, the union was able to show the public, more clearly than any press statements, its desire to maintain service. In the past, whether by strike or by lockout, telephone workers on the streets carried the full blame for deteriorating service and for forcing the dispute. With the union in control the pressure was now on the company.

Aside from public support, the situation at B.C. Telephone had been closely monitored by the province's labour central, the B.C. Federation of Labour. The Federation and the International Woodworkers of America (I.W.A.) had intervened along with the telephone workers in opposition to the B.C. Telephone rate increase. With the province-wide take-over of telephone buildings, the Federation called a special meeting of affiliate staff and proposed a strategy of support for the telephone workers as well as three other groups of workers on strike at the same time. The Federation characterized the disputes as part of a wider campaign by the Employers Council of British Columbia to "stone wall" on collective bargaining, using courts, injunctions, and industrial inquiry commissions to drag out disputes and avoid bargaining. In response to this employer offensive, the Federation announced that it would initiate an "escalating programme of economic action" in support of the striking workers. The Federation president promised, "we will win these strikes using the full force of our militant tradition." The Federation president characterized this new stage in the dispute as "industrial relations war on the employers of British Columbia."[13]

The following day, leaders of the B.C. Federation of Labour underlined their support of the occupation by touring the occupied William Farrell building at 768 Seymour Street in Vancouver. The visit boosted the morale of the telephone workers by demonstrating the support of the Federation. Commenting on the significance of this tour, the Vancouver *Province* termed the action an endorsement of the T.W.U.'s takeover, warning that it constituted a "recipe for anarchy." "Now that the precedent of supporting a takeover of property has been set" asked the *Province*, "in the future might we not expect to see, for example, longshoremen taking over the wharves? Bus drivers seizing their buses? Tellers taking over banks? All could be equally justified."

The occupation coincidentally occurred at a fortuitous time in world events. Throughout the occupation, the press carried stories on the occupations of factories and worksites in Poland by the Solidarity trade union. Most Western leaders were publicly defending the Polish workers and condemning the Polish government. This stance in effect gave legitimacy to occupations as a form of popular dissent.

The openness with which the union welcomed reporters into the occupied buildings made it clear that the workers felt they had nothing to hide and did not fear public scrutiny. The press tours also allowed the union to reject company allegations that damage was being done to equipment. As well, the occupiers had a chance to make their case to the press, explaining firsthand many of their longstanding grievances.

Finally, the vulnerability of the equipment in the buildings occupied by the union made it highly unlikely that the police would risk a surprise expulsion or raid. In fact, as far as the police were concerned, until the courts presented them with a warrant, the occupation was part of a labour dispute and they had no plans to intervene. For its part, the union had guaranteed that no damage to equipment would take place. But the situation could change quickly with an attempted expulsion of the workers. While the union had asked workers passively to resist an expulsion attempt, under the heat of such a confrontation it would have been difficult to predict the reaction of the workers or the police. As well, any action taking place in one part of the province could instantly be communicated to all other occupied centres. After all, the workers were occupying the province's central communication network. In addition to British Columbia's intraprovincial telecommunications links, the occupiers handled telecommunications to Asia, Canada's west coast defence communications network, and national television and radio connections. Any attempt to isolate one exchange would require a complete communications shutdown for cities or even regions. To risk such a communications shutdown was unthinkable.

Before the extension of the occupation across the province, the company was in the process of seeking contempt charges against the union for the Nanaimo takeover. B.C. Telephone charged that the December 1980 injunction specifically prohibited sit-ins, and the mass occupation was in contempt of this injunction. A court date was set for Monday, 9 February, and over the weekend the occupiers discussed the possible outcome of the court hearing on the contempt charges.

In its defence, the union argued that the occupation was provoked by the company's suspension of telephone workers in Duncan and Nanaimo. The union's lawyer outlined the peaceful nature of the sit-ins and noted that there had been no damage to company equipment. The occupation had in fact defused the mounting antagonisms at the telephone company. By implication, the interests of the public had been served by the continuation of the telephone service by the union. In an affidavit to the court, a union official from Nanaimo stated, "it is my opinion and the unanimous opinion of the executive of Local 3 [Nanaimo] of the Telecommunications Workers Union that we have averted a much more serious confrontation between the union and the Company" and that relations between the workers and lower management had improved as a result of the occupation.[14]

The court rejected the union's argument, denouncing it for setting itself as sole arbiter of "what is in the best interests of the public, the union members, and even of the company." Finding the union guilty of criminal contempt, the judge charged that "a more blatant affront to the authority of this Court, the law and of the basic principles of an ordered society would be difficult to imagine." The court ruled that the union would be fined an undetermined amount and that the fine would be increased for each day the union continued in the occupation. The sentencing was suspended for two days, as the court awaited the union's response to the order that it evacuate the buildings.

While the union had pledged to remain in the buildings until a contract was signed, the union leadership felt that with the court conviction they would eventually be forced out. The discussion turned to whether or not to follow through with the tactic of passive resistance. The union executive felt that the tactic would divide the union, with some members opting to remain in the buildings until carried out and others walking out on their own. The solidarity, co-operation, and general good feeling built up during the occupation would be lost if some workers left the buildings out of fear of arrests, or physical intimidation. As well, the confrontation with police inherent in the tactic might lead to damage and violence which, regardless of circumstances, would be blamed on the union. The union would lose the support it enjoyed to date.

A second tactic—defiance of the court order—was discussed, but the majority view was that this would lead to the smashing of the union. With the union convicted of criminal contempt, the T.W.U. was no longer taking on just the telephone company. Defiance of the court order meant the union had to contend with the police, the courts, and the military—in short, the Canadian state.

Neither of these two alternatives were considered realistic, and so the union executive decided to order an end to the occupation. With the workers on the street and public sympathy behind the union, they reasoned, the dispute could still be won. In a communication sent to the occupied buildings, the union leadership commended the telephone workers for the occupation, stating "we have proven that our disciplined membership is willing and able to provide the people of British Columbia with telephone service despite countless management provocations designed to lock us out." It described the court ruling as "granting the company the lockout which B.C. Tel has not been able to achieve on its own" and promised escalation in the form of a province-wide strike. The statement included instructions to be followed during the evacuation of the buildings. Anticipating that the company would accuse workers of sabotage, the union instructed local areas to arrange for tours of all occupied buildings before they were vacated. After establishing that no telephone equipment or facilities had been damaged, the workers were to leave the company premises together in a disciplined, orderly march out.[15]

Most of the buildings were vacated later Monday evening or early Tuesday morning. The one exception was 768 Seymour, B.C. Telephone's "nerve centre." The tour of the twelve-floor building started at 9:00 A.M. on Tuesday and ended with a march out at noon. Trade unionists, largely construction workers from downtown Vancouver, left their job sites shortly before noon and gathered in front of the B.C. Telephone building in a massive show of solidarity. The demonstration filled the street and crowded into a four-storey parking garage opposite the B.C. Telephone building. At noon, the telephone workers marched out of the building led by a unionist playing the bagpipes. It took a full twenty minutes for the workers to file out of the B.C. Telephone building.

For the first few days of the all-out strike, local areas sent flying pickets to shut down anything remotely connected with B.C. Telephone. The union leadership warned that the union was awaiting sentencing on conviction for contempt of a court injunction and that further violations of the injunction would leave the union in a precarious position. Local strike captains were told to restrict picketing to two workers per building entrance. The return to the streets after the five-day occupation left emotions running high. During the occupation, T.W.U. members had been working long and hard staffing the exchanges; once on the streets, they wanted to force an immediate settlement.

With the end of the occupation, the federal labour minister sent his senior mediator to end the dispute. Negotiations were started but broke off after six days when the company demanded that any settlement be contingent upon a further telephone rate hike. The demand shocked even the mediator who claimed that "we have an agreement, but I can't cope with a situation where one party [B.C. Tel] puts a third party [C.R.T.C.] into the picture." The rate increase in the collective agreement was, in the words of the mediator, "a new experience in any mediations I've been involved in." The federal labour minister called it "bizarre" and characterized the demand as "totally outside the field of labour relations. . . . I am not aware in my experience of any occasion in history in which any utility company ever before thought to put such a clause in a collective agreement," he explained.[16]

The newspapers were also quick to condemn the company's proposal. The Vancouver *Sun* termed it "corporate blackmail," charging that "with one crude slash the company has cut its own credibility in this dispute." The *Province* termed the company's proposal "preposterous," stating that "no company can expect a guaranteed recovery of its costs and such a suggestion can come only from someone dwelling in Never-Never Land."[17]

In response to the public outcry, the company agreed to reopen negotiations with a new mediator; on 2 March a tentative agreement was reached. But the dispute was far from over. During the course of the strike, B.C. Telephone supervisors had fired a total of twenty-four unionists for strike-related activities. The union regarded these firings as victimizations and insisted that the back-to-work agreement allow all employees to return to work. The union contended that if it allowed the company to get away with these firings, "every struck employer would simply fire strikers to weaken the union and break the strike."[18]

The company argued that the fired employees had "abused their strike privilege," a statement which infuriated trade unionists, who felt that strike action was a right not a privilege. B.C. Telephone proposed that the union seek reinstatement of the twenty-four through the grievance procedure. The company urged that the strikers return to work until the fate of the twenty-four was settled. This proposal was rejected by the union and on 6 March, talks broke off once again.[19]

In the last week of February, the B.C. Federation of Labour announced that one-day general strikes were to be held in different regions of the province in an escalating campaign in support of the telephone workers. The Federation warned that the one-day actions might culminate in a province-wide general strike. Nanaimo, where the occupation had begun and a city noted for its strong labour traditions, was appropriately chosen as the centre for the first strike.[20]

On Friday, 6 March, Nanaimo was shut tight for one day. Ferries, buses, Harmac Pulp and Paper mill, Crown Zellerbach, MacMillan Bloedel, Assembly Wharves, SuperValue, Safeway, Overwaitea, construction sites, provincial government offices, liquor stores, federal government offices, post offices—every work place with a union was closed from midnight Thursday to midnight Friday. The press condemned the solidarity action, but despite these criticisms the Federation announced that the second solidarity action would take place on 20 March in the East Kootenays, an important resource centre for mining and forestry.[21]

On 14 March, the union and company agreed to a back-to-work arrangement. Subject to membership ratification of the contract, all employees were to return to work on 23 March. The evening before the return to work, a sole arbitrator was to submit a binding interim decision on the twenty-four fired workers; he had the power to recommend suspension of any or all of them. Those suspended would report to work on the morning of 23 March but would leave immediately. They would collect their full salary pending the final outcome of the arbitration.[66] .flhyxnpo following week the union held ratification meetings around the province. On 20 March, the contract was adopted and the following day the agreement was signed. The B.C. Federation of Labour postponed indefinitely its second one-day strike.

With the return to work of the telephone workers, the arbitrator brought down his interim decision that ten employees were to be temporarily suspended. A little over a week later, in his final report, he ordered full reinstatement of these suspended employees, arguing that the strike was basically free of violence. With 10,000 workers on strike, he argued, "the mathematics of the dispute indicate that there were hundreds of confrontations daily between union members and supervisors." "I can say," he continued, "that there was not so much as a bloody nose in those hundreds of individual confrontations that took place." B.C. Telephone immediately announced that it would appeal the "binding decision" to the Supreme Court of British Columbia.[23] After a confrontation lasting 536 days, including a four-month selective strike, a seven-day occupation in Nanaimo, a five-day province-wide occupation of telephone exchanges, a one-day general strike in Nanaimo, the intervention of the federal labour minister, the provincial labour minister, the provincial leader of the opposition, and half a dozen mediators, the telephone workers had concluded another collective agreement.

In a long-term sense, the telephone workers' occupation represented the possible development of a new and different type of workers' consciousness in North America, demanding a re-evaluation of the assumptions of the modern labour-management relationship—which gives management control over the organization of labour and the design of production and tools. A central driving force giving impetus to this new consciousness is management's introduction of new technology, removing the worker's control over his or her product, deskilling him or her, and threatening job loss. While the telephone workers are in an industry on the leading edge of the new technology, there is much in the specific case of the telephone industry which is also generally true about the introduction of the new technology in other industries, including restructuring of work, deskilling, and fear for job security.

The telephone workers' intervention into the C.R.T.C. hearings crystallized the new consciousness, with the workers allied with labour, community, and consumer groups in the role of experts in the telecommunications industry. After close to a century of scientific management and deskilling, the telephone workers still recognized that they were the basic producers and as such the experts on work in the industry, with a right to voice opinions on organization and decision in the work place. With every increasing technological change and the accompanying radical restructuring of work, the workers recognized the urgent need for them to assert their voice and their concerns in the work place, before it was too late.

The dilemma facing the telephone workers was that at just such a time as they began to recognize the need to assert more control over decision-making in the work place, they lost the industrial strength to win such major concessions from the company: they lost the ability to shut down production. Also in this respect, the experience of the telephone workers is not significantly different from what is happening in many organized work places where workers have experienced a continual weakening of their strike weapon: through automation and the inclusion of non-bargaining unit professionals into the industry; through legislative weakening of the right to strike such as in the B.C. Essential Services Act; or through the role of the courts in curtailing strike activity. It is valuable to remember that the telephone workers' action came out of a position of weakness not of strength. One suspects that, if the members had not feared a lockout, had trusted the company promise of job security, and had felt that they could assert sufficient pressure on the company through more traditional industrial actions, the occupation would not have occurred. Industrial peace will not necessarily be the outcome of the weakening of the industrial strength of unions through technological change and automation.

It is also instructive to note the speed at which the telephone workers' consciousness changed from 1969 to 1981. Little more than a decade before the occupation, the telephone workers were widely characterized within the labour movement as a "company union." In the 1969 strike, the union executive worried that they could not bring their members out on strike. By the 1981 occupation, the union executive was seriously troubled that it could not persuade workers to end the occupation.

While it would be wrong to argue that the 1981 telephone workers' occupation marks the shape of things to come in industrial relations in Canada, it is important to recognize that specific tactics employed by the workers could be widely applied in a variety of industries, and that many of the problems which drove the telephone workers to take such a radical action are appearing increasingly in other work places.

NOTES

1. Department of Labour, Letter from D. S. Tysoe to W. P. Kelly, Director, Conciliation and Arbitration Branch, 26 May 1969.
2. Linda Rolufs, testimony, C.R.T.C. Hearings 1980.
3. Rod Hiebert, testimony, C.R.T.C. Hearings 1980.
4. John Johnson, testimony, C.R.T.C. Hearings 1980.
5. Rick Gordon and Ken Hansen, *Technological Change at B.C. Telephone: a Case Study*. Report by TDS Limited (Vancouver: June 1983).
6. Elaine Bernard, *The Long Distance Feeling: A History of the Telecommunications Workers Union*, Vancouver: New Star 1982), pp. 152-82.
7. Vancouver *Province*, "Tel union can return but ...," 10 February 1978, and "Long, ruthless battle seen at B.C. Tel," 24 September, 1980.
8. T.W.U. Intervention to the C.R.T.C. Hearings on B.C. Telephone Company's Request for a Rate Increase, 31 July, 1980, U.B.C. Library, Special Collections. See also testimony at C.R.T.C. Rate Hearings, Vancouver, 30 September through 4 December 1980.
9. B.C. Telephone *Bulletin*, 23, no. 192 (3 December 1980).
10. Telecom Decision C.R.T.C., 81-3, U.B.C. Library, Special Collections. British Columbia Telephone Company general increase in rate, 29 January 1981, pp. 15-16.
11. Vancouver *Sun*, "'Desperate' Workers Seize B.C. Tel Office," 4 February 1981. The Nanaimo *Times*, "B.C. Tel 'Under New Management'," 5 February 1981.
12. T.W.U. Press Release, 5 February 1981.
13. B.C. Federation of Labour, Press Release, 7 February 1981. Vancouver *Province*, "Recipe for Anarchy," 10 February 1981.
14. B.C. Telephone Company and Telecommunications Workers Union, Reason for Judgement, C804526, Vancouver, 9 February 1981.
15. T.W.U. Press Release, 9 February 1981.
16. *Sun*, "Regan Rips 'Bizarre' B.C. Tel," 19 February 1981.
17. *Province*, "Preposterous Proposal," 19 February 1981. *Sun*, "Corporate Blackmail," 20 February 1981.
18. Letter to the Membership, Bill Clark, 5 March 1981. U.B.C. Library, Special Collections.
19. *Province*, B.C. Telephone Advertisement, 8 March 1981.
20. Calgary *Herald*, "B.C. Labour Group Planning Rotating General Walkouts," 4 March 1981. B.C. Federation *Labour News*, 2, no. 1 (March 1981).
21. *Sun*, "Regional Walkout Brings Island Area to Standstill," 6 March 1981.
22. Arbitration Award, Allan Hope, B.C. Telephone and T.W.U., 24, 25, 26, 27, 30 March 1981. If the arbitrator decided to suspend or dismiss the employee(s), the union would have to reimburse the company for the employees' wages.
23. Hope's award only applied to twenty-three members. One of the fired employees, Mort Johnsen, had brought a libel suit against B.C. Telephone when he was fired on charges of destroying company property. The company later apologized, explaining that it was a case of mistaken identity. On receipt of a written apology Johnsen dropped the suit against the company.

12

The Rise of Non-Manual Work
in British Columbia

RENNIE WARBURTON
and
DAVID COBURN

INTRODUCTION

"The growth of the white-collar labour force is one of the most out-standing characteristics of the economic and social development of the twentieth century."[1] The full emergence of the "non-manual" or "white-collar" sector of the labour force has led to widespread research, theoretical debate, and political commentary.[2] In the social science literature, several basic questions have been raised, such as are workers in this sector becoming more like manual workers in terms of their class position, work situation, market conditions, union activities, and political preferences? Or are they part of a "new middle class" with its own distinct characteristics and activities which serves as a buffer between labour and capital? Or are they in ambiguous or contradictory positions, as suggested by writers like Crompton and Wright?[3] Or, as many North American analysts claim, are they best understood as individuals occupying numerous or continuous strata of status and prestige for whom class analysis is an outmoded and inaccurate perspective? In Canada, Clement, Denis, Guindon, Johnson, Lowe, Marchak, Milner, and Rinehart are among those who have begun the task of describing, analyzing, and explaining the increasing proportion of non-manual workers and outlining the implications of this process for class structure, labour relations, and politics.[4]

In British Columbia, longstanding working-class-based political activity and a strong labour movement testify to the constant presence throughout the province's history of struggles over wages, working conditions, and wider issues concerning the distribution of wealth and power. But there is an enormous gap in the literature on B.C.'s labour history which, despite concluding that British Columbia has been one of the most class-polarized provinces in Canada, has concentrated almost entirely on the experience and activities of miners, fishermen and forestry workers to the neglect of the "non-manual" or "white-collar" sector.[5] During the latter part of the nineteenth century, manual workers in the primary industries were among the most militant and radical in all of Canada, forming the core membership of early socialist movements and the most active unions. In recent years, however, disputes involving government, telephone and hospital workers, physicians, professors, teachers, police associations, nurses and others, some of which have led to strike activity, indicate the need for research and analysis of the situation of "white-collar" workers in the province.

For convenience we define "white-collar" or "non-manual" members of the labour force as comprising managers, proprietors, professional and technical workers, clerical, recreation, sales, and service workers.[6] Taken together, these occupations now include about two-thirds of the total work force. Although the more traditional of them, that is administrators, managers, clerks and other office workers, salespersons, nurses, and teachers, have been employed in the province for over one hundred years, they have either been ignored or considered largely irrelevant elements in historical accounts of labour, socialist movements, and the working-class experience. This is particularly true of the newer types of white-collar worker, such as social workers, computer programmers, researchers, laboratory technicians, and library personnel. Although foreshadowed by employees' associations among such groups as government workers and nurses, white-collar unions have been a recent development. But now bodies such as the Canadian Union of Public Employees, the British Columbia Government Employees' Union, the Telecommunications Workers' Union, and the Hospital Employees' Union are in the forefront of labour relations activity. These trends make it imperative that we study both the rise to prominence of non-manual workers in the labour force and their place within the overall social structure.

The presence of a large number of women in certain types of white-collar work is of central importance and has recently led a major researcher in this field to call for an examination of "the connections between the sex structure of work arrangements, the family system and the subordinate position of women within it, and the persistence of class-based inequalities in the larger society." He goes on to add that the presence of working-class women in the office may constitute the only real form of proletarianization . . . the crux of the issue is how researchers can most accurately identify the class position of women."[7]

It is not possible to deal with all these major issues in this paper. In what follows we 1) document the rise of non-manual workers in the province, showing the huge increase in the service sector and in the numbers and proportions of female employees, many of them concentrated in subordinate and poorer-paid positions, and 2) present a modified Marxist political economy perspective as a way to begin to account for these trends. The organization of reproduction as well as production is considered essential for an adequate discussion of women's employment. But this can only be examined in this paper against the backdrop of the rise of monopoly capitalism, the differentiation of capitalist activity which it implies, and the rise of the modern state.

NON-MANUAL WORKERS IN BRITISH COLUMBIA 1881-1981

Occupation

In the past century, the proportion of non-manual workers in the British Columbia labour force increased almost fivefold (see Table 1). The proportion of white-collar workers doubled between 1881-1901 and was followed by a second spurt in 1911-21, but the major growth has occurred in the past thirty years when non-manual workers moved from a minority to a sizeable majority (66 per cent) of the labour force.

Some light can be shed on the nature of these changes by breaking the labour force into the more traditionally used categories of "white-collar" (managerial, professional, clerical, and sales), "service" (service and recreation) and "blue-collar" (manual) categories. It is apparent that the main "trade-offs" have been between the "traditional white-collar" and "blue-collar" sectors (Figure 1). While the service category has shown a small but steady increase, the percentage of blue-collar workers in the labour force has plummeted, primarily because of the decline in the number of agricultural and primary production workers. This has been accompanied by a corresponding rise in white-collar work.

There are, however, two distinct occupational distributions, one for men and one for women. Throughout the twentieth century, most women workers have been concentrated in non-manual jobs (Table 1). During 1891-1921, a time of some of the most intense labour struggles in the province, at least three-quarters of all non-manual workers were men, and they have shown an increasing tendency to move into white-collar rather than manual work, particularly during and after the Second World War (Table 2). Nearly 60 per cent of all new male jobs between 1941 and 1981 were non-manual. However, while at least 60 per cent of the non-manual labour force was male until 1951, the male *proportion* in that sector has been steadily declining. The increasing feminization of the non-manual labour force is thus not the corollary of an absolute decline in the *numbers* of male employees in that section but of a great upsurge of women in the labour force, nearly all of whom have become clerical, sales, service, professional, technical, or managerial workers. Between 1891 and 1981, the percentage of women who were employed outside the home in British Columbia increased from about 12 to 56 per cent. The period of accelerated growth of non-manual employment after the Second World War has thus coincided with the increasing feminization of that sector. By 1971, there were approximately equal numbers of male and female workers; more recently, there is an excess of female over male workers of 12 per cent.

Closer examination of the trends within the non-manual sector reveals that the changes in individual categories among men have not been great; all categories show a more or less steady increase (Table 3). The most rapid growth patterns occurred among "managers and proprietors" between 1941 and 1951 and among "professional and technical workers" between 1951 and 1961. The Second World War marks a major transition period before the rapid expansion of these two occupational categories.

The female non-manual sector, however, has shown quite dramatic changes over the years. The most pronounced of these changes has been in the clerical and service divisions. From 1891 to 1971, these two groups showed inverse growth trends. Clerical work as a percentage of the female labour force increased from 1.2 per cent to 37 per cent, while the service sector declined from 33 to 23 per cent over the same period. A closer look at this latter decline shows that the single largest change for women occurred between 1911 and 1921, when the service category fell from almost 42 to just over 28 per cent of the female labour force. Then, after increasing between 1921 and 1941, it decreased rapidly again from 36 to 23 per cent in the 1950's. Another notable change was in the high proportion of women in the "professional and technical" category in the 1921 census (21 per cent); this number had declined to 15 per cent by 1971. The female "managers and proprietors" formed an increasing percentage of the female labour force between 1931 and 1961 but by 1971 had dropped by one percentage point. The "commercial and financial" group (which since 1921 has included "sales") has actually declined since 1951.

A comparison of the occupational distributions of women and men indicates differences in labour market segmentation. Men tend to be in the higher and women in the lower status occupations in each of the broad categories. In 1971, for example, 13 per cent of non-manual male workers were "proprietors or managers," compared to only 4 per cent of the females. In the "professional" category, the largest female groups throughout the years have been teachers and nurses, as compared to predominantly male professors and physicians.[8] But most remarkable is that almost 60 per cent of all female workers were in the "clerical" and "service and recreation" sectors in 1971. The data for both British Columbia and Canada as a whole shows women confined to particular occupations and occupational groups.

Industry

The occupational distribution in British Columbia is at least in part a function of the province's underlying industrial structure, which can be fairly easily described because of its basic continuity since the late nineteenth century. Shearer has noted:

> The economic base of British Columbia ... involves primarily the extraction and processing of a few natural resources, principally forest and mineral resources. Fishing and agriculture are important, but in much lesser degree, although the recreational use of resources is a rapidly increasing component of the economic base."[9]

Directly or indirectly, forestry has influenced the employment of about one-half of the province's labour force and accounts for about 66 per cent of the province's exports.[10] Nevertheless, while the provincial economy continues to be largely dependent on the export of semi-processed resources, the extractive industries have employed an increasingly smaller percentage of the labour force, mainly because of the use of more capital-intensive, highly mechanized production methods.

Using census data, McInnis has calculated industry classifications comparable over the 1911-61 period for all the major regions in Canada.[11] We have updated his British Columbia data to 1971, adding roughly comparable 1981 data from the Labour Force Survey (Table 4). Remarkable trends appear over the seventy-year period: for example, the increase in the percentage of the labour force in the service industries (from 12.6 to 30.7), and the decreases in both agriculture (from 11.8 to

2.1) and in the primary sector as a whole from 27.3 to 7.4. Both "trade" and "finance, insurance, and real estate" show steady increases. The most significant change, however, is the percentage employed in "manufacturing," which was steadily increasing until 1951 and has been declining ever since. The current British Columbia labour force comprises a very small proportion of primary sector workers (7.4 per cent), a shrinking secondary manufacturing and construction sector (22.0 per cent), and a huge tertiary sector employing over two-thirds of all B.C. workers (70.6 per cent).

There are three possible ways in which the industrial composition of the labour force can be related to the occupational trends discussed earlier.[12] The growth in the proportion of non-manual workers may have involved 1) their employment in greater numbers within existing industrial sectors, 2) the rise of newer, predominantly non-manual industrial sectors such as "financial" or "service" or 3) the interaction between the two.

Based on a method used by Singelmann and Browning, comparisons were made of the net shift in occupational distribution in 1941-71. Table 5 reveals that all three processes are at work.[13] But while all of the non-manual categories increased during the period, the only manual group to gain was that of "craftsmen and operatives." There have been large shifts among occupational categories independent of growth in the labour force. As we have already seen, the major changes have been away from primary and labouring occupations toward "clerical," "professional and technical," and "managerial" groups.

A comparison of the non-manual and manual groups as a whole, however, indicates that about three-quarters of the shift from manual to non-manual work can be explained by changes in the British Columbia industrial structure: 129,292 out of a total net shift of 169,615. There have been large shifts between industries, and those gaining the most are the ones already predominantly white-collar in nature.[14] For more specific occupational categories, clerical workers show trends which somewhat contradict the results for non-manual workers as a whole. While the other non-manual categories (such as "managers") show larger "industry shift" than "occupational shift" effects, the proportion of the growth in clerical workers in the labour force because of the increases *within* industries is over twice that resulting from changes in industrial structure. On the other hand, both "sales" and "service and recreation" categories would actually have lost proportionately if there had only been within-industry compositional shifts. They gained only because of the large shift to these two categories because of increases in sales and recreation industries. Overall, these detailed comparisons reveal that the "service and recreation" group has been the main beneficiary of changes in industrial structure and clerical workers the main beneficiaries of occupational composition changes within industry.

Discussion

In the absence of detailed research into the growth and decline of particular industries and occupations in the province, a thoroughgoing explanation of the rise and feminization of non-manual work in British Columbia is not possible at this time. However, we are persuaded that a modified Marxist political economy perspective is appropriate. That is, British Columbia's changing economy and social structure are best understood in relation to a developing capitalist mode of production which was introduced by Europeans in the nineteenth century. Seccombe has recently modified traditional Marxist approaches by placing reproduction processes—the production of labour-power on a daily and generational basis—at the centre of analysis; he argues that, together with production of the means of subsistence and of the means of production themselves, reproduction is not a "superstructural" element but a basic ingredient of particular modes of production and specific social formations.[15] In this way the position of women in all societies, which is dependent on conceptions of wife/motherhood and is organized within household/family/kin relations, is analyzed as part of the basic forces and relations of production and reproduction.

In adopting this approach, we acknowledge that technological change, the growth of large, complex bureaucratic organizations, new forms of communication, the expansion of leisure activities, and advances in prosperity have all been involved in the rise of non-manual employment. But there are major shortcomings in theories which emphasize such processes as merely part of the logic of industrialization, bureaucratization, modernization, or the advent of the post-industrial or service society. Most important is their tendency to see these developments as unrelated to concrete social relations, particularly those involving power and interests. Whether, how, and to what extent new forms of activity such as technological processes or work organization are to be introduced is usually decided by men in positions of authority within corporate or governmental organizations. Property ownership, especially that which confers control over capital expenditures, is a fundamental condition of the exercise of such authority. The class relationship between employers and those who produce the commodities and services they sell is the primary context for decisions about adopting new technology or work organization.[16]

By not making these social relations explicit, most orthodox social scientific approaches provide only partial accounts of the rise of non-manual employment; thus, they serve as ideological screens which obscure class relations, sometimes to the extent of denying their very existence in favour of an atomized hierarchy of prestige or income levels. Orthodox social science has also failed to present an adequate approach to problems of gender and women's oppression. Theories of sex role socialization are of limited value in explaining the movement of women into the work force and into certain kinds of white-collar work in particular.[17]

Following the above modified Marxist approach, we note that accumulation takes place within capitalism through a steady increase in surplus value. The production of relative rather than absolute surplus value became the prime means of capital accumulation; this occurred through the introduction of more efficient technology and the use of management techniques or work fragmentation. Rising rates of relative surplus value thus provide the basis for the expansion of corporate enterprise and for the employment of increasing numbers of workers who are unproductive (in the sense of not contributing directly in their own activity to the production of surplus). In the following discussion, we stress: 1) the growth of large-scale corporate organizations as a primary feature of the transition from competitive, entrepreneurial to monopoly (perhaps more appropriately "oligopolistic") capitalism, 2) the expansion of state organizations, and 3) the feminization of subordinate forms of white-collar work. These trends have been accompanied by the decline of self-employed members of the labour force; the differentiation of capitalist activity, whereby various specialized workers take over many tasks previously performed by capitalist employers themselves; and a general increase in the use of female labour power.

FROM ENTREPRENEURIAL TO MONOPOLY CAPITALISM

During the nineteenth century, when capitalism first established a foothold in British Columbia, it coexisted with other modes of production, including those of the native peoples and also petty or independent commodity production where the owners of capital goods and resources used their own labour (or that of their households) to produce saleable commodities or provide services.[18] But capitalism tends to supersede petty commodity production, partly because of the high levels of accumulation made possible by its superior productive capacity. This process was greatly helped in British Columbia by concessions to corporations from governments in the form of subsidies, tax benefits, and legal access to land and resources.

Malcolmson's research shows clearly how, after completion of the Canadian Pacific Railway in 1886, the legal framework of state activity shifted away from supporting independent producers towards catering for resource companies.[19] The formation of British Columbia Packers' Association in 1902, through the acquisition of forty-two canneries, and the arrival of large American lumber companies at the turn of the century were early landmarks in the trend towards monopoly capitalism.[20] By 1980, the four largest canning companies accounted for 82 per cent of all salmon canned in the province and 84 per cent of herring roe.[21] In the forest industry, Marchak noted the following data on corporate concentration in 1978:

> At present, ten companies control between 80 and 93 per cent of the forestry resource in each of the seven forestry districts, own about 35 per cent of the lumber facilities, 90 per cent of the pulp facilities, 100 per cent of the paper facilities, and 74 per cent of the plywood and veneer facilities."[22]

In manufacturing, the trend towards oligopolistic concentration has been steady for the past one hundred years. In 1881, 16.4 per cent (68 of 415) of manufacturing establishments in the province produced 69.1 per cent of total product value in that sector.[23] By 1975, 4.9 per cent (154 of 3,131) produced 90.3 per cent of total product value in manufacturing.

From the labour force point of view, 33 per cent of all employees in manufacturing in 1979 worked in establishments which employed 500 or more; and 56 per cent were in establishments with 200 or more. Less than 10 per cent were in establishments with fewer than 20 employees. More importantly, non-production workers comprised 34 per cent of the largest establishments (those with over 500 workers), 19 per cent of the moderate (200-500 workers), and only 12 per cent of the smallest (less than 20 workers). Thus, 65 per cent of non-production workers in manufacturing in 1979 were in plants with 200 or more employees.

In the retail merchandising trade, 6.8 per cent of all stores had 61 per cent of total sales by 1971. In retail services, a traditional field for small or independent businesses, 71 per cent of sales were controlled by only 7.7 per cent of establishments.

The precise significance of the above trends towards monopoly capitalism for the spread of non-manual work lies in the diversification of tasks carried out in large bureaucratic organizations. In the early stages of industrial capitalism, the owner-entrepreneurs were personally responsible for and involved in all aspects of the activities of the enterprise: employing, organizing, and supervising workers, and co-ordinating production, transportation, distribution and so on. These tasks and many newer ones are now carried out by specialized personnel. Financing, marketing, supplying raw materials, advertising, and data processing are all examples of what Crompton calls the "differentiation of capitalist activity."[24] These changes involve an increase in the proportion of administrative, professional, technical, and clerical workers within industries, as well as the rise of predominantly white-collar industrial sectors, such as advertising, communications, or banking. Control over the labour process has also been extended by the application of "scientific management" techniques in imposing stricter forms of work discipline on employees.[25] As Marglin has shown, this was not simply a move towards greater efficiency but also a means of controlling potentially recalcitrant workers.[26] It led to the growth of several strata of productive workers with different job tasks, rates of pay, and differing work privileges. As well, more people were needed to administer and monitor these processes.

One major example of the expansion of white-collar work is provided by clerical workers. According to Lowe, there was in Canada as a whole an administrative revolution in the first three decades of this century. He observed that increasing company size, resulting from growth, mergers, and takeovers, generated the need to organize and control bigger and more geographically dispersed production and distribution units. With the increase in size of the clerical and administrative functions came the need to control administration itself, a problem related to the growth of management consulting and such new occupations as systems and budgetary analysis.

All the above examples of occupational diversification are closely related to the processes of production and the realization of surplus. They are organizational measures taken by occupants of distinct class positions as the owners and controllers of capital.

We recognize that, in the absence of data on the extent to which British Columbia conformed to the above general trends, these comments are merely tentative efforts at theoretical analysis. Table 6, however, shows that, although British Columbia has had a larger tertiary sector than other Canadian regions since 1911, the proportions across Canada are remarkably similar. In Table 7, regional similarities in occupational distribution are also apparent.

THE GROWTH OF STATE INSTITUTIONS

We have already noted the role of government in assisting capital accumulation directly through favourable legislation and access to resources. Provision of transportation routes, including railroads, highways, air routes, and ferries, easy access to energy sources, especially electrical power, and scientific and technological research have all been major state services to corporate capital. The state's contribution to re-producing a stable and co-operative labour force and maintaining support for the existing political and economic order lies in the fields of educa-tion, labour relations, and health, welfare, and recreational services. Many of those services were introduced to cope directly with problems of unemployment, poverty, industrial and social unrest, and worker-supported political opposition.

Recently released data provide a broad picture of the size of the public service in the government of British Columbia since 1872 (Table 8). There was a threefold increase before 1900 and an increase of more than four times between 1901 and 1921. From then until after the Second World War the figure grew to over 7,000 employees. By 1961, it reached to over 10,000 and in the prosperous 1960's it climbed towards the 30,000 mark. The figure for 1981 showed that there were over 43,000 provincial government employees. This number is almost identical to that for employees of the federal government within the province, which by June 1981 was 43,259, up from 19,546 in October 1959.[27]

But the state has far greater influence on employment than simply on its own employees. Wide sectors of society, including educational and health sectors, depend directly or indirectly on state financing. Defining public employment more widely to include educational and institutional workers in hospitals, charitable and religious institutions, as well as gov-ernment employees provides further evidence of the huge growth of state-dependent employment. Between 1947 and 1975, public employ-ment in the province increased from 35,851 to 229,885 workers, a six-fold increase, over twice that for the labour force as a whole.[28]

Although we do not have a breakdown of these figures along occupa-tional lines, the 1971 census showed that 81 per cent of employees in British Columbia in the "public administration" sector fell into our defi-nition of the non-manual catgegory.

FEMINIZATION

We have shown that female workers have formed a growing propor-tion of the provincial labour force since the turn of the century, the ma-jority of them occupying subordinate positions in the "clerical" and "service and recreation" sectors. Even in the "professional and techni-cal" and "commercial and financial" fields they tend to find themselves in relatively powerless, dependent, and lower-paid situations compared to male workers.

In order to account for these trends, we suggest an analysis, following Seccombe, which accommodates both the domestic and the occupational division of labour, that is, social reproduction as well as the production of surplus value through goods and services. During the early development of capitalism in Europe and Eastern North America, women and children were employed as wage-labour on a large scale. As a result of male workers' struggles for a living wage, the displacement of labour power by machinery, and pressures from the male-dominated labour movement, women and children were removed from many industrial establishments. This led to their domestication and to the undervaluation of housework within the sexual division of labour. The mainly single women who did take up employment were paid low wages partly because of the application of patriarchal ideology in the form of sexual discrimination and because of the need for reduced labour costs on the part of profit-making enterprises.

As the clerical and service sectors grew around the turn of the century, women workers were preferred because they cost less to employ, were prepared to carry out menial tasks, could work on a part-time basis, did not expect promotion, and were unlikely to unionize. According to Lowe's research on clerical workers, fragmentation of clerical tasks and speeding up of correspondence were accomplished effectively by employing women.

Although it is no longer the case, married women used to provide a reserve labour force which could be drawn upon when needed, such as during the two World Wars. Men were not attracted by clerical and service work because there was little chance for upward mobility or comfortable salaries. Patriarchal relationships, though not originating under capitalism, have thus been reproduced at both the domestic and paid-employment levels, each reinforcing the other. The subordination of women in the traditional professional fields (such as male physicians directing female nurses) indicates a similar type of patriarchal control.

The feminization of white-collar work mainly involves the employment of married women; this has also been facilitated by the shorter length of reproductive activity. The definition of what constitutes an acceptable standard of living, as defined to a large extent by commercial advertising, has also been a major factor encouraging married women to take paid employment.[29]

Production, reproduction, and consumption must be analyzed under changing historical conditions in order to reach a fuller explanation of the trend to greater women's employment in the white-collar sector. The use of women workers to weaken employee solidarity must also be considered. Rosenthal and Bernard present evidence of such behaviour in a dispute involving telephone workers as early as 1906.[30]

CONCLUSION

Although we have presented evidence to show that similar patterns in the rise of white-collar work can be found in various parts of Canada, subsequent research would likely show unevenness in the differential impact of industrial development, geographical location, and the place of a given region in the national and international economic orders.[31] For example, Vancouver's position in trading patterns and the impact of the West Coast climate on tourism may have had a significant influence on B.C.'s slightly higher proportion of service industry workers.

We noted at the outset the neglect of non-manual workers in historical studies of labour and politics within British Columbia. The question of their class position and class activities is of crucial significance for an understanding of social structure and change within the province. What part, if any, did they play in the intense industrial struggles of the past? Does the rise of non-manual work imply a reduction or exacerbation of the conflict between capital and labour? Have white-collar unions emerged in response to work degradation and proletarianization? What differences exist between the newer white-collar unions and the more traditional ones in the forest, mining, and other industries? What role do female employees play in the structure of class and in forms of industrial and political action? In our subsequent research we expect to shed light on these matters by analyzing in greater specificity and depth the labour-market situation, working conditions, and class-related activity of non-manual workers in British Columbia.

NOTES

This paper is reprinted from B.C. Studies 59 (Autumn 1983). We thank that journal for permission to reprint it and the following for their assistance: the Social Sciences and Humanities Research Council of Canada for research funds; Kenneth Allison, Lesley Biggs, Stephen Scott, and Zane Shannon for research assistance; Elaine Bernard, Gene Errington, William Ccarroll, and Graham Lowe for comments on earlier drafts.

1. R. M. Blackburn, Union Character and Social Class (London: B. T. Batsford, 1967), p. 11.
2. For example, ibid., M. Crozier, The World of the Office Worker (Chicago: University of Chicago Press, 1971); C. Jenkins and B. Sherman, White-Collar Unionism: The Rebellious Salariat (London: Routledge and Kegan Paul, 1979); J. Kocka, White-Collar Workers in America 1890-1940 (London: Sage Publications, 1980); D. Lockwood, The Blackcoated Worker: A Study in Class Consciousness (London:

George Allen and Unwin, 1958); C. W. Mills, *White-Collar* (New York: Oxford University Press, 1951).

3. R. Crompton, "Approaches to the Study of White-Collar Unionism," *Sociology* 10 (1977):407-26; R. Crompton, "Trade Unionism and the Insurance Clerk," *Sociology* 13 (1979):403-26; E. O. Wright, *Class, Crisis and the State* (London: Verso, 1978).

4. G. W. Lowe, "The Administrative Revolution: The Growth of Clerical Operations and the Development of the Modern Office in Canada, 1911-1931" (Ph.D. diss., University of Toronto, 1979); L. Johnson, "The Development of Class in Canada in the Twentieth Century," in Gary Teeple, (ed.), *Capitalism and the National Question in Canada* (Toronto: University of Toronto Press, 1971); R. Denis, *Luttes de classes et la question nationale au Québec: 1948-1968* (Montreal: Presses Socialistes Internationales, 1979); P. Marchak, "Women, Work and Unions," *International Journal of Sociology* 5, no. 4(1975-76):39-61; H. Milner, *Politics in the New Quebec* (Toronto: McClelland & Stewart, 1978), Chapter 4; J. W. Rinehart, *The Tyranny of Work* (Toronto: Academic Press, 1975).

5. See A. R. McCormack, "The Emergence of the Socialist Movement in British Columbia," *BC Studies* 21 (1976):3-27; M. A. Ormsby, *British Columbia: A History* (Toronto: Macmillan, 1958); P. A. Phillips, *No Greater Power: A Century of Labour in B.C.* (Vancouver: B.C. Federation of Labour and the Boag Foundation, 1967); M. Robin, *The Company Province*, Vols. 1 and 2 (Toronto: McClelland & Stewart, 1972, 1973); C.A. Schwantes, *Radical Heritage: Labour, Socialism, and Reform in Washington and British Columbia, 1885-1917* (Vancouver: Douglas & McIntyre, 1979).

6. The dividing line between non-manual and manual workers is notoriously ambiguous; see, for example, G. S. Bain and R. Prince, "Who Is a White-Collar Employee?" *British Journal of Industrial Relations* (1972):325-29. Although the categories used here are broad, they merely help to sketch the rise of non-manual work. Obviously, more detailed analysis is necessary to reveal the full complexity of the situation. A major problem is presented by the inclusion of "proprietors" because, from the theoretical standpoint which informs this paper, they belong either to the capitalist class or the petty bourgeoisie rather than that of the working-class proletariat.

7. Graham S. Lowe, "Class, Job and Gender in the Canadian Office," *Labour/Le Travailleur* 10 (Autumn 1982):37.

8. In 1911, there were 1,735 female teachers and nurses compared to 547 males, and only 28 female professors and physicians as compared to 431 males. In 1971, there were 25,070 women in nursing and teaching and 9,080 men in the same occupations. The same census reports 780 female professors or doctors and 6,070 men. Even within the non-university teaching category, 74 per cent of female teachers were in elementary or kindergarten schools while 71 per cent of the males were in secondary teaching.

9. R. A. Shearer, "The Economy of British Columbia," in R. A. Shearer, J. H. Young, and G. R. Munro, *Trade Liberalization and a Regional Economy: Studies of the Impact of Free Trade on British Columbia* (Toronto: University of Toronto Press, 1971), pp. 3-42. See also R. E. Caves and R. H. Holton, "An Outline of the Economic History of British Columbia, 1881-1951," in J. Friesen and H. K. Ralston (eds.), *Historical Essays on British Columbia* (Toronto: McClelland & Stewart, 1976).

10. R. Schwindt, *The Existence and Exercise of Corporate Power: A Case Study of MacMillan Bloedel Ltd.*, Commission on Corporate Concentration, Study No. 15 (Ottawa: Queen's Printer, 1977), p. 5.

11. R. M. McInnis, "Long-Run Changes in the Industrial Structure of the Canadian Work Force," *Canadian Journal of Economics* 4, (1971):353-61; R. M. McInnis, "Long-Run Trends in Industrial Structure of the Canadian Work Force: Regional

Differentials, 1911-1961'' (unpublished paper, Department of Economics, Queen's University, 1973).

12. Following J. Singelmann and H. L. Browning, "Industrial Transformation and Occupational Change in the U.S., 1960-70," *Social Forces* 59 (1980):246-64.

13. At the basis of the procedure is the calculation of the shifts among occupational categories independent of the growth of total employment (the net shift). The number of workers in each occupational category is then calculated as if there had been only shifts because of changes in industrial structure but not "within industry" shifts in occupational composition, thereby producing "industry effect." The remaining shift totals are those resulting from within-industry shifts plus interaction effects. The procedure is then reversed by calculating the number of workers in each occupational group had there been only "within-industry" changes but no shifts in industrial structure. This produces "occupation effects." The "interaction effect" is then obtained by subtraction of the industry and occupation effects from the total net shift. In order to calculate the effects of within-industry and industry shifts on occupational composition, one must have comparable matrices for occupations and industrial sectors of the labour force over time. Such a matrix is available for British Columbia for 1971 based on the 1961 occupation and industry classifications as applied to a random sample of the census. A complete occupation by industry matrix had been published for the 1941 occupation and industry classifications and, although they are not commensurate with the 1961 classifications, this matrix was recalculated to match the 1961 (hence also the 1971) sample classifications, thus permitting an analysis of the major recent growth in non-manual occupations 1941-71.

14. While these findings largely reflect the widespread trends in industrial structure that we illustrated earlier, the results should not be extrapolated further back. We suspect, for example, that earlier increases in the non-manual categories (say between 1881 and 1921) were owing more to compositional shifts within industries than to changes in industrial structure. See Lowe, "The Administrative Revolution."

15. W. Seccombe, "Marxism and Demography," *New Left Review* 137 (January/February 1983):22-47.

16. For a cogent and empirically well-documented application of this approach in Canada see W. Clement, "The Subordination of Labour in Canadian Mining" *Labour/Le Travailleur* 5 (Spring 1980):133-148.

17. P. and H. Armstrong, *The Double Ghetto: Canadian Women and Their Segregated Work* (Toronto: McClelland & Stewart, 1978), Chapters 5 and 6.

18. J. D. Malcolmson, "Resource Development and the State in Early British Columbia" (M.A. thesis, Simon Fraser University, 1980).

19. Ibid., p. 66.

20. C. Lyons, *Salmon: Our Heritage* (Vancouver: Mitchell Press, 1969), p. 492; J. C. Lawrence, "Markets and Capital: A History of the Lumber Industry of British Columbia" (M.A. thesis, University of British Columbia, 1957), p. 37.

21. P. H. Pearse, *Turning the Tide*. Final Report of the Commission on Pacific Fisheries Policy (Ottawa: Ministry of Supplies and Services, 1982), p. 163.

22. P. Marchak, "Labour in a Staples Economy," *Studies in Political Economy* 2 (Autumn 1979):10.

23. Sources of manufacturing data include Canada Year Book, 1927, 1922-23, 1927, 1952-53 and a series on manufacturing statistics for various years. Statistics Canada Catalogue no. 31-203.

24. Crompton, "Approaches to the Study of White-Collar Unionism."

25. See H. Braverman, *Labour and Monopoly Capital* (New York: Monthly Review Press, 1974); and Rinehart, *The Tyranny of Work*.

26. S. Marglin, "What Do Bosses Do?: The Origins and Functions of Hierarchy in Capitalist Production," *Review of Radical Political Economics* 6, no. 2 (Summer 1974):60-112.

27. *Federal Employment in Canada* (Ottawa: Statistics Canada), Ref. HA-72-004, Dec. 1981.
28. D. K. Foot (ed.), *Public Employment and Compensation in Canada: Myths and Realities*, Institute for Research on Public Policy, Vol. 1 (Scarborough, Ontario: Butterworth, 1978).
29. P. and H. Armstrong, *The Double Ghetto*, pp. 147ff.
30. Star Rosenthal, "Union Maids: Organized Women Workers in Vancouver, 1900-1915," *BC Studies* 41 (Spring 1979):36-55; Elaine Bernard, *The Long Distance Feeling: A History of the Telecommunications Workers' Union* (Vancouver: New Star, 1982), pp. 32ff.
31. V. Burris, "Class Formation and Transformation in Advanced Capitalist Societies: A Comparative Analysis," *Social Praxis* 7, nos. 3-4 (1980):147-79.

TABLE 1: NON-MANUAL WORKERS AS A PERCENTAGE OF THE MALE/FEMALE/TOTAL LABOUR FORCE* IN BRITISH COLUMBIA, 1881-1981

	Males	*Females*	*Total*	*Number in Labour Force*
1881	—	—	14	17,701
1891	22	46	26	48,032
1901	25	77	28	81,276
1911	23	76	27	205,062
1921	31	84	37	218,660
1931	28	84	36	305,890
1941	29	86	39	312,758
1951	36	83	47	437,688
1961	43	88	55	560,462
1971	45	90	60	824,489
1981	48	91	66	1,354,000

*Omitting from the Labour Force totals the "occupation not stated" category.

1. 1881, 1891—calculated from the 1881, 1891 censuses by the authors using the 1961 census occupational classification. The 1881 census does not break down occupational data by gender.
2. 1901—detailed occupational distributions are not available at the provincial level for 1901. Non-manual/manual totals were calculated using broad occupational categories in which linear extrapolations 1891-1911 had to be made in separating "Trade and Finance" workers in 1901 from the "Transportation" category.
3. 1911-21—from the 1961 census (historical series).
4. 1931-61—from the 1971 census (historical series).
5. 1971—from the 1971 census.
6. 1981—from the June 1981 Statistics Canada Monthly Labour Force Survey.
The non-manual/manual divisions in this paper are largely based on broad census categories of occupation. The 1971 census, for example, includes twenty-four occupational categories of which eleven are non-manual; the 1931 census includes fourteen broad categories, four non-manual. Census occupational and industrial classifications frequently change from one census to the next; hence detailed occupation/industry distributions are not directly comparable, although broader groupings are generally roughly comparable. Fortunately the censuses themselves provide comparable historical occupation/industry data across four or five census decades in the historical series accompanying most censuses. Overall, then, there is good comparability for the manual/non-manual split 1911-81, while the 1881-1901 data are estimates or were calculated by the authors from detailed occupational data.

Figure 1. Trends in the Percentage of White-collar, Service, Blue-collar Occupations in the B.C. Labour Force 1911-81.

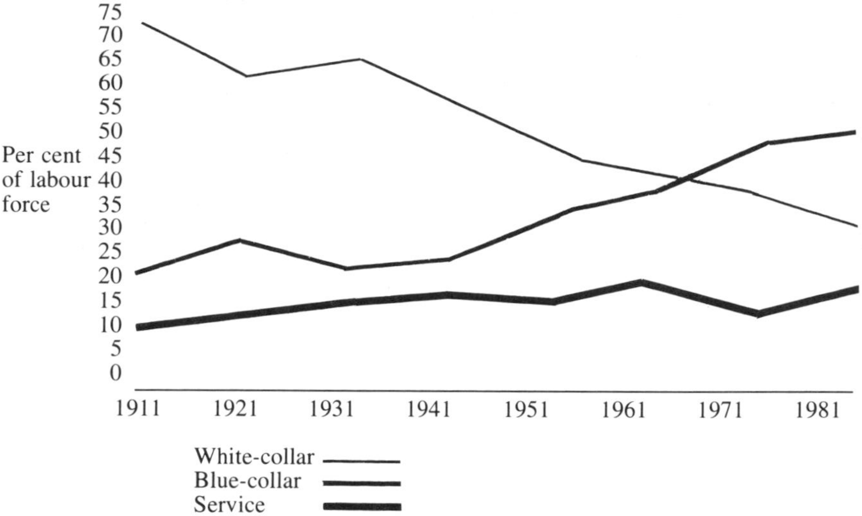

Sources: See Table 1.

TABLE 2.   MALE AND FEMALE WORKERS AS A PERCENTAGE OF THE NON-MANUAL LABOUR FORCE IN BRITISH COLUMBIA, 1891-1981

	Male	Female	M/F Ratio	Number in non-manual labour force
1881	—	—	—	2,478
1891	88	12	7.3	12,566
1901	84	16	5.2	23,032
1911	77	23	3.4	55,183
1921	74	26	2.8	81,698
1931	67	33	2.0	111,203
1941	61	39	1.6	121,144
1951	60	40	1.5	205,830
1961	57	43	1.3	307,744
1971	49	51	1.0	489,318
1981	44	56	0.8	891,000

No breakdown by gender is available for 1881. See Table 1.

TABLE 3. PERCENTAGES OF THE MALE AND FEMALE LABOUR FORCE IN THE NON-MANUAL OCCUPATIONAL CATEGORIES IN BRITISH COLUMBIA 1891, 1911-71

	Males								
	1891	1901	1911	1921	1931	1941	1951	1961	1971
Managers and proprietors	7.6	—	6.4	9.8	7.3	7.3	10.6	12.2	12.9
Professional and Technical	3.8	—	3.0	4.0	4.2	5.0	5.8	8.1	9.9
Clerical	2.2	—	3.2	5.0	4.5	4.3	5.7	5.9	5.8
Commercial and Financial (including Sales after 1911)	—	—	4.4	5.6	5.5	5.0	5.3	6.3	6.3
Service and Recreation	8.4	—	5.6	6.6	6.9	6.9	8.8	10.0	9.6

	Females								
	1891	1901	1911	1921	1931	1941	1951	1961	1971
Managers and Proprietors	1.8	—	1.6	2.9	2.5	3.3	4.5	4.7	3.6
Professionals and Technical	10.5	—	12.8	21.2	18.2	16.5	14.4	15.4	15.0
Clerical	1.2	—	13.3	22.0	20.2	19.8	31.7	32.8	37.2
Commercial and Financial (including Sales after 1911)	—	—	6.4	10.1	9.1	9.8	11.0	10.8	9.6
Service and Recreation	33.0	—	41.7	28.1	34.3	36.5	23.2	24.6	22.6

See Table 1.

TABLE 4. BRITISH COLUMBIA LABOUR FORCE INDUSTRIAL STRUCTURE, 1911-1981

Sectors	1911	1921	1931	1941	1951	1961	1971	1981
PRIMARY								7.4
Agriculture	11.8	16.7	14.8	13.2	6.3	4.1	2.7	2.1
Forestry	5.9	6.0	5.4	5.9	5.7	3.8	3.3	
Fishing and Trapping	2.3	2.5	3.3	3.2	1.2	0.8	0.5	5.3
Mining	7.3	5.4	4.4	4.6	2.6	1.5	1.8	
SECONDARY								22.0
Manufacturing	17.2	17.0	16.6	20.2	22.6	20.2	17.5	14.4
Construction	15.4	7.0	8.1	6.3	7.0	7.1	7.8	7.6
TERTIARY								70.6
Transportation/Communication/ Utilities	9.7	11.3	10.6	9.1	10.0	9.7	8.8	10.0
Trade	9.5	12.2	13.3	14.2	16.7	17.7	17.6	18.0
Finance Insurance/Real Estate	2.6	2.3	2.6	2.5	3.3	4.0	5.0	5.5
Service	12.6	15.4	17.2	17.3	17.1	22.0	26.9	30.7
Public Administration	5.6	4.2	3.7	3.5	7.4	9.1	7.8	6.4

Dr. McInnis kindly provided his data for British Columbia. We standardized 1971 British Columbia census data on industry with McInnis's classification. The 1981 industry data from the Labour Force Survey differ only slightly from the rest. 1911-1961—McInnis, unpublished data; 1971—Canada Census; 1981—Canada Labour Force Survey, June 1981.

TABLE 5. CHANGES IN THE OCCUPATIONAL STRUCTURE AND ITS COMPONENTS, BRITISH COLUMBIA, 1971-74

| | | Components of net shift | | |
| | | | Occupation effect | |
Occupational category	Net shift	Industry effect	(within industry)	Interaction effect
Managers	25,061	16,340	6,681	2,040
Professional and				
Technical	41,959	23,527	19,496	−1,064
Clerical	81,288	20,413	46,843	14,032
Sales	8,171	21,104	−6,928	−6,005
Service and Recreation	13,136	47,908	-24,434	-10,338
TOTAL NON-MANUAL	169,615	129,292	41,658	−1,335
Transportation and				
Communication*	−12,899	4,587	−15,760	−1,726
Craftsmen and Operatives	14,820	4,006	19,935	−9,121
Primary*	−97,779	−-103,870	28,160	−22,069
Labourers	−73,749	−34,013	−73,987	34,251
TOTAL MANUAL	−169,607	−129,290	−41,652	1,335

*These categories were developed by excluding non-manual workers from each of the two industrial categories involved.

1941 census occupation by industry matrix converted to 1961 classifications; 1971 census occupation by industry matrix converted to 1961 classifications.

TABLE 6. PERCENTAGE OF THE LABOUR FORCE IN BROAD INDUSTRY GROUPS, B.C., ONTARIO, ATLANTIC, 1911, 1951-81 (OMITTING THE "UNCLASSIFIED")

| | | Primary | | | Secondary | | | Tertiary | | |
Differences*		BC	Ont	Atl	BC	Ont	Atl	BC	Ont	Atl
146	1911	28	36	51	32	29	19	40	36	30
103	1951	16	14	29	29	39	21	56	48	49
81	1961	10	10	17	27	34	21	63	56	62
71	1971	8	6	10	25	34	25	66	61	65
64	1981	8	5	10	23	30	22	70	64	68

*Differences among the three regions comparing all possible pairs and using percentage differences across ten broad industry categories: e.g., Agriculture (B.C. -Ont.) + (Ont.- Atl.) + Manufacturing (B.C.-Ont.)

1911, 1971 from McInnis, 1973; 1951-1961 from 1971 Canada Census historical series; 1981 from Canada Labour Force Survey, June 1981.

TABLE 7. NON-MANUAL OCCUPATIONS AS A PERCENTAGE OF TOTAL
LABOUR FORCE, B.C., ONTARIO, ATLANTIC REGION, 1931, 1971
(OMITTING "NOT STATED")

	1931			1971		
	BC	Ont	Atl	BC	Ont	Atl
Managerial	6.6	6.2	4.8	9.7	8.6	7.8
Professional and Technical	6.2	6.4	5.3	11.6	14.5	13.9
Clerical	6.8	8.5	4.5	16.5	17.7	13.0
Sales	6.0	6.1	4.0	7.4	7.3	6.1
Service	10.8	9.1	8.8	14.0	12.1	14.8
Total Non-Manual	36.4	36.3	27.4	59.2	60.2	55.6

1971 Census historical series.

TABLE 8. NUMBERS EMPLOYED IN THE PROVINCIAL PUBLIC SERVICE IN
BRITISH COLUMBIA

	Permanent	Temporary	Total
1872	85	6	91
1881	54	1	55
1891	98	20	118
1901	319	16	335
1910	293	266	559
1912	824	N/A	824
1921	1,262	93	1,335
1931	1,313	135	1,448
1941	1,489	362	1,851
1951	7,494	500	7,994
1961	8,763	1,470	10,233
1971	16,011	13,130	29,141
1981	33,108	10,044	43,152

This table is abridged from a document tabled in the provincial legislature on 15 April
1982 and provided to us by the Public Service Commission. Figures for 1910 and 1912
are included because those for 1911 were not available.

13

The Class Relations of Public Schoolteachers in British Columbia

As Harp and Betcherman (1980) have pointed out, the prominence of public school teachers as a political and economic force in Canada in recent decades calls for a sharper analysis of their class position, including the influence of ideological and political factors on their activities. This paper deals with the experience of public school teachers in British Columbia where in 1983 the teachers' union, the British Columbia Teachers' Federation (B.C.T.F.), was the third largest labour organization and where teachers have become a visible force in the province's political arena.

SOCIAL CLASS, THE STATE, AND PROFESSIONALISM

Teachers are among the numerous white-collar or non-manual workers whose rise to prominence in the bureaucratic corporations and state institutions of advanced capitalist societies during the present century has raised problems for the analysis of social class (Warburton and Coburn, 1983). As was pointed out recently, participants in the debate fall broadly into Weberian and Marxist camps (Abercrombie and Urry, 1983:2).

Both perspectives include examples of concern over the extent to which loss of skills, loss of authority, routinization of work tasks, mechanization, and other changes in working conditions imply a change in the class position of non-manual workers. However, the Weberians on the whole maintain that differential salaries, fringe benefits, promotion opportunities, discretionary authority, credentialism, and subjective class-consciousness imply distinct differences between the middle and working classes.[1]

Among Marxists, who see ownership of the means of production as fundamental, there are three basic positions. Poulantzas (1975), Ehrenreich and Ehrenreich (1979), Burris (1980), and Abercrombie and Urry (1983) still argue for the existence of a separate middle class, variously referred to as the "new middle class," the "professional-managerial class," or the "service class." Their approaches emphasize the distinctive political and ideological position of the group concerned, with a focus on such characteristics as unproductive mental labour, social reproductive functions, credentialism, subjective perceptions of class location, and separate cultural interests.

The second kind of Marxist approach is that of Crompton (1976), Crompton and Gubbay (1977), Wright (1978; 1980), and Harris (1982) who emphasize the ambiguities or contradictions found in the objective class position of many white-collar workers, that is, their dependence on selling their labour power to gain a living combined with their performance of the global function of capital in contributions to management, social reproduction, and the maintenance of law, order, and social control. Teachers in particular, while having been proletarianized economically (they are wage-earners) are seen by these analysts as located between the petit bourgeoisie and the proletariat because they operate an important ideological state apparatus in helping to socialize workers to accept the capitalist system. Their part in the distribution of life chances and their professional orientation are also seen to separate them from the working class.[2]

The theoretical position taken here is closest to that of the third Marxist group which argues that teachers became part of the working class when they became wage-earning employees. In this group are Ozga and Lawn (1981), who correctly point out that much Marxist theorizing on class location is deficient because it is carried on at a highly abstract level, separate from studies of the actual labour process, working conditions, and, most importantly, class struggle, in which particular groups of workers are involved. On the basis of their historical analysis of the experience of British teachers, they argue strongly that teachers have much in common with the traditional working class, particularly their basically antagonistic relations with their employers, their historical struggles for working-class education, their vulnerability to redundancy and increased workloads, and the lack of convincing evidence that teachers have antagonistic relations with other workers or that they passively collaborate in general with the state at the ideological and political levels.

Ozga and Lawn stress the need to see classes as sets of antagonistic social relations, asserting that the common interests of many mental and manual, productive and unproductive workers, outweigh their differences. They follow Hunt (1977) in attempting to bring economic, political, and ideological factors together into a single dynamic situation; in other words, they reject the base-superstructure approach. In order to do this for teachers they examine the labour process, proletarianization, and trade-union activity. They also claim that teachers have used the ideology of professionalism to change their work content and conditions in a manner that questions straightforward assumptions about their collaboration with the state.

In writing about the state in nineteenth-century British Columbia, Malcolmson (this volume) describes it as both a product of, and a participant in, the process of social class struggle. Since public school teachers are typically involved in conflicts over remuneration which put them in competition with members of all classes for access to the economic surplus and since the state broadly caters to capitalist class interests, their clashes with the state can be seen as aspects of social-class struggle. As Poulantzas (1978:132) remarked: "The state is the condensation of a relationship of forces between classes and class fractions, such as these express themselves, in a necessarily specific form, within the state itself."

Analyses like that of Muir (1969) tend to obscure the class aspects of teachers' relationship with the state. In his overview of Canadian teachers' organizations, Muir, who saw the B.C.T.F. as the vanguard, detected three distinct periods in their development. The first, from 1900 to the 1930's, saw "significant social and educational advancement" and the formation of provincial teachers' organizations. In that period teachers' qualifications were upgraded, their position in the community elevated, and the basic elements provided for "the establishment of a profession." The second period, which stretched from the 1930's to the 1960's, saw teachers' economic position change from that of underpaid individuals to "a highly organized professional group, receiving a relatively appropriate level of remuneration." The more recent third period Muir saw as involving less emphasis on the economic and more on professional development—teacher certification, aides and assistants, and in-service training programmes.

There is a certain, but only partial, validity in this analysis. It was consistent with many optimistic views expressed by those who saw in the prosperous 1960's evidence in advanced industrial societies of progressive modernization, educational development, and accompanying professionalization. But such analyses overlooked class relations and the uneven development of capitalist economies. Muir did not deal with the impact of the inter-war Depression, nor did he foresee the recession in the late 1970's and early 1980's and its effects on state revenues and the reductions in government spending which have resulted in teacher dismissals and the lost opportunity to practise their skills. They have simply been thrown on the labour market in a manner quite inconsistent with certain aspects of the professional self-image which both their employers and their associations have helped them cultivate.[3]

This paper shares the perspective of Ozga and Lawn, who maintain that professionalism must not be seen as a fixed concept for labelling teachers and distinguishing them from other non-professional groups, but as a dynamic element in their situation which both they and the state exploit as part of dialectic of control and resistance. They also note that assumptions about teachers moving consistently towards professionalism mask the contradictory and dynamic components of teachers' experience with union activity as a response to changing conditions of work. Unionization and strike activity have been teachers' primary forms of resistance against conditions threatening to their status and individualistic professional self-image. Ironically, it was the incompatibility between their professional ideals and their conditions of employment which led to organization and later to unionization.

PUBLIC SCHOOL TEACHERS IN BRITISH COLUMBIA

What follows is an overview of the situation of public school teachers in British Columbia from the mercantile colonial period to that of state monopoly capitalism, paying particular attention to crises, particularly economic recessions, and the contradictory operations of the state. The focus is on teachers' position in the class structure, their role in developing the public education system, their working conditions, and their collective organization and relations with employers.

COLONIAL YEARS: THE CREATION OF A TEACHING LABOUR FORCE AND THE ONSET OF STRUGGLE

The early colonial, pre-capitalist period saw teachers engaged in the education of the children of Hudson's Bay Company officials. The first teacher whom the company employed, Reverend Robert Staines, served as both chaplain and schoomaster at Fort Victoria (Johnson, 1964:16). His work, and that of his wife who taught the officers' daughters, was clearly to provide children of the relatively privileged in colonial society with the personal qualities and attributes necessary to their station in life and possible professional careers on returning to England. Roman Catholic children of French-Canadian packers, voyageurs, and labourers employed by the Company received some instruction from an Oblate priest. Schools for the "labouring and poorer classes," as Governor Douglas called them, were established in Victoria and Esquimalt in 1852, and Reverend Edward Cridge, Staines's successor, was asked in 1855 to hold examinations and report on pupils' progress and conduct (Johnson, 1964:17–19). References to the labouring classes may be seen as unusually clear demonstrations of class consciousness on the part of the colonial elite.

The first report of the inspector of common schools in the Colony of Vancouver Island in 1856 indicated the state's interest in social reproduction. It contained a reference to the need for a girls' school for the labouring class where "those who are likely hereafter to perform so important a part in the community in the capacity of wives and mothers" could be educated (MacLaurin, 1936:298).

Campaigns for a secular public education system were led by journalists and reformers Amor de Cosmos on the Island and John Robson on the mainland, both of whom were familiar with Ryerson's Ontario system as well as those in the United States. Robson advocated educational reform on the grounds that immigrant numbers were increasing, more and more were juveniles, and a better class of immigrant would be attracted by the existence of public schools. Both he and de Cosmos suggested using land to provide endowment funds for educational financing. Their battles with the colonial elite on these issues may be seen as manifestations of shifts in the class configuration of the colonies, that is, the rise of bourgeois elements as rivals for power with the colonial state elite (Malcolmson, 1980).

During the years leading up to British Columbia's entry into Confederation, economic recession followed the Gold Rush boom. The colonial state was unable to pay teachers for work they had done. Revenue shortfalls, the result of reductions in the amount paid in customs and export duties, in land values and sales, in mining licences and road tolls, as well as fewer people, led to impoverishment of teachers in the colonial schools. John Jessop, who later played a leading role in developing British Columbia's public education system comparable to that of Ryerson in Ontario, was one of several teachers whose salaries were reduced and who were told that owing to financial stringency, the schools would be closed (MacLaurin, 1936:30, 69). The Board of Education informed the governor of the newly united Colony of British Columbia of the "almost destitute condition of the teachers" (Johnson, 1971:57). Jessop responded by opening adult evening classes for which fees could be charged, that is, a kind of independent commodity service.

In October 1869, Jessop presented a petition to the governor on behalf of Victoria teachers, outlining their poor treatment, including arrears in salaries and rents amounting to $3,918. In 1870, in what Johnson (1971:61) calls the first teachers' strike in Canadian history, Jessop and a colleague wrote to the *Colonist* newspaper saying they were withdrawing their services because of "non payment of the monies due to us." They had received only six months' pay during the previous eighteen months. Their schools remained closed for two years.

Although teachers such as Jessop had initially set up their own curricula, scope for teachers' autonomy in this area was rapidly reduced as state authorities took over. The Common School Ordinance of 1869 placed all authority for the schools of British Columbia under the governor-in-council, which body was to create school districts, apportion the school grants, appoint, examine, and remove teachers, decide on textbooks, and make rules or regulations for managing and governing common schools. Teachers were thereby subordinated in dependent positions where they were obliged to use prescribed textbooks, even though neither a specific course of study nor a set of requirements for use existed. The situation may be seen as the first attempt by the employer state to control the teaching labour process.

In this colonial period, there is thus clear evidence that shortage of revenues placed education in an adverse competitive position relative to the colonial government's other objectives. Public education was not strongly supported, and teachers were poorly paid, dependent employees engaged in a struggle to improve their economic well-being. They were not valued by the alliance of state and capital which ran the colony's affairs even though legislation had been passed, in 1865 on Vancouver Island and in 1869 in the joint colony, incorporating education into its fold.

It should be noted that British Columbia was not yet very far along the road of capitalist industrialization which would result in the demands for a large, educated labour force. Neither the fur-trade nor the gold-mining era involved settled, permanent communities. Education was seen as vital for the cultural reproduction of the colonial elite, and while approval existed for missionaries' educational efforts with native Indians, merely the beginnings of an education existed for the poor and labouring classes. The teachers of the latter, who numbered nineteen by 1871 and are estimated to have been educating about 20 per cent of school-age children, were treated as expendable workers and forced to suffer penury

(MacLaurin, 19326:121; Johnson, 1964:44). Leading teachers such as Jessop prepared for struggles that lay ahead, not only over teachers' pay and working conditions but over the formation of an adequate public education system itself (Johnson, 1964:45). These struggles are evidence that the state had become an arena for the pursuit of education workers' goals.

POST-CONFEDERATION AND THE SHIFT TO INDUSTRIAL CAPITALISM

The establishment of public education in the new province began with the Public Schools Act of 1872. Co-drafted by Jessop, the legislation was modelled on Ryerson's system in Ontario. That system, as Schechter (1977) has pointed out, was designed to instill habits of discipline, punctuality, and good conduct in the working class, to subordinate workers in the class structure, and to maintain order and social stability in place of crime and social unrest. Curtis (1983), however, criticizes Schechter and points out that education in Upper Canada was a struggle over who would rule and how. He notes the disjuncture between educational reform and economic development, arguing that the former did not seek to discipline workers not yet in existence. Educational reformers were interested in constructing a public, in creating a sphere of classlessness in which the state could rule. Such an analysis must be examined as appropriate to British Columbia case. Clearly the Robson and de Cosmos were engaged in defining a new type of state formation. Although British Columbia's public school system also existed before industrial capitalism was established in the province, schooling was already seen as necessary for the children who would become merchants, shopkeepers, clerical workers, and others who served the independent commodity-producing activities of miners and gold-prospectors.

Jessop became the first superintendent of education, the most powerful position in a centralized education system, which granted his department the right to control teachers' working conditions, salaries, qualifications, and autonomy (Putnam and Weir, 1925:16). One of his first acts was to set up annual teachers' conferences, called "institutes," where discussion of teaching methods and of the working of the provincial school system took place. They were annual gatherings aimed at furthering the professional education of the teachers and communicating the Education Department's views to them. They were "initiated, sponsored, encouraged, financed and largely directed" by the department. This was another way to draw teachers into the state formation. Although these gatherings of practising teachers helped foster solidarity and esprit de corps among teachers and were actually the forerunners of the British Columbia Teachers' Federation, Muir (1969:27-9) has correctly noted that they were dominated by the ministry and neither expressed teachers' professional autonomy nor attempted to solve their economic, professional, or occupational problems.[4]

That uniformity and control were more important than actual material taught is indicated by the absence of a prescribed course of study, as distinct from a list of subjects and prescribed textbooks, until 1880. Because he regularly visited all the schools personally, Jessop was very successful in imposing uniformity and constraint through textbooks (Van Brummelen, 1983-4:4). The use of competitive examinations for entrance to high school, which began in 1876 when the first high school in the province was opened, was designed to control teachers. Jessop openly stated that failure to pass students would argue strongly against the efficiency and capability of the teacher (MacLaurin, 1936:276-77). Jessop also introduced a teacher-certification system, based on examinations prepared by himself and other teachers, which granted three classes of certificate with A and B levels in each. His concern over teachers' general well-being, as shown by his efforts to improve their salaries, was thereby combined with an interest in helping upgrade their qualifications as a means of exerting quality control over their performance.

Pressure towards universal and compulsory public education accompanied the expansion of industry. Only just over half of all eligible children were in attendance in the 1870's. In a manner suggesting the application of norms of industrial production, the Board of Education set up rules and regulations making teachers' salaries dependent on levels of student attendance. Salaries ranged from $80 a month for at least forty students to $50 for at least ten (Johnson, 1971:143). According to Johnson (1971:43), teachers were often paid less than unskilled labourers; for example, in 1876 the average teacher's salary was $644.41 compared to $912 for an assistant gaoler, $720 for a "turnkey," $720 for a convict guard, and $758 for a printer's assistant.

On the basis of such comparisons the struggle for better rewards took place. Having already paid off salary arrears at the end of his first year as superintendent, Jessop recommended salary increases of 20 per cent, noting that "common farm hands" could, during the busy seasons, clear as much again as the educated school teacher. By 1874 the thirty-two teachers in the province were being paid salaries comparable to those paid in Ontario (Johnson, 1964:49). Jessop pressed the provincial government to contribute to a teachers' superannuation fund, but this did not come about for another fifty years. He also concluded that, in order to attract better-qualified people and to raise the status of teachers, higher qualifications were necessary. Merit should be rewarded by higher salaries, more secure employment, and promotion.

In 1885 the first continuing teachers' association in the province, the Victoria Teachers' Association, was formed. According to Johnson (1964:238) its purpose was to increase the efficiency of teachers, securing "greater uniformity in teaching methods and organization and correcting prevailing faults" while also "promoting professional knowledge and co-operation with the Department." Although this was the beginning of a professional association which would eventually protect teachers' interests, the Victoria Teachers' Association was actually part of the apparatus aimed at improving their efficiency, professional development, and co-operativeness as state employees.

In 1904 a resolution to form a British Columbia teachers' union along the same lines as the British National Union of Teachers was defeated, but it provides evidence that solidarity among teachers had increased. A certain number felt that they needed to organize for self-protection and advancement. Teachers at that time were "denied the opportunity to discuss openly their economic problems and other grievances" (Johnson, 1964:239). They also "followed, almost without question, their superiors in education; they knew their proper places and, in general, refrained from any kind of self-assertive action" (Paton, 1964:25).

Johnson (1964:93) refers to certain less scrupulous school boards which allowed overcrowded school rooms in order to maintain high daily attendance levels on which revenue was at that time based. Another way to meet financial exigency was to keep teachers' salaries to a minimum. Teachers' salaries were already related to the overall balance between the state and the interests of capital, the latter competing for state revenues.

Rural teachers were particularly hard-hit by this situation. The creation of rural school districts in 1906, which reduced the number of school boards in rural areas from 127 to 21, was seen by school inspectors as an important breakthrough which, in addition to being more economical and efficient, would bring teachers higher salaries and greater security of tenure. The provincial grant system was actually changed to encourage school boards to improve teachers' salaries by providing dollar-for-dollar supplementary grants up to $100 for boards which paid teachers above the minimum.

Dunn (1978:31) has pointed out that rural situations involved poorly qualified teachers, high teacher turnover because of the low pay, and adverse working conditions, which included squabbles between inspectors and those local parents powerful enough to bring about dismissal of a teacher. Throughout the province attempts were made to respond to the situation by raising teaching standards through expansion of the inspectorate. Teachers were obliged to co-operate in ensuring universal school attendance by reporting student absences to locally appointed truancy officers. All of these processes exemplify externally imposed working conditions which circumscribed teachers' autonomy and reinforced their position as dependent employees subject to state control.

There is evidence that teachers' salaries increased substantially following the turn of the century (Johnson, 1964:96). Much of this was a function of the increase in prosperity which accompanied expanding construction, forestry, and mining industries. This economic growth also enabled provisions to be made in 1910 for school library expansion, medical inspection, and night classes.

The 1911 Census of Canada reported that there were 1,217 female teachers in the province and 491 males, a ratio of almost two and a half to one. There had been only a few more women teachers than men recorded in 1881 and 1891.[5] It is clear that the employment of female teachers on a large scale accompanied British Columbia's rapid growth as an industrial region. Many female teachers began to perform teaching work that had been carried out by men at an earlier period, paralleling to some degree the shift in clerical work which Lowe (1982) has documented in the early decades of this century. Since women teachers were paid less at this time and had to leave their jobs if they married, they were clearly a source of cheaper labour power. That women teachers generally possessed fewer qualifications conveniently justified their receiving lower salaries. More indicative of patriarchal practice, however, was the belief that women were better suited to teach primary grades. Consequently the gender ratio rose to a peak of 3.4 by 1921 only to fall to 1.6 twenty years later, after the rise of secondary education. The latter created more opportunities for male teachers but the overall female-male ratio has remained remarkably stable for the past forty years. In the secondary sector the female-male ratio has ranged between 0.4 and 0.5 since 1951. In the primary sector the comparable range has been from 2.2 to 2.3.[6]

RECESSIONS, STRIKES, AND UNIONIZATION

The formation of the British Columbia Teachers' Federation in 1917 represented an effort to meet the province's educational needs and to improve teachers' well-being under appalling working conditions. The primary aims of its founders were: 1) collective bargaining to improve salaries; 2) a provincial pension scheme; 3) statutory sick leave; 4) improved contracts with tenure protection and a board of reference; 5) a code of ethics to raise the standards of professional behaviour and representation of the association on boards and committees which control teaching conditions (Paton, 1964:13-14, quoted in Skolrood, 1967:2).

Owing to the economic downturn prior to World War I, the salaries of teachers actually deteriorated between 1913 and 1920, falling far short of cost of living increases (Skolrood, 1967:64). The argument for salary raises was that teachers tended to lag behind those with comparable training and experience and that improved pay and working conditions were necessary to attract desirable recruits (Skolrood, 1967:65). In 1920 the federation proposed a minimum annual salary of $1,200.

The first of two significant teachers' strikes took place in 1919 after a prolonged and unsuccessful struggle which included reductions of already low salaries; negotiations with the Victoria School Board had deteriorated sufficiently for teachers to decide to withdraw their labour for two days.[7] And the strike was successful. The intervention of the provincial Department of Education resulted in teachers gaining nearly all they asked for, a situation in which the state acted to protect teachers against the school boards.

Two years later in New Westminster a week-long strike took place when the school board refused to meet the teachers or to submit the dispute to arbitration. The outcome was, once again, favourable to the teachers. Both strikes led to the provincial government taking steps towards submitting unresolved disputes to arbitration, thereby incorporating teachers' struggles into an institutionalized state apparatus (Thompson and Cairnie, 1973:5).

All that the fledgling B.C.T.F. could offer the New Westminster strikers was moral support. There was no financial or other assistance available since the federation was a loose organization of autonomous associations engaged in lobbying local school boards and the provincial government. The B.C.T.F. was not yet officially recognized as the organized representative of the province's teachers. Nevertheless, the 1920's saw the B.C.T.F. primarily engaged in the battle for higher salaries, particularly minimum salaries, and locally established salary schedules (Thompson and Cairnie, 1973:7). These were among the "urgent matters" which the 1924 membership campaigners claimed would be settled if every teacher gave active and loyal support to the federation. These mobilization efforts proved successful when, five years later, the "first real salary scale" for teachers in British Columbia was granted in Vancouver. In 1932 the provincial government set wage minima of $780 for elementary, and $1,100 and $1,200 for high-school teachers (Johnson, 1964:242-43).

Teachers' dependence on relations between the state and capital was demonstrated by a series of salary cuts during the Depression period. In

1935 teachers in outlying areas were organized into the Rural Teachers' Association which devoted ten years towards achieving parity of salaries with city teachers. Parity was eventually reached in the same year (1945) as the termination of the practice of requiring female teachers to resign their posts when they married!

In 1937 the provincial government, under pressure from the B.C.T.F., moved further to combine mediation with control. It effectively established compulsory arbitration in salary disputes, although there is some evidence that teachers refused to take advantage of it on the grounds that it was unbecoming to professionals (Skolrood, 1967:138). The government also made concessions to teachers by providing for bargaining over single salary schedules. Formerly, salary minima were first negotiated before bargaining took place over salaries above the minimum (Thompson and Cairnie, 1973:5).

The drive for pensions which Jessop had initiated in 1876 culminated in legislation in 1929 implementing a fund into which teachers paid 4 per cent of their annual salaries and the government $25,000 per year (Johnson, 1964:246). Subsequently, in 1940, and in response to federation pressures, the scheme was placed on a more secure footing by the Teachers' Pension Act, in which the provincial government accepted responsibility for securing the fund, again demonstrating its responsiveness to the teachers in certain circumstances.

A primary issue over which British Columbia's public school teachers have always been divided, and one which expresses the contradictory aspects of their class activities, is that of affiliation with the labour movement. It was actually approved at the 1943 annual meeting, but controversy still raged within the B.C.T.F. over the next decade. In 1953, after teachers had denied active support to striking school janitors in Richmond, the profession-minded moderates took advantage of the requirement that an application be made for affiliated status with the newly formed Canadian Labour Congress to persuade enough delegates to vote against affiliation.

By the 1940's 80 per cent of teachers were members of the B.C.T.F., and automatic membership became an issue. The arguments in favour were that it would relieve the federation from the necessity of regular membership drives, enhance professional morale, enable insistence on high ethical standards, and teachers would be closer in professional standing to doctors and lawyers! A referendum on the issue had been passed in 1937, but strong minority opposition led to a prolonged series of discussions and proposals, culminating in its eventual approval by the B.C.T.F. Convention in 1944. Three years later the provincial government made membership in the B.C.T.F. a condition for employment.

However, later events were to show that this was by no means a permanent achievement. It became a part of subsequent struggles between teachers and the provincial government.

During the Second World War there was further concerted action regarding salaries. The B.C.T.F. was strengthened in 1940 when it moved from being a loose organization of federated teacher locals to a strong provincial association to which members owed their primary allegiance (Johnson, 1964:242). The federation's magazine, *The B.C. Teacher,* announced in September 1942 that the federation had adopted an "all-out" policy for action:

> In carrying out these plans, and in improving the salaries of low paid teachers, the Federation will also be fighting the battle of Councils, the School Boards and the over-burdened tax payers, in a most effective fashion . . . based on the fundamental procedure of using the combined, unified and collective strength of the Federation, and bringing it to bear on *any* and every portion of the province where satisfactory solutions of salary difficulties can not be obtained (Skolrood, 1967:135-6).

In a strike vote 57 per cent of teachers in the province saw striking as the only means to attract public attention to the deplorable salary conditions in country districts. The strike itself did not materialize, but in 1944 their objectives were met after the Cameron Report advocated a salary grant structure based on the scale current in the more favoured areas of the province. It was at that time too that female teachers began to receive the same rates of pay as males in comparable positions (Johnson, 1964:244).

ADVANCED CAPITALISM, POST-WAR PROSPERITY, AND THE CURRENT RECESSION

In 1944 the editor of the *B.C. Teacher* (Sept.-Oct. 1944:4) called on his colleagues to push for improvements in salaries, pensions, tenure, teaching conditions, and schools generally. In the same publication the president of the B.C.T.F. insisted on the need to have every "teacher, parent and citizen" demand that the development of education receive priority in future planning efforts. The twin goals of advancement of material benefits and improved educational services have since been major federation objectives.

The state, however, further moved to impose institutionalized procedures on its teachers. In 1958 changes were made in the Public Schools Act making conciliation compulsory and requiring the conciliator to submit unresolved disputes to arbitration. These requirements were incorporated into a mandatory timetable for negotiation, conciliation, and arbitration, all of which must occur between September and December of each year. These constraints show that institutionalized collective bargaining exemplifies state intervention into industrial relations which contains class conflict by legally restricting its scope. This practice compels parties to bargain by means of a series of procedures designed to resolve disputes in a manner minimally disruptive to the ongoing operations of the system (Huxley, 1979). In the case of British Columbia school teachers, the short period of negotiation and resolution avoids strikes while preserving the bargaining process (Thompson and Cairnie, 1973). Teachers' leaders, however, have pressed from time to time for full bargaining rights, including the right to strike, through which treatment the B.C.T.F. has compared itself several times to workers not normally considered "professional."

On the other hand, the provincial government and the school trustees have usually interpreted teachers' professional responsibilities, sometimes described as "essential services," as implying that they are unlike other workers. There have, however, been occasions when the B.C. School Trustees Association (B.C.S.T.A.) has behaved like an industrial employer in requesting lockout privileges.[8]

The attainment of automatic membership in 1947 greatly strengthened the federation as a whole, facilitating its usefulness as a supplier of information and tactical advice to local associations involved in the bargaining process. But the improved settlements teachers achieved have frequently been rejected by the Ministry of Education, and the provincial government has occasionally introduced legislation placing ceilings on teachers' salary increases.[9]

Apart from salaries and battles over class sizes as an element in working conditions, (a continuing issue today) the other prime area of struggle has been pensions. Actuarial evaluations had resulted in decreases in pension benefits between 1941 and 1960 (Johnson, 1964:247), and the provincial government had plans to reduce its own contributions. This reduction was cancelled under pressure from the B.C.T.F. but later reinstated. The B.C.T.F. accused the government of channelling pension funds into B.C. Hydro development projects. The issue came to a head in 1971 when, after the province's teachers voted 88 per cent in favour of striking, they walked out for one day to press the provincial government to improve benefits paid to retired teachers.[10] Such developments support the contention of this paper that teachers are involved in class struggle.

There were other incidents which led to growing animosity between the B.C.T.F. and the provincial government in the late 1960's. The government curtailed expenditure on school operations and construction for which it was attacked by the federation. It accused the latter of dabbling illegitimately in politics, for the 1968 A.G.M. of the B.C.T.F. in fact decided that the organization would take part in the next (1969) provincial election by identifying issues and seeking candidates' support. The government removed automatic membership in the B.C.T.F. in 1971. In response the federation planned during the months before the 1972 election to levy a day's pay from members for political purposes. An injunction was secured by the government to prevent such action. The teachers responded by forming a separate organization, the Teachers for Political Action Committee. The consequences of this explicit move into the parliamentary political arena are still manifesting themselves.

The election of the New Democratic Party (N.D.P.) to office in 1972 was seen by politicized teachers as a victory. Teachers received several benefits under that government in the areas of pensions, reinstatement of automatic membership, bargaining rights, and cordial relations with the Ministry of Education. But dissatisfaction with lack of progressive development in education continued. After teachers in Surrey embarked on a one-day strike to enable many of them to travel to Victoria to protest the high pupil-teacher ratios, the Barrett government agreed to reduce class size by 1.5 per year over a three-year period.

An interesting development during the years of N.D.P. government was the submission of a draft "Teaching Profession Act," designed to bring teachers' control over their own occupation closer to those enjoyed by medicine and law. It laid down minimum requirements for entering the profession and provided for majority B.C.T.F. membership on a proposed teacher certification board. The federation was to be granted legislated authority to establish procedures for evaluting members' competence and to govern their ethical behaviour. The draught was submitted to the Ministries of Education in the N.D.P. government and its successor in 1977. The B.C.T.F. continued to identify it as a major priority in its *Members' Guide*.

One of the first moves of the newly elected Social Credit government in 1975 was to rollback arbitrated salary awards to teachers, and confrontation was thereby rapidly renewed. A number of improvements to the pension plan were implemented in 1980, but changes in indexing methods were strongly opposed. Conflict between the B.C.T.F. and the provincial government has sharpened during the current period of austerity. Cutbacks in funding have put thousands of public school teachers out of work. Continuing increases in grants to independent schools add more fuel to the fire. They leave the government open to the charge that it is weakening the public education system while strengthening a private, elitist system alongside it.

The 1980 A.G.M. of the federation decided to make full bargaining rights, including all terms and conditions of work, a priority. A campaign was launched which in some districts included working to rule and bans on extracurricular activity, resulting, according to the federation, in gains being made.[11] In 1981 teachers in Terrace struck for six days in a dispute over personnel rights and in that year bargaining resulted in average salary increases of 17.25 per cent. That was the last year before the current period of government cutbacks.

Kratzmann et al. have summarized the working situation facing teachers today compared to fifty years ago. Referring to the "comprehensive, diverse and demanding set of job specifications," they cite one teacher as having observed:

> teachers are not psychologists, social workers, leisure activity directors, entertainers, annual curriculum revisers, filing clerks, computer experts, record keepers, telephone receptionists, duplicating clerks, disability analysts . . . these are but a few of the supplementary roles that have been added to, or elbowed out, the traditional teaching role (1980:19-21).

Flanders (1980) found evidence of widespread resentment among teachers in British Columbia to such bureaucratic measures. Stress and burnout are frequently found among teachers because of an intensified labour situation and degradation of working conditions.

The B.C.T.F. played a leading part in the Solidarity movement which opposed various pieces of 1983 provincial legislation and budgeting. In this movement teachers stood shoulder to shoulder with other labour groups in a manner inconsistent with the assumption that teachers' interests differ from those of other workers. Cuts in education have been a major part of Social Credit policies, and almost 60 per cent of the province's teachers voted for participation in the escalating strike action which Solidarity used to mobilize opposition. Ninety per cent of teachers stayed away from work when the time for action came, including, at one point, a majority of principals.[12]

In the spring of 1987 the Social Credit government passed its new Teaching Profession Act, which puts control of teachers' qualification, professional conduct and professional development in the hands of a Teachers' College run by a board made up of government appointees and elected teachers' representatives. The act grants full bargaining rights, including the right to strike, to teachers' organizations in each school district, thereby forcing the B.C.T.F. to start organizing its members afresh on a district by district basis. At the same time teachers are to be subject to the provisions of Bill 19, the new Industrial Relations Reform Act, which threatens to reduce the powers of organized labour severely. Already teachers are not participating in extracurricular activities and have withdrawn their labour for one day, together with other workers in the province. Other forms of protest are planned.

These moves occurred two years after this paper was originally completed. But they represent the continuation of a clearly visible trend in teacher-government relations, involving a struggle for improved working conditions and rights which these educational workers consider important not only to their well-being but also to that of their students.

CONCLUSION

This overview of the history of teachers and their organizations in British Columbia shows that considerable improvement in teachers' economic well-being, working conditions, and participation in the making of educational policy and practice over the past century have been the result of their success in organizing and putting pressures on their state employers. Militancy, including occasional withdrawal of labour power, has recurred throughout the province's history. The record before the recent uproar over Social Credit austerity policy shows that when strike action has arisen, which has typically been after a prolonged dispute, desired results have been achieved, for example, recognition of teachers' associations as bargaining agents, and improvements in salary and pensions.

Provincial politicians and school trustees have been more eager to guard the public purse and keep property taxes down than to pursue educational expansion. The latter has only been seriously considered when high levels of prosperity have prevailed.

It cannot be said, therefore, that there has been a consistent movement towards professionalism, if this term means autonomy and power as found in the traditional professions of medicine and law. The kind of professionalism that has been achieved is one which emphasizes quality of service, increasing educational qualifications, access to such policy-making bodies as Ministry of Education committees, the policing of members' conduct and performance, and salary levels comparable to those of simiarly qualified workers. In the crucial areas of determining who their clients will be, what remuneration they will receive, and what services they may offer (that is, what they may teach) teachers are heavily constrained. Their labour power continues to be formally subordinated within a state bureaucracy, and their class struggle is conducted within state institutions.

Professional aspirations have proven useful to teachers in their relations with employers, resulting in representation of the B.C.T.F. on all advisory committees in the Department of Education dealing with teachers' working conditions. They have also helped them to claim salaries commensurate with those who possess comparable qualifications. But professionalism has been a two-edged sword. The other edge enables the government, the press, and others to discredit militant teachers, especially those who contemplate withdrawing their labour, as irresponsible, unprofessional, and insufficiently dedicated to duty and service. As a consequence there is much popular support for reducing social services like education and exerting more control over teachers' working conditions and life-chances.

In the face of the fiscal crises of the past few years governments have sought to "rationalize" state expenditure, particularly in the areas of health and education. Funds that are saved through redundancies, keeping down teachers' salaries, or reducing educational funding, are available for capital investment, low-interest loans, and subsidies to corporations, highway construction or debt payments to large financial institutions (Magnusson, Carroll, Doyle, Langer, and Walker, 1984). The reluctance of many school boards and the government of British Columbia to take seriously teachers' goals of decreased class sizes is evidence of their interest in intensifying teachers' "productivity." Even the more independent medical profession has had to cope with this trend in negotiations over fee schedules for medical insurance plans. Teachers, faced with working conditions which never resembled those of physicians in terms of autonomy, have used union strategies to protect their interests, joining together with other state employees.[13]

The political polarization which has prevailed in British Columbia for over a decade is reflected clearly in battles between moderates and progressives within the B.C.T.F. Many teachers are in the position of having benefited from the post-war period of economic growth in terms of personal comforts. It takes a great deal of effort for such people, particularly in households with two well-paid income earners, to analyse critically the role of the state and its relations with the corporate business sector. Their often dedicated commitment to serving their students and the community, which reflects traditional concepts of women's subservient roles, also inhibits such teachers when it comes to taking a stand against their employers.

It is evident that British Columbia's public school teachers have always been dependent wage-earners engaged in social class struggle. As the province shifted from its initially colonial position, the state, faced with responsibilities for capitalist expansion and social and cultural reproduction, moved quickly to control and centralize the education system. Although school boards have been a concession to local democracy, until recently they have included a disproportionate number of businessmen and others eager to keep down taxes. During recessionary periods and the First World War, pressures to rationalize and economize proved irresistible. Teachers responded with action ranging from outbursts of protest to establishment in a single organization of a province-wide labour union and professional association. Development of industrial relations in other sectors of the economy and the increased strength of the province's labour movement led the teachers into the collective bargaining process and to confrontations and struggles resembling those involving unionized workers generally. Their bargaining rights are, however, confined to salary matters. North's (1964) study documents the evolution of industrial relations in this area, arguing that conflicts between teachers and school boards have been exacerbated by 'erroneous' government policies.

The teachers' working-class position, however, contradicts their professional ideology according to which provision of services always takes priority over self-interest. This prevents the B.C.T.F. from pursuing closer relations with other elements in the labour movement. Formal affiliation with labour lasted only ten years. But since 1973 the B.C.T.F. has maintained liaison with the Canadian Labour Congress and the B.C. Federation of Labour through exchange of observers. Recent developments, however, including the opposition to the 1983 provincial budget cuts and the current protest against Bills 19 and 20, seem to have brought these parties closer together.[14]

In his study of the Nova Scotia Teachers' Union, Watson (1960:301) emphasized the success which followed the adoption of union tactics. In the light of his findings and the evidence provided in this paper, Harp and Betcherman's (1980) conclusion should probably have been that the Quebec teachers had a highly realistic analysis of their situation, that is, they rejected the contradictory implications of the professional model, accepted that their position was one shared with the working class, and proceeded to pursue policies consistent with it. Although Quebec teachers may not have attained their objectives, the success of organized teachers in British Columbia and Nova Scotia when they have behaved like the organized working class suggests that their economic conditions, political effectiveness, and service to future generations might be greater if they sharpened their working-class consciousness and allied with other organizations, particularly labour unions. Given the significance of gender issues among teachers, one of the bridges towards such an alliance is afforded by those feminist groups which see clearly the inextricable aspects of class and gender relations.

NOTES

Thanks are due to the Social Sciences and Humanities Research Council of Canada for Research Grant No. 410-80-0700, to William Broadley, William Carroll, David Coburn and Roy Watson for comments on a draft of this article and to the Records Department of the British Columbia Teachers' Federation for access to materials. The article is published with the permission of the *Canadian Review of Sociology and Anthropology;* it is a slightly revised version of a paper with the same title which appeared in that journal in May, 1986.

1. See Mills (1951), Lockwood (1958), Dahrendorf (1959), Giddens (1973), Parkin (1979).
2. The problem of locating teachers in the class structure is also apparent in Marchak's (1975) outline of the class structure of British Columbia. Since they do not control industrial wealth they may be placed in Class 3, the working class. But they possess 'more personal job control with respect to job content, pacing, daily quantity of work' etc. than typical working-class employees and would on that score be placed in Marchak's Class 2, the managerial class.
3. Many of these unemployed teachers are women. The female presence among school teachers and recent researches on the position of women in capitalist societies raise important questions concerning the relationship between class and patriarchy (MacDonald, 1980). Apple (1983) has drawn attention to how the largely female occupants of lower-level teaching positions, compared to primarily male holders of the positions of school principal and supervisor, are evidence that the education system reproduces the patriarchal relations of the wider society as well as, indeed as part of, the reproduction of the labour force generally. Schooling is a major means of securing the consent of workers' children to the capitalist order and the consent of girls to the sexual division of labour (Stanworth, 1982).

    The position of female teachers is therefore an important locus for studying struggles around gender as well as class. In the space of this article, however, gender cannot be given the prominent position it deserves in a full analysis of the situation. For an interesting study of the experience of one assertive female teacher in 1894 see Pazdro (1980).
4. See also Charlesworth, n.d.
5. Calculated from statistics on occupations from various Censuses of Canada.
6. Calculated from *Salaries and Qualifications of Teachers in Public Elementary and Secondary Schools*, Statistics Canada.
7. Victoria *Colonist*, September 1918-December 1919. Minutes of the Victoria School Board, 1918 and 1919.
8. Vancouver *Sun*, 21 December 1981, "BCSTA wants lockout rights." Victoria *Times*, 9 May 1973, 'BCSTA resolves to lockout teachers in salary negotiations deadlock'. See also B.C. Department of Education correspondence dated 28 Sep-

tember 1939 on pensions issues. British Coilumbia Provincial Archives, 451, Box 17, No. 3.

9.   For example, Bill 3, 1972. See *The B.C. Teacher*, Jan.-Feb. 1984:116.
10. B.C.T.F. *Newsletter* Vol. 10, 1970-71.
11. B.C.T.F. *Newsletter* Vol. 22, 1982-83, p. 100.
12. Magnusson and Langer, 1984. *B.C. Teacher*, Jan.-Feb. 1984:139.
13. Women's issues have been strongly represented in the B.C.T.F. during the past ten years. The federation has a statement of policies and procedures on the status of women. It has been suggested in the *B.C. Teacher* (Oct.-Nov. 1984:7) that female teachers comprise 92 per cent of part-time teachers and two-thirds of those on temporary contracts, implying a renewed trend toward the employment of women as cheaper labour.
14. *B.C. Teacher*, Jan.-Feb. 1984.

REFERENCES

Abercrombie, N. and J. Urry. 1983.
   Capital, Labour and the Middle Classes. London: George Allen and Unwin.
Apple, M. 1983.
   "Work, Class and Teaching." In S. Walker and L. Barton (eds.), *Gender, Class and Education*. London: Palmer Press: pp. 53–69.
Burris, V. 1980.
   "Capital Accumulation and the Rise of the New Middle Class." *Review of Radical Political Economics* 12(1) (Spring):17-34.
Charlesworth, H. n.d.
   Teachers Institutes. Unpublished manuscript in possession of B.C.T.F.
Crompton, R. 1976.
   "Approaches to the Study of White-collar Unionism." *Sociology* 10(3):407-26.
Crompton, R., and J. Gubbay. 1977.
   Economy and Class Structure. London: Macmillan.
Curtis, B. 1983.
   "Preconditions of the Canadian State: Educational Reforms and the Construction of a Public in Upper Canada, 1837-1846." *Studies in Political Economy* 10(Winter):99-122.
Dahrendorf, R. 1959.
   Class and Class Conflict in Industrial Society. London: Routledge and Kegan Paul.
Dunn, Timothy A. 1978.
   Work, Class and Education: Vocationalism in B.C.'s Public Schools 1900-29. M.A. thesis, University of British Columbia.
Ehrenreich, B., and J. Ehrenreich. 1979.
   "The Professional-Managerial Class." In P. Walker (ed.), *Between Labour and Capital*. New York: Monthly Review Press.
Flanders, T. 1980.
   Summary Report: Professional Development Study. Vancouver: B.C. Teachers' Federation.
Giddens, A. 1973.
   The Class Structure of Advanced Societies. London: Hutchinson.
Harp, J., and G. Betcherman. 1980.
   "Contradictory Class Locations and Class Action: the Case of School Teachers' Organizations in Ontario and Quebec." *Canadian Journal of Sociology* 5(2):145-62.

Harris, K. 1982.
  Teachers and Classes: A Marxist Analysis. London: Routledge and Kegan Paul.
Hunt, A. 1977.
  "Theory and Politics in the Identification of the Working Class." In A. Hunt (ed.),
  Class and Class Structure. London: Lawrence and Wishart.
Huxley, Christopher. 1979.
  "The State, Collective Bargaining and the Shape of Strikes in Canada." *Canadian
  Journal of Sociology* 4(3):223-39.
Johnson, F. Henry. 1964.
  A History of Public Education in British Columbia. Vancouver: University of British
  Columbia Press.
— 1971. *John Jessop: Goldseeker and Educator: Founder of the British Columbia
  School System*. Vancouver: Mitchell Press.
Kratzmann, A., T.C. Byrne, and W. H. Worth. 1980. *A System in Conflict*. Edmonton:
  Alberta Labour.
Lockwood, D. 1958.
  The Blackcoated Worker. London: Allen and Unwin.
Lowe, G. 1982.
  "Class, Job and Gender in the Canadian Office." *Labour/Le Travailleur* 10
  (Autumn):37-64.
MacDonald, M. 1980.
  "Schooling and the Reproduction of Class and Gender Relations". In L. Barton et al.
  (eds.), *Schooling, Ideology and the Curriculum*. London: Palmer Press.
MacLaurin, D. L. 1936.
  *The History of Education in the Crown Colonies of Vancouver Island and British
  Columbia* (2 vols). Unpublished doctoral dissertation, University of Washington.
Magnusson, W., and M. Langer. 1984.
  "The 'New Reality' in Education." In W. Magnusson et al. (eds.), *The New Reality:
  The Politics of Restraint in British Columbia*. Vancouver: New Star.
Magnusson, W., W. K. Carroll, C. Doyle, M. Langer, and R. B. J. Walker. 1984.
  The New Reality: the Politics of Restraint in British Columbia. Vancouver: New Star.
Malcolmson, J. 1980.
  Resource Development and the State in Early British Columbia. M.A. thesis, Simon
  Fraser University.
Marchak, P. 1975.
  "Class, Regional and Institutional Sources of Social Conflict in B.C." *B.C. Studies*
  27(Autumn):30-49.
Mills, C. W. 1951.
  White-Collar. New York: Oxford University Press.
Muir, J. Douglas. 1969.
  "Canada." In Albert A. Blum (ed.), *Teacher Unions and Associations: A Compara-
  tive Study*. Urbana: University of Illinois Press: Chapter 1.
North, R. A. 1964.
  The British Columbia Teachers' Federation and the Arbitration Process. M.A.
  thesis, University of British Columbia.
Ozga, J., and M. Lawn. 1981.
  Teachers, Professionalism and Class: A Study of Organized Teachers. London: Pal-
  mer Press.
Parkin, P. 1979.
  Marxism and Class Theory: A Bourgeois Critique. London: Tavistock.
Paton, J. M. 1964.
  "The Quest for Corporate Status." *The B.C. Teacher* 44(1):13-14.
Pazdro, R. J. 1980.
  "Agnes Deans Cameron: Against the Current." In B. Latham and C. Kerr (eds.), *In

Her Own Right: Selected Essays on Women's History in B.C. Victoria: Camosun College: pp. 101–24.

Phillips, P. 1967.
"Confederation and the Economy of British Columbia." In W. G. Shelton (ed.), *British Columbia and Confederation.* Victoria: Morriss Printing.

Poulantzas, N. 1975.
Classes in Contemporary Capitalism. London: New Left Books.
—1978. *State, Power, Socialism.* London: New Left Books.

Putnam, J. H., and G. M. Weir. 1925
Survey of the School System. Victoria: King's Printer.

Schechter, S. 1977.
"Capitalism, Class and Educational Reform in Canada." In L. Panitch (ed.), *The Canadian State: Political Economy and Political Power.* Toronto: University of Toronto Press: pp. 373–416.

Skolrood, A. H. 1967.
The British Columbia Teachers' Federation: A Study of its Historical Development, Interests and Activities from 1916 to 1963. Ph.D. diss., University of Oregon.

Stanworth, M. 1982.
Gender and Schooling. London: Women's Research and Resource Centre, Pamphlet No. 7.

Thompson, M., and J. Cairnie. 1973.
"Compulsory Arbitration: The Case of British Columbia Teachers." *Industrial and Labour Relations Review* 27(1):3-17.

Van Brummelen, H. 1983-4.
"Shifting Perspectives: Early British Columbia Textbooks from 1872 to 1925." *B.C. Studies* 6(Winter):3-27.

Warburton, R., and D. Coburn. 1983.
"The Rise of Non-Manual Work in British Columbia." *B.C. Studies* 59(Autumn):5-27.

Watson, Roy E. L. 1960.
The Nova Scotia Teachers' Union: A Study in the Sociology of Organizations. Ph.D diss., University of Toronto.

Wright, E. O. 1978.
Class, Crisis and the State. London: New Left Books.
—1980. "Varieties of Marxist Conceptions of Class Structure." *Politics and Society* 9(3):323-70.

14

Conclusion: Capitalist Social Relations in British Columbia

RENNIE WARBURTON

In most of the foregoing episodes in the formation, experience, and development of the British Columbia working class, the authors acknowledge, if only implicitly, the importance of studying the processes they examine within the context of capitalist development. It is the aim of this final chapter to tie some of the papers together by outlining the key features of capitalism and how they have structured some of the developments discussed. We consider the analysis of capitalism in the specific historical context of British Columbia and Canada to be indispensible for an understanding of the province's development.

Following from this, our discussion of class conflict is intended to show that it has been and continues to be a dominant feature of B.C. history and social structure. We also argue that the salience of ethnic relations in the province can best be understood in terms of the placement of peoples of diverse origins within the structure of class and power; it is not simply a manifestation of prejudice or the clash of cultures. Finally we maintain that the state's role in B.C., though generally biased in favour of the interests of capital, is more complex, contradictory, and autonomous than simplistic concepts of "the capitalist state" imply.

In first outlining the main features of the capitalist mode of production, we do not claim that capitalism "explains everything" that has happened in British Columbia. There are clearly levels of historical and sociological analysis that are necessary supplements to the essentially economic sociology outlined here. Early in the present century, for example, Max Weber (Gerth and Mills, 1948:180-93) and more recently Harre (1979), have noted that the pursuit of prestige, honour, and social recognition has been an important feature of human social relations. A useful insight has been provided by Barbalet (1986), who points to the normative interests peculiar to specific occupational strata within the working class which they pursue in struggles with employers; a good example is the concept of "academic freedom" cherished by university teachers. There are numerous other factors, such as culture, families and households, communities, group dynamics, and ideological and political forces, which are necessary for historical explanation. Our position, therefore, cannot be accurately described as "economic determinism" if that term means that "everything is determined by economic factors." What we contend is that in a predominantly capitalist society, the ownership and distribution of wealth and property, combined with the dominant relations between labour and capital, tend over time increasingly to condition, limit, and constrain most forms of activity in that society. But social conditions and relations at any particular time are not simply the results of economic forces. A mode of production is also a mode of appropriation and a mode of reproduction. Political and other forms of struggle are themselves significant social processes which in certain circumstances directly influence economic relations.

Yet capitalism has a tendency to penetrate all aspects of social life and to modify existing culture and social relations. Religion, education, literature, art, and many other non-economic elements of societies dominated by capitalism have been made into commodities in the market place or otherwise influenced by capitalist relations. For example, organizations whose primary goals are not economic become investors and consumers.

Most of the above papers deal with relationships in the world of work and employment and must therefore be interpreted within a framework that is both economic and sociological. The following summary of the principal elements of capitalism and its development, including the patriarchal gender relations it has preserved, provides the outlines of such a framework. Because of the paucity of material in the book dealing with women, we have chosen to include only passing references to gender power and the sexual division of labour. This must not be taken as evidence that we consider gender relations less significant than class relations.

THE CAPITALIST MODE OF PRODUCTION

It is of paramount importance to note that the main features of the capitalist mode of production are social relations which follow from the rights of property-owners and the obligations of wage-earning employees

(Clement 1986:16). The crucially important capitalist relationship involves the payment of wages to formally "free" workers by owners of the means of production or their agents in exchange for the workers' labour power, the latter being defined as the physical or intellectual capacity to produce or deliver goods and services. Workers' labour power is used to produce commodities for sale at a profit. The source of the capitalist's profit is the surplus value produced by workers, that is, the value of what workers produce is more than what they receive in wage payments. In response to those who see this as a dogmatic assertion or merely ideological premise, we note the time, energy, and resources which employers devote to collective bargaining, labour relations, and to reducing labour costs, particularly in response to intensely competitive circumstances, such as those prevailing during recessions.

Capitalist employer-worker relations, therefore, are inherently conflictual because increased labour costs *ceteris paribus* imply reductions in profit. Wage-earners and owners comprise the two major classes in capitalist societies. Capitalists command considerable power as owners of corporate property and in their dealings with employees whose power lies in collective organization. Power relations thus lie at the heart of the capitalist social order. Employers use their rights as owners to make decisions about production or wage payments which directly affect workers' material circumstances. And because workers' labour is the source of profit, the principal contradiction of capitalism is that between capital and labour. The two terms presuppose each other and reciprocally condition each other's existence (Larrain 1983:153). Conflict between these two major classes is endemic to capitalist societies.

The growth of unions, strikes, and labour-based political parties are forms of working-class activity which express the capital-labour contradiction as workers attempt to further their interests in struggles against their employers. Those struggles occur at various levels. In the economic sphere, wages, working conditions, job security, and fringe benefits are the central issues. Politically, workers' parties fight for state-funded programmes such as better and cheaper, sometimes free, health and educational services, income redistribution, pensions, welfare, and unemployment benefits. On the employers' side, associations of employers or businessmen represent the interests of capital in the economic sphere. In politics, the major bourgeois parties cater primarily to the overall, long-term interests of capital, which is why studies of campaign contributions to Canadian political parties show large corporations making equal contributions to both the federal Liberal and Progressive Conservative parties.

Capital-labour employment relations did not exist in pre-capitalist societies. Although immediately pre-capitalist, that is, feudal, societies were class-based, their class structure revolved around the control of land and reciprocal obligations between propertied lords and labouring serfs. Capitalist relations resulted from specific changes in the organization of European and North American economies between the sixteenth and nineteenth centuries. A major aspect of the establishment of the capitalist mode of production has been the creation of formally "free" labour, that is, of large numbers of people no longer tied to their plots of land, their village or tribal communities, or to independent commodity production, and often obliged to relocate in search of employment (Pentland 1959). During that process, labour was also transformed into a commodity, that is, it could be exchanged for money in the form of wages. One well-researched example of the making of part of the labour force of British Columbia is provided by Muszynski's (1986) study of shoreworkers in the fishing industry.

Independent commodity production, where the worker-producer is also the proprietor, preceded capitalism, but persists alongside it (Johnson 1981; Christensen 1982; Muszynski 1984; Conley, this volume). In Canada many fishermen, farmers, and loggers have remained independent commodity producers, but because of difficulties such as inability to obtain credit, loss of markets, and drops in prices, many have been obliged to relinquish their independence, selling out and moving into the capitalist labour force. Capitalist expansion therefore produces the decline of the self-employed independent commodity producers. And although Cuneo (1984) has recently demonstrated that in certain economic sectors there has been a recent increase in petty commodity producers, contradictions between capitalism and independent commodity production have been a central feature of Canadian economic and political history (Johnson 1972; Craven and Traves 1979). But Canada as a whole, and British Columbia even more so, is largely divided between employers and wage-workers.

Capitalist growth requires technological progress because it is a means to save on labour costs or to produce more saleable commodities. But within capitalist contexts this has not occurred as a separate, autonomous process involving the spontaneous invention of new production methods. Rather, technology is developed within the social organization of capitalist production, and because it is frequently designed to reduce labour costs, it is often a matter of dispute between workers and management.

Competition leads to the buying out of smaller and weaker firms and the amalgamation of companies; the result is the formation of large, oligopolistic corporations, many of which are international. The biggest of them are wealthier and more powerful than the majority of nation states in the world (Barnet and Mueller 1974). These multi-national corporations compete internationally by making decisions about investment in the context of class struggle and class-structured prospects for producing, appropriating and realizing surplus value at given times and in particular places (Carroll 1985; 1986). The availability of resources, transportation facilities, and taxation levels in a given region are contextual factors to be considered. Low-wage areas where the working class is fragmented by gender or race or is unorganized or coerced are attractive to foreign investors.

Accumulated capital is largely reinvested, usually in further commodity production, in order to maintain profit rates. Consumption and the realization of profit depend on the system constantly reproducing itself, which it does partly through the economy as the result of the competitive actions of many capitalists in their efforts to accumulate capital from profits. This occurs in a market place which has become worldwide in scope as capitalist operations expand, first domestically and then in foreign areas.

Capitalist reproduction also occurs in various settings: the family-household, state agencies dealing with education and health, working-class institutions like friendly societies, charitable, philanthropic, and church organizations, and companies which provide employee welfare benefits (Dickinson and Russell 1986:11-12). Women play a crucial role in these spheres of social reproduction as mothers, teachers, nurses, volunteers, clerical workers, and in other female ghetto-type occupations. In certain industries, notably garment-making and fish-processing, women's labour contributes directly to the production of surplus value (Armstrong and Armstrong 1984; Musjinsky 1984; Gannage 1987).

Because of the imperative of capital accumulation, social or collective needs of human beings are frequently unmet. The extent to which they are met frequently depends on the strength of labour unions in obtaining benefits for their workers and the amount of pressure that political organizations representing the interests of the working class as a whole can put on the ruling class or its political representatives to make concessions in the form of social programmes. In the advanced capitalist regions of Europe, North America, Australasia, and parts of the Middle East, welfare states have thereby been created as part of a class compromise.

The last point we wish to make in this sketch of capitalism is that development occurs under specific geographical conditions which include available resources, suitable climate and topography, the proximity of markets, and various forms of transportation. But according to the perspective taken here, some of these, for example, climate and topography, are to be understood as specific facilitating, limiting, and constraining conditions while others have themselves been produced in the process of capitalist growth itself e.g. transportation and markets (Harvey 1985:146). None of them can be considered a more basic determinant of development than the dynamics of capital accumulation are. The province of British Columbia is a distinctive territory where particular forms of production and consumption, patterns of labour demand and supply, and particular physical and social infrastructures are found. It is part of a national and international structure of imperialism and finance capital, where capital is invested and withdrawn whenever profitable.

This outline of the capitalist mode of production is a statement of its overall tendencies. They occur with varying degrees of complexity and in specific geographical and historical circumstances. In the following overview of the period in British Columbia's history covered by contributors, we first discuss class conflict and then ethnic relations, noting the state's role in each and closing with an overall assessment of that role.

CLASS CONFLICT IN B.C.

In B.C., capitalist development did not simply occur as a result of internal forces such as the much-vaunted ventures and adventures of European pioneers or the "builders" of the province discussed by Taylor (1982). It emerged as a set of relations between workers and capitalists in the province and between workers in B.C. and capitalists in places as far away as London, Montreal, and New York. Most recently employers of workers in the province have also come from Japan and New Zealand. The economy of British Columbia became a part of the international capitalist system in the nineteenth century at a time when corporate capital had already been accumulated on a large scale in central Canada, Britain, and the United States, all developed centres of industrial capitalism. Corporations in those advanced regions have invested in resource extraction, transportation, communications, and manufacturing in the province.

The chapters by Malcolmson and Phillips cover crucial aspects of capitalism's beginnings in the province. Malcolmson is concerned with the state's relation to underlying class forces and relations. One of his most important observations concerns the need to see the state as both a product of class struggle and a participant in it. He cites an alteration in the regional configuration of social classes, involving the rise of independent commodity producers during the Gold Rush and a new class of merchants in Victoria. That period saw the decline of the Hudson's Bay Company, a monopolistic corporation which served as an arm of the British state, and the growth of a separate state apparatus which regulated land settlement and resource extraction. The colonial state also assisted economic development with road construction for transportation of products for export. Among the forces leading to the amalgamation of the Island and Mainland colonies and later the entry into Confederation was the loss of state revenues and rising public debt with the decline of the Gold Rush era. Malcolmson interprets the movement towards entry into Confederation in 1871 partly as a result of British interest in imperial control of Canada as a whole and of British Columbia specifically. But it was also a strategy which suited the purposes of both interior miners and owners of coal and timber companies, who were attracted to responsible government because they felt they would be able to pressure it to operate in their interests as developers and accumulators of capital. Thus, the initial struggles for control of the state took place between various fractions of the emergent bourgeoisie rather than between employers and workers.

As Phillips points out, it was not only the Gold Rush and the influx of people that were crucial in the transformation of B.C. from a colonial trading outpost into a developing region. It was the types of social relation between capitalist employers and their wage-earning employees that had long-run significance. Early gold-mining consisted of large numbers of individual miners engaged in petty commodity production where competition was eventually limited by a state licensing system. But, as Phillips notes, a portion of the profits made during the Gold Rush era provided the capital that later helped to expand and diversify the economy.

The first capitalist relations of production were established on Vancouver Island by the Hudson's Bay Company (Mackie 1984). However, until the completion of the railroad across Canada, independent commodity production remained the dominant economic activity. The completion of the Canadian Pacific Railway brought major capital investment, both foreign and central Canadian, in lumber, mining and smelting, which gave rise to a growing working class and a local Vancouver bourgeoisie of merchants, real estate speculators, mining promoters, and saw-mill owners. It also led to what was to become a distinctive presence in British Columbia—resource-exporting, oligopolistic corporations controlled from outside the province (Resnick 1985; Marchak 1986). By the century's end the provincial state was actively encouraging large-scale capitalist production through coal and fish exports, forest licensing and, railway promotion.

Throughout the period discussed by Malcolmson and Phillips, the late nineteenth and early twentieth centuries, an industrial working class was created, a development which had deep, long-term implications for British Columbia. Phillips details the conflict between Scottish miners and their Hudson's Bay Company employers which occurred as early as 1850. Strikes followed at regular intervals in the ensuing decades and beyond: workers in the resource industries struggled for living wages and satisfactory working conditions. The state generally sided with the employers, early examples being the granting of coal rights on Vancouver Island as a reward to the elder Dunsmuir for helping to resist strikers, and the use of the militia to break coal-miners' strikes. For several decades mining employers managed to prevent the formation of unions when they used foreign or Asian labour and exploited ethnic divisions between miners.

Class struggle also became manifest on the political front. Organized working-class pressure led to the election of two labour representatives to the provincial legislature in 1890 and eventually to reforms which included workers' compensation, safety regulations, and an eight-hour day in the mines. The rise of large industries, several with hundreds of workers, and the spread of industrial unionism also pushed workers' politics in a socialist direction. Malcolmson implies that the institutionalizing shift to party politics was in response to the challenge of an independent, class-conscious labour movement and the need to maintain a stable investment climate. The influence on state reorganization of particular forms of economic and class struggle was apparent in that situation.

Conley's chapter on the salmon fishery at the outset of the twentieth century illustrates the complexity of class relations produced by the differential property rights of cannery owners, independent commodity-producing fishermen, and wage-earners. In the context of expanding companies, advancing technology, and rivalry between Japanese fishermen and others, he highlights conflicts between fishers and canners and among fishers themselves, focusing on workers' cycles of social reproduction. Wage-earning fishermen moved between various occupations throughout the year to maintain their cycle of reproduction and in some cases to save enough to become owners of the means of production themselves. Others remained part of a reserve army of labour which helped keep down the price paid by canners for the fish. Simple commodity producers carried on different types of production or alternated fishing with wage labour in other sectors, some of which, such as railway construction, logging, and sawmilling, paid more and thus threatened to lure fishermen away from the canners.

The subordination of most simple commodity producers, except trollers, to the canners was a significant process in the establishment of capitalist relations in the fishing industry. Companies addressed the labour problem on the Fraser River by granting fishers mortgages on boats and nets and advances for food and supplies. Fishermen thus became deeply in debt to the canning companies to which they sold their fish. Clement (1986:62) refers to the outcome of the canners' strategy as "a distorted form of petty production" which subordinates producers and provides a steady labour force while giving the appearance of petty bourgeois relations of production. Fishermen also became bound to the canning companies through renting company housing and contracting with them. Canners' interest in profits came into conflict with fishermen's concerns to maintain a living wage.

Fishermen themselves responded to these pressures with collective (mainly strike) action, making demands on the canneries or trying to control fishing opportunities. Conley notes that the reproduction cycles of the fishermen shaped their capacity to mobilize for collective action. For example, simple commodity-producers sought exclusive fishing rights because they felt the use of increasing numbers of wage-earning fishermen kept prices down. Those in the New Westminster area who were full-time fishers had enough solidarity, owing to their settled residence and long-term fishing experience, to make them a strong political force. Although they too were a socially cohesive group, native fishermen lacked political clout because of their subordinate relations with the federal government. Similarly, the solidarity of the Japanese was frustrated by racist opposition. In fact, their competitiveness made Japanese fishermen the object of defensive, exclusionary, co-operative action by Canadian and native fishers. On the other hand, in the strike of 1913 five thousand Canadian, native, and Japanese gillnetters united across racial lines (Clement 1986:38).

Conley's paper fits in well with the research findings of Marchak (1984a) and her colleagues on the complexities of the fishing industry. An element making for intense competition is the mobility and relative unpredictability of fish. But although the property relations involved are less tangible than those surrounding other resources, they do determine the structure of power, with B.C. Packers obtaining "as much of the resource as it can probably market" and the banks receiving considerable sums in interest payments (ibid:64). Various forms of conflict characterize the fisheries, not the least important of which is that between fishers who see themselves as independent commodity producers and those who identify with wage-earners.

A petty bourgeoisie was present in British Columbia from an early stage. Its origins lie in the farmers who received land from the Hudson's Bay Company and the merchants who supplied the gold prospectors. Together with the early lawyers, doctors, and other independent professionals, these groups may be seen to comprise the "old" middle class, a term which is virtually synonymous with "petty bourgeoisie." Cuneo's

(1984) analysis of this class's experience in Canada shows that, although the proportion of the population in the petty bourgeoisie has been in decline as the shift from entrepreneurial to monopolistic, state-sponsored capitalism has occurred, there has been an increase in certain areas, for example, real estate and automobile dealerships and other retail services, during the period of economic boom in the decades preceding the current recession.

New Westminster was not the typical resource-based class-polarized company town on which the generalizations about labour radicalism in Western Canada by Drache (1984) were founded. It was a diversified industrial and manufacturing centre with a substantial non-manual segment of the labour force. Seager shows how, despite several setbacks to the union movement, workers' industrial and political activities in the early twentieth century in New Westminster, which included forty-eight strikes and lock-outs, were important mobilizing events which paved the way for the subsequent rise of support for social democratic politics at the expense of revolutionary socialism. The general strike in 1919 in support of the Winnipeg strikers was referred to by one prominent labour spokesperson as "class war." However, although labour militancy declined after 1919, capital and labour did not abandon class struggle.

Seager's research also provides further evidence that, in appropriate circumstances, male and female workers from different racial and ethnic groups are quite capable of co-operative industrial and political action. These findings are evidence against Ward's claim that race is a more basic divisive factor in the province's history than class (Ward, 1980). So also is the work on farmworkers by Dutton and Cornish showing how vulnerable they are to accidents, poisoning, low wages, and appalling working conditions. With the help of workers of various ethnic origins they are embarked on a unionization course in an effort to cope with their contradictory class circumstances.

Class conflict in the forest industry in the period discussed by Marchak evidenced union militancy to secure high wages and other benefits, goals that were attainable during the post-Second World War economic boom. But the decline of international markets, withdrawal of capital from the province by corporations facing acute international competition, and consequent persisting high unemployment levels have ruined many logging communities and destroyed local economies in B.C. The prolonged forest strike in 1986 saw workers continuing the struggle for benefits in the face of corporations calling for wage rollbacks, although recent data show the forest companies as having boosted profits in 1986.

The Fraser Mills strike of 1931 reported on by Meyers was a successful one. It was a response by millworkers and their families to wage cuts

—for some workers the sixth in eighteen months. Noting a tendency among historians to dismiss the strike as merely another example of communist agitation, Meyers maintains that its eventual success was the result of competent leadership, community organization, solidarity, and workers' class-conscious determination in the face of wages that fell faster than prices. This included co-operation across gender, ethnic, and religious lines which proved even stronger than the support given to the employers by the provincial government.

The workers in the B.C. Telephone strike of 1981 studied by Bernard were opposing technological change, specifically computerization of work, which threatened some workers' jobs. Solidarity with other labour groups, consumers, and communities, support from the press and disciplined, and responsible tactics (for example, guarantees of no damage to equipment) enabled the telephone workers to win their battle. Bernard sees the strike as an example of change in labour tactics away from simply totally or partially withdrawing labour towards taking over the workplace itself.

Class conflict in the province recently took another new form. In 1983 a conservative Social Credit government was re-elected. Justifying its actions in terms of an ideology of restraint, it confronted the labour movement and many working people in the province by introducing legislation which contained a concerted attack on working-class benefits and organizations (Marchak 1984). In response a variety of groups coalesced into the Solidarity movement (Carroll 1984; Palmer 1986).

(Solidarity can be described as a populist social movement because its adherents were trying to protect the rights and benefits of consumers and a range of underprivileged groups in general. It was an alliance between an organized segment of the working-class, that is, the union-sponsored Operation Solidarity component, and women's, church, and human rights groups, and community organizations. Many of its supporters were totally unaware of their class circumstances, and many would have resisted the suggestion that they were engaged in class-based action. Nevertheless, most of them were actual or retired wage-earners or members of wage-earners' families or unemployed (and thus potential) wage-earners. In July and through October of 1983 the Solidarity Coalition mobilized tens of thousands of British Columbians to demonstrate their opposition to Social Credit policies in the streets of Vancouver and Victoria. Nowhere else in Canada outside Quebec could confrontations and demonstrations on such a scale have taken place.)

Legislation was introduced in the spring of 1987 which bore certain similarities to that of 1983. Bill 19, the Industrial Relations Reform Act, is aimed at organized labour and weakens the position of unions in the

province. Bill 20, the Teaching Profession Act, weakens the power of
the B.C. Teachers' Federation by forcing teachers to organize all over
again on a district by district basis for collective bargaining purposes.
Teachers are also subject to Bill 19 and will be governed by a "professional agency," staffed by government appointees and elected teacher
representatives, to oversee standards and qualifications. The provincial
government is using state power to divide school teachers who have
formed an organized political opposition in recent elections. One consequence, evidence of an open division among teachers, is the formation
of a new, conservative, non-union organization by non-politicized
teachers at the local level. Warburton's chapter shows that this type of
confrontation between teachers and government is but the latest phase in
teachers' struggles against their state employers evident since the beginnings of the public school system.

Teachers belong to what is often called the "new middle class," the
upper stratum of white-collar workers which includes employed professionals, semi-professionals, technicians, and service workers with higher
education. The division between higher and lower status "white collar"
sectors was recognized by Marchak (1975) in the only explicit analysis of
the province's class structure to date. She noted the significance of factors like educational level, technical expertise, authority, working conditions, degree of organization and bargaining power in differentiating
among "white-collar" workers.

Our position is that because they sell their labour-power as a commodity in exchange for wages, most non-manual or service workers, including especially those who do routine clerical or sales work, but also
teachers and nurses, have always belonged objectively to the working
class. White-collar workers have been proletarianized in the sense that
more and more of them are employed, paid wages (or salaries), and are
subject to the authority of others. There is also a definite transition to
salary-earning employment among the traditional professions such as
medicine and law which is changing the class position of their prac-
titioners from the petit bourgeoisie towards that of the working class.

These processes have led to a steady increase in union organization in
the white-collar sector, involving co-operation with other branches of the
labour movement; this behaviour clearly does not conform to that characteristic of the so-called "middle class," that is, doctors, lawyers, and
other professionals. Several of what are now leading white-collar unions
were formerly professional associations whose use of collective bargaining methods to obtain improvements in salary and other benefits pushed
them towards unionization. An extended implication of the processes
outlined in our chapter on non-manual work is that the expansion of state

activities in response to the needs of the capitalist system and the demands of labour has created a public sector labour force which competes for surplus capital with the corporate sector. Public school teachers, government employees, and nurses all fall into that category. In 1983 four out of the five largest unions in British Columbia represented white-collar workers.

The persistence of struggles involving various elements in the working class is why we insist on the contemporary relevance of a class conflict model to the analysis of British Columbia's political economy. Union organization, collective bargaining rights, higher wages, better working conditions, retirement benefits, and job security have been the subject of workers' actions in the above papers. These are the concerns of employees who live mainly by the sale of their labour and whose life-chances — of obtaining benefits such as employment, living or higher wages, high living standards, higher education and good health — are largely dependent on their relations with employers who belong to the capitalist class. This is a material fact of life in our society, not an ideological bias on our part.

But the practices involving class relations have been obscured by many ideological perceptions of the situation, including the divisions between mental and manual labour, "white" and "blue" collar workers, and public and private sectors. Relations involving male and female, old and young, central and peripheral region, and "white" majority and ethnic minority complicate the structure of societies like British Columbia. Space and the limitations in the content of the book preclude us examining all of these factors. However, because ethnic relations figure so prominently in several of the papers, we offer the following discussion of them.

ETHNIC RELATIONS IN B.C.

Native Peoples

Following Rex (1986) we distinguish between situations of benign and malign ethnicity. A benign ethnic relation is one that presents no problems for the parties concerned: their different origins are not seen to imply inherent or socially ranked statuses; they accept each other as equals. Residential neighbours or members of the same labour union whose racial or ethnic differences are irrelevant to their shared social ties and form no basis for mutually tense or hostile relations provide examples of benign ethnic relations.

Sociologists and historians in British Columbia, however, have devoted much attention to the malign type, notably racist opposition to native peoples and Asians. It is Rex's contention, based on detailed comparative study of ethnic (including race) relations in various societies, that malign ethnic relations are marked by "conflict, discrimination, oppression and exploitation" (1986:79). Many relations between native and non-native and between Asian and so-called "white" persons in British Columbia are of this type.

The presence of native peoples in the original communities and their confrontation with the fur trade and later with colonial expansion, settlement, and capitalist development marks the starting point for a sociological history of B.C. During the era of the fur trade, relations between Europeans and indigenous North Americans were initially reasonably harmonious. Each had something to offer the other; furs were exchanged for such practically useful objects as guns, axes and knives. Then, as Bourgeault (1983:51) put it:

> Eventually, the labour process went more and more into the production of goods as a commodity for exchange in excess of what was needed to live. The surplus-labour of the Indian, which previously had been appropriated communally, was increasingly appropriated by the merchant capitalist, resulting in the creation of surplus-value from the circulation of commodities in the European marketplace.

This statement was made with regard to the situation of Indians and Métis on the prairies, but even allowing for the fact that many coastal native groups traditionally produced surpluses for ceremonial consumption and to augment the wealth of ruling elements, the observation is applicable to British Columbia during the fur trade. Large profits were made from the sale of furs produced by native labour (Warburton and Scott, 1985).

But the indigenous peoples of British Columbia, many of whom, particularly on the coast, had developed not only viable but highly sophisticated cultures and economies, experienced humiliating and in some cases disastrous consequences at the hands of (often sincerely well-meaning) Europeans and Canadians. The current disadvantaged position of many native peoples is primarily a consequence of the destructive impact of Euro-Canadians' use of power to impose their forms of economic activity and culture on pre-existing cultures and modes of production. It is a reminder that the present social order is the product of a particular set of historically specific human activities, including coercion. It is not the result of a linear progression of human achievement, the expression of biological forces, or the mere juxtaposing of diverse cultures. Tennant (1983:8) has reminded us that even today:

> destruction of the natural environment by logging, mining, pipeline construction and electricity production remains a constant threat to many Indian communities. Takeover of aboriginal land and resources is not something which occurred only at some indeterminate point in the past.

The recent controversies over Meares and Lyell Islands are obvious cases in point (Kennedy 1985).

In the early development of the province when control over resources was crucial, the primary resource for the early settlers was land that for thousands of years had been used by aboriginal inhabitants. Kew observes that the federal and provincial governments unilaterally decided which lands would be opened for European settlers and resource companies, leaving small "reserves" for the native groups. A unique feature of the situation of native peoples in British Columbia is that no treaties were signed with the federal government. But Kew's account shows how the Indian Act and later an oppressive education system were used to undermine native cultures, control their behaviour, and shape their social structures to accommodate to European ways.

The involvement of the indigenous people in the capitalist economy took several forms. Many were able to carry on traditional activities as trappers, hunters, and fishermen, operating as independent commodity producers and selling their products to wholesalers and retailers or directly to customers. Mackie's (1984:273ff) research shows that Indian wage labour in the colony dates back to 1849 when they began work for the Hudson's Bay Company and other enterprises, mainly in forest products, mining, and agriculture. They were paid in kind with blankets, beads, and tobacco, thus having no opportunity to "buy land, form joint-stock companies or run for legislative office" (Mackie, 1984:277). Later they entered the labour market on a transient or full-time basis where they have laboured side-by-side with other workers in all of the province's major industries (Knight, 1978). As Conley's essay indicates, many natives were in both independent commodity production and in the capitalist wage-labour market. An unknown number carried on marginal, often seasonal, economic activity, moving from one type of production to another during alternating periods of employment and unemployment.

The political activity of native organizations has typically been aimed at the well-being of their own people rather than at broader reforms. Increased self-determination, economic development, the satisfactory resolution of land claims, and disputes over hunting and fishing have been high on their priority list. These are objectives which are not direct products of their traditional cultures but are responses to their subordinate position in Canadian society.

Although native people have often found themselves part of a reserve labour force together with members of other minority groups and subject to similar racist slurs, abuse, and discrimination, they are a special people because of their unique political and legal position. The Canadian constitution and the Indian Act grant them special privileges and rights, some of them, like aboriginal rights, yet to be determined. They are not therefore simply an ethnic or racial group among the many others found in Canadian society.

As Carstens (1971) has pointed out, their situation is a result of "class, not culture." He emphasizes their underprivileged placement in the structures of property ownership, economic activity, and political power. Bourgeault (1983:45) too is convinced that class exploitation and oppression are the basis of native people's modern history. Although Tennant (1982:3-4) is reluctant to refer to the situation in terms of social class, in discussing Indians as victims of internal colonialism and as subjugated peoples, he notes that they were restricted in their use of land and resources, administratively supervised to varying degrees, and subject to social discrimination, suppression of culture and denial of political and other freedoms. There is an undeniable class element in these processes. And, as Bourgeault points out, liberation from exploitation and oppression cannot be accomplished without the support of the working class (ibid.:74).

Asian Immigrants

The initial formation of the province's working class largely involved imported labour, particularly Scottish, English, and Chinese miners and later the Chinese workers without whose labour the C.P.R. might never have been completed. Willmott has provided evidence that the early Chinese enjoyed cordial relations with whites, receiving the right to own property and being seen as "good for business" (Wickberg et al., 1982:42-43). And Creese notes in her contribution to this volume that there was little political agitation against Asians prior to railroad construction and industrialization.

Creese's study focuses on the way they were organized into the lowest working-class sectors as a result of colonialism, capitalist development, and immigration policies. In adopting different policies towards Asian immigrants from those applied to Americans and Europeans, the federal government created an ethnically segregated labour market. But even before the importation of thousands of Chinese workers as cheap labour to build the railroad, ethnic segmentation of the labour market was well under way in road construction, mining, and canning. Completion of the C.P.R. and a large influx of British immigrants led to acute competition for employment. The Chinese workers' willingness to work for low pay can be explained as one aspect of the competition among workers in desperate need of employment. The lower subsistence levels of Asian peasants are also a relevant consideration. This competitive situation included the interests of employers in reducing labour costs by paying Chinese workers 30 per cent less wages than the British. Employers also used Chinese workers as strike-breakers, thereby aggravating racist reactions.

The situation of Japanese fishermen is comparable. Conley notes that they were productive enough to successfully compete against "whites" and Indians. When Japanese fishermen capitulated to employers during strikes, "Whites" and Indians responded by requesting limits on the number of licences granted to the Japanese. In order to provide fishing opportunities to soldiers returning from the First World War, severe cuts were made in licenses issued to the Japanese.

Beginning in the coal mines in the 1870's, Euro-Canadians organized into unions from which the Chinese were excluded. Racism in the labour movement, according to Creese, was a form of "immature" class consciousness, racist animosity expressing the interests of a particular group of workers but blocking class consciousness among workers collectively. Asians were scapegoated and subject to racist hostility as Euro-Canadians fought to preserve their jobs and maintain access to the labour market by calling for the exclusion of Asians from the province. That the Canadian state eventually acceded to the demands of labour groups for Asiatic exclusion, thereby denying employers access to cheap labour, raises questions for the theory of the capitalist state.

Asians were also excluded from several Canadian political and cultural organizations, leading them to create institutions of their own for support. These include the Chinese benevolent associations, perpetuations of Chinese customs, language, and family traditions. As Creese points out, ethnic cultural practices, far from being themselves the sources of conflict, are responses to unequal social relations in which ethnically or racially identifiable immigrants are placed in subordinate social positions.

Partly in response to hostility in the Euro-Canadian working class, particularly in the unions, a significant minority of Asians embarked on small business activities. This placed them in competitive relations both with one another and with others of European or Canadian origin, the latter relationship adding fuel to the fire of anti-Asian sentiments.

Rejecting those explanations of racism which stress primordial prejudice and the imperialist power of the British as well as those which see capital directly dictating racist immigration policy, Creese accepts Bonacich's findings that the source of much racism lies in competition among workers. Creese goes on to note how the state created segmented labour markets when it forced Asians into a marginal status by denying them equal legal and political rights. It recognized their short-term usefulness as cheap labour but did not see them as settlers. Malign ethnic relations thus developed as employers sought to maintain access to cheap immigrant labour, thereby dividing the working class. Workers opposed Asian immigrants as a threat to their interests. Both parties eventually agreed that Asians should be denied political rights. In fact, they were not granted the right to vote in B.C. until after the Second World War.

It is important to note that in different circumstances co-operation occurred between Asians and Canadian workers, for example in the Fraser River fishing strikes between 1900 and 1925 and in the shingle mills. Seager and Meyers both provide other examples of inter-ethnic co-operation. And, as noted by Dutton and Cornish, unionized Canadians and minority workers have combined in support of the farmworkers' unionization campaign. These events suggest that it is not the personal characteristics of members of ethnic groups nor their different cultures which determine racial and ethnic antagonism or exclusion, but rather the context in which they encounter one another, particularly competitive or oppressive situations. Malign relations of this sort are not alternative relations to those between classes; they are part and parcel of class conflict. It is therefore the organization of persons of different national or racial origins into economic and social structures that makes ethnicity or race significant.

THE STATE

There is much evidence to show that the state in capitalist societies has close relations with the capitalist class, helping development by providing corporations with subsidies, access to resources, tax concessions, infrastructural services such as railroads, highways, and ferries, and supplies of industrial power (Panitch 1977). The state also supplies a labour force that is able to comply with the requirements of the workplace. Immigration policy in Canada has been a major means of supplying such labour. But several actions taken by the state in the episodes reported in this book suggest one cannot assume that the state always acts in the immediate interest of all capitalists, a prime example being the federal government's support of workers' demands for reductions in Asian immigration. Another example is that under pressure from labour, it has also granted rights to strike and to workers' compensation.

The state also mediates conflicts by providing arenas — through conferences and institutionalized, legal disputation methods — in which the conflicts can be fought over and, in the case of class conflict, temporarily resolved. For example, industrial and political conflicts are channelled into collective bargaining and parliamentary institutions respectively. The involvement of the courts in labour disputes has also been a significant venture by the state into the arena of class conflict. While noting appropriately the need to take into consideration political forces like nineteenth-century British imperialist interests, Malcolmson sees the state as "both a product of and a participant in the process of class struggle," part of the balance of class forces. At any particular time the state expresses the prevailing results and form of the class struggle, including the continual pressure from workers for greater recognition and benefits. This is apparent in several of the above contributions.

In the late nineteenth century capitalists held government office while continuing to participate directly in corporate affairs. After Confederation the provincial government actively encouraged trends towards large-scale capitalist production in mining, forestry, and the fisheries through a generous licensing system, railway and road construction, land grants, and cash subsidies. Malcolmson notes that after 1886 much of the best agricultural land in the province was occupied under the provincial government's settlement policy, with the C.P.R. taking over the largest acreages. And Kew's account of the shunting of native people on to reserves shows how state action deprived them of access to land at the same time as they became local pockets of labour for the emerging industries. But state control of them through the Indian Act helped to prevent them from competing effectively in the economy against the Euro-Canadian settlers.

Towards the end of the nineteenth century, as Phillips's discussion shows, the growth of full-scale capitalist production and the emergence of a wage-earning working class faced with harsh working conditions and low wages led to industrial disputes, strikes, and workers' trade union and political movements. In this process the state protected established proprietorial interests. Repressive labour legislation was used to frustrate worker resistance, and the militia or the police were frequently used to break up disputes or to coerce workers. The organization of workers was undertaken in the face of intimidation from employers and from the state. Legal and illegal methods were freely used to prevent the formation of labour unions.

Yet workers' political activity did lead to the election of provincial parliamentary representatives; an independent class-conscious labour movement, openly committed to socialism, posed a threat to ruling interests early in the twentieth century. According to Malcolmson one response was the adoption of the party system in 1903, which ensured government stability and facilitated further capitalist growth, particularly in the mining and forest industries.

Early in this century the federal government aided canning companies rather than independent fishermen by placing limitations on numbers of fishing licences (Ralston, 1965:42-43). In his contribution to this volume Conley provides examples of other federal action in support of companies, including pressure on Indian fishermen to break a strike and the introduction of a boat-rating system. In more recent times it has underwritten "petty commodity production by providing loans, grants, allowances, subsidies and tax benefits, overwhelmingly for this section of capital" (McMullen, 1984:84). However, McMullen points out that control over allocation of production and products, and prices and markets rests with local and transnational capital groupings. Direct bank capital control has also become prevalent as a result of loans to fishermen.

In the forest industry, as Marchak indicates, the issuing of licences to permit capital investment and the use of direct capital subsidies have been key instruments whereby the provincial state has encouraged corporate growth. The most recent Forest Act in 1978 went further than ever in granting long-term tenure to the big forest companies which have squeezed out smaller competitors. The failure to implement fully the principles of sustained yield management, to which lip service had been paid since the Sloan Commissions of the 1940's and 1950's, can also be seen as a result of the favourable treatment given to the largest enterprises (Marchak 1983:56-57). The bias of the state towards capitalist class interests has enabled the severe depletion within less than one hundred years of what was once thought of as an inexhaustible timber supply.

The ease with which resource capital has penetrated British Columbia is therefore attributable to encouragement and incentives provided by the provincial government. Only minimal efforts have been made to encourage local manufacturing. Because of the low level of diversification in its economy, the province has always been vulnerable to international economic cycles and is now in an extremely precarious position in the face of a shift in world economic activity, particularly the competition from low-wage regions, an important example of class-structured prospects for producing, appropriating and realizing surplus value in given times and places (Marchak, 1984:23).

Among the more prominent forms of state expansion in the past fifty years have been advances in workers' pensions, health insurance and social welfare provisions, human rights and labour legislation. These provisions were not introduced because of the benevolence of the ruling elements but as a response to contradictions and pressures within the society. They are also ways of integrating subordinate classes into the social order by responding to strong, organized working-class pressure, most of it through political parties, some of it expressed in legal battles. State services provide important means for the state to legitimize its role as an arbitrator within the capitalist order. And the reproduction, through state institutions such as schools and hospitals, of a generally compliant labour force helps to provide the stable conditions for that continuing production, distribution, and consumption on which the accumulation of capital depends.

State concessions to workers imply that the state acts with a certain independence from the interests of capital. It possesses relative autonomy in that it may take action that is not in the direct interests of all capitalists. In his recent theoretical discussion of the state, Bandyopadhyay (1986:206) cites the specific interests of state agents, including career development and employment stability on the part of government employees, and the scope and power of bureaucratic directors which operate strategically side-by-side with the constraints on the state to assist in capital accumulation. The existence of capitalists with separate, competing interests precludes the state from simultaneously satisfying all the particular interests of capitalists through public policy. Also important is the state's interest in maintaining the private economic sector because it is dependent for revenue on the taxes paid by workers and corporations (Bandyopadhyay, 1986). Another source of pressure on governments to provide some benefits for workers is their dependence on working class voters for re-election purposes.

The austerity measures introduced by various governments in recent years, including that of British Columbia, are part of a process of restructuring the international division of labour in response to global crisis and in the interests of capital (Marchak, 1986). They involve cutting back on government expenditure to make more capital available to assist corporate investment and using restrictions on collective bargaining to drive down wages. The current Canada-U.S. free-trade negotiations are efforts to secure access to markets and labour for capitalist interests on both sides of the border.

Because the state responds to the prevailing manifestation of class conflict in which it is also a direct participant, we suggest that the future of public policy and the development of British Columbia will be determined to a considerable extent by the balance of class forces. Unlike the situation prevailing in an earlier period covered by several of the above papers, when the working class was comprised mainly of male labourers today's working class includes large numbers of "white-collar" and professional employees, many of them female. This shift has far-reaching implications for the theory and practice of class struggle because women workers fight for their rights as women as well as as workers. Organized women are already a considerable political force with which the state and the capitalist class have to reckon seriously. Women's groups will continue to challenge the status quo and the connections between class and gender make it impossible for the labour movement and progressive parties and organizations to neglect women's issues. In the long run it could also prove impossible for women's groups to ignore the part played by class relations in women's oppression.

The present British Columbia and federal governments like to portray their actions as neutral and intended to be in the best interests of everyone. However, it is quite clear that many of their recent actions towards workers are far from neutral, but rather are part of an assault on the rights and privileges of the working class, once thought to be secure and permanent. Far from merely negotiating with unions, these governments are more or less openly joined with business representatives in trying to weaken unions. Bill 19 and 20, introduced and passed in the provincial legislature in the spring of 1987, are cases in point. The open class warfare waged by the state and sections of capital against the organized working class has rarely been more obvious.

The working class, defined objectively as those who sell their labour, is large and complex. Working class consciousness and actions are still far from being cohesive and solidarist, due in large part to divisions among workers based on such factors as gender, ethnic relations, unionized versus non-unionized workers, public versus private sector workers, and status and income differences, all of which are difficult for workers' movements to overcome. Nevertheless, as Wood (1986) has pointed out, the working class has a special position in the capitalist economy and society. It is the primary exploited class; it is the producing class without which capital could not continue to be accumulated; and as the collective producer it has the capacity to found a new mode of production which would eventually abolish capitalist exploitation. The extension of popular political participation from the merely electoral to the economic sphere would be a logical step towards the evolution of full-blown democracy.

Whether or not the working class's power to cause such change will be realized depends on overcoming the above-mentioned divisions among workers. It also depends on the use of possibilities to mobilize working class political potential (together with that of women) through parliamentary and extra-parliamentary processes. It would involve exposing the flaws inherent in the existing bourgeois and patriarchal social and economic order. The required change can take place at several levels: in the household and in the community as well as in the workplace and the political arena. It may also require convincing capitalists themselves of the major flaws in the system. And what happens in British Columbia will, of course, be influenced by developments elsewhere in the global village which we humans all inhabit. The world is presently in a critical phase of intense class and gender struggle in which the parameters have been set by capitalist development.

There is a large variety of groups outside of the labour movement and workers' parties which acknowledge the destructive and oppressive elements in capitalism. Included are not only certain women's groups but also environmentalists, peace organizations, human rights groups, socially active churches, native Indian groups, and community organizations. To many who are involved in these movements an economy based on the imperative of profit accumulation and the power of private owners of the means of production is a barrier to the satisfaction of human needs in a democratic, peace-loving, co-operative, and egalitarian society. Many are themselves workers or members of workers' families and they support local community-based economic and social development as advocated in recent policy proposals (Magnusson et al., 1986). The attainability of those goals and the establishemnt of a post-capitalist mode of production requires that large numbers of workers and their families recognize the class nature of their society, the class conflict in which many of them are embroiled, and the need to take power away from the ruling class.

In the future development of British Columbia, class struggle, and particularly the degree of strength the working class can muster, will continue to play the major role it has played in the past. The dissemination of knowledge about the episodes examined in this volume is intended to be a small contribution to the education of those involved.

REFERENCES

Armstrong, P. and Hugh Armstrong. 1983.
The Double Ghetto: Canadian Women and Their Segregated Work. Toronto: McClelland and Stewart.
Bandyopadhyay, P. 1986.
"Theoretical Approaches to the State and Social Reproduction." In James Dickinson and Bob Russell (eds.), *Family, Economy and State: The Social Reproduction Process Under Capitalism*. Toronto: Garamond, 1986: Chapter 7, pp. 192–222.
Barbalet, J. M. 1986.
"Limitations of Class Theory and the Disappearance of Status: The Problem of the New Middle Class." *Sociology* 20:4 (November):557-576.
Barnet, R. J. and R. E. Mueller. 1974.
Global Reach: The Power of Multinational Corporations. New York: Simon and Schuster.
Bourgeault, R. 1983.
"The Indians, the Metis and the Fur Trade." *Studies in Political Economy*, 12 (Fall):45-80.
Carroll, W. K. 1984.
"The Solidarity Coalition." In W. Magnusson et al. (eds.), *The New Reality: The Politics of Restraint in British Columbia*. Vancouver: New Star.
—. 1985. "Dependency, Imperialism and the Capitalist Class in Canada." In R. Brym (ed.), *The Structure of the Canadian Capitalist Class*. Toronto: Garamond: pp. 21–52.
—. 1986. *Corporate Power and Canadian Capitalism*. Vancouver: University of British Columbia Press.
Carstens, P. 1971.
"Coercion and Change." In R. J. Ossenberg (ed.), *Canadian Society: Pluralism, Change and Conflict*. Scarborough: Prentice-Hall: Chapter 6, pp. 126–45.
Christensen, E. 1982.
"Aspects of the Crisis in Petit Commodity Production in the Okanagan Valley." *Alternate Routes*, 5:1-25.
Clement, W. 1986.
The Struggle to Organize: Resistance in Canada's Fishery. Toronto: McClelland and Stewart.
Craven, Paul and Traves, T. 1979.
"The Class Politics of the National Policy, 1872-1933." *Journal of Canadian Studies*, 14 (Fall):14-38.
Cuneo, Carl. 1984.
"Has the Traditional Petite Bourgeoisie Persisted?" *Canadian Journal of Sociology* 9:3 (Summer):269-302.
Dickinson, James and Bob Russell. 1986.
Family, Economy and State: The Social Reproduction Process under Capitalism. Toronto: Garamond.
Drache, Daniel. 1984.
"The Formation and Fragmentation of the Canadian Working Class, 1820-1920." In *Studies in Political Economy* 15 (Fall):43-89.
Gannage, C. 1987.
"A World of Difference: the Case of Women Workers in a Canadian Garment Factory." In H.J. Maroney and M. Luxton (eds.), *Feminism and Political Economy: Women's Work, Women's Struggles*. Toronto: Methuen: Chapter 8, pp. 139–66.
Gerth, H. and C. W. Mills. 1948.
From Max Weber: Essays in Sociology. London: Routledge and Kegan Paul.
Harré, R. 1979.
Social Being. Oxford: Blackwell.

Harvey, D. 1985.
"The Geopolitics of Capitalism." In D. Gregory and J. Urry (eds.), *Social Relations and Spatial Structures*. London: Macmillan: Chapter 7, pp. 128–63.
Johnson, L. 1972.
"The Development of Class in Canada in the Twentieth Century." In G. Teeple (ed.), *Capitalism and the National Question in Canada*. Toronto: University of Toronto Press.
—. 1981. "Independent Commodity Production: Mode of Production or Capitalist Class Formation?" *Studies in Political Economy* 6:93-112.
Kennedy, D. 1985.
"Belonging to the Land: The Meaning of Meares Island." *Canadian Forum* (June/July):8-18.
Knight, Rolf. 1978.
Indians at Work. Vancouver: New Star.
Larrain, J. 1983.
Marxism and Ideology. London: Macmillan.
Mackie, R. J. 1984.
"Colonial Land, Indian Labour and Company Capital: the Economy of Vancouver Island, 1849-1858." M.A. thesis. University of Victoria.
Magnusson, W. et.al. 1986.
After Bennett: A New Politics for British Columbia. Vancouver: New Star.
Marchak, P. 1975.
"Class, Regional and Institutional Sources of Conflict in B.C." *B.C. Studies* 27 (Autumn):30-49.
—. 1983. *Green Gold: The Forest Industry in British Columbia*. Vancouver: University of British Columbia Press.
—. 1984a. "Introduction." *Journal of Canadian Studies*. Special Issue on Fisheries (Spring) 19:1.
—. 1984b. "The New Economic Reality: Substance and Rhetoric." In W. Magnusson et al (eds.), *The New Reality: The Politics of Restraint in British Columbia*. Vancouver: New Star.
—. 1986. "The Rise and Fall of the Peripheral State: The Case of British Columbia." In R. Brym (ed.), *Regionalism in Canada*. Toronto: Irwin: pp. 123–59.
McMullen, J. L. 1984.
"State, Capital and Debt in the British Columbia Fishing Fleet." *Journal of Canadian Studies*. Special issue in the Fisheries, 19:1 (Spring):65-88
Muszyinski, A. 1984.
"The Organization of Women and Ethnic Minorities in a Resource Industry: A Case Study of Unionization of Shoreworkers in the B.C. Fishing Industry, 1937-1949." *Journal of Canadian Studies*. Special Issue on Fisheries, 19:1 (Spring):89-107.
—. 1986. "Class Formation and Class Consciousness: The Making of Shoreworkers in the B.C. Fishing Industry." *Studies in Political Economy* 20 (Summer):85-116.
Palmer, B. 1986.
Solidarity: The Rise and Fall of an Opposition in British Columbia. Vancouver: New Star.
Panitch, L. 1977.
The Canadian State: Political Economy and Political Power. Toronto: University of Toronto Press.
Pentland, H. Clare. 1959.
"The Development of a Capitalistic Labour Market in Canada." In *Canadian Journal of Economic and Political Science* 25:4, 450-461.
Ralston, H. K. 1965.
"The 1900 Strike of Fraser River Sockeye Salmon Fishermen." M.A. thesis, University of British Columbia.

Resnick, P. 1985.
  "The Ideology of Neo-Conservatism." In W. Magnusson et al (eds.) *The New Reality: The Politics of Restraint in British Columbia*. Vancouver: New Star.
Rex, J. 1986.
  Race and Ethnicity. Milton Keynes: Open University Press.
Taylor, G. W. 1982.
  Builders of British Columbia: An Industrial History. Victoria: Morriss Publishing.
Tennant, P. 1982
  "Native Indian Political Organization in British Columbia, 1900-1969: A Response to Internal Colonialism," *B.C. Studies* 55 (Autumn).
—. 1983. Preface to "British Columbia: A Place for Aboriginal Peoples." *B.C. Studies* 57 (Spring).
Warburton, Rennie and Stephen Scott. 1985.
  "The Fur Trade and the Beginnings of Capitalism in British Columbia." In *Canadian Journal of Native Studies*. 5:1, 27-46.
Ward, W. P. 1980.
  "Class and Race in the Social Structure of British Columbia, 1870-1939." *B.C. Studies* 45 (Spring):17-35.
Wickberg, E. et al. 1982.
  From China to Canada: A History of the Chinese Communities in Canada. Ottawa: Minister of Supplies and Services.